Barnett

Meot
KiBBEY
489-5481

Home
Cell

1851 SACRAMENTO DIRECTORY AND HISTORY

The earliest illustration of the site of Sacramento City, then called *Sutter's Embarcadero.*
The view is to the east toward the future location of I Street, and the date is July to October 1848.
George McDougal's store ship *Providence* is at the center, and Mr. Stewart's log cabin above it.

FACSIMILE REPRODUCTION OF
THE CALIFORNIA STATE LIBRARY COPY OF

J. HORACE CULVER'S

SACRAMENTO CITY DIRECTORY
FOR THE YEAR 1851,

WITH
A HISTORY OF SACRAMENTO TO 1851,
BIOGRAPHICAL SKETCHES,
AND
INFORMATIVE APPENDICES

By

MEAD B. KIBBEY

CALIFORNIA STATE LIBRARY FOUNDATION
SACRAMENTO, CALIFORNIA
2000

The illustrations on pages 6, 8, 9,10, 42, 65, 66, 101, 113, 147, were provided by the Director of the California State Library's Special Collections Branch, Gary Kurutz, who also corrected many errors in the original text. The illustrations on pages 2 and 14 were provided by James Henley, director of the Sacramento Archives and Museum Collections Center. The photograph on page 104 was provided by Burnett Miller of Burnett & Sons. The two illustrations on page 138 were provided by James B. McClatchy. The photograph on page 157 was provided by John Wheaton. The engraved bookplate illustration on page 194 was provided by the Houghton Library, Harvard University. The rest of the illustrations came from the author's collection. The front cover illustration was derived from the first seal of the City of Sacramento, and was designed and drawn by Alison B. Kibbey.

Catherine Rodebaugh gave invaluable assistance in research at the City Cemetery, proofreading, and in sorting and copying illustrations. My wife, Nancy Kibbey, provided essential editorial aid and advice. J. S. Holliday was a constant advisor, and rewrote several passages of my sometimes obscure prose.

John Gonzales and Sibylle Zemitis of the California History Room of the California State Library provided invaluable support in providing access to illustrations and histories of obscure pioneer Sacramento citizens. Fr. Steven Arvella provided valuable information on early Sacramento churchmen and on the McClatchy family history.

DEDICATION

To James Horace Culver, a California Pioneer who had a vision of Sacramento's future and the energy, scholarship, and faith to publish a directory and history of the city in the second year of its existence. He perhaps had read John Greenleaf Whittier:

I hear the tread of pioneers,
Of nations yet to be;
The first low wash of waves where soon
Shall roll a human sea.

JAMES HORACE CULVER
Born in 1814 in Pennsylvania, and died in 1864 in Sacramento. During
December 1850, he wrote the first book printed in Sacramento, which was also
the first city directory on the Pacific Coast containing street address numbers.

TABLE OF CONTENTS

Jedediah Strong Smith 1799 - 1831

While hunting beaver (in 1827), he became the first U.S. citizen to see the future location of Sacramento City, and commanded the first group to travel overland to California and Sacramento from the United States.

Sacramento City, Looking east at Front Street, from I Street to a little south of J Street, in the fall of 1849.
The City Hotel (at left), opened in November 1849 and built from Sutter's former grist mill, appears unfinished. While under construction, it was used for a grand ball on July 4, 1849. The Eagle Theater, the city's first, is by the sailboat's mast.

Interior of California Indian Dance House or *Kum*.

These were the largest buildings in a village and were also used for meetings and as a residence for the chief's family. The entrance faced east, and the roof was covered with soil over rushes. Forbes, *Upper California*, 1839.

PREFACE

Sacramento in 1850 was the ultimate expression of that peculiarly American phenomenon — the boom town. Unlike most such early settlements in California, the town kept growing and after 150 years is still expanding. On January 1, 1851, when J. Horace Culver finished publishing his 1851 Sacramento City Directory (reproduced here), the city's first building was two years old, and the city government had been operating for fourteen months. The earliest business men had moved in from Sutter's Fort, many of them had failed, and the Fort itself had been sold by Sutter.

The populace continually arrived, moved, and often departed the area, at a remarkable rate. The growing size of Sacramento City was not like a pool filling, but rather a river becoming wider. As an example: 37 names are listed on page twelve of this 1851 directory and two years later in the 1853 directory, not one is listed in the same business at the same location. Eight of the 1851 names were still listed in Sacramento; one had retired, a doctor had become a real estate agent, a merchant had entered a partnership and moved four blocks away, a lawyer had become a merchant, an express agent a printer, a bricklayer a builder, a blacksmith changed employers and moved three blocks, and the eighth had moved across town. Even the directory's publisher, J. H. Culver had changed from an auctioneer at 4th and J Streets to a lime dealer at 2nd and L Streets. Furthermore, in just two years, 78% of the businesses and people listed on that randomly selected page of the directory had apparently left town. An example of this turmoil may be seen in an entry in the 1856 directory giving the history of the City Market (a butcher shop):

> Opened in Sept. 1849 by Morse & Dunning; in April 1850, Morse sold out his interest to A. Wollerston; in the summer of the same year Dunning sold out his interest to the same gentleman, who conducted it alone until September [1850], when he sold to F. W. Fratt & E. Pierce. In December, same year [1850], Pierce sold to A. W. Burns & Joe Heywood, and in the same month [Dec., 1850] Fratt sold out to David Molena. In May, 1851 Burns sold to Molena; in summer following [summer of 1851] Molena sold to Chas. Coil, after which Coil sold to Ferris & Fountain. . . .

The entry continues through nine more lines, but this gives a good picture of the rate of change. One wonders if those early owners were really more interested in selling butcher shops than meat.

Only a few years before, in April of 1848, the site of Sacramento City was uninhabited except for the hut of an Indian ferryman and an Indian sweat-house in a forest of Sycamores, "dense and green, guarding a mighty solitude." A muddy ox wagon road led away from the river to Sutter's Fort. Fifteen months later a city council was in office, and in nineteen months Sacramento citizens had voted to approve a city charter and the city seal which appears on the cover of this book. And all this occurred before California was even a State. Sacramento's population came from dozens of countries and represented many ethnic backgrounds, but the "establishment" was essentially Anglo–American, mainly from east of the Mississippi River.

During the first eleven months of 1850, the citizens of Sacramento had suffered from a seemingly endless succession of disasters. Flood, Riots, Financial Panic, and Pestilence had all taken their toll in that short period. If the biblical Four Horsemen of the Apocalypse (Rev. 6: 2-8) had been seen riding down K Street, citizens would only have warned those equestrians on the strange horses that they didn't look strong enough to survive in Sacramento City.

Through all this, in 1850, building stores, offices, long levees, and houses rapidly continued in the city. A traveler, who spent seven days in Sacramento, complained of the garbage problem in almost clinical detail and then as an afterthought said that during his short stay 50 buildings had been completed.

The existence of the first book published in Sacramento, J. Horace Culver's *The Sacramento City Directory* dated January 1, 1851, has been well known among Californian historians, but copies are so rare (three were known) that few have had access to it. Their interest may have also been affected by an 1871 description of it as a mere pamphlet and "more or less an abortion."[1] In previously editing a reproduction of the California State Library's copy of the 1853 Sacramento Directory, I was given access to an old photocopy of Culver's 1851 directory in order to trace some of the names in the 1853 book. I quickly realized Culver's directory was much larger than I had

---

1. *The Sacramento Directory, 1871* (Sacramento: H. S. Crocker & Co., 1871) page 3, "The first Sacramento Directory bears the date January 1st, 1851. It is a small 12mo. pamphlet, . . .This is very scarce, and has been considerably sought for within the last two years. . . . There is a copy in the State Library; James Anthony & Co. [publishers of the *Sacramento Union*] have one, and possibly the Pioneers [Sacramento Pioneer Association] another, though an agent we sent to their rooms to search for it could not find it. . . .Since '51 there has been, with probably the exception of '52, at least one Sacramento Directory of some kind issued annually. . . .but with the exception of those published in 1853 *et seq.* by Samuel Colville, and those compiled more recently by Robert E. Draper, every one of the series has been more or less of an abortion."

expected, containing 96 pages, including some very informative advertisements and twelve pages of what he termed "historical notes." Richard Quebedeaux, writing in 1992, lists three copies in libraries, and adds the mysterious information "The copy once at the California State Library has been missing for years."[2]

Because of the absence in Sacramento of an original 1851 copy, I started to work with Dr. Bonnie Hardwick of The Bancroft library on the idea of reproducing their copy. Suddenly in September 1997, Gary Kurutz, head of Special Collections at the California State Library, called with some remarkable news. He had been conducting a tour of the library for a group from the California legislature led by Jeffrey Volberg of the Senate Committee on Constitutional Amendments, and they asked to see material in the temperature controlled vault where the rarest and most valuable items are located. In this room the unusual and earliest California directories are kept together on a section of eight shelves. While the group examined some rare books, Gary Kurutz checked an obscure corner for other documents that might be of interest.

An archival envelope bearing the cryptic word "directory" and filed with its old library number caught his eye. Opening it, he found a magnificent copy of the long missing Culver's 1851 directory bound in tree leather with gilt spine lettering and edge decoration! Seeing this original, and the obvious care with which it had been bound, I felt even more strongly that this wonderful early book had to be reproduced for modern readers who could then judge for themselves the work of its almost unknown author (see biographical sketch on page 115).

I have added a condensed history, which includes information gathered on a 1999 sea voyage my wife and I took from Rio de Janeiro to Valpariso around Cape Horn, some illustrations, 55 biographical sketches, a conversion table for old addresses to the modern equivalent, and five appendices to give the general reader a glimpse of Sacramento and its citizens up to the first day of 1851.

Despite great effort, no information could be found on the sixteen women listed in the directory, explaining why none are included in the biographical material starting on page 93 (see also page 174).

M. B. K. November, 1999

---

2. Richard Quebedeaux, *Prime Sources of California and Nevada Local History/ 151 Rare and Important City, County, and State Directories/ 1850 - 1906* (Spokane, Washington, The Arthur H. Clark Company, 1992) pp. 106-108

The sidewheel steamer *New World* docked at the foot of K Street in 1850.

This daguerreotype is the earliest known photograph of the Sacramento City waterfront, and of the *New World*. Early in 1850, this ship had just been completed in New York, but was under attachment and occupied by sheriff's deputies. On Saturday, April 13, 1850, Captain Edgar Wakeman gave them unlimited bar privileges and began a "test run." When 3 miles at sea, he answered their inebriated protests by putting them in a rowboat and pointing them toward the coast. The ship was too fast to catch with that head-start, and made a safe trip to San Francisco, arriving in July 1850 with 300 paying passengers picked up on the way. J. B. Starr's two story auction house at the south corner of Front and K Street is just in front of the *New World's* smoke stack.

A HISTORY OF SACRAMENTO TO 1851

January 1, 1851 in Sacramento, was not just the first day of a new year and the end of an old one. It marked the publishing of Sacramento's first book, James Horace Culver's *Sacramento City Directory for the Year 1851*. While it made economic sense for the publisher to call this the 1851 directory, it really was the directory of Sacramento for November and December, 1850. Every fact had been gathered and the text completed in that year and its only connection with 1851 was its date of publication and the author's desire to have it seem current for all of the ensuing year.[3] In subsequent years, the Sacramento directories came out later in the year and contained entries for the year of publication. Culver's directory was the first on the Pacific Coast to use street address numbers.

Four months before, on September 1, 1850, Charles P. Kimball published his *San Francisco City Directory* without address numbers, and in his conclusion (page 129) wrote,

"In conclusion, we shall touch upon but two things, about which little has been said by others but which we think are of importance, and first, the one brought more particularly to our notice as connected with this work that of numbering the Streets.

Under the present [un]settled state of change it is very plain that all plans of numbering the buildings will very soon become defective from the building-up and tearing-down process continually going on, nor will it be likely to be better for some time to come. If then a plan could be adopted giving the location quite accurate, and still independent of the buildings. We think it worthy the consideration of the public."

He goes on to propose exactly the Sacramento system, then in use for over 20 months. His second problem involved indiscriminate ringing of church bells which confused members of volunteer fire departments—proposed solution; ring church bells only at fixed times.

---

3. The persons known to have been residents of Sacramento, who left before August 1850, and the partnerships listed, suggest Culver began gathering data no earlier than September, 1850. Persons who arrived and partnerships formed up to mid-December are included. Frederick Roe, who was lynched on January 26, 1851, is listed, and on page 58, Peter H. Burnett, who resigned on January 9, 1851, is shown as Governor of California. A. P. Catlin, an attorney prominent at the time of the Squatter Riots, went to Morman Island in October or November, 1850 and is not listed. These facts would tend to verify that all entries were tabulated in November to late December, 1850.

The end of 1850 was also accompanied by the departure, and often the fiscal ruin, of most of Sacramento's earliest hard charging businessmen and the end of the influence of the city's wild and audacious first pioneers. Gone from the scene are the names of John A. Sutter and his son John Jr.; Sam Brannan who was California's first millionaire; Hardin Bigelow who, as the first mayor, was shot and wounded in the squatter riots; James Marshall of gold discovery fame; Edward C. Kemble, editor of Sacramento's first newspaper; George McKinstry, the first sheriff; and even a listing of the name "New Helvetia" was absent.

In 1850, the citizens would have known of all these early names plus the identity of dozens of other pioneers who came to Sutter's Fort from 1840 to 1848, and Sacramento City in 1849, but many of the old timers had died, moved elsewhere, or were no longer active enough to be listed in the directory. A new group with different ways of getting things done was in place, and their names appeared in this first directory.

The start of the transformation of the Sacramento region from a sparsely settled,[4] quiet, and largely agrarian region to a roaring economic maelstrom and outpost of the distant United States, slowly began many years before the arrival of Captain Johan Augustus Sutter in 1839. It is very tempting to begin with that date as many of the early historians did so, but the earliest Native Americans came here surely before 8,000 B.C.[5] and hunters, trappers, and explorers had been visiting the area since at least 1775.

NATIVE CALIFORNIANS BEFORE THE EXPLORERS

Any history of the inhabitants of California before the arrival of European explorers is complicated by a number of factors, the most important of which may be listed as follows: the large number of separate tribes or groups, the unchanging nature of the buried artifacts

---

4. The native Indian population of the state has been estimated at 135,000 to 300,000 in 1770, but by 1841 had been terribly decimated by forced removal to the missions (where most eventually died), diseases introduced by returning mission Indians, and by Canadian and American trappers.

5. Robert F. Heizer, *Handbook of North American Indians*, (Washington: Smithsonian Institution, 1978) p. 3. Native Indians with many similar customs had reached Tierra del Fuego at the southern tip of South America about 4,000 years ago.

making dating difficult, the absence of a written language, and the natives' lack of information about other areas (few if any of the Indians interviewed had ever been more than forty miles from their place of birth). Those abducted to the missions and some working for Sutter were exceptions, but they were gone by 1870. The terrible decimation of the Native Californian population amounted to over 85% between 1770 and 1910, with some tribes becoming extinct. By far the largest numerical losses occurred before 1847, in the era of Spanish and Mexican rule, and before the gold seekers arrived. Early writers used spiritedly abusive descriptions of the native people to report every piece of adverse information they saw or heard, while making no effort to learn the history or customs of this ancient civilization.

There is also the fact that the translation of Indian words and descriptions of early customs are based on interviews with survivors. The first serious efforts to collect such information were in 1870 when some Indians who had been born before 1848 were still living. Unfortunately the majority of recorded interviews occurred after 1910 when the information was only available from persons who had not been alive at time of the Gold Rush. The later comments are often given the same weight as those from eye-witnesses while in fact their replies were influenced by some of the enormous cultural changes resulting from contacts with the American and European immigrants.

In the area within 120 miles of Sacramento, some ten to fifteen Indian groups, all of the same general ethnic type, lived in separate regions and spoke separate but somewhat similar languages. Their habits remained unchanged over a very long period. Careful excavations made since 1900 indicate that some shell mounds (so called, because they contained more than 50% cast-off mollusk shells) near village sites in Emeryville, Berkeley, and elsewhere around San Francisco Bay were used for 3000 years from around 1200 B.C. to A.D. 1800, with almost a constant population and type of artifacts interred. As mentioned by Dr. A. L. Kroeber;

> In a word, the basis of culture remained identical during the whole of the shell-mound period. . . . It means that at the time when Troy was besieged and Solomon was building the Temple, at a period when even Greek civilization had not yet taken on the traits that we regard as characteristic, . . . and our own northern ancestors dwelled in unmitigated barbarism, the native Californian already lived in all essentials like his descendant of today. In Europe and Asia, change succeeded

change of the profoundest type. On this far shore of the Pacific, civilization, such as it was, remained immutable in all fundamentals.

The permanence of Californian culture, therefore is of far more than local interest. *It is a fact of significance in the history of civilization* [Italics added].[6]

Subsequent archeological research has shown that between 9000 and 1000 B.C. important cultural and territorial changes occurred, but for the later period mentioned by Kroeber, changes were slight. Somewhat similar mounds have been found in the Sacramento area near Indian village sites, but the main constituents there are ash and bones of mammals rather than the mollusk shells found around the Bay. The information on age and consistent culture which can be obtained, tends to show that in the Sacramento area *Nisenan* and *Miwok* Indians had also occupied the same locations for thousands of years.

It appears that much of the culture of the California Indians had spread over a huge area of the Americas several thousand years before the arrival of Europeans. Shell mounds two to four thousand years more recent than those in California have been excavated in Tierra del Fuego 6,700 miles to the southeast. They used shell money in both places, built similar huts, and piled sea shells nearby.

Tierra del Fueugan hut and shellmound, 1839

The *Nisenan* reckoning of time within the period of one year was based on the lunar cycle, and among those around Sacramento, the year comprised twelve lunar months. These were named for seasonal conditions, like "Grass" for March or "Acorns ripen" for August, and began in the spring without any reference to astronomical observations. Since twelve such

6. A.L. Kroeber, *Handbook of the Indians of California*, (Berkeley: California Book Company, Ltd., 1953) p. 930. This book provided most of the information used in this section. There have been many newer discoveries, but Kroeber supplies a good framework of the history of these most interesting people. He includes a bibliography with comments on the special information provided in many of the 415 titles listed.

periods are 354.36 days, an adjustment was needed every three years so that the names of the months would continue to agree with actual conditions. This may have been done by inserting an un-named month or by some other means, but the method is not now certain. A new moon was considered favorable for weather, health and crops if its horns pointed up and unfavorable if they pointed horizontally.

Sacramento was in the territory of the southern section of the Maidu group, and this large sub-group is now referred to as the *Nisenan*. Based on a map (Plate 37) in Kroeber, *Handbook of California Indians* the *Nisenan* territorial boundaries are:

> Commencing at a point on the Sacramento River near Hood about ten miles south of the mouth of the American; thence north along the Sacramento to Knight's Landing; thence due north until opposite Marysville; thence northeast to the Feather River and up the Feather to Honcut Creek; thence northeast through Brownsville, Challenge, Woodleaf, La Porte, and Gibsonville to Pilot Peak; thence south along the Sierra summits passing west of Lake Tahoe to Echo Summit on Highway 50; thence west a little south of Highway 50 to the point of beginning.

Their neighbors to the north were the north-eastern and north-western Maidu, to the east the Washoe, to the south the Miwok, and to the west the Wintun or Patwin.[7]

The *Nisenan* of Sacramento used polished and drilled sea-shells from the coast as money.[8] If this were true from the earliest days of their history, as some authorities believe, they were using a form of

---

7. The Maidu and Nisenan are now considered along with the Miwok, Wintun, Costanoan, and Yokut groups, to be members of the *PENUTIAN* family. Careful analysis of their languages disclosed underlying similarities. In the Wintun, Maidu, and Yokut languages derivatives of *pen* as in *pene, ponoi,* and *panotl* were used in the sense of "two." In the Costanoan and Miwok "two" was *uti.* Combining these two roots gave Pen-uti-an, and modern linguistic scholars manufactured the word describing the family of languages and the area occupied by its users. The California Indians had no equivalent word, and after reading the description above of the boundary of just a single sub-group, one can see it made far more sense to create a descriptive word than to describe the areas occupied by the six members of the family.

8. Barclay V. Head, *Historia Numorum,* (Oxford: Clarendon Press 1911) p. 643 where he quotes Herodotus as stating that this is the first instance known of striking coins of gold and silver. "Electrum" was mixture of the two metals, found in nature.

currency before the first electrum coins were issued by the Lydians in Asia Minor in the seventh century B.C. The individual shells were of low value and the owners threaded them on thongs of set lengths of three up to 30 feet for convenience in handling or storage. A very valuable form of shell money, *Dentalium Indianorum*, which came from Vancouver Island was used by the Yoruk Indians near Eureka, but was only rarely seen by the *Nisenan*. They regarded it more as we would think of jewelry, and it had no fixed value among them. The Dentalia shells could not be harvested at will because the mollusks producing them lived in water from 3,000 to 14,000 feet deep. A few of the shells were washed ashore at certain points around Puget Sound.

The value of the *Nisenan* shell money expressed in dollars was fairly well understood after the Gold Rush period. The value of the standard *Nisenan* clamshell bead currency called *Howok*, was reported in the 1870s as, "1160 pieces, stringing 30 feet, average thickness per bead a little less than a third of an inch, valued at $230, or five to a dollar. The largest beads, nearly an inch in diameter, four to a dollar. . . . These native appraisals are much higher than any reported from the Pomo or Southern Californians; which fact seems to be due to Maidu remoteness from both sources of supply."[9]

Among the *Nisenan*, legal disputes arose on a regular basis, and in common with the neighboring Maidu, settlement was based on certain well understood principles. They did not individually own land, but recognized the right of possessing locations such as a fishing spot, an eel hole, or a grasshopper hole. Personal property could be owned by men directly, or by women and children with a male trustee such as a brother or relative acting on their behalf. Hugh Littlejohn specifically mentions personal ownership of rabbit nets, quail nets made of women's hair, fishing poles, and certain oak trees growing immediately adjacent to the owner's residence.[10] Women personally owned, without a trustee, baskets, cooking utensils, acorn pestles, mats, blankets, digging sticks, seed beaters, and basket-making supplies. Due to the custom of burning all the personal property of a man at his funeral ceremony, there was little to be inherited.

Theft of material possessions within the community was

---

9. Dr. A.L. Kroeber, *Handbook of the Indians of California,* p. 421

10. Hugh W. Littlejohn, *Nisenan Geography,* (Typed manuscript at Sacramento Archives and Museum collection, 1928) p. 22.

punished by reprisal. If the thief were caught, he had to pay the owner something of equal value, and unlike our modern debt collection process, if he did not pay, the owner could kill him.

Loans and debt payments occurred, with the latter process sometimes accelerated by the use of "Dunning Sticks." These were pieces of round wood about four inches long painted with red and black rings, and tied together like the rungs of a small rope ladder. They were tossed into a debtor's house as an unsubtle reminder that payment was expected in the near future. An example found in 1876 had six sticks, and is now in the Smithsonian Institution.[11]

Murder, rape and similar serious offenses were often followed by retaliatory killing, sometimes preformed by a hired shaman or "medicine-man." Mediation efforts were made by the headman, assisted by hired go-betweens, to avoid such revenge killings, and if successful the matter was settled by property payment. The amount of this payment was simplified because every person had a fixed value determined by bride price, the price paid for his or her mother in marriage. Among the Shasta Indians where dentalia shells were used for money rather than jewelry, an average bride price was one or two deerskins, fifteen to 20 dentalia shells, ten to fifteen strings of round clamshell beads, and 20 to 30 red woodpecker scalps.[12] The values of all these items were known in relation to the value of the others so that the price could, for instance, have been set entirely in woodpecker scalps. It is interesting that payment was preferred in a variety of goods—almost as if the recipients were building a portfolio of family wealth. Bride prices among the *Nisenan* would probably have been of roughly equal value, but paid in items more available in the valley.

Indian houses in the Sacramento area were of three types, the individual residence, the sweat house, and in major villages, the dance or meeting house called a *kum*. The residence was from ten to fifteen feet in diameter and framed with cut saplings placed in holes at the perimeter and then bent toward the center and tied in place. The earth within the circle was frequently excavated to a depth of twelve to 24 inches. The frame was covered with tules or branches leaving a hole at the top for smoke and as an entrance for the more agile members of

---

11. Norman Wilson and Arlean Towne, in *Handbook of North American Indians,* (Washington: Smithsonian Institution, 1978) Volume 8, p. 393.

12. Shirley Silver, *Handbook of North American Indians,* Vol 8, p. 214.

the family. A low doorway at ground level, often facing east, was used as a regular entrance. The outside was then covered with a thick layer of earth, leaving the whole structure strong enough to allow several people to sit on top.

The sweat house was built in the same general form, but of smaller size and with lighter framing. These houses could accommodate up to six men and were usually built near a pond or stream where they would swim at the end of the sweating period. An Indian sweat-house was described as being near the river and the future site of Sacramento's J Street on April 17, 1848, by the editor of the *California Star,* Edward Kemble.[13] Although a large number of tents are also shown, possibly the remains of the same structure is just visible on a small hill in a lithograph of flooded Sacramento City drawn on January 1, 1849, by George Casilear and Henry Bainbridge. In the text below the image, the hill is described as being "*Sa'cum,* a knoll built by Indians and the only dry spot visible for miles."

The circular dance house belonged to the village and was 30 feet or larger in diameter. Around the smoke hole at the center, two or four large vertical posts were set in the ground which had previously been excavated to a depth of a yard or more. One of the posts was notched to make a ladder for access to the roof. Rafters were then placed between the central posts and a ring (about two thirds the diameter of the house) of beams supported by smaller and shorter vertical posts. Rafters extended down from this ring to a circular mound of earth at the wall of the structure. A ground level entrance was provided and the rafters were covered like the individual residences. When not being used for ceremonies, the dance house was often occupied by the headman and his family.

Between the mouth of the American River and Folsom there were ten village sites whose Indian names are known, and more than these probably existed before 1839. At least four sites lay within the city limits of modern Sacramento; *Momel,* at about Fifth and Richards Boulevard, *Sama,* at Fifth and J Streets, *Yalisuni,* near 30th and B Streets, and another at the City Plaza on J Street.

The ferryman and his hut maintained by Sutter at the Sacramento Embarcadero (Kemble quote page 57) honored an Indian tradition

---

13. Edward C. Kemble, *A Kemble Reader,* Edited by Fred B. Rogers, (San Francisco: California Historical Society, 1963) p. 132.

observed by the Yurok and very probably the *Nisenan*.[14]   Free ferriage was at all times to be rendered, even to those who could not reciprocate because of being boatless or in chronic poverty. The custom was based on the assumption that ferriage was a primal necessity which at times everyone needed and at other times could supply.

Although some tribes in southeastern California seemed to almost relish warfare, the *Nisenan* tended to be peaceful, and organized battles or campaigns were rare. The few that occurred usually resulted from trespass and ranged from random feuds between families to raids and surprise attacks involving whole villages or even communities. The tactics and weapons of the *Nisenan* were not effective against organized forces of the Spaniards and Mexicans. Later, after suffering the ravages of disease (see page 33) they were even less able to resist attacks by groups of the Anglo-Americans. In the foothills and mountains, members of other tribes would occasionally kill a few soldiers or settlers, but these events did not permanently halt the advance of the miners and settlers into even the most remote Indian territories.

EXPLORATIONS AND VISITS BEFORE 1839

In the spring of 1772 the Spanish explorer, and first governor of California, Pedro Fages, was the earliest to record having seen the Sacramento Valley, which he did from the hills behind modern Antioch. On this same expedition his colleague, Fr. Juan Crespi, had named the combined Sacramento and San Joaquin Rivers, below their juncture, *The Great River of Our Father San Francisco,* and stated its mouth to be located in latitude N37° 54' (off modern Richmond). Even if he meant the east end of Susuin Bay in latitude N38° 03', he was still only about nine miles off, which was quite good for an observer using an astrolabe and outdated tables intended for Spain.[15] Fages mentions seeing large

---

14. A.L. Kroeber, *Handbook of California Indians*, p. 35.

15. Theodore E. Treutlein, *Fages as Explorer, 1769-1772*, (N.P., California Historical Quarterly, Winter 1972) Vol li, No.4, p. 351. Latitude measurements are mentioned in *The Anza Expeditions of 1775-1776, diary of Pedro Font*, Frederick Teggert, editor, (Berkeley: Academy of Pacific Coast History, 1913) Vol 3, No. 1, pp. 7-8.". . .the observations that I was able to take with the astronomical quadrant. . . .I calculated the latitudes by some tables...As these tables are for the meridian of Cadiz [Spain], and for the years 1756, 1757, 1758, and 1759, they require two corrections; and although the latitudes I set down are in accordance with the observations that I made, endeavoring to employ in the tables the two corrections necessary for the calculation, I

Indian villages (rancherias) and many friendly Indians with whom he exchanged small gifts.

Juan Bautista Anza again reported seeing the valley from the same hills in 1776, but the first recorded visit into the Sacramento Valley did not occur until 32 years later.

— § —

Ensign,[16] or Alférez, Gabriel Moraga was about 42 years of age and had been in the Spanish army in California for 24 years when he was ordered by the governor of the province, Don Josef Joaquín de Arrillaga to explore the "rivers of the north." In a footnote in Vol II page 571, Bancroft mentions Moraga was described by a contemporary as a tall, well-built man of dark complexion, brave, gentlemanly, and the best Californian soldier of his time.[17] On September 25, 1808, with a corporal, eleven privates, and probably an Indian interpreter, he departed on horseback from Mission San Jose and traveled to the northeast. They reached a lake near modern Tracy, turned southeast, and forded the San Joaquin river a few miles south of the mouth of the Stanislaus. They rode 9 miles east of the San Joaquin and turned north west to reach the Stanislaus, which he had named the "Guadalupe" on his 1806 San Joaquin Valley exploration. For two days they explored the river, from its mouth up into the foothills and crossed it from the south bank on September 30, 1808.

As they moved north, Moraga's group stayed several miles east of the San Joaquin, and later the Sacramento River because of the difficulty of traveling through the tule swamps adjacent to the main rivers. He had been instructed to explore the rivers encountered, locate Indian rancherias or villages, look for possible Mission sites, and to

---

record in all the observations the meridian [noon] altitude of the lower limb [bottom edge] of the sun, as given by the quadrant, for the greater satisfaction of the learned."

16. The term "ensign" now refers to the lowest commissioned rank in the U.S. Navy, ranking with a second lieutenant in the U.S. Army or a sub-lieutenant in England. In 1806, when Moraga received this rank, it was also the lowest commissioned rank in the British army, and was changed later in the nineteenth century. Bancroft just uses the Spanish rank "Alférez."

17. Donald C. Cutter, editor, *The Diary of Ensign Gabriel Moraga's Expedition of Discovery in the Sacramento Valley, 1808,* (Los Angeles: Glen Dawson, 1957) p. 7, paraphrases this remark. Moraga's relatively low rank after 25 years of service and despite his accomplishments, may have been due to his having entered the service as an enlisted man.

recapture *cimarones* (escaped Mission Indians). Moraga was already a very experienced military man and seemed to realize that with only twelve men, he would not accomplish much exploration if accompanied by vocal and unwilling prisoners. His diary mentions no *cimarones*.

Unfortunately, most of his entries are short and do not mention the spaces between rivers because without water, they would not be suitable mission sites. One of his longer descriptions covers October 4, 1808 when he was at the Mokelumne River looking north to the Cosumnes and his first view of the Sacramento Valley:

> This morning I climbed a rather high hill which is at the end of the low, hilly land to the north, [possibly near the site of the modern Camanche Reservoir] and looking at a distance in that direction I perceived a plain filled with oaks and with a few low, somewhat grass-covered hills. There is an arroyo with some water in a few rather large pools, and two moderate sized springs of water.
>
> It is seen that the plain runs from north to east.[18] To the north no sierra can be seen and to the east only a few low hills. If perhaps there is a sierra in one direction or the other, I have not been able to see it because of the excessive haze that exists. At about 5 leagues distance [13 miles] a grove of trees was sighted that indicated a river [the Cosumnes River] that comes out of a north easterly direction. Coming forth into the valley it flows toward the south.
>
> I returned to the camp where I arrived about noon. Then I dispatched the corporal in a northwesterly direction to examine the aforementioned grove. He returned at about 10 P.M., and having searched the grove, he found a river similar to those already mentioned. In all the country explored around the Río de la Pasión [the Mokelumne] the only things found were good plains for sown crops, pine timber up river where it leaves the sierra, and the fact that water can be drawn from the river.[19]

On the next day, they covered nine leagues (about 25 miles) and camped by the Cosumnes River which they named the San Francisco.

---

18. At its southern end the Sacramento Valley runs about N 30° W and Moraga occasionally wrote "east" where"south" would have been more appropriate.

19. Cutter, *Ibid*, p. 17

The entry for the next day, October 6, 1808, reads:

> Today, I sent four men upstream to explore it [the Cosumnes] to the place where it leaves the sierra. They found good plains, pine timber and many Indians. I went north-northwest with two men and after about 5 leagues (13 miles) I found a river which runs from north to south. It carries more water than any of the others except the San Joaquin. This is all for today.

Because of the diary entry for the next day, most historians believe that it was the American River that Moraga discovered on October sixth, and it is true if his camp had been further up the Cosumnes at present-day Wilton, the American would have been fourteen miles away to the north-northwest. However at that point the American is flowing, with many short bends, almost due west, and in October would be carrying little more water than the other rivers to the south. If he had camped further down on the Cosumnes, the Sacramento River, a bigger river which does flow north to south would have been thirteen miles away.

They left the camp on the Cosumnes the next day, October 7, 1808, travelled north about nineteen miles and stopped at the American River between modern Rancho Cordova and Folsom. They named the river *Las Llagas*, and Moraga rode eleven miles up stream to the beginning of the mountains (possibly at Folsom or the forks of the American). He turned back because of darkness, but noted several large logs along the bank which had been washed down during winter floods.

Unfortunately for the story of Sacramento, no entry in Moraga's diary has been preserved for October 8th. There is an entry for every day of the 20-day trip except the day that he might have explored the future site of Sacramento. The entry for the following day mentions that they "broke camp, and moved to the river we discovered yesterday, which we named the Sacramento [it was a Sunday]." He adds:

> There are many Indians on this river, and they showed themselves completely hostile, for this afternoon I sent three men to ford the river, and having found a ford, they crossed. On seeing them the Indians on the other side took up arms against them. They lightly wounded one soldier, cutting one of his nostrils by a sharp object which they threw at him on a stick like a lance, which they use with a flint blade. The result of the

matter was that one Indian was killed, and the rest jumped into the river and swam across.

These Sacramento Indians may have been hostile, but they were certainly brave. Moraga's men, the first foreigners to visit the Valley, wore arrow-proof vests made from five layers of sheepskin, steel helmets, and long swords. They were mounted on horses, which the Indians had never seen, and carried muskets. The Indians had only throwing sticks, bows, and arrows. He further mentions that the river measured 465 feet across with a uniform depth from shore to shore of four feet two inches.[20]

The following day, Moraga and his men forded the Feather River which then appeared (and still does) to be just a continuation of the main Sacramento River. They continued to march north-northwest past the Marysville Buttes which they noted, but did not name although they were the first non-Indians to see them. On October 11th, 1808, they travelled in the same direction along the east bank of the Upper Sacramento River, which they named the Jesús María thinking it was a separate tributary of the Sacramento.[21]

They met 130 armed Indians with whom Moraga spoke through an interpreter, asking what they wished. They wanted to know if the Spaniards would harm them. After Moraga told them no, the Indians immediately loosened their bows, approached the mounted soldiers, and made signs for them to dismount. Moraga and four others did so, and the Indians carefully inspected the horses before offering to trade their

---

20. This was on October 9, when the mountain snows had melted away, and well before the rainy season. The rivers were at their lowest point so that it would be unlikely that the Feather River would be either that wide or deep. On October 30, 1837, a skilled navigator, Captain Edward Belcher, visited the juncture of the Sacramento and Feather rivers, and reported the water too shallow for the ships boats. Others reported a shallow ford across the mouth of the Feather which Indian hunters crossed without horses during the fall. Moraga may have reached the Sacramento a bit below the point where the Upper Sacramento flows into the Feather from the west, that is, near the modern I-5 bridge above the Sacramento International Airport..

21. Moraga and some other early explorers have been regarded as having made a serious mistake in regarding the Feather River as a continuation of the Sacramento River. At the point of juncture, the Sacramento is flowing to the east and the Feather is flowing east south-east as it does for several miles above the juncture. The Upper Sacramento after several bends of over 100 degrees flows due north into the junction. Both rivers drain thousands of square miles and are fed by many smaller rivers and creeks; in the case of the Upper Sacramento, the longest being the Pitt River. Moraga's decision made on the spot from the back of a horse, and without any possible knowledge of the relative lengths of the rivers, seems really quite logical — even sitting at a desk with a modern map of California.

weapons for the animals. The offers were not accepted, but about 60 of the Indians continued to peaceably follow the Spaniards for over 20 miles to a point on the Upper Sacramento. A competent expert has estimated this was near the present site of Butte City, west of Oroville where state highway 162 crosses the Sacramento.[22]

Here they decided to turn back, crossing the Feather River farther north than before, and reached the American on October 13, 1808. The next day, Moraga sent the corporal downstream with four men, but they couldn't reach its mouth, and the site of Sacramento, because of the abundant tules. This may have been true of the north bank of the American, but Sutter and his later visitors seemed to have no such problem along the south bank in the dry season. In a later part of his report, Moraga stated that they found eleven Indian rancherias along the American River.

Moraga continued south into the San Joaquin Valley, turned to the west, and reached Mission San Jose, his starting point, on October 23, 1808. He had ridden over 600 miles, named four new rivers and one creek, and counted 33 previously unknown Indian rancherias. Gabriel Moraga continued to serve in the Spanish Army and his army record of 1820 stated that he had participated in 46 expeditions, and ten battles. He died in about his 58th year and was buried on June 15, 1823, in the mission cemetery at Santa Barbara.[23]

— § —

On October, 15, 1811, an exploring party of over 60 persons in several boats, under command of Sergeant Sanchez departed from the presidio of San Francisco. They went up the San Joaquin River, crossed over to the Sacramento River and returned on October 30, 1811, this being the first recorded instance of navigation on the Sacramento.

— § —

On May 13, 1817, Don Luis Antonio Argüello in his launch, *San Rafael* in company with Fr. José Ramón Abella of the San Francisco Mission and Fr. Narciso Duran of Mission San José in their launch *San José* started a thirteen-day expedition up the San Joaquin

---

22. Cutter, *Ibid*, p. 21 and endnote 31, p. 34.

23. Bancroft, *History of California*, Vol. II, footnote p. 571

and Sacramento Rivers.[24] As one would expect, Father Duran did not spend a lot of time in determining their daily positions, and most of the nine pages of his text concern the baptism of Indians, the heavy rainstorms, and descriptions of the terrain. He expressed distances in leagues, which later British navigators said were from two and a half to four English miles, but were usually considered for Spanish California to be 2.75 miles. He expressed the courses followed using eight compass directions, North, Northeast, East, and so forth. Occasionally, following their route is made more difficult by passages such as the one for May 16, 1817:

> ...Either this stream or the former is the main stream of the Sacramento. All along this river it is like a park, because of the verdure and luxuriance of its groves of trees. Still, it is difficult to land, because everything is inundated, due to the rise in the rivers from the melting snow. We stopped at six o'clock, having rowed eight leagues toward the northeast, north and somewhat to the northwest.

The table below gives some possible locations of Fr. Duran's stopping places estimated from a careful reading of Duran's diary and the belief that his "league" was about 2.75 statute miles, or 14,520 feet.

Stop	Location	Latitude	Longitude
START	Beach at Presidio of S. F.	N37°-48'-18"	W122°-27.6'
May 13, 1817	Point San Pablo	N37°-57.7'	W122°-25'
May 14	Collinsville, mouth Sac. R.	N38°-05'	W121°-51'
May 15	Above Rio Vista	N38°-12'	W121°-40'
May 16	Near Ryde on Sac. River	N38°-15'	W121°-33'
May 17	North end Steamboat Slough	N38°-18'	W121°-34'
May 18	Above Hood nr. Stone Lake	N38°-24.5'	W121°-31'
May 19	Sacramento Weir	N38°-36.3'	W121°-33.3'
May 20, 1817	Highest point, 2 miles above Highway 5 bridge, near Sacramento International Airport. Cut cross in oak tree.		

This listing may give the reader the impression that the stops shown are known exactly since a minute of latitude is only about one mile. The latitude and longitude are given to assist a future reader in

---

24. Fray Narciso Duran, *Diary during Expedition on the Sacramento and San Joaquin Rivers in 1817*, Edited by Charles Edward Chapman, (Berkeley: Academy of Pacific Coast History, 1911) Volume 2, No. 5. It consists of 21 pages, the even numbered pages in the original Spanish, and the odd or right-hand pages having the English translation.

locating the points on a map, not as proof that Fr. Duran actually stopped there. The bearings he reported are probably fairly accurate because it is reasonable to assume that this group carried one or more magnetic compasses for direction, but his method of determining the distances covered is not mentioned. On the open sea or in calm water, he could have multiplied their speed by the time on each leg of a course, but most of the time they were in swift currents and yet he gave the distances over the ground.[25] With these reservations, modern computer generated maps were used to approximately trace Fr. Duran's route and estimated stopping places.

His knowledge of the delta region seems to have been quite extensive because he knew the names of numerous Indian tribes and the supposed locations of some of their larger villages. When he was at Hood overlooking the level plain to the east around Stone Lake, (May 18, 1817) he recognized the Sierra Nevada, saw the snow, and mentioned the then-supposed fact that they might be seeing white rocks. This illusion can be seen at Carrara in Italy, when looking at the site of the distant marble quarries, but in this part of California, any "white rocks" seen from the valley, on the mountains, even in May, are really just snow. In his entry for May 20th (page 15), while going to the northwest on the Sacramento River near Verona, Duran noted:

> ...The vast lands to the end[26] of the Sierra Nevada be examined, which lands, it is likely, may be settled by innumerable natives. Once the pass in the Sierra is discovered, which the said end seems to offer, we would be able to ascertain the truth of what the Indians have told us for some years past, that on the other side of the Sierra Nevada there are people like our soldiers. We have never been able to clear up the matter and know whether they are Spanish from New Mexico, or English from the

---

25. Treutlein op. cit (p. 9) Fr. Pedro Font remarks about leagues "Finally, I wish to state regarding the leagues which I set down, that I have calculated them according to a measured league which I walked at a marching pace; they are Mexican leagues of five thousand yards or three thousand geometric paces [the Oxford English Dictionary cites a 1559 writer who stated this was five feet]. . . .Spanish leagues consist of four thousand geometric paces or 6666 yards and 2/3. . .according to Father Flores in his *Clave Geográfica.*"

26. Fr. Duran's Spanish text uses the word *Remate*, which can be translated as both "end" and "pinnacle." If he intended the latter meaning, he was thinking of exploring to the east rather than finding some end to the Sierra to the north. From Verona, on a clear day, passes between the highest peaks of the mountains around Donner Pass are visible about 85 miles away to the north east.

Columbia, or Russians from La Bodega.

At about ten leagues to the northwest of this place we saw the very high hill called by the soldiers that went near its slope *Jesús María* [the Sutter Buttes are 31 miles to the northwest of Verona].

He also understood that the San Joaquin and the Sacramento were the only two rivers in the Delta and did not spend time looking for other mythical rivers as did some later explorers.

We cannot be sure why Duran did not mention passing the mouth of the American River, when a few days before he had noted the smaller Steamboat and Sutter sloughs. A possible explanation could be that in May, the Sierra snow is rapidly melting causing heavy flows in the American River. The site of modern Sacramento and the point where the American joined the Sacramento River were quite low in 1817 and may have presented the appearance of a huge marsh rather than the juncture of two rivers.

In the afternoon of May 20, 1817, the exploring party turned back down the Sacramento, making good speed because of the strong current and reached the mouth of the San Joaquin River on May 22nd. After going up the San Joaquin and doing more baptizing and exploring, they turned back in the afternoon of May 23 and reached the beach of the Presidio of San Francisco at dawn, May 26, 1817.

— § —

In October or November, 1824, Otto von Kotzebue, post captain of the Russian Imperial Navy and commander of the Russian frigate *Predpriatie,* came by ship's boat up the Sacramento River. The highest point he reported reaching was in latitude N 38° 27', corresponding to a location on the river above Clarksburg and a mile below present-day Freeport. This was, before the founding of Clarksburg and Freeport, a relatively uninteresting part of the river, providing no real geographic reasons for turning back. Kotzebue may well have reached the mouth of the American River, then at latitude N 38° 35' only eight miles farther north. Errors in latitude, and even more in longitude, were very common with early California explorers for a number of reasons.

As an example of this problem, Jean J. Vioget (see footnote 69, page 74) in 1841, prepared an early map of the Sacramento region which showed New Helvetia (Sutter's Fort) in Latitude N 38° 45' 42", or just above Riego Road in modern Sutter County, and about thirteen miles north of its actual location in Sacramento. This map was used by Sutter in obtaining the New Helvetia grant, and the incorrect latitude was the basis of the "Squatter Riots."

Also in support of the conjecture that Kotzebue reached the site of Sacramento is the fact that on an 1833 Spanish map, the American River was shown as the "Ojotska" which seems more Russian than Spanish, although "ojota" was a Spanish word for a sandal worn by Indian women. Somewhat similar to Ojotska is a Russian word which is the root of the verb "to hunt" and pronounced *oho'tit'sya*. Perhaps this would indicate that Kotzebue had noted the presence of Native Indian hunters who traded otter and beaver skins at the missions. Later when American hunters frequented it, the Ojotska became *Rio de los Americanos*, or as we know it, the American River.

He also made a rather amazing prophesy for a visitor to California in 1824:

> It has hitherto been the fate of these regions, like that of modest merit, or humble virtue, to remain unnoticed; but posterity will do them justice; towns and cities will hereafter flourish where is now desert. The waters, over which scarcely a solitary boat is seen to glide, will reflect the flags of all nations, and a happy, prosperous people, receiving with thankfulness, what prodigal Nature bestows for their use, will disperse her treasures over every part of the world.[27]

Kotzebue hoped that this happy result might be caused by Russian occupation as indicated by the following quotation: "I could not help speculating upon the benefit this country would derive from becoming a province of our powerful empire, and how useful it would prove to Russia."[28]

Kotzebue reported extraordinarily abundant game, and mentioned seeing a bear swimming after a deer in the Sacramento River by moonlight. His ship, the *Predpriatie* had anchored in San Francisco Bay on October 8, 1824, and he departed on December 6.

— § —

---

27. Otto von Kotzebue, *Kotzebue's New Voyage Round the World in the years 1823, 24, 25, and 26* (London: 1830) Vol. II pp. 71-150. This citation is from Hubert Howe Bancroft, *History of California*, (San Francisco: The History Company, 1886) Vol. II, pp. 522-524.

28. Cited by Dr. J.D.B. Stillman, *Seeking the Golden Fleece*, (San Francisco: A Roman & Co., 1877) p. 312.

Early in 1827, a trapping expedition headed by the American frontiersman, Jedediah Smith, first crossed the American River, (which they named "Wild River"), while headed north along the Sacramento. They returned in April, and spent a little time at a camp on the American River. Later research has caused some modern historians to believe this camp was at or very near the present location of California State University, Sacramento. In the first week of May 1827, Smith's party attempted to cross the Sierra by going up along the American River. They were turned back by the deep snow encountered and moved to the south on the Stanislaus River. On May 20, 1827 Smith, with one other man, started up that river and in only eight days made the first eastward crossing of the Sierra by non-Indians.[29]

— § —

The first hunting expedition of the Hudson's Bay Company to reach the area of Sacramento was led by Chief Trader Alexander R. McLeod.[30] In his written report of the trip, he mentions that, on August 8, 1829, while camped on the Cosumnes River, he received a letter from a local settler named William Welsh. He also mentions seeing large numbers of California Indians, and at another point being opposed by 400 Indians armed with bows and arrows. This particular group was dispersed by a show of force, although in other instances small parties of trappers were killed. In late 1832, the Hudson's Bay Company sent another party to California from Vancouver, Washington under the command of John Work.[31] On February 24, 1833, he reported seeing in the vicinity of present-day Oroville, "four villages with 40 to 50 houses in each and there is another large village a little way ahead of us."

— § —

With John Work in 1833 came the most deadly killing force ever released against such a high proportion of the populace of a large

---

29. Dale L. Morgan, *Jedediah Smith and the Opening of the West* (New York: Bobbs-Merrill Co., 1953) pp. 210, 211.

30. Doyce B. Nunis Jr.,editor, *The Hudson's Bay Company's First Fur Brigade to the Sacramento Valley: Alexander McLeod's 1829 Hunt*, (Sacramento: Sacramento Book Collectors Club, 1968).

31. Bonita Louise Boles, *The Advent of Malaria in California and Oregon in the 1830's*, (Sacramento: Sacramento County Historical Society, 1990) Golden Notes Vol 36, No. 4, p. 4.

area. This force was the malarial parasite carried to California in the bodies of the trappers and transmitted by the female *Anopheles* Mosquito. It was silent, invisible, and quick; and against it, the unfortunate Indians had no defense. The forbearers of the trappers had lived with malaria for hundreds of generations, and many, many had died, but by a process of natural selection, the survivors had a genetic resistance. The trappers got sick, shook with fever, and took quinine, but after long suffering and many relapses, they usually recovered. The California Indians had lost no ancestors to malaria, had no access to, nor understanding of quinine, and simply died. They were a very spiritual people who believed that sickness was either caused by a spell cast by an evil person, or resulted from some transgression by the victim. In addition, their religious beliefs included great respect for their ancestors, and the funeral rites that were necessary to ensure their passage into the spirit world. The mass dying must have had a particularly terrible effect on the few survivors. A piteous example being a statement by Chief Factor John McLoughlin of the Hudson's Bay Company "The Indians . . . frightened at the mortality amongst them came in numbers to camp alongside of us giving as a reason that if they died they knew we would bury them. Most reluctantly . . . we were obliged to drive them away."[32]

Within a few months travelers were noting the prevalence of sick Indians and by the next year, whole villages were abandoned and the bones of the former occupants left unburied. Many of the surviving Valley Indians attempted to migrate to the territories of the Sierra tribes, where it would be an understatement to say they were not welcome. Quoting the final words of Boles' article, "Instead of fighting a human enemy, the Native Americans fought and lost the battle with a life-form that was both invisible and incomprehensible to them." By 1837, the Sacramento Delta, and the valley as far up as Marysville was almost devoid of native residents. Even Sutter in 1839 is reported having recruited Indian workers from as far north as Redding.

— § —

While there appears to be no written account of an 1832/33 visit to Sacramento by John Cooper, he must have visited here because he showed an interest in settling a little to the east of the site later

---

32. Bonita Louise Boles, ibid.

occupied by New Helvetia. John Bautista Roger Cooper (1792-1872) came to California in 1823 as captain of the Boston ship *Rover*. In 1827, he was baptized and added the Spanish name "Bautista" to his original given names of John Roger, and signed bonds for Jedediah Smith.[33] Cooper applied for a Mexican land grant south of the American River in 1833, but allowed the application to lapse. The grant was trapezoidal in shape, about nine miles on each side, with the top and bottom running east/west and the sides about N30°E. The southwest corner was in the general vicinity of Power Inn and Fruitridge Roads in modern Sacramento, and thus no part of the proposed grant touched the later site of Sutter's Fort. Accompanying the grant application was a manuscript map, the earliest known of the Sacramento area, and eight years older than Jean Jaques Vioget's map, mentioned in connection with Sutter's title to New Helvetia on pages 74 and 75, following.[34]

— § —

H.M.S. *Sulphur* commanded by Captain Sir Edward Belcher, R.N. (1799 -1877) anchored in company with H.M.S. *Starling* at Yerba Buena, in San Francisco Bay on October 19, 1837. Five days later an exploring party with the *Starling* and five boats started for Sacramento.[35]

It was after a long summer, and before the season of winter rains, so the river was low. As a result the *Starling,* on the advice of the pilot, was left in the vicinity of present-day Benicia, and the group continued in the boats. The actual location of the *Starling's* anchorage was merely reported as 36 nautical miles from Yerba Buena and might have been on the Martinez side. Belcher also noted that the pilot's

---

33. Hubert Howe Bancroft, *History of California* (San Francisco: The History Company, 1886) Vol. II pp. 765-766 and at the end of succeeding volumes, in the *Pioneer Register* section. This register lists literally thousands of persons who were in California before January 1, 1849, some with multi-page biographies.

34. Cooper's application and his original 1833 map are in the California State Archives, and they were located by Allan R. Ottley to be used by James Henley in his 1969 book *City of the Plain.* Bancroft included the Voiget map in his *History of California*, Vol IV, page 230, because he thought it was the first map of the Sacramento region.

35. Then, as now, in the navy, a ship is not a boat. A boat can be hoisted aboard a ship, but not the reverse. This fact is mentioned, because seafaring explorers considered it obvious and did not always make clear that their boats were taken up the rivers while their ship remained anchored in or near the bay.

opinion proved incorrect and the *Starling* could have proceeded much farther up the river.[36]   On the way up the Sacramento he remarked on the purity of the water:

> About twenty miles above the Starling's anchorage [thus very near modern Rio Vista] we found the water perfectly sweet; we therefore became not only relieved of the weight of this necessary article, but were enabled to luxuriate in draughts of the purest we had tasted for many weary months. To seamen such a luxury seldom occurs, and it is one a landsman can scarcely appreciate. I suspect, however, that the waters of the Sacramento would obtain their preference over all others.

No particular mention was made of the American River, although he had local Indian guides who should have known of its existence. Belcher's highest ascent of the Sacramento was to the promontory at the mouth of the Feather River, which he named *Point Victoria.* This was reached after six days travel, on October 30, 1837, and reported to be in latitude N38° 46 '47", longitude 47 minutes 31.5 seconds east of the Yerba Buena observatory (or W121° 37' 22"). By modern reckoning this is less than one third of a mile south of the present location of the junction of the Sacramento and Feather Rivers. Belcher, a highly experienced surveyor, knew the possible inaccuracies of longitude so far from fixed points, and the far smaller inaccuracies in comparing the longitudes of points separated by short distances and over relatively brief periods of time. He therefore listed the longitude as, "0° 47' 31.5" east of the observatory on Yerba Buena." His care and his confidence in the observation was indicated by the fact that .5 second of longitude at latitude 38° is about 40 feet. He was well aware that the location of the observatory would continually be more accurately fixed by future observations and would thus allow its refined longitude to be applied to the location of the junction point. The words "on Yerba Buena" could be taken to mean "on the island of Yerba Buena" or he could have meant "the observatory at Yerba Buena," as the town of San Francisco

---

36. H.M.S *Sulphur* was fitted as a surveying vessel of 380 tons, with a compliment of 109 men. H.M. Schooner *Starling* of 109 tons, commanded by Lieutenant H. Kellett, was fitted as a tender. Both vessels departed Plymouth on December 24, 1836. Mentioned in Captain Sir Edward Belcher, RN *Narrative of a Voyage Round the World preformed in Her Majesty's Ship Sulphur, during the years 1836 - 1842* (London: Henry Colburn, 1843) Vol I pp. xvii, 118-135.

Point Victoria at juncture of Sacramento and Feather Rivers

This photograph was taken October 25, 1998 looking west. The Sacramento River comes in from the south at the left, and the Feather River (which seems larger) enters from the northwest at the right. The mouth of the Feather here was, and still is, fairly shallow, and was a summer crossing place. Fremont is thought to have used this ford on July 10, 1846 in his 4-day march from Sonoma to Sutter's Fort with about 200 men. Sutter anchored here in 1839 before returning to ascend the American River. MBK photo.

was then called. If the first meaning is taken, *Point Victoria* would have been several miles to the east of the river, but if one assumes he meant the "observatory" was on or near Telegraph Hill in modern San Francisco, at longitude W 122° 24' 17" his location of the junction would have been very near the middle of the confluence of the two rivers on a point separating them at the present time. This point is located 21 miles along the river road (or "Garden Highway") above modern Sacramento, measured from the bridge at the mouth of the American River, and is quite near the hamlet of Verona (from 1849 to 1906 called "Vernon"). Belcher wrote of their visit here as follows:

> About half way up [the Sacramento River] we observed Indians on our right, but were apprised of their friendship by our guide, who brought their pass from the General Vallejo, "to absent themselves from the mission San José, in order to make treaties with natives or wild Indians;" or in other terms, to make trade for peltry, &c. Two of these volunteering to join our party, and hoping through them to get into communication with others, by whom we might be supplied with venison &c., we willingly took them into our boats.
>
> On the 30th [of October, 1837], about four P.M., we found the deep boats stopped at a point where the river forked. Lieutenant Kellett was dispatched to examine the main stream [Then and now, at this point the mouth of the Feather River appears to be the continuation of the of the Sacramento River and the Upper Sacramento actually comes in at a sharp angle from the left], but returned without having passed out of sight, reporting "no water for our lightest boats." The natives also assured us that this was the ford where hunters cross.
>
> I landed at "the Fork," which was named Point Victoria, and found the natives had but shortly fled, leaving a large stock of acorns, and all their provisions, fires, &c., behind.
>
> Every experiment was resorted to in order to get an answer from them. The natives who accompanied us called loud enough, and doubtless [they] were close to us ambushed, but afraid to reply. I therefore attached a knife, some tobacco, and beads, and left them to be picked up when the natives returned.

Belcher and his party spent the night near *Point Victoria* and left other presents the next day, but were unable to come within speaking distance of the local Indians.

Queen Victoria succeeded to the throne of Great Britain on the morning of June 20, 1837, and this obscure point was named four months and ten days later on October 30, 1837. It is possible that Point Victoria on the Sacramento could be the first geographic feature on earth, among the thousands of lakes, rivers, mountains, and cities, named for that illustrious queen.[37] There is also a possibility that news of Victoria's becoming Queen of Great Britain had not reached the *Sulphur* by October 30th, but her name had been carried on the Sacramento expedition on the bow of one of the ship's boats making the trip. Belcher seems to have been interested in Victoria even when she was a young princess, because in 1830 he supervised the building of a ship's boat in England, which he named *Victoria* and first used in exploring Africa, and later shipped aboard the *Sulphur*. In late 1839 he sold that boat on the coast of Mexico at the port of San Blas (between Mazatlán and Puerto Vallarta) and wrote:[38]

> I found the ship [*HMS Sulphur*] too deep to be agreeable, having immersed her copper; and having previously obtained the permission of the Admiralty, I disposed of the *Victoria* to Mr. Forbes, for £100. This was one of the two vessels constructed in 1830, under my superintendence, for the African survey; and the same which, under my present first Lieutenant (Monypenny), in 1833, by mistaking my orders, made her passage from Gibraltar to England. Having done her duty well during ten years, connected with several of our establishments, we parted with her with mixed feelings; one of satisfaction—that of being relieved from her weight; but the other of regret, arising from the loss of an old aid and pet, and the certainty that she never could be kept as she had been under the pendent [of the Royal Navy].

After much difficult surveying as they proceeded down the Sacramento River, Captain Belcher's party reached the *Starling* on November 18, 1837. Belcher also mentioned that while he and his men in the boats had often been hungry, game was remarkably plentiful around the *Starling*. In an interesting comparison with the equipment now considered essential for killing an elk, he mentioned that near the *Starling* one of these creatures had been dispatched by a sailor using

---

37. On a visit in April, 1998 to a small marina overlooking Point Victoria, I was told by the owner that he had never heard the point called by any name, but old Indian arrowheads used to be found there.

38. Captain Sir Edward Belcher *ibid*, Vol. I p.344.

only an oar. Belcher's sole further comment on this rather remarkable feat was that the meat was "coarse." His lack of enthusiasm may have been the result of a mental calculation of the value of a good oar 17,000 miles from England compared to that of some tough elk meat.

The whole party returned to the *Sulphur* at Yerba Buena on November 24th. Belcher's ships left San Francisco Bay at the end of November 1837.[39] During the *Sulphur's* stay in the bay, the sergeant and corporal of marines, the carpenter's mate, and several men and boys deserted. Diligent efforts were made to recover them, but four years later Commander Charles Wilkes (See Appendix D) noted the former English marines were rather unhappily hanging around New Helvetia.

EXPLORATIONS AND VISITS FROM 1839 TO 1846

In August 1839, and probably on or about August 9, 1839, Captain John A. Sutter left Yerba Buena in charge of a group intending to set up a permanent settlement in the Sacramento Valley.[40] Sutter led the way in a four-oared pinnace followed by the chartered schooners *Isabella* and *Nicolás,* commanded by William Davis and Jack Rainsford. Accompanying Sutter were eight or ten Kanakas he had brought from the Hawaiian Islands and five to seven "white men" who were artisans. The cargo included stores of provisions, ammunition, implements and three small cannon from Honolulu.

About a week later, the schooners anchored near Point Victoria (thus verifying Belcher's prediction in 1837 that this was the limit of navigation on the Sacramento for sea-going sailing vessels) and Sutter and his pinnace rowed fifteen miles further up the Feather River. The fleet then, on August 16, 1839, dropped down the Sacramento and went some three miles up the American River where they unloaded on the south bank quite near the modern railway bridge over the American River and the former city dump. Sacramentans have not always been so casual in commemorating this historic spot; before it was used as a dump, Sutter built his tannery there, and it was later occupied by a

---

39. Hubert Howe Bancroft, *History of California* Vol.IV pp.142-145 mentions this visit to San Francisco Bay and the trip up the Sacramento. For some reason he found Belcher's location of *Point Victoria* "altogether unintelligible," and believed *Point Victoria* and *Elk Station* to be the same, although Belcher did not use them interchangeably.

40. Hubert Howe Bancroft, *ibid* Vol IV, pp. 130. In this same Volume pp. 122-139, Bancroft provides a detailed history of John A. Sutter's life before this trip and more on the first year after his arrival at the settlement later named *New Helvetia,* and now part of Sacramento.

large gravel pit.

In Bancroft's words (Vol IV, p. 131):

> The schooners started in the morning on their return, carrying back several of the men who had intended to remain, and were saluted at parting with nine guns, which made a sensation among Indians, animals, and birds.
>
> Sutter was now left to carve his fortunes in the wilderness, his companions being three white men whose names are not known, ten Kanakas including two women, an Indian boy from Oregon, and a large bull-dog from Oahu. A site for permanent settlement was at once selected about a quarter of a mile from the landing on high ground, where two or three grass and tule houses were built by the Kanakas, more or less in the Hawaiian style, on wooden frames put up by the white men. Such were the primitive structures of California's later capital, and they were ready for their occupants early in September.

Although it was August, and the rivers were low, Sutter seemed to have listened to the local Indians, and to avoid winter flooding, he moved inland about a mile to a small rise in order to build a fort, farm, and trading post. Sacramento has had many floods in the 160 years since his selection of this location, but the site of his fort has never been under water — difficult to reach at times, but always dry.

About a year later, a group of settlers arrived on August 17, 1840 by land from Bodega. They had come down the coast from Oregon by ship, and with the aid of the Russians, Peter Lassen, William Wiggins, and four others had made the trip from Bodega to New Helvetia in 12 days. Their progress had been slow as they apparently wanted to avoid notice by the Mexican authorities of their entrance into California.

Wiggins noted that Sutter was living in an adobe house of 3 rooms, the fort not having been begun. Lassen went on to San Jose, where he was a blacksmith during the winter of 1840-1841, and Wiggins left for Dr. Marsh's ranch near Mount Diablo. The other four, who had traveled with Sutter in earlier years, remained at New Helvetia as his employees.

— § —

On January 22, 1840 Captain William Dane Phelps, master of the merchant trading ship *Alert,* departed from Boston bound for the California coast, where he made a series of trips between San Diego and San Francisco, gathering hides and selling goods brought out from New England. On February 4, 1841, during one of his visits to San Francisco Bay, he met Captain John Sutter, and had dinner with him aboard the *Alert*. Sutter invited his new friend to come up to see his thriving settlement at New Helvetia.[41]

CAP'T. WILLIAM PHELPS
1802-1872

A few months later Captain Phelps returned to the bay, and on July 27, 1841, at 11 A.M., left the *Alert* for Sacramento in a boat with four hands and an Indian pilot. He had expected to go with several other boats from nearby ships, but at the last minute amid claims that it was a bad season of the year, the river was low, the weather was hot, the mosquitos ravenous, and the Indians fiercely antagonistic, his friends refused to go along. Phelps had also been assured that no ship's boat had ever ascended the Sacramento, and he desired to be the first. His boat actually had been preceded by a veritable armada of ships' boats, but his at least, was the first flying the American flag.

With a fair wind and favorable tide, they entered the Carquinez Straits in five hours, and finally encamped on the bank of the river at 11 P.M., where he reckoned they were 95 miles from the *Alert*. Although the heat was very oppressive, they started rowing and sailing at 5 A.M. on the 28th and, with several rests under the trees, stopped again at 11 P.M. to camp by the river. The next day, July 29, 1841, Captain Phelps reached New Helvetia where he was greeted with a military salute and a fine dinner. This was a very fast trip to Sacramento and demonstrated his skill as a sailor as well as the strength of the southwest winds which frequently during the summer blow up through Carquinez Straits from San Francisco Bay.

---

41. William Dane Phelps, *Alta California, 1840-1842,* introduced and edited by Burton Cooper Busch, (Glendale, California: Arthur H. Clark Company, 1983) p.107. Captain Phelps traveled inland as well as up and down the Coast of California, picked up a lot of information, and recorded it in great detail in his most interesting journal of some 291 pages including illustrations. Three appendixes cover the ship's rules [the first of which is "no profanity"], Prices of goods at California, ["scalping knives $6.00"], and vessels encountered on the California Coast with rig, captain, flag of registry and tonnage for each. There follows a very complete index.

He describes the rest of his evening without mentioning, for obvious reasons, the "ravenous mosquitos:"

> The weather being very warm, and the temporary house in which Capt. S. Now lives abounding in fleas, a tent was pitched for me near the house, and being very tired I retired to bed & was soon asleep. But long before morning I was routed from my camp by an army of fleas who had found me out and were drawing on my being at a merciless rate. Giving my bedding a good shaking and myself a thorough scratching, I returned to my quarters again and slept soundly until after sunrise.

It is clear from Phelps' remarks that at the time of his visit, Sutter had not completed Sutter's Fort and even the large central building was still under construction. Just to the northeast of New Helvetia, across the American River, John Sinclair, a Scotchman and former employee of the Hudson's Bay Co., had a large ranch which Phelps visited on July 30th in company with Captain Sutter. Later in that day he and the captain rode around some of Sutter's holdings, and Phelps mentioned seeing a huge wheat field surrounded by the longest fence he'd ever seen. He estimated its length as being about three miles. Sutter and Sinclair also dug ditches around smaller fields to keep in the cattle, but no mention is made of the method used for the owners to enter such areas. A small draw-bridge or a filled section of ditch with a gate may have served to provide access.

On July 31, 1841, Phelps went back to Sinclair's ranch and was taken on an elk hunt, during which, late in the day, he was successful in killing a wildcat in a tree. About eight miles farther up the river, Phelps who was a remarkably good shot for a seafaring man, while standing up in his stirrups, killed an elk with a single shot to the head from about 60 yards away. Phelps attended a big going-away party at the Fort on the evening of August 2, 1841, and departed the next day, accompanied by John Sinclair who was going to San Francisco to take a ship for Hawaii to transact some business for New Helvetia.

The next morning, Phelps set out from Sacramento for the *Alert* in San Francisco Bay, and after fighting adverse tides and very strong winds, reached her at 10 A.M. on Sunday, August 8. His passenger, John Sinclair, was just able to book passage on the *Lama* which sailed for the Sandwich Islands on the following day. The U.S.S. *Vincennes* arrived on August 14, 1841, under the command of Lieutenant-Commander Cadwalader Ringgold, USN, and Phelps was welcomed aboard and asked innumerable questions about conditions on the California Coast. His entry for August 17 mentions piloting the *Vincennes* over to Whaler's Harbor (near modern Sausalito) and goes on to say:

> . . . Dined in the ward room & supped in the [Captain's] cabin. Capt. R. was much pleased with my account of the Sacramento and intends to explore it as far up as possible, feels much interested in Capt. Sutter's settlement and said that he would certainly visit him even if it were a hundred miles out of his way. I felt glad that he determined to explore the river hoping that his expedition up there would be of service to Cap. Sutter, and feeling not a little pleased that I myself forestalled (i.e. obtained) the honour of mine being the first American boat that ascended this river, which must in after years be alive with navigation.

After gathering more hides from around the bay, and loading wood and water, September 3, 1841, Phelps and the *Alert* left San Francisco Bay bound for San Diego with stops en route.

Aboard the *Vincennes,* Captain Ringgold prepared for the largest naval expedition on the Sacramento River up to that time.[42]   On August 20, 1841, he departed with Dr. Pickering (naturalist), six junior officers, an Indian pilot, about 60 men, and 30 days provisions in six boats. They reached camp on the American River opposite Sutter's New Helvetia, after a very fast trip, on August 23. Ringgold's extensive observations are included in the five-volume report of Commander Charles Wilkes, U.S.N., in command of the expedition. Wilkes was very strong minded, and very probably extensively edited Ringgold's report to bring it into agreement with Wilkes rather unfavorable view of California and his somewhat unsympathetic opinion of its inhabitants. While undoubtedly intelligent, Wilkes was blunt, highly opinionated, and always self-righteous. These are not generally endearing characteristics, and frequently brought him into open conflict with colleagues and those under his command. Unfortunately for Wilkes, these same sentiments were felt by some of his superior officers,

---

42. Although Cadwalader Ringgold had the permanent U. S. Navy rank of Lieutenant Commander in 1841, he had been temporarily placed in command of the *Vincennes,* and as such would be referred to as "Captain" by the ship's company.

Sutter's Fort looking almost due north in July of 1849 with the remains of the adobe-walled corral in front

The Fort is the only building in the original Sacramento city limits whose walls run true north-south and east-west, and may have been laid out using the North Star. The small building formerly occupied by the *Placer Times* can be seen at the extreme right. Sutter had sold out and moved to the Hock farm on the Feather River. The Fort was then in the early stages of ruin with portions rented out and a hospital inside the walls. From an illustration opposite page 62 of *California Illustrated* by J. M. Letts published in 1853.

and on two separate occasions he was tried by court-marshall during his long navy career (1818-1873). He completed his 2,800 page, hand written autobiography in 1875, and it was finally set in type and published by the U.S. Navy in 1978.[43] More famous admirals like Chester Nimitz or George Dewey had biographical material published while they were still on active duty, and the 103 year delay for Wilkes may be a record for all time. Despite his problems, he was an excellent observer, and in command of the first U.S. Navy group in the Sacramento Valley. Part of his original instructions and the details of his visit to the Sacramento Valley, from his California report appear in Appendix B, page 305.

— § —

Captain William Phelps in the *Alert* returned to Yerba Buena on March 28, 1842 and two days later departed from the ship for the Sacramento River with the cutter, a crew of "the 2nd officer, 4 stout hands, and an Indian pilot." The next day, after many hours of hard rowing in heavy rain, the weather cleared and they anchored at 11 P.M. to sleep in the crowded boat. Across 157 years of time the old sea captain's description of that moment on the Sacramento River is still moving. He wrote:

> . . . The moon rose about ½ past 11, and as it shed its bright beams upon the silver surface of the beautiful river, and the lofty sycamores throwing their broad shading along the margin, a picture was presented on which the eye could dwell with much pleasure. As I sat in the stern sheets of the boat gazing on the lovely scenery around me, I felt no inclination to sleep. The river at this place was broad; on either side were spread thick primeval forests, where the axe never resounded. All is quiet save the chirping of the cricket and gentle ripple of the eddies as the majestic torrent moves in solitary grandeur to mingle with the sea. . . .Here its waters are seldom disturbed by the oar, occasionally the solitary hunter paddles his canoe along its margin to entrap the Beaver, or monthly a boat from New Helvetia drops down with its rapid current, else all is silent.

---

43. William J. Morgan, et al., editors, *Autobiography of Rear Admiral Charles Wilkes, U.S. Navy, 1788-1877,* (Washington, D.C.: U.S. Government Printing Office, 1978). Wilkes began writing this work in "horrendous handwriting" at age 73 and wrote without chapters and very few paragraphs. To the editors, the autobiography seemed a vast collection of phrases, with little punctuation and almost no complete sentences. This style of presentation is certainly part of the reason for the delay in publication.

At noon on April 2, 1842, three days after leaving the *Alert* they reached Sutter's "embarcadero" at the site of modern Sacramento. The road to Sutter's Fort was impassable due to flooding and the Indian pilot was sent to the Fort to obtain a horse. By wading and swimming, he covered the 2-1/4 miles and reached Captain Sutter in about two hours. At 4 P.M., a "bidarka" or Eskimo kayak which Sutter had obtained from the Russians arrived, manned by two Kanakas. Sutter sent a note with them, explaining that a horse could not reach the embarcadero, but the visitor should sit in the center "hole" of the kayak and trust to the skill of his boatmen. Phelps described the craft as being about sixteen feet long, covered with seal skins, very light and buoyant, and extremely ticklish (likely to capsize). The trip involved fighting heavy currents through the trees and constant care to avoid being impaled on broken stumps, but after a half hour they reached the fort where the water was so high the boat came almost to the walls.

He passed Sunday April 3rd, reading and conversing with Sutter. Phelps congratulated him on halting the practice of paying the Indians on the Sabbath, and earnestly begged Sutter not to complete a distillery then being planned. He also described to Sutter a newly invented threshing machine which would greatly facilitate the preparation of grain after harvesting. Sutter tried to order one from Consul Larkin in Monterey, but was unsuccessful because the device had never been seen on the California coast.[44] The next day after breakfast Phelps rode for fifteen miles with John Sinclair to look at the country. He noted, "Nothing can exceed the beauty and richness of the lovely plains covered with luxuriant feed and a vast quantity of flowers of every hue and of great variety,"

On April 6, 1842, Phelps departed with his crew in the cutter for San Francisco Bay, and, after a trip which included a long visit with four Hudson's Bay Company trappers near modern Rio Vista, reached the *Alert* at 4 P.M. on April 8th. Captain Phelps continued trading along the California Coast until December 30, 1842, when he set sail for Boston. In his last entry he mentioned that he had visited San Francisco seven times, Monterey thirteen times, Santa Cruz three times, Santa Barbara and San Pedro each seventeen times, San Diego nine times, and several coastal stops.

---

44. Reuben C. Underhill, *From Cowhides to Golden Fleece, Unpublished Correspondence of Thomas O. Larkin*, (Stanford University: Stanford University Press, 1939), p. 43.

In all they had "hove up" the anchor on 131 occasions.

— § —

For a few years after 1842 , the coastal trade by Yankee ships wanting to explore the Sacramento River seemed to decrease. Sutter's launch made regular trips to San Francisco Bay and Fort Ross, the Sacramento Valley had been examined, and settlement was beginning. California's interior had lost some of its mystery. Visits by boats may have occurred from time to time, but explorers who left written records were not coming from the Bay. An exception was John Yates, an English sailor who was born near Liverpool in 1806, and went to sea when he was thirteen. After years of sailing to Australia, in the slave trade to Africa, and many trips to South America, he arrived in Yerba Buena from Mazatlán in 1842. Shortly after that, he became the captain of the small schooner, *Sacramento*, Sutter's launch. Yates tended to have a drinking problem, which may have contributed to his running the *Sacramento* on the rocks at Fort Ross on June 30, 1844. The schooner was eventually repaired, but in 1846 or '47, Yates gave up river sailing, obtained some land and combined farming with his drinking.

On May 11, 1847, in his forty-first year, he was married at Sutter's Fort to sixteen-year-old Eliza Booth, who had been living with her family at the Nye ranch on the Yuba River near its juncture with the Feather. He then took his new bride and her large family up the Feather River to his farming operation. They expected to see a grand California rancho, but instead found a run-down shack, uncultivated land and two Maidu women who claimed to be Yates' wives. The two excess "wives" refused to leave, the family all came down with fever, and in a short time they left Yates and his Indian consorts. Eliza's family moved down the Feather River to become the unwelcome guests of Heinrich Lienhard who was then managing Sutter's garden at the former Indian rancheria of Mimal on the west bank of the river a few miles below Marysville.[45] There they received informal medical care from Lienhard who saved all but the bride's youngest sister. About this time, the bridegroom, John Yates traveled down the river to the Fort and on June 1, 1847, he registered his branding iron and ear mark with Justice of the Peace, John Sinclair.

---

45. Heinrich Lienhard, *A Pioneer at Sutter's Fort, 1846 - 1850,* Edited by Marguerite E. Wilbur, (Los Angeles: The Calafía Society, 1941), pp. 59-62.

Yates remained in California until 1851, but seemed to have had absolutely no interest in gold mining. He sent a long letter from his home in Hawaii on May 10, 1872, to the historian, Hubert Howe Bancroft, in which he described some events of his earlier life, but told particularly of a trip he made up the Sacramento Valley in 1842 and his friendly reception by the local Native Indians.[46] He also had fond memories of the generosity of his old employer, Captain Sutter.

— § —

Visitors and settlers had been coming overland to Sacramento since the time of Jedediah Smith in 1827, but in the 1840s their numbers steadily increased. For the year 1843 about 50 or 60 people from outside California visited the Fort, and Bancroft,[47] mentions the names of members of two parties, in one of which were included Samuel J. Hensley and Pierson B. Reading both of whom became prominent in early Sacramento history. (See pages 121 and 150.)

— § —

After a most difficult, 33 day, winter crossing of the Sierra, a hungry and exhausted exploring party led by Captain John Charles Frémont arrived at New Helvetia on March 6, 1844. They were given food, supplies, and a most genial welcome by Captain Sutter. They had entered California near modern Markleeville, Alpine County, and gone north to the headwaters of the South Fork of the American River. They followed it down to Coloma, then through its junction with the North Fork, through Folsom, and finally crossed it near modern H Street to reach the Fort. Along the route, on February 14, 1844, Frémont and Charles Preuss climbed Red Lake Peak (10,061 feet), and from it they made the first recorded sighting of Lake Tahoe, which they called *Mountain Lake*. They had entered the mountains with 67 horses and mules, and 33 reached the Sacramento Valley, "and they were only in a condition to be led along." Most of the others had been killed for food, as had a little dog named *Clamet* they had brought all the way from Oregon.

---

46. John Yates, *A Sailor's Sketch of the Sacramento Valley in 1842,* introduction and notes by Ferol Egan, (Berkeley: Friends of the Bancroft Library, 1971), pp. 11-25.

47. Hubert H. Bancroft, *ibid,* Vol. IV, pp. 300-303.

The mountain Indians had traded a small amount of pine nuts and fifteen pounds of salt for some trinkets, but really all the men and animals were starving when they reached New Helvetia. The next day, on March 7, Frémont gathered some supplies and rode back to reach the main part of his group and they met very near the present site of Folsom Prison. In his words, "Mr. Fitzpatrick and his party, travelling more slowly, had been able to make some little exertion at hunting, and had killed a few deer. The scanty supply was a great relief to them; for several had been made sick by the strange and unwholesome food which the preservation of life compelled them to use. We stopped and encamped as soon as we met; and a repast of good beef, excellent bread, and delicious salmon, which I had brought along, was their first relief from their suffering of the Sierra, and their first introduction to the luxuries of the Sacramento [and to the justly famous generosity of Captain Sutter]."[48]

— § —

From 1844 through 1847 the number of overland immigrants intending to become farmers and tradesmen increased each year, and even though they did not always remain in the Sacramento area, "Sutter's Fort" was their most frequent initial destination. Captain Sutter had always imagined New Helvetia as the center of an inland empire under his personal ownership and control. He realized that the flood-free area around the Fort was too small to accommodate a large settlement and for his dream to become reality, a larger and dry area adjacent to the Sacramento River was needed.

He selected a site to be called *Sutterville* facing on the river and about one-half mile below present-day Broadway. On January 28, 1846, Sutter's diary mentions Mr. (Henry) Trow was cutting stakes to be used in laying out a new town. The survey was completed by Hastings and Bidwell about a month later, and soon thereafter Sutter erected the new town's first building. A brick kiln was set up and the first regular brick building in California was completed at Sutterville in the next year by George Zins, a German who had arrived at the Fort in 1846.

Thousands of miles from Sacramento, an event occurred which

---

48. Bob Graham, *The Crossing of the Sierra Nevada in the Winter of 1843-44,* (Sacramento: Bob Graham, Publisher, 1996) p. 60. Also, Brevet Captain J.C. Frémont, *Report of the Exploring Expedition to the Rocky Mountains in the Year 1842 and to Oregon and North California in the Years 1843-44,* (Washington: Senate Document 174, 1845).

would completely alter the political climate of California and the course of John Sutter's empire centered at the fort. In May of 1846, The United States and Mexico declared that a state of war existed between them, and this situation continued until the Treaty of Guadalupe Hidalgo was signed on February 7, 1848. At the start of this war, the United States had a small standing army of a few thousand men, and since gaining independence had engaged in two wars. The war of 1812 had been fairly successful despite the burning of the White House, but Great Britain had been occupied with affairs in Europe at the time and had not devoted its full attention to fighting the Americans. The Seminole Wars (1817-1818 and 1835-1842) were costly and vicious guerilla affairs. They cost over $40,000,000 and the United States lost as many as 2,000 soldiers killed in action. Although Spain did cede Florida to the United States in the Transcontinental Treaty which ended the first Seminole War, taken together, these wars were by no means a triumph of American arms.

Because of this record, the European Powers, and to an even greater extent, Mexico, felt that the Mexican Army of over 50,000 trained veterans would, in 1846, make short work of the North Americans. The actual result was that within eighteen months, Mexico lost almost half its claimed territory, and had its Capitol occupied by the Americans under General Winfield Scott. Historian Gary Kurutz[49] cites two factors possibly affecting the outcome the War with Mexico:

First was the availability of many graduates of the United States Military Academy at West Point in the grades of lieutenant and captain and particularly those trained as military engineers after 1817 when Col. Sylvanus Thayer became superintendent. Some examples in this group are; Jefferson Davis, Ulysses S. Grant, Thomas "Stonewall" Jackson, Robert E. Lee, and William Tecumseh Sherman. Second was the excellent quality of the United States Navy, its ability to closely cooperate with the Army, and to use its Marines and sailors ashore when needed. This was particularly true in California where Commodore R. F. Stockton's proclamation of August 17, 1846 said;

TO THE PEOPLE OF CALIFORNIA
On my approach to this place with the [naval] forces
under my command, José Castro the Commandant General of

---

49. Author, Principal Librarian, and Head of Special Collections of the California State Library at Sacramento—in a conversation with the author in May 1999.

51

California, buried his artillery and abandoned his fortified camp "at the Mesa," and fled toward Mexico.

With the sailors, the marines, and the California Battalion of mounted Riflemen, we entered the "City of the Angels," the Capitol of California on the 13th of August and hoisted the North American Flag.

The Flag of the United States is now flying from every commanding position in the Territory, and California is entirely free from Mexican Dominion.

The Territory of California now belongs to the United States and will be governed as soon as circumstances may permit, by officers and laws, similar to those by which the other Territories of the United States are regulated and protected.

But until the Governor, the Secretary, and Council are appointed, and the various civil departments of the Government are arranged, military law will prevail, and the Commander-in-Chief will be the Governor and protector of the Territory . . . [there follow a series of rules applying to the conduct of the civilian population of California, ending with]

. . .All persons are required as long as the Territory is under martial law, to be within their houses from 10 o'clock at night until sunrise in the morning.

R. F. STOCKTON, Commander-in-Chief, and Governor of the Territory of California. Ciudad de los Angeles, August 17th, 1846.[50]

The news traveled fairly quickly to Sacramento where American type political officers seemed desirable or at least fashionable. On September 28, 1846, the first election in Sacramento was held at Sutter's Fort for the office of Magistrate of the Sacramento District. There were fifteen voters listed by name, none of whom remained in Sacramento to be shown in the 1851 directory. The result was reported by the judge of the election as;

The candidates and the number of votes were: John Sinclair, 15; Jared Sheldon, 8; J. A. Sutter, 1.

The subscribers certify that the above is a correct register and poll of votes for the election of a magistrate of the Sacramento District, held at Fort New Helvetia, on the 28th

---

50. Monterey *Californian*, Extra Edition, September 5, 1846 page 1, Column 1.

day of September, A.D. 1846.[51]

J. A. Sutter, *Judge*

G.[Gardner] T. Wyman
J.[James] Tyler

Considering the fact that all the judges, including Captain Sutter were listed voters, and the Captain was a candidate, he should have fared better in the election. Perhaps it was just that 23 of the 24 voters thought it was time for a new alcalde.

— § —

Even before the war started, the Navy Department had sent ships to California to ensure that the essentially undefended area would not be taken over by Great Britain. In the very first days of the war (they left New York on July 14, 1846), Lt. William T. Sherman and five other army officers commanding an artillery company went around Cape Horn to Monterey, California in the old navy store ship *Lexington*. They carried a large number of cannon, small arms, and quantities of ammunition for both with the expectation that they might have to fight their way ashore. In a letter written June 30, 1846, from Pittsburgh, Pennsylvania, Sherman said "Ordered to California by Sea around Cape Horn! Is this not enough to rouse the most placid? . . .I have the fullest confidence in the officers with whom I am to go, and believe I shall be benefitted in every way by the change. We shall be pioneers at least in a far off world."[52]

Before Sherman's departure, two remarkable events had occurred which forever changed the influence of the United States on the west coast of North America. Unknown to the people on the eastern seaboard, at about noon on July 7, 1846, the flag of the United States was raised by Commodore Sloat over the custom house at Monterey, the old capital of the Californias. And by a treaty, signed June 15, 1846 between the United States and Great Britain, the Oregon territory, south of the 49th parallel of latitude came under the

---

51. From a file seen before 1890 in the office of the San Francisco County Clerk and cited by Win. J Davis, *Illustrated History of Sacramento County,* (Chicago: Lewis Publishing Company, 1890), p. 20.

52. M. A. DeWolfe Howe, Editor, *Home Letters of General Sherman*, (New York: Charles Scribner's Sons, 1909), p. 34.

sovereignty of the United States.[53]   Thus in the 22 day period between those dates, the United States had obtained sovereignty of the Pacific Coast from Cape Flattery at the mouth of the Strait of Juan de Fuca, to the border of Lower California. Within eight months the conquest had been extended to Cabo San Lucas at the southern tip of Baja California in Latitude N 22° 50'. For comparison of the distance on the Atlantic side, this would encompass the coast from Corner Brook, New Foundland to a point eighteen miles south of Havana, Cuba.

In the evening of July 10, 1846, Mr. William Scott arrived at Sutter's Fort with a copy of Commodore Sloat's proclamation and an American flag he had been given by Captain John B. Montgomery of the USS *Portsmouth* then anchored at Yerba Buena (later, San Francisco). Probably after seeing Captain Sutter, Scott rode a short distance to Col. Frémont's camp on the American River where the news of Commodore Sloat's proclamation was warmly received.[54]   The next morning the flag of the United States was raised for the first time over New Helvetia, then referred to as "Fort Sacramento."[55]

The key points of Alta California were quickly occupied by the Americans, but the flag was not hoisted in Baja California until March 30, 1847. On that date, under the command of Lieutenant Benjamin F. B. Hunter, 140 sailors and marines from the USS *Portsmouth* (still commanded by Captain John B. Montgomery, USN) landed at San José del Cabo near Cabo San Lucas, and without resistance from the local citizens, hoisted the flag of the United States as the *Portsmouth,* anchored in the harbor, fired a 21 gun salute. Captain Montgomery issued a proclamation which read in part:

> . . .in virtue of authority vested in me by the Naval Commander in Chief of the U. States in the Pacific, by reason of the belligerent relations now existing between the U. States of America and the Republic of Mexico; I do hereby in the name of the U States take formal possession of the Town and

------

53. Peter H. Burnett, *An Old California Pioneer,* (Oakland, California, Biobooks, 1946), p. 143.

54. Monterey *Californian*, May 10, 1847, page 1, column 1. This was the first newspaper published in California, and started August 15, 1846. Its first mention of Sacramento or New Helvetia was on September 17, 1846.

55. Hubert Howe Bancroft, *ibid*, Vol V, p. 244 (in footnote).

jurisdiction of San José in California; in token whereof I have
this day caused the Flag of the U. States to be hoisted in the
town of San José. . .[56]

Within a few months, brave and determined Mexican volunteers
with regular officers from the mainland were attacking the American
positions in Baja California, and a desperate example occurred at San
José del Cabo in November of 1847. Lieutenant Charles Heywood had
been left on November 9th, in an old mission building, converted into a
make-shift fort. He had landed with four passed midshipmen, 20
marines, a nine-pounder cannon, 75 carbines, and ammunition, On
November 16, 1847, they were attacked by 150 men. After three days
of fighting they were presented with a surrender demand which they
immediately refused. Two days later they were finally saved by the
arrival of two American whaling ships that landed a band of 60 whalers
"half in uniform of red shirts and banners; armed with muskets, lances,
spades (huge sharpened instruments used for cutting blubber) and even
harpoons." They "came in very good order, presenting a formidable
appearance. . ." These unusual reinforcements remained until relieved
by the arrival of the USS *Southampton* on November 26.[57]

This represented just one of the low points in the American
efforts to establish control of Baja California, but fighting continued
until April 1848 when the last of the Mexican leaders was captured and
returned by US forces to Mazatlán on the mainland. News of the final
ratification of the treaty which ended the Mexican War, returning Baja
California to Mexican control, was received there on June 13, 1848.
The last American presence was the USS *Dale* which departed from
Cabo San Lucas on September 21, 1848.

By the terms of this treaty, California and New Mexico were
purchased from Mexico, and these territories may well have been slowly
settled and integrated into the United States as had occurred in
Oregon, Louisiana, and later Alaska. In northern California this
tranquil possible change was accelerated to a degree unique in history
by another much smaller event which occurred about 50 miles from
Sacramento in January, 1848–just fourteen days before the treaty date.

---

56. Doyce B. Nunis, jr., Editor, *The Mexican War in Baja California,* (Los Angeles:
Dawson's Book Shop, 1977), pp. 22-23 and end note 16, p. 76.

57. Nunis, *ibid,* p. 39.

GOLD AT SUTTER'S MILL

Through many difficulties, Sutter's efforts at establishing a mini-empire around New Helvetia had proved successful, until he was essentially ruined by what one would expect to be the ultimate good fortune; gold was found on January 24, 1848 in almost unlimited quantities on public land near his own holdings. Shortly after the discovery, in a unique original document now in the possession of the California State Library, Sutter and his agent who had actually discovered the gold, James Marshall, obtained a lease for the area around the discovery site signed with the marks of local Indian chiefs.

California had just been purchased from the Mexican government, and was then under the military governor, Colonel R. B. Mason, at Monterey. Hoping for the governor's approval, Sutter and Marshall sent the proposed lease, which made absolutely no mention of the gold, to Monterey for ratification. This was denied for the amazing reason that since Indians could not own land in California (by a Mexican law inherited by the Americans under the terms of the peace treaty), they could not sell or lease it.

The news of the gold at Coloma spread slowly at first and Edward C. Kemble, the nineteen-year-old editor of the San Francisco *California Star,* heard the first mention in early March 1848. Some native Californian, the rumor went, a hard rider with a fast horse, had ridden from across the river opposite Sutter's Embarcadero to the ranches back of Benicia, crossed the Carquinez Straits by boat, passed through Livermore Pass and San Jose to San Francisco in just two days. He had brought a report that some of Sutter's men had found gold on the American Fork. Despite the incredible effort on the part of this forgotten courier, the news was not generally accepted as being important and the *Star* did not give it any space.

A few days later, Sutter's launch, the *Sacramento,* arrived at the beach in San Francisco after a four-day trip down the river and brought four passengers. Kemble did not pick up much news in questioning them, until one of the passengers said that if he would "come up to the store" the passenger would show him something. This proved to be a few thin flakes of a dull yellow metal wrapped in a little rag, and accompanied by the remark that "that there is gold, and I know it and I know where it comes from." Kemble and the others in the store were not impressed and the *Star* was published that night without any mention of possibly the greatest "scoop" of the 19th century. A small amount of gold and a lot of rumors continued to come down from Sacramento, and early in April, Kemble decided to join the first group of prospectors from San Francisco to go to the mines after gold was discovered.

In a small, progress-fighting sailboat named *Rainbow* (as a steamboat named *Sitka* it had reached Sacramento on November 21, 1847), Kemble, George McKinstry, and Major Pierson B. Reading (see page 150 following) and his Indian servant took passage to Sutter's Fort with William A. Leidesdorff's young clerk, George R. Glidden, as captain. Unlike some 200,000 prospectors who followed, they neither expected nor wanted to find rich mines at Coloma. They had publicly discounted in San Francisco the importance of the small quantities of gold they had seen, and made this trip to prove the wisdom of their pronouncements.[58] The trip to Sutter's Embarcadero took about six days and Kemble described the scene as it was on Monday, April 17, 1848, twelve weeks to the day, after the discovery of gold at Coloma:

> The picture of your wilderness . . . the site of the embryo city and capital of a great state—rises before me as I recall the memories of this time and trip. A forest of noble sycamores, dense and deep, guarding a mighty solitude like a vast army of giants in array, their bright green banners mirrored in the clear stream. Not a human habitation in sight save the Indian ferryman's hut about the foot of [modern] J Street, and an Indian-sweat house, a hundred yards, perhaps, above.
>
> Moored to the bank was the pioneer of your present commerce and navigation, an Indian canoe. A broad, well-

---

58. Bancroft in his *History of California*, Vol. V, pp. 576-581 mentions that about October 23, 1847, it was reported in the *California Star*, that the first steamboat on San Francisco Bay had been delivered to its new owner, William A. Leidesdorff. Later called the *Sitka*, it was a side wheeler with a very small engine, and was 37 feet long, nine feet wide, depth of hold 3-1/2 feet, and drew 18 inches of water.

After two trial runs on the Bay to Santa Clara and Sonoma, she left San Francisco for Sacramento on November 15, 1847. Aboard were about ten passengers including Leidesdorff and George McKinstry, the first sheriff of the Sacramento district, headquartered at Sutter's Fort. The trip took six days and seven hours, which compares rather unfavorably with Captain Phelp's time of two days in a sail boat. Sacramento's first steamboat visitor returned to San Francisco, and as she departed from Sacramento a large wagon and ox team crossed the river, headed for the Bay. The oxen beat the *Sitka* to Benicia by four days. The *Sitka* finally made it to San Francisco, and the next day was sunk at her anchorage, where Battery Street is now located, by a south-east gale. She was promptly raised, had her engine removed, and was transformed into a sailing launch with the new name, *Rainbow.*

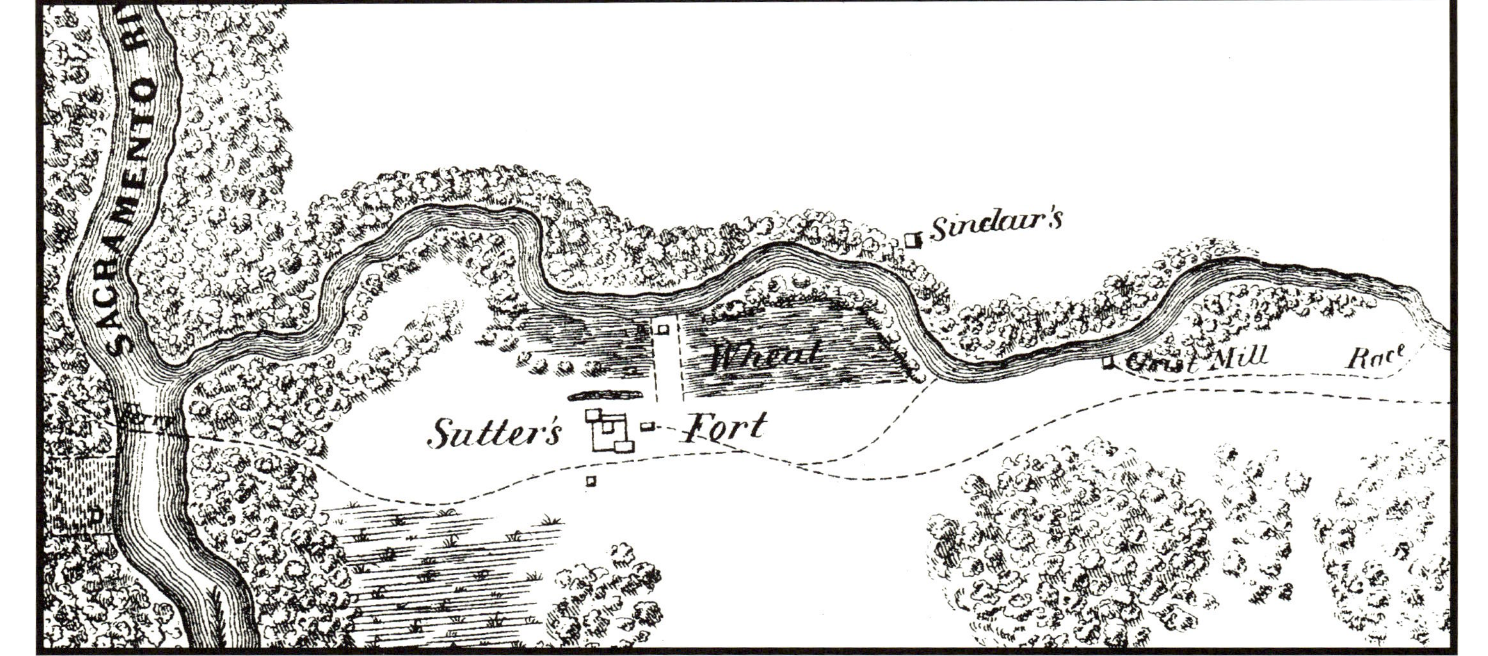

Lt. William T. Sherman's Map July 20, 1848, of Sutter's Fort before the founding of Sacramento City

Sutter's Indian ferry (a large canoe) across the Sacramento left from modern I Street. The small building above the Fort on the American River was Sutter's tannery. The Grist mill on the south side of the American River (at modern Watt Avenue) was moved to Front Street and became the City Hotel in the fall of 1849. The rancho of John Sinclair, Alcalde of the Sacramento District, is north of the American River. The location of his house was on the west side of modern Howe Ave. between Northrop and Hurley. Just to the right of the Fort was the "hospital" and later probably the location of Sacramento's first newspaper, the *Placer Times*.

From Ex. Doc. 1, President Filmore's address to Congress, December 5, 1848, Col. R. B. Mason's report, Map 23.

> beaten road, laid by the wheels of that twin-pioneer of your commerce, the "adobe cart". . . led back from the river's bank, the only clearing visible in all this waste and solitary place. [About taking passage in the Indian's ferry, he added] . . . In riding in these frail, tilting canoes, it is sometimes thought the part of prudence to part one's hair exactly in the middle.
>
> The setting sun was throwing a flood of mellow light beneath the arching branches, brightening the silver shafts of the cottonwood and turning to molten gold the miniature lakes spread on every side. Ah! Those miniature lakes—pools in a vale of misery; prophets of the floods to come that were to drown the fortunes of thousands in subsequent times.[59]

That evening they stayed at the Fort with Captain Sutter who displayed no confidence in the importance of the gold discoveries. Because of his anxiety for the progress of the sawmill rather than an interest in the mining activities, he agreed to accompany Kemble's group to Coloma. Sutter had been there once before, in March, and had brought back the first remittance of treasure from the northern mines of California—a few grains of gold stopped in the quill of some mountain bird. Again quoting Kemble's narrative:

> There was, then, Captain Sutter, Major Reading, McKinstry, and the editor aforesaid [Kemble, then nineteen years old], with two Indian "boys," Antonio and Jose, favorites of the Captain, to look after the horses and make camp, and the party started at an early hour, because it was not expected to reach the mill before the next day. Captain Sutter, singular as it may seem, is a very poor horseman. Rarely in those days did he ever venture on the back of a horse; riding a mule in preference. On this occasion he was mounted on a favorite mule called Katy. Frequently that morning in crossing marshy places or ascending slippery paths the Captain would fall to the rear and be heard in low tones of earnest expostulation with his mule; "Now den Katy—de oder foot! God bless me Katy—de oder foot, child!"
> . . .[arriving above Coloma] Straight before them, seeming so very near in the transparent atmosphere of that early morning, rose in solemn majesty the hoary heads of the Sierras. . . . The course of the river is lost to the eye in the dense growth of the

---

59. Edward C. Kemble in *Sacramento Daily Union*, April 5, 1873.

> forest—we can scarcely catch at this distance the sound of its
> white, flashing waters. Only one sign of life, and that is a thin,
> blue column of smoke ascending dreamily from the depths of the
> vale, marking the locality of the lumbermen's camp. . . . On a
> beach of land near the base of the long hill we are descending
> under majestic, spreading trees, we spy the camp of Marshall
> and his companions. It is a rude bivouac in the open air, with
> blankets, smoke-blackened kettles and tins and provender sacks
> and boxes strewed all around, as though the men were on a
> march. . . . the lumbering crew . . . were sitting or sprawling on
> the ground about the smoldering fire. They hardly returned our
> greeting as we rode up. It was apparent from the first moment
> we came in sight we were unwelcome guests.

While Sutter went off with Marshall to inspect the mill, the rest of
the party tried to obtain information on the gold from the lumbermen.
It would have been easier, in Kemble's words, "opening oysters with a
wooden toothpick" than finding out from these people where and how
much gold was found. Eventually Major Reading borrowed an Indian
water tight basket and dug up some earth from the mill race. He took
this to the water's edge and panned several shovelfuls down to the
black sand. When he returned to the group, and was asked about the
gold he had found, he said, "not enough to buy a drink." Kemble duly
noted in his memorandum book the word "humbug," and further
practical investigation by the visiting prospectors was halted.

That evening, around the fire, Captain Sutter through one of his
boys acting as an interpreter and turning it into Spanish, assisted in
questioning some local Indians who had come in to see the captain.
Kemble was surprised to learn that the Indians had known of the
existence of the gold for many generations, but it was considered to be
owned and guarded by evil spirits (later that same year Karl Marx
published *The Communist Manifesto* which tended to support this view).
The Indians seemed to not know the value of the yellow metal, and the
visitors made the unlikely assumption that the early mission padres had
knowledge of the gold mines and had spread the rumor among the
Indian proselytes so that the mines could be worked sometime in the
future for the church.

The prospectors returned to Sutter's Fort and departed for San
Francisco on April 24, 1848, without any quantity of gold, but secure in
the knowledge they had been right in stating that the mines on the
American River were not rich. In the next issue of the *California Star*

after his arrival in San Francisco, Edward C. Kemble "denounced the whole theory and alleged success as an arrant cheat and imposture."

Within less than a month of this statement, emigrants on the trail to California heard (in Kemble's own words written later in 1873) "thundering in the rear with hot breath and flashing eyes the messengers that spoke one word and that word the electrifying monosyllable that fired the hearts of all travelers . . . that cry of "GOLD." The other newspaper in San Francisco, *The Californian*, suspended publication on June 2, 1848, due to the departure of its employees for the mines, and Kemble temporarily closed the *California Star* on June 14th to return to the northern mines.[60]

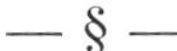

A highly reputable American, Thomas O. Larkin, who had been in California for sixteen years, visited the American River mines in June of 1848 when the site of downtown Sacramento was still a forested wetland. The "Gold Rush" from the United States had not really started, gold was so plentiful that crime did not either pay or exist, and a sort of glorious anarchy prevailed over all of Northern California. A feeling for the times may be gained from a few excerpts from the letter Larkin wrote to the U.S. Secretary of State upon his return to Monterey. This informative letter is included in its entirety in Appendix C on page 317.

> During my visit I was an interpreter for a native of Monterey, who was purchasing a machine or canoe [a"rocker"]. I first tried to purchase boards and hire a carpenter for him. There were but a few hundred feet of boards to be had; for these the owner asked me fifty dollars per hundred ($500 per M), and a carpenter washing gold dust demanded fifty dollars per day for working. I at last purchased a log dug out, with a riddle and sieve made of willow-boughs on it, for one hundred and twenty dollars, payable in gold dust at fourteen dollars per ounce. The owner excused himself for the price, by saying that he was two days in making it, *and even then demanded the use of it until sunset* [italics inserted]. My Californian has told me since that himself, a partner and two Indians obtained with this canoe eight ounces the first and five ounces the second day.

---

60. *A Kemble Reader*, edited by Fred B. Rogers, (San Francisco: California Historical Society, 1963), p. 125.

Under ordinary circumstances the sieve, needed to keep larger rocks out of the riffle box below, would have been made of heavy wire mesh or a metal plate with holes punched in it, instead of the far less durable "willow boughs." The eight and one half ounces of gold required for the purchase would be worth $2,571.00 at 1998 prices. The fact that the moment of transfer of ownership was part of the purchase contract shows the rewards expected in even a few hours of use. Larkin also gives estimates of the number of miners then working, the income obtained, and the chaotic effects on the very fabric of society around the Pacific Rim.

> A complete revolution in the ordinary state of affairs is taking place; both of our newspapers are discontinued from want of workmen and the loss of their agencies; the alcaldes have left San Francisco, and I believe Sonoma likewise; the former place has not a justice of the peace left.
>
> The second alcalde of Monterey today joins the keepers of our principal hotel, who have closed their office and house, and will leave tomorrow for the golden rivers. I saw on the ground a lawyer who last year was attorney general of the king of the Sandwich Islands, digging and washing out his ounce and a half per day; near him can be found most of his brethren of the long robe, working in the same occupation.
>
> ... To conclude; my letter is long, but I could not well describe what I have seen in less words, and now can believe that my account may well be doubted; if the affair proves a bubble, a mere excitement; I know not how we can all be deceived, as we are situated. Governor Mason and his staff [including Lieutenant William Tecumseh Sherman] have left Monterey to visit the place in question, and will, I suppose, soon forward to his department his views and opinions on the subject.

Colonel Mason did, in fact, on August 17, 1848, send a long and highly informative report to General R. Jones, adjutant general of the Army at Washington, D.C. While Colonel Mason mentions several instances of the disruptive effects of the gold fields, the following lines from his message seem to say it all:

> A soldier of the artillery company returned here [Monterey, California] a few days ago from the mines, having been absent on furlough twenty days; he made by trading and working during that time $1,500. During these twenty days he was travelling ten or eleven days, leaving but a week, in which he

> made a sum of money greater than he receives in pay, clothes, and rations during a whole enlistment of *five years* [Italics added]. These statements appear incredible, but they are true.

The information contained in these reports reached Washington in the early fall of 1848 and Colonel Mason sent about 230 ounces of California gold to the Secretary of War. Secretary Marcy turned it over to the treasury, where it was promptly minted into 1,389 quarter eagles (2-1/2 dollar gold pieces) dated 1848 with the legend "CAL" above the eagle on the reverse. President Polk also verified the importance of the gold discovery in a speech to Congress on December 5, 1848. On a truly national scale, the stage had been set for the rush to California of 1849/50.

Back in Sacramento, Captain John Sutter was profiting very little from the trade serving the needs of the miners. Sam Brannan, a Mormon Elder, who had come out to California in the *Brooklyn* had been the first to rent space at the Fort and opened a general merchandise store in October, 1847. Some of the very first gold dust used for purchases came over his counter there. Sutter's son, John Sutter, Jr., had arrived, and to avoid some creditors, Sutter had conveyed his Sacramento holdings to the young man. The son, at the suggestion of Brannan, hired a U.S. Army topographical engineer, Captain William H. Warner, to lay out and survey a town to be called Sacramento City. Warner was assisted by Lieutenants O. C. E. Ord and William T. Sherman, and work was commenced in the fall of 1848. The blocks were 320 east to west x 340 feet north to south (including the 20 foot wide alley), the streets 80 feet wide, except M Street which was 100 feet wide, and the blocks between 12th and 13th Streets were 340 x 400 feet. The streets near the river must have been staked out by December 1848, because a store had been completed near the foot of I Street, and Brannan had built one at the foot of J before the first lots were auctioned on January 8, 1849.

The winter of 1848/1849 was fairly mild, and the possibility of future flooding of the town site west of 12th Street did not seem to bother the buyers who rapidly started building. In the words of Dr. John F. Morse, writing in 1853 in Colville's *Sacramento Directory*:

> From the commencement of the town of Sacramento, until the first of June [1849], the progress of improvement was comparatively gradual. The immigration was limited in contrast with what followed, and yet it evolved a most interesting period

in the history of the Levee City. Everything wore such an anomalous appearance; there was no law, system, nor consistency, and yet there was no absolute disorder or discord. The whole fabric of society was little less than chaos, and still there was a oneness and harmony in its movements, which can scarcely be paralleled in the annals of the world. . . . There was no moral restraint, and yet for months there was never a community more perfectly exempt from violence and immorality. There was really no government, no acknowledged standard to regulate the concessions and mutual forbearances . . . there was such a glorious and intoxicating equality, such a total dependence upon an innate chivalry; such a uniformity of rights, and utter dethronement of the uncomfortable distinctions of society, that any man could reign as peasant, nabob, or king, without fear of incurring odium, or the possibility of giving offense.[61]

In describing Northern California later in 1849, and by extension, the conditions in Sacramento, Bancroft said in his *History of California*, Vol. VI, p. 439, "Never was there a place or people where the changes of life, its vicissitudes and its successes, were brought out in such bold relief as here. The rich and the poor, the proud and the humble, the vile and the virtuous, changed places in a day. Wild speculation and slovenly business habits, together with the gambling character of all occupations, and the visitations or benign influences of the elements and a thousand incalculable incidents usually classed in the category of luck were constantly lifting up one and pulling down another."

— § —

In June every avenue of immigration was opened, and thousands upon thousands began to concentrate at Sacramento, the gateway to the Northern Mines. Morse said that on June 26, 1849, Sacramento had about 100 houses, many covered with canvas.
By October, Sacramento's first brick building 60 x 40 feet and two stories high was completed, and by the end of 1849, there were over 800 structures in the city. The estimates are quite rough because buildings were being finished at an incredible rate (about one building

---

61. Samuel Colville, *Sacramento Directory for the Year 1853-54*, Mead Kibbey , Editor, (Sacramento: California State Library Foundation, 1997) pp. 35-36. In 2000, available from the publisher, telephone (916) 447-6331.

every one and one-half hours of the working day, or 50 in one week). One hundred seventy structures can be counted between I Street and the north side of L Street in a lithograph drawn of Sacramento City sometime in the fall of 1849 by G. V. Cooper. In another view, showing the city flooded on January 1, 1850, 220 are shown in the same area. Because of the perspective and the trees, areas beyond 3rd Street and to the north I Street and south of L Streets are not clearly visible. A census of 800 tents, houses, buildings, and lean-to's would not be an unreasonable total estimate.

A newspaper article published in Boston on January 5, 1850, described interviewing returning Californians at Panama and mentioned one had said that "Sacramento is a hot, dusty, filthy place, and if the wind blew there as at San Francisco, it would be impossible to live. But it has increased astonishingly. It now has a three-story house called the City Hotel, several zinc stores, a number of wooden ones, and tents, gambling-houses and boarding houses of all descriptions and sizes. . . .A man who planted a garden near Sacramento City, had cleared $10,000 from it, after paying a man $3,000 to assist in the cultivation."

In addition to overland immigrants, the majority of whom passed through Sacramento, 762 ships departed from eastern ports of the United States and Canada for San Francisco by way of Cape Horn during the thirteen months from December 7, 1848 to December 31, 1849. Approximately 27,000 passengers were carried this way in addition to thousands who came through Nicaragua, across Mexico, or over Panama. Some of the American ships only stayed a week or two in San Francisco

Bark rigged sailing ship

Bay and then brought their passengers or cargo directly to Sacramento.

The first example was the bark *Whiton* under Captain Roland Gelston, which came around the Horn from New York to San Francisco in 140 days, and 23 barks, nineteen brigs and 21 brigantines

arrived in Sacramento from the offshore routes the same year (1849).[62]
After a short stop in the Bay, the *Whiton* then made the trip up the
river to Sacramento in the "remarkable" time of 72 hours.   Reporters
of that day did not seem to realize that both Captains Ringgold and
Phelps, years before, had made the trip in boats in 72 hours or less.
The *Whiton* was of 241 tons burden and drew nine and a half feet of
water, making her the heaviest vessel to reach Sacramento up to that
time. She arrived on May 4, 1849, with "her royal yards crossed," that
is her high yard arms carrying sail were at right angles to the ship as
she would travel at sea and not rigged fore-and-aft to avoid trees on the
river. Part of her cargo was sold directly from the ship to retail
customers and the balance delivered to local merchants who had moved
to Sacramento City from the Fort. The trend had already begun and
her arrival only confirmed the wisdom of deserting Sutter's Fort for the
Embarcadero.

Brig sailing close-hauled

Another example was the
bark *Strafford* which arrived in
Sacramento around the middle of
September 1849, carrying William
R. Wheaton (see biography pages
157-169), and was later used for
two or three months as a prison
brig at the foot of I Street. It
departed from Sacramento in May
of 1850 and was replaced as a
floating jail by the *La Grange*, a
259 ton bark which had arrived in San Francisco September 17, 1849,
carrying its owners. She was anchored in the River about where the I
Street Bridge is now located, and remained there until damaged in a flood
and auctioned off by the city to Chinese ship-breakers.

— § —

Most people have at least once in their lives been present when
history was being made, and more often than not the event's
importance only became clear at a later date. Other great moments are
seen by only a few participants as in the signing of a peace treaty, or

---

62. Jerry McMullen, *Paddle-Wheel Days in California,* (Palo Alto: Stanford University
Press, 1944) p. 18. The steam sidewheeler *Senator,* 226 feet long and 750 tons first reached
Sacramento in November of 1849, and many other steamers followed. By 1850, Sacramento River
travel was largely by paddle-wheel steamers.

the invention of the transistor or telephone. Only rarely are thousands and thousands present when an event occurs which they all know at the time will change the history of the world. They may not talk about it, but they absolutely never forget. A twentieth century example of such an occasion was the Normandy Invasion. About 100 years earlier the young men who took part in the Gold Rush also changed history and themselves forever. They knew they were living through an epochal event, but in this case almost all of them who survived were overjoyed to talk about it. As soon as they left home, the writing began in diaries and letters and upon arrival here, swelled to a torrent of printed articles, books, pamphlets, magazines, newspapers, drawings, paintings, photographs, engravings, wood-cuts, maps, lithographs and closely written (writing paper was scarce in the mountains) manuscripts. A few authors who had never been within a thousand miles of California, wrote and published almost-believable stories of adventures here.[63]

Another factor adding fascination to the adventures of the Gold Rush participants was the danger of disease and accidents in that wild country. As pointed out by author and eminent historian, Dr. J. S. Holliday, there was something else, "Most of all, families [back home] feared *moral* dangers, the sinful temptations; drinking, swearing, gambling, violation of the Sabbath, fornication and adultery, all of which everyone (particularly hometown preachers) believed to be unrestrained in that new Gomorrah." [64]

"I might add, with a smile, that most Argonaut accounts adamantly proclaimed disapproval of, even shock at the extent of these practices. Indeed no letter, diary, or reminiscence—published or manuscript—[that I, J. S. Holliday, have seen] indicates that the writer had personally succumbed to any of these immoral temptations."

---

63. Gary F. Kurutz, *The California Gold Rush, A Descriptive Bibliography of Books and Pamphlets Covering the years 1848-1853*, (San Francisco: The Book Club of California, 1997) 798 pages. In this monumental work entailing ten years of research, the author lists and describes 707 books and pamphlets about the Gold Rush written in Dutch, English, French, German, Spanish or Swedish. And all these were written just in the period from 1848 through 1853, although a few were published later.

64. Dr. J. S. Holliday in the *Introduction* to Gary F. Kurutz, *The California Gold Rush*, p. xxiv. — Author's Note: The bracketed exception is added because I have seen an 1860s letter written from St. Louis, Sierra County, which carefully describes the writer's adventures with a recently arrived "new Dutch girl." In addition the California State Library reputedly has a manuscript of a more graphic nature on the same theme, but not knowing its name, I have not had the courage to ask for it by referring only to the subject matter.

Remarkably, the flow of writing has never stopped. The Spanish-American War was fought 50 years after the Gold Rush yet little is written of it today, but the grand-children of the grand-children of the 1848 authors are still pouring out a river of literature on the "Days of Gold." As early as 1854 the author of the Sacramento City Directory, Samuel Colville, saw the beginnings of this phenomenon when he wrote in his introduction only five years after the founding of the city:

> It was the original design of the compiler of this work, to embrace within its pages a synoptical history of Sacramento, . . . but the experience obtained in collecting the prominent material of which it is composed, convinced him that the design was impracticable.
>
> Sacramento contains too much history to justify an imperfect condensation. Her trials, her triumphs, and her glories have become the theme of millions, and her fame, therefore, is composed of more elements than a mere chronological table could present.

From the summer of 1849 to the end of 1850, when Culver stopped gathering information for this directory, Sacramento produced history at a furious pace. Some of the events are mentioned in Culver's fourteen-page "Historical Sketch" (see pages 261-274), which is really the earliest history of Sacramento ever published. He included a small error when he said on page 262, "The blocks are 320 by 400 feet, divided by 20 feet alleys running east and west." In fact the blocks are 320 feet from east to west, and 340 feet from north to south so that after taking out the 20 foot alley, the usable space is 320 feet on each side. The blocks lying between 12th and 13th Streets are an exception because they are 340 feet from north to south, but 400 feet from east to west. Books published well into the twentieth century repeat his error, and show the author read Culver's history or an authority who had done so.

A much better history, usually cited as Sacramento's first, was of 40 pages, written by Dr. John F. Morse and published in the 1853 Sacramento City Directory (for a description see page 178). Both of these historians covered many commercial stories and Culver provided some very informative material on early shipping. Since most Sacramentans seemed to have led relatively happy lives, bad news stories and particularly those of natural disasters were of great interest and several important items, with a couple of short, happy ones, are included below:

THE FLOOD OF JANUARY, 1850

Although there had been flooding in January of 1847, the winter of 1848/1849 had been fairly mild, and the citizens of Sacramento City were not expecting the continuing rainfall which started November 2, 1849. By the end of that year, 27 inches had fallen and some of the lower portions of the city were flooded. After a few dry days, in the evening of Tuesday, January 8, 1850, torrential rains fell which melted snow in the mountains and caused the American River to flood over its banks in the vicinity of Sutter Lake which lay just north of I Street from Front to 6th, (later occupied by the Southern Pacific Railroad Shops).

By Wednesday afternoon, water surged down 2nd and 3rd Streets carrying all sorts of merchandise that had been stored on sidewalks and in rear yards, and on the morning of January 10, the whole city up to a mile from Front Street was under water with the exception of a small rise at the City Plaza at 10th and J and an even smaller Indian mound on the north side of J near 4th Street which became crowded with tents. Alonzo Delano, a miner and correspondent for the New Orleans *True Delta* newspaper, climbed a mountain adjoining the Yuba River where he was working to observe the devastation in the Sacramento Valley below him. "I had an extended view, I estimated that at least one quarter of this Earthly Paradise, this charming and fertile Valley (oh!) was under water. Hundreds of cattle and mules were drowned and floated down to rejoice with the aromatic scent of their putrid carcasses on the refined olfactory nerves of the citizens of Sacramento." [65] This same correspondent mentioned that a short time later he visited a friend, Mr. Spencer, who lived on the east side of the Feather River between the Yuba and Bear Creek. His friend said that during the recent flood he had saved himself only by crawling to the roof of his house, at least 30 feet above the river, and that one of his neighbors had traveled about fifteen miles east to the foot of the mountains in a sailboat.

---

65. Irving McKee, Editor, *Alonzo Delano's California Correspondence,* (Sacramento: Sacramento Book Collector's Club, 1952), p. 41.

Flooded Street Scene in the Winter of 1849 - 1850.

This engraving appears on page 150 of Frank Marryat's *Mountains and Molehills*, published in 1855.

In Sacramento City, the first floor of the new hospital of Drs. John Morse and Jacob Stillman at 3rd and K Streets was flooded over six feet deep and they were driven to the attic. Here in a space 35 x 55 feet, three doctors and a cook lived and attended to about 35 desperately sick patients. Some were dying on the floor of the attic, and those who had died were sewn up in blankets and sunk in the water in a room below at street level.

Dr. Stillman describes the scene:

> *January 12th*—The water is still rising. Tents, houses, boxes, barrels, horses, mules, and cattle are sweeping by with the swollen torrent, that is now spread out in a vast sea farther than the eye can reach. There are few two- story houses, and as the water rose, which it did at the rate of six inches an hour, men were compelled to get outside. To-day there is no first floor in the city uncovered, and but for the vessels in the river, now all crowded with people, there is no telling what numbers have perished.
>
> . . . Men continue to come, begging to be taken in or bringing some valuables for safe keeping. Now that the doorways are inaccessible, they come in boats to the second-story windows. . . .Today we went out in a boat to find some blankets, but in vain. We returned with some drift-wood for fuel. All means are in use to get about — bakers' troughs, rafts, and India rubber beds. . . .The yelling for help by some man on a roof, or clinging to some wreck — the howling of a dog abandoned by his master — the boisterous revelry of men in boats, who find all they want to drink floating free about them — make the scene never to be forgotten. . . . I have some misgivings about our fate, but sure I am that we will not desert the sick, and if we are swept away, we will all go together.
>
> It is late and for two days and nights I have not slept. I shall lie down, and if the worst comes, I have taken precautions to have you get this letter.
>
> *Sunday, January 13th [1850]* — Yesterday we found it necessary to bury the dead. I spoke a whale boat that was passing, made an agreement for the use of it in the afternoon for $40 and deposited three bodies in it. They had been sewed up in blankets and sunk in the first story. We fished them up with a hook and line and laid them in the bottom of the boat.
>
> . . . [Three of us] with the two sailors owning the boat, started for land, which we could see with a glass from our window in a south-easterly direction from the town [possibly the

> site of the city cemetery at 10th and Broadway]. Of course,
> coffins were out of the question, and we dug a large square
> grave, at the foot of an oak. . . . In digging the grave we found
> a large root of the tree intersecting the pit in both directions
> . . . grown together in that position. By chopping it off at the
> ends, the root formed a perfect cross, which we planted at the
> head of the grave, and then covered the mound with soft, green
> sod.[66]

Dr. Stillman reported that by the 23rd, the water had left the first floor of the hospital although it was still three or four feet deep in the street. They found four barrels of pork, one of beef, and a case of wine which were not on the premises when the flood came. Without hesitation the good doctors appropriated them as a contribution to the support of the destitute people thrown upon the charity of the hospital.

Dr. John Morse in his history of Sacramento written in 1853 describes the sad end during the flood of another slightly less noble Sacramentan. Two gentlemen named Boyd & Davis were connected with a lumberyard on Front Street and were very actively making coffins. They also offered a transportation and burial service using a boat they had built before they realized the profit margin in coffins. This funeral barge was rowed by two of their employees, one of whom Dr. Morse described as being a Dutchman very suspicious regarding banks, so that he kept $2,000 in hard-earned gold on his person. The two were dispatched on a rush job and carelessly loaded the coffin containing a customer crossway in the rowboat. They had just reached deep water, when the coffin slipped to one side capsizing the boat.

The Dutchman, who was known to be a strong swimmer shouted to the other man to hold onto the coffin while he swam ashore for another boat. In this effort he proved unsuccessful and despite great exertion, he drowned while his colleague rode ashore on the coffin which had been built "very tight." Dr. Morse related these facts, and then made comments indicating that this was a lesson on the evils of greed. He apparently failed to realize that $2,000 in gold, even at the depressed price of $16 per ounce then prevailing, weighed only 8.12 pounds under water — hardly enough to sink a strong and motivated swimmer. It was really a lesson in not trying to swim in heavy boots

---

66. Dr. J.D.B. Stillman, *Seeking the Golden Fleece*, (San Francisco: A Roman & Co., 1877), pp. 149-152.

and rain gear while yelling instructions.

Another adventure which is difficult to confirm, but so interesting that it is included here, involves a very fool-hardy river captain and a couple of merchants with an eye for publicity. Alonzo Delano reported that during this flood, the water was so deep on J Street that a small steamer delivered a cargo directly to Starr, Bensley & Co.'s store at 58 J (224 J, new style, now under the freeway). It seems particularly difficult because in a birdseye view of Sacramento drawn in January of 1850, a tree is shown growing in the middle of J Street, quite near the front of their store.

Sacramento finally dried out, and by April 8th the last serious rains had ended. The onslaught it had faced can be judged by a single statistic. Culver reported that in the period from November, 1849 to May of 1850, the rainfall in Sacramento was 42 inches,[67] while the long-term average is about seventeen inches.

— § —

In contrast to the effects of the January flood, a small but happy event occurred on August 5, 1850, with arrival of the brig *Merchantman*. The ship had sailed by way of Cape Horn from Boston to the Sacramento Levee, the first to do so without stopping at San Francisco. The cargo, which would have only been of modest interest in foggy San Francisco, was entirely of ice, from New England and packed in sawdust for insulation. This may have resulted from an oversupply of the product in New England ports as reported in the following item from a Boston newspaper on January 5, 1850:

> *The Ice Trade*—The ice trade between the United States and England, at one time opened under favorable auspices, has been entirely superseded by the ice from Sweden and Norway. This ice is delivered in London at the same price which ice is sold for in Boston. Norway ice, in immense blocks, of great thickness, is sold in the Thames at 15s. sterling [then $3.75] a ton, while American costs delivered there 40s. a ton, 25s.[then $6.25] freight, and 15s. cost of the ice.[68]

---

67. A number of other sources state the total as only 36 inches; quite convincingly because they give the total for each individual month of the season.

68. The *Boston Cultivator* (newspaper), January 5, 1850, p. 7, column 5.

73

The trip to California was about five times as long as to London, and guessing $33.25 per ton freight would be close. Adding that to the Boston price of $3.75 would give a delivered price at Sacramento of $37.00 per ton or 1.85 cents per pound, compared to the 30 cents selling price. "Economic Sense" hardly covers the 1,621% profit accruing to the adventurous operators who made this gamble.

Ice and frozen snow had previously been brought down from the Sierra Nevada Mountains by mules to the road and then to the valley by wagons, and cost $1.00 per pound in Sacramento. The *Merchantman's* cargo was unloaded at the foot of K Street and promptly sold for 30 cents per pound to be used in drinks and a little in desserts. The Common Council voted a free berth to the vessel during delivery and passed a resolution of thanks to the captain "for a liberal supply of the cool article."

THE SQUATTER RIOTS OF 1850

SQUAT: To settle upon new, uncultivated, or unoccupied land without any legal title and without the payment of rent (origin, U.S.). The earliest use of the word in this sense found in the Oxford English Dictionary, was written in the Mississippi Territorial Archives in 1800.

A problem of land titles to lots in Sacramento City had been brewing since about October 1849, when it became apparent that lots close to the river were extremely valuable, many were vacant, and some of those Americans who arrived later in 1849 wanted to occupy them at little or no cost to themselves, despite the fact that the lots had been paid for by others. They based their claim on a mistake made by the surveyor, Jean Jacques Vioget,[69] who prepared the map, probably in the fall of 1840, which Sutter used in obtaining his grant dated June 18, 1841, from the Mexican Government. At the time of the grant, the Mexican lands in California had been obtained from Spain for no cost, the square miles in the state far exceeded the number of Mexican

---

69. Jean Jaques Vioget, was born in Switzerland about 1801, arrived in California in 1837, was master of the ship *Delmira*, made the first town survey of San Francisco in 1839, and built a house there. He also did land surveying, operated a billiard saloon, commanded other vessels, and later owned a San Francisco hotel, the *Portsmouth House*. Bancroft describes Vioget as a jolly, musical sort of fellow, speaking several languages, a sailor, surveyor, and hotel-keeper of some skill. Hubert Howe Bancroft, *History of California*, Volume V, p. 764.
Vioget, in 1837, painted an attractive view of Yerba Buena when the village consisted of two houses.

citizens, and most of the interior of the state had never been seen by the authorities making the grants.

The map clearly shows the intended scope of the grant extending to a point well south of present day Broadway to include later Sutterville and the Sacramento Zoo. The northern boundary of the grant was the Marysville Buttes. Sadly for Sutter, although not required on all Mexican land grants, the map also included erroneous latitudes for Sutter's Fort, the Marysville Buttes, the point at the mouth of the Feather River, and most importantly, the southern edge of the grant. The surveyor, Vioget, had given latitudes that averaged about thirteen minutes to the north of the correct latitudes. The southern boundary was labelled nine minutes too far north and actually was the correct latitude for modern Rio Linda about nine miles north of Sutterville and the zoo. Unfortunately, the grant to Sutter simplified the description of the land to be transferred from the usual bounds of geographic features to (English translation recorded February 6, 1851):[70]

> GRANT—Dated June 18, 1841.
> Eleven Leagues of land, bounded on the north by the "Three Peaks," in latitude thirty-nine degrees, forty-one minutes, and forty-five seconds north; on the east by the margins of Feather river; on the south by latitude thirty-eight degrees, forty-nine minutes and thirty two seconds north, and on the West by the Sacramento river.

In a subsequent deed dated October 14, 1848, from John A. Sutter, (Sr.) to John A. Sutter, Jr., the intended width of the "margin of the Feather river" was cleared up by the inclusion of the words, ". . . east to the Rio de las Plumas and three leagues beyond said river.." The error regarding the southern boundary was also repeated in this deed, recorded in Sacramento Deeds Book A, page 1, in late 1848 or very early in 1849.

Using the true latitude for the highest point of the Marysville Buttes, N 39°-14'-07", and moving east toward the Feather River, the eastern bank at the same latitude is at longitude W 121°-37'-33". Continuing east along the same latitude for three leagues or nine miles to a point just above Honcut, Yuba County, whose longitude is

---

70. J. J. Buckley, *Abstract of the Records in the Office of the Recorder of Sacramento County,* (Sacramento: manuscript copy, March 27, 1889), pp. 1-6 covering Lot 2 in the square between N & O and Front & Second Streets. (author's collection).

W121°-29'-28". Moving south along this meridian, to Sacramento, the line passes through the Garden Center of McKinley Park, the intersection of Santa Inez Way and I Street, and 39th and T Streets, all east of the Fort and west of other grants in the area. Considering the area shown on Vioget's map this would be one reasonable interpretation of "margin of Feather river" as the eastern boundary of Sutter's 1841 grant.

Sutter's son began selling Sacramento lots, and one such transaction, for $2,000, recorded in a deed dated March 20, 1850, covers lot two in the block or square between N and O and Front and Second Streets. This lot is now under the freeway to the west of Crocker Park. The original survey laid out eight lots in each block except those between 12th and 13th Streets, and odd shaped blocks along the American River to the north of I Street. In June of 1850, he made a huge sale to Samuel Brannan which did not specify which blocks were involved, but the records afterward include many partnerships, mortgages, and resales to others. The price of only $56.81 per lot may have included other considerations, but the sale was partly made to induce Brannan and his fellow merchants to remain, rather than moving to the cheap (or even free) lots in Sutterville.

> By a deed, dated June 11, 1850, John A. Sutter, Jr. conveyed 2,200 town lots in Sacramento city to Samuel Brannan for $125,000, $25,000 down and the balance in three equal payments in three, six, and nine months from July 1, 1850.

This transaction represented 275 blocks of eight lots each, and from its terms appeared to allow Brannan and his assigns the right to select those they wanted from all then unsold. In addition several others obtained large holdings like this, one of the more notable being Albert Priest and Barton Lee acting as Priest, Lee & Company. If one ignores the facts that Sutter had, by 1849, occupied the land for ten years, borrowed money against it, added numerous improvements, and had been recognized as the owner by the Mexican authorities; further ignore that the map submitted to obtain his grant clearly showed the area intended; and ignore article X of the treaty of Guadalupe Hildago,[72] signed February 23, 1848, by which the war between the United States and the Republic of Mexico was ended—then the original owner of the land underlying the lots, J. A. Sutter, Sr., did not own them and could not legally sell them.

In that event the lots and the lands of Sacramento City might be considered United States land or "public domain" not previously filed on by the occupants or "owners" and therefore available for homesteading by others.[71] It was a little stretch to apply a law that was twelve years from passage and required "working" the land, to a city lot someone else had bought and paid for, but fine details of land ownership and use by previous owners were seldom of concern to the newer immigrants in the early days of California.[72]

Based on this reasoning, a group of immigrants led by Dr. Charles Robinson, from Fitchburg Massachusetts, a college graduate, physician, and later the first governor of Kansas, formed the Sacramento City Settlers Association, December 7, 1849, at an evening meeting. Semantics are, as in most human conflicts, important here. Robinson's group and their sympathetic historians referred to their adherents as "settlers" and those who held title under Sutter's grant as "speculators," while the Sutter people and their historians called Robinson's men "squatters" and the old owners "landholders."

The Robinson people, as suggested by "Sacramento City" in the name of their association, did not attempt to take up any of the tens of thousands of unclaimed acres outside of Sutter's grant to the south or west of the city across the Sacramento River. They did occupy city lots that others had purchased from Priest, Lee or Brannan, and when the

---

71. The Homestead Movement became active in the U.S. about 1830, when western farmers began asking that 160 acre portions of the United States public domain be given to settlers willing to work the land. In 1848 the Free Soil Party included a plank in the party platform urging distribution of public land to settlers free of charge. The southern slave holders, large eastern landowners, and employers opposed this view. As a result no legislation was passed until the Civil War when southerners were expelled from Congress, and the Republicans passed, and Abraham Lincoln signed, the Homestead Act on May 20, 1862. The act provided 160 acres of public land to any citizen, or citizenship applicant, either 21 years old or head of a family who had lived on and cultivated the land for at least five years.

72. ARTICLE X, "All grants of land made by the Mexican government, or by the competent authorities, in territories previously appertaining to Mexico, and remaining for the future within the limits of the United States, shall be respected as valid, to the same extent that the same grants would be valid if the said territories had remained within the limits of Mexico..."
30th Congress, Executive Doc. 52, *The Treaty between THE UNITED STATES AND MEXICO,* In executive session, Senate of the U.S. (Washington: 1848) p. 49.
ARTICLE XII "In consideration of the extensions acquired by the boundaries of the United States, as in the fifth article of the present treaty, the government of the United States engages to pay to that of the Mexican republic the sum of fifteen millions of dollars. . ." ibid, p. 52. This sum was paid three million dollars in July, 1848, and three million a year for the next four years with interest on the unpaid balance of 6%. The magnitude of this total, if allowed to accumulate at the same 6% interest, would be more than ninety six billion dollars on December 31, 1999.

owners attempted to build on the lots the Squatters interfered by force. Both the settlers and the landholders attempted to suppress the activities of the other side by burning down their shacks, erecting and tearing down fences, giving fiery speeches at public meetings, posting inflammatory broadsides, and taking legal actions (usually by the landholders). The real problems began when the leader and later founder of the squatter's association, Dr. Charles Robinson, built a house on city land near the river on the north side of I Street where the Discovery Museum is now located. On September 7, 1849, Henry A. Schoolcraft, alcalde of the Sacramento District, petitioned the City Council to remove the house, and it was subsequently torn down. The next day, Robinson entered a suit against the City on account of the destruction of his private property, and the suit was decided against him.[73]

About the middle of October 1849, Z. M. Chapman went upon a piece of unoccupied land outside the city limits beyond the Fort, and commenced cutting timber for a cabin, claiming 160 acres. Pierre B. Cornwall of Priest, Lee & Co. owned this land by purchase from Captain Sutter. Various attempts by the owner to stop Chapman from cutting the trees and an offer to allow him to continue occupancy during the winter were unsuccessful. A law suit was filed by Cornwall and a jury decided in favor of the owner. Chapman was waited on by the sheriff with a writ of ejectment, but he refused to vacate the premises. The sheriff returned with a posse of 50 men, who pulled down the house after removing Chapman's portable property. This occurred on a Saturday, and on Monday the house was rebuilt by squatter sympathizers. The following Tuesday evening, while the squatters were having a meeting and passing resolutions, the one-day-old cabin was burned down by anti-squatter forces. Another cabin soon appeared on the same site, but due to the arrival of the flood season, ill health from exposure, and a lack of enthusiasm for Sacramento real estate, Chapman went back to the States and never returned to Sacramento to press his claim.[74]

Samuel Brannan, the earliest merchant and the largest

---

73. *History of Sacramento County,* (Oakland: Thompson & West, 1880), p. 50. Dr. Morse gives the petition date as December 7.

74. Bruce Cornwall, *Life Sketch of Pierre Barlow Cornwall,* (San Francisco: A. M. Robertson, 1906), pp. 38-43. P. B. Cornwall's own statement of this matter is reproduced in full.

landholder in Sacramento City made a clever counter move to the Squatter claims. On December 7, 1849 he issued the following proclamation claiming a settler's right to 160 acres in the city:

> NOTICE TO SQUATTERS AND TRESPASSERS — FAIR WARNING.— Whereas, some persons have decided that Capt. John A. Sutter has no right or title to the ground upon which Sacramento City is located, and such being the case in their legal judgment and sovereign opinion, the undersigned would now respectfully notify the citizens of Sacramento City that he lays claim for one hundred and sixty acres, (being the first settler and improver,) commencing at the corner of J street, at the old store of S. Brannan & Co., and running up J to Second street, adjoining the line of pre-emption of Priest, Lee & Co., on said street; extending south between Second Street and the Sacramento river, to cover one hundred and sixty acres, and all persons located on the same are hereby notified that they will be held responsible for ground rent from this date, and had better call on the subscriber at once and negotiate satisfactory arrangements for the future possession of the same.
>
> S. BRANNAN.[75]

The mention of Priest, Lee & Co.'s claim indicates that the second earliest merchants in the city had filed, or were expected to file, a similar claim east of 2nd Street. Brannan had come up with an interesting fall-back defense against the Squatters, but it seemed to have no effect on their efforts to take over the property of the landholders.

After the flood in 1850, so many squatters located along the waterfront that it became difficult for cargoes to be landed, and access to the storeships was blocked. Sam Brannan, a large land holder and merchant with a loud voice and fiery temper, led an armed group that started early in the day by tearing down a structure that Dr. Robinson had rebuilt on I Street at the river's edge. They continued the destruction as they moved south past J Street, and by sunset every obstruction had been removed from the levee. On a smaller scale, such events continued through the summer and finally resulted bloodshed and death to members of both parties.

---

75. Daniel J. Thomas, *History of Sacramento*, in *Sacramento City Directory for 1871* (Sacramento: H.S. Crocker & Co., 1871), p. 68.

Location of Madden's shack at 2nd and N Streets
Photograph taken in 1999

On May 10, 1850 John P. Rogers (Governor Burnett's brother-in-law) and DeWitt J. Burnett commenced an action in the recorder's court to remove John T. Madden who had "squatted" on a lot they owned at the southeast corner of 2nd and N Streets. He had entered upon the property about March 1, 1850 and built a small house. Despite an extremely active defense over many weeks, the plaintiffs prevailed, and Madden lost his final appeal on August 10. Dr. Robinson and the squatters were outraged by the decision and gathered about 200 men to defend Madden's house from any action by the sheriff. They also issued a manifesto printed on a large broadside which refused recognition of both the State and City governments and ended with, "but the property and lives of those who take the field against them [the squatters], will share the fate of war."

On the 13th, James McClatchy and Michael Moran were taken into custody at the Madden house for resisting the efforts of the sheriff to enforce the writ of ejectment. They could not or would not make the $2,000 bail and were placed aboard the prison brig *La Grange* anchored in the river at the foot of H Street. On the morning of August 14, 1850, Sheriff McKinney seized a house on 2nd Street near L in accordance with a court order. A party of 30 squatters under the leadership of James Maloney, a veteran of the Mexican War, retook the house. Maloney, on horseback and armed with a sword and pistols, marched his party down L Street to the levee and turned north toward the prison brig. He and his men were followed by a crowd of citizens, who thought he planned to release the prisoners. The whole affair

80

seemed rather more a spectacle than a coming tragedy, and the spectators laughed and shouted.

At the same time, the mayor, Hardin Bigelow, could no longer blind himself to the necessity of asserting his authority, and rode up and down the streets making his proclamation to the people to sustain law and order. Many then ran for arms. The squatters continued up the levee to I Street, paused a short time, and marched up I Street to 3rd where they turned right or south, still followed by a laughing, jeering crowd. When they reached J Street, the mayor ordered the citizens in the vicinity to arrest the armed squatters, and with three cheers they followed. The two groups approached each other on J Street with the squatters drawn up on 4th Street facing the south side of J Street. The mayor and sheriff rode up and ordered them to lay down their arms and yield to arrest. While the two were still advancing, Maloney gave the order to fire and was heard to say distinctly "shoot the mayor." The firing was returned by the armed citizens, a general battle ensued, and the squatters fled, leaving a field of blood.

The mayor received at least four serious wounds and fell from his horse, after which he stood up, took a few steps, and fell again. He then said the citizens must protect themselves, for he was disabled and could do no more. He was taken to the Columbia Hotel at 21 Second Street (921, new style) where he received medical attention until he could be moved to Dr. Stillman's. Mayor Bigelow recovered in a maimed condition after five weeks "care and attendance" at Dr. Stillman's house in San Francisco (costing $2,238) — only to die there of cholera on November 27, 1850. The following day, he was buried in Sacramento with full military honors, having served in the Illinois Mohawk War. He was laid to rest next to Sheriff McKinney in the New Helvetia Cemetery at 31st and J Streets. Upon the abandonment of New Helvetia Cemetery in the 1950's the mayor's remains were moved, and his grave is now just inside the Broadway gate of the City Cemetery next to that of John A. Sutter, Jr.

In addition to the mayor, the assessor, James. M. Woodland, was shot in the groin and died from loss of blood within minutes. He was unarmed and attempting to reason with the squatters at the moment he was killed. Jesse Morgan, said to have been recently arrived from Millersville, Ohio, who was seen aiming at the mayor, was killed by a shot through the neck. The fight had reached 4th and K Streets where the military leader of the squatters, James Maloney was effectively using his saber, when he had his horse shot from under him

at the northeast corner of 4th and K Streets by a bullet from the rifle of
Dr. T. J. White. Maloney, with an injured leg and encumbered by his
saber scabbard, crawled to the alley (Oak Street) on the east side of 4th
Street between J and K Streets (in 1999, under the Down Town Plaza
movie theater). He then stood up and attempted escape through the
alley toward 5th Street, but the city recorder, B. F. Washington, killed
him by a shot through the head. One other man was killed, but in the
confusion his name was not recorded.

Dr. Robinson, the head of the squatter association, was
wounded in the lower part of his body, hid in a nearby house, and was
later in the day captured, and carried to the prison brig on a cot. Mr.
James H. Harper, former city clerk, was badly but not dangerously,
wounded while supporting the sheriff. Others were wounded to varying
degrees including the leg wound to a child of the same Mr. Rogers who
filed suit against Madden occupying the lot at 2nd and N Streets.[76]

Shortly after the battle at 4th and J Streets, the city council met
and appointed Captain J. Sherwood, Assistant City Marshall, and
B. F. Washington, City Marshall. General A. M. Winn issued a
proclamation, declaring the city under martial law, and ordering all law-
abiding citizens to form themselves into volunteer companies. Even
before the meeting, the lieutenant governor, John McDougal had left
on the steamer *Senator* for Benicia to obtain military assistance. He
rode directly from the riot scene, and departed so hurriedly that he left
his horse standing on the levee.

Henry Caulfield,[77] a contentious little rascal and very poor shot
had been seen aiming at the mayor. Although not so regarded by
witnesses, this was no threat to the city's chief magistrate. Caulfield, in
1851, cornered a hated judge in a small courtroom, fired five shots at
him — and missed every time. He escaped from the riot area toward
Brighton (east of 70th and R Streets) "obtaining" a horse along the
way. A group of citizens, including some authorities, learned of his
probable destination and rode out in pursuit, overtaking him about a
mile from Brighton. He was riding at a gallop, a reasonable pace

---

76. Hubert Howe Bancroft, *History of California*, Vol VI, pp. 328 - 335 in footnote 24
which is quite possibly the longest ever printed in English. Some additional data came from
Thompson & West, *History of Sacramento County*, 1880, pp 50-56. Both of these authorities
quoted an article in the August 15, 1850 issue of the Sacramento *Placer Times*.

77. For a biography of Caulfield see page 107 following.

considering the appearance of the crowd overtaking him, when a man named Latson got close enough to grab the fugitive's coat, but was unable to hold on. Caulfield, who must have realized his ineptitude with firearms, finally had a target that he could not miss, a man only a few feet from him. He aimed his rifle at Latson and pulled the trigger — it misfired. Latson was carrying a heavy pistol, which he immediately used as a club to knock Caulfield off his horse.

The rest of the party agreed that this treatment should have killed most men, but the almost indestructible ruffian survived to be promptly arrested by Sacramento County Surveyor John G. Cleal. The prisoner was secured to the saddle with his feet tied under the horse's belly and his hands secured behind him. He was brought by the party down J Street at a furious pace with his hat off and his face covered in blood and dust — as they headed for a tall tree on the levee. Their intentions regarding Caulfield and the tree were obvious to the recently deputized Dr. J. D. B. Stillman, who ran to the river to stop the proposed hanging. For some reason they changed course and delivered the fugitive to the prison brig.

A little earlier, Dr. Stillman, the same doctor who had stood by his patients during the January flood, had been told by someone that Dr. Robinson was wounded and hidden in a house on 4th Street —in Stillman's own words:

> I reported the matter to B. F. Washington, [newly appointed] Acting Marshall of the city, who directed me to procure what help I could, and take him [Robinson] dead or alive.   Dr. Robinson was the leading rioter, and had done more by his talents than any one among them to bring on the trouble. I took two men, armed like myself with double-barrel guns [smooth bore muzzle loaders with round bullets], and entered the house where he was said to be hidden. The proprietor stood at the head of the stairs leading to the second floor, and, presenting his shot-gun, threatened to shoot if we came up; but one of the men who followed me, seeming to think this was a good chance to kill somebody, "covered" the man with his gun, and told him to lay down his arms, or have a large hole made in his body. He obeyed, when we told him to go into a room, where we shut him up.
>
> Then we searched the house, and found the doctor in the back room, lying on a bed. I examined him, and found a bullet wound of small size in his left side; but it seemed to be superficial, and his pulse was not affected. . . . I pressed a cot

and four men, under the war power conferred upon me (for the city was under martial law), and compelled the men to carry our prisoner to the prison-brig, while we escorted him to prevent rescue.[78]

By that evening the city was filled with rumors of an impending attack by the squatters coming from the east or south. Defending Sacramento were over 200 volunteer police plus one infantry company of militia under Captain Sherwood, another under Major Snyder, and the artillery under Major Fowler. Despite the fears of more trouble the night passed without further military action, and the defending forces prepared for the ceremonies of burying the dead.

The next day, Thursday, August 15, 1850, the city was quiet in the morning, although it was rumored the squatters intended to bury their dead at the same time and place as the ceremonies for Assessor Woodland. As a result, the coffin was followed by many city officers and Captain Sherwood's infantry, which included Dr. Stillman, and every man had been issued ten rounds of ammunition. Behind this company as they slowly marched to the City Cemetery at 10th and Y Streets (now Broadway), were many armed citizens on horse back. No enemy appeared, and J. M Woodland was quietly laid to rest.

As soon as the funeral services were over, Sheriff Joseph McKinney, with about twenty mounted citizens rode off rapidly across the plains to apprehend some squatters who had gathered at a road house, called "the Five Mile House," near Brighton. This establishment was owned by a Mr. Allen. They approached the house as darkness fell, divided into three groups and the sheriff's group entered. He immediately observed ten men with guns and ordered them to lay down their arms. The occupants began shooting and total confusion reigned as the sheriff stepped just outside the door to call up assistance. At this point he was shot by Allen with a heavy duck-gun and died almost instantly. The fire was instantly returned by others and Allen was severely, but not fatally wounded. He escaped, bleeding, up the river and was never arrested.

Two squatters, M. Kelly, and George W. Henshaw were killed, and two of the sheriff's party wounded. Reinforcements for the sheriff arrived, banged on the door of the house, and so frightened Allen's wife, who was ill in bed, that she died of a heart attack.

---

78. Dr. J. D. B. Stillman, *ibid*, pp. 173-175.

Four prisoners were taken, John Hughes, James Coffman, William B. Cornogg, and another unnamed. The party returned to Sacramento, leaving the sheriff's body at the Fort and taking the captives to the prison brig despite many offers and shouted suggestions that they be hung on the spot. Earlier in the evening the Common Council had met and appointed its president, Demas Strong, to be acting mayor, replacing the wounded Mayor Bigelow. At about 9 P.M., shortly before the arrival of the prisoners from Brighton, Col. E. J. C. Kewen dashed into the Common Council meeting and announced that the sheriff and ten men were killed, and the squatters in force were marching into town. Although largely untrue, the effect of these statements on the city fathers can only be imagined. From the contemporary newspaper description, it must have been like hitting a beehive with a shovel.

They ordered the alarm sounded, mounted and armed citizens and soldiers were dispatched to the east end of J and K Streets, pass words issued, and patrols set up to protect against arsonists in the southern part of the city. Councilman J. R. Hardenbergh commanded one of the mounted patrols and Councilman C. A. Tweed, the other. Dr. Stillman was detailed to anti-arson duty and told of his group patrolling up and down the lonely streets with fixed bayonets, stopping every man for the countersign, and if he could not give it, marching him home. With their leaders in prison, the whole city full of armed citizens, and regular army infantry and artillery reported on the way from Benicia, the squatters, as far as records indicate, did not even consider the feared "invasion." In reality, by midnight of the 15th, the violence had ended.

Very early the next morning, Friday, August 16, the *Senator* returned with the lieutenant governor and 150 men under arms in two companies of volunteers; the California Guard under Captain W. D. Howard, and Protection Engine Company, of the fire department under Captain Shay. It became obvious that the situation was under control, and possibly to keep the new arrivals occupied, they were asked to join a large procession forming on J Street for the sheriff's funeral. There is no record of anyone complaining of this duty, but the August afternoon temperature in Sacramento is usually over 90°F and frequently exceeds 100 degrees; the volunteers were wearing heavy San Francisco uniforms and carrying their guns. The distance to the old cemetery was over 2-1/2 miles and the roads were dusty. Despite these factors, a large cortege marched out to Sutter's Fort, received the body of Sheriff Joseph McKinney, and carried him to the old New Helvetia Cemetery on the north side of J just east of 31st Street (now Alhambra Boulevard). All the bodies in this location were exhumed between 1954 and 1957 and moved elsewhere. The sheriff's body now lies under a monument erected by the Sacramento County Sheriff's Department in the New Helvetia section of the East Lawn Cemetery. Sheriff McKinney was very highly regarded by the citizens of Sacramento; a contemporary referring to him as, "our brave young sheriff." His wife followed his body to the cemetery, and her obvious sorrow at his loss was deeply moving to all those present.

In Sacramento City, that day the City Council appointed Coroner P. F. Ewer as acting sheriff to replace the fallen Joseph McKinney, and the following dispatch was received by General Winn:

SAN JOSE, August 15, 1850

To Brig. Gen. A. M. Winn, Second Brigade, California Militia:

SIR: — It having been made to appear to me that there is a riotous and unlawful assembly, with intent to commit a felony, at Sacramento City, in Sacramento County, you will therefore order out the whole of your command, to appear at Sacramento City, on the 16th day of August, 1850, or as soon as thereafter as practicable, and you will take command of same, and give all the aid in your power to the civil authorities, in suppressing violence and enforcing the laws. Should the force ordered out not be sufficient, you will forthwith inform me accordingly.

Your obedient servant,
PETER H. BURNETT,
Governor of California and Commander-in-Chief.

Dated the 17th, a reply was sent by Demas Strong, president of the common council and acting mayor which said in part;
". . . after the unexpected riot of the 14th instant, a police force of 500 men was authorized to be raised, and B. F. Washington, Esq., appointed as Marshal to take command, aided by Capt. J. Sherwood. Thus far, this force has proven itself capable of sustaining our laws and protecting the property of our citizens, without military aid, and . . . there is no great probability of such aid being needed."

By this letter the acting mayor officially recognized the fact that was obvious to the citizens—the riots were over.

THE BUSINESS PANIC OF 1850

The questions raised by the squatters regarding Sutter's title were eventually settled in favor of the landholders, but not before a crash in land values had occurred in Sacramento. Other factors also contributed, including; unsecured loan and sometimes even mortgage rates of 10% per month, a really remarkable lack of experience on the part of the city's bankers, and large expenditures for freight by merchants having branches in the mining country. The immigrants of 1849 and early 1850 were often men who brought money, and even after they had passed through the financial filter of San Francisco, or a visit to the mines, some had money to start businesses in Sacramento. Prices had risen to unsustainable levels, and only a trigger was needed to start a downward spiral that only the strongest and most frugal would survive. Dr. John F. Morse in his 1853 history described the plight of inexperienced merchants:

> Whilst public confidence continued to flood the city with the means of progress and the facilities of growing exchanges, nothing was easier than the management business that was never subjected to any test of strength; but when . . . [large and financially sound suppliers] began not only to withhold expected supplies, but to demand the return of those already furnished [on credit], then did the perils of the experimenters in business begin to appear. Then did this conglomerated mass begin a fermenting process which had no end but explosion; an explosion that shook Sacramento to its foundations.

The first banker to fail was Barton Lee in late August, representing a capital of $1,500,000, who assigned all his assets to his creditors and closed his doors.[79] A few days after, he was followed by Hensley, McKnight and Hastings, and shortly after that by Warbuss and Company. A number of the leading merchants followed, and in a few weeks, the intoxicating progress of the city was arrested by a complete prostration of confidence in the value of real estate and the worth those

---

79. The early Sacramento bankers and merchants operated as individual proprietorships and partnerships, not as corporations. As a result, they were personally responsible for the company debts to the absolute limit of their possessions. When the business failed, they lost everything — home, real estate, furnishings; everything but clothing and tools. "Assigning Assets" meant they avoided declaring bankruptcy by quickly giving everything to the creditors, although the effect on the debtor was far more serious than going through a modern bankruptcy.

whose wealth derived from it.[80]   It is impossible to attach an exact number to the losses experienced, but an idea can be derived from assessed valuations of real estate in Sacramento City. In 1850 before the crash, the amount was $7,654,794. The population was increasing, and buildings were being rapidly constructed, but in 1851, the assessed value had dropped to $5,400,481, a decline of almost 30% in a single year. The value of Sacramento real estate slowly increased over the years, but the 1850 assessment was not surpassed for 22 years, until 1872.

— § —

A wildly happy celebration occurred in Sacramento when the first news of the admission of California to the Union as its 31st state arrived on October 19, 1850. The fast steamer *New World* brought the news from San Francisco where it had arrived the morning before with the steamer *Oregon* from Panama. The ship had been supplied with a large flag reading "California is a State" which it displayed as it entered the Bay with all her bunting flying. The feelings in San Francisco were instant and extreme. Business was suspended, the courts adjourned and the whole populace, frenzied with delight, gathered at Portsmouth Square to celebrate. Guns boomed from the ships and the shore, bonfires blazed at night, processions formed, bands played, and the people in every way expressed their joy. Nine days later a huge formal celebration was conducted with the flying of a 31-star flag representing the admission of the first American state on the Pacific Coast. A really enormous parade followed which is described by Bancroft in volume VI. pages 348-349. Even the *London Times*, reported on this event;

> Forgetting for a moment the decorative features of this exhibition, let the reader consider the extraordinary character of the facts it symbolized. Here was a community of some hundreds of thousands of souls collected from all quarters of the known world — Polynesians and Peruvians, Englishmen and Mexicans, Germans and New Englanders, Spaniards and Chinese — organized under old Saxon institutions and actually marching under the command of a mayor and aldermen. Nor was this all, for the extemporized state had demanded and obtained its admission into the most powerful federation in the world, and was recognized as part of the American Union. A third of the

---

80. Thompson & West, *ibid,* p. 134.

time which has been consumed in erecting our house of
parliament has here sufficed to create a state with a territory as
large as Great Britain, a population difficult to number, and
destinies which none can foresee.

California was indeed huge compared to the other states then in
the Union. The combined area of the seven New England states plus
New Jersey, New York, and Pennsylvania was 182,092 and that of
California 188,892 square miles.

Under ordinary circumstances, as the residents of the second
city of California, Sacramento's citizens would have celebrated in a
similar, if slightly more modest fashion. They did experience at least a
day or two of pure joy, but then with almost biblical force, they were
struck by an irresistible natural scourge.

THE CHOLERA EPIDEMIC AT SACRAMENTO

*CHOLERA: An acute bacterial infection of the small intestine
caused by VIBRIO CHOLERAE and characterized by massive diarrhea with
rapid and severe depletion of body fluids and salts. The vibrio enters the
body via the mouth, usually in water or foods contaminated by sewage,
and the diarrhea is caused by a toxin excreted by the VIBRIO CHOLERAE
bacteria. This toxin activates an enzyme system in the intestine that causes
the rapid excretion of body fluids containing bicarbonate and sodium. The
incubation period is normally twelve to 28 hours. Severe dehydration is
followed by intense thirst, lowered blood pressure, and loss of
consciousness after which the patient may die in shock. The disease
normally runs its course in two to seven days.*[81]

On October 20th, the day after the *New World* brought the news
of California's becoming a state, an immigrant was found at dawn on
the Sacramento levee, dying of cholera. It was known that the *Oregon*
and other ships had recently brought the disease to San Francisco from
Central America. As a result, at least one contemporary newspaper,
Dr. Morse in 1853, and other later writers, reported that the infection
was brought to Sacramento from San Francisco by the *New World*. In
fact cholera had been raging on the Atlantic seaboard in late 1848 and
by the spring of 1849 had reached Missouri in time to afflict the
departing overland emigrants. They, like all other Americans, were not

---

81. Encyclopædia Britannica, *Micropædia*, 1994, Vol 3, pp. 258-259.

prepared to battle this foe, and Bancroft estimated that 5,000 died as a result. At least some survived, carrying westward the tiny *Vibrio Cholerae* in their bodies. On September 5, 1850, cholera broke out in a small party of immigrants nearing the Bear River, and eight died in three hours. It had already appeared in Placerville on August 1, and before October 20 could easily have reached Sacramento.

Whatever the direction from which it came, the next day four fatal cholera cases were reported, and six the day after. Within six days fatalities reached such a level that timely burial of the dead became difficult. On October 23, the deaths reached thirteen, and continued to rise until the thirty first, when 51 occurred, of which 39 were from cholera and eleven from the kindred disease of dysentery.[82]

The citizens of Sacramento were generally familiar with similar, but smaller outbreaks — either by having personally seen the afflicted, or by having talked to those who had done so. But here the mounting death toll became terrifying, and hundreds left the city in every direction to the extent that Dr. Morse estimated only 20% remained. He also noted that the victims did not seem to be confined to those of intemperate and irregular habits. In a few days many of the most substantial citizens had died as a result of the sweeping epidemic.

The Sacramento correspondent of the *San Francisco Alta California* wrote:

> This city presents an aspect truly terrible. Three of the large gambling resorts have been closed. The streets are deserted, and frequented only by the hearse. Nearly all business is at a standstill. There seems to be a deep sense of expectancy, mingled with fear, pervading all classes. There is an expression of anxiety in every eye, and all sense of pecuniary loss is merged in a greater appreciation of personal danger. The daily mortality is about sixty. Many deaths are concealed and many others are not reported. Deaths during the past week, so far as known, 188.[83]

Despite these remarks, there were many who stayed and attempted to alleviate the suffering of the sick and dying patients.

The doctors of the community were outstanding in this respect.

---

82. H.S. Crocker & Co. *Sacramento Directory, Commencing January, 1871,* pp. 77-78.

83. *San Francisco Alta California,* November 4, 1850.

Of them it was said, " The rapid spread of the epidemic gave to the physicians of the city no rest day or night. As might be expected, they were falling like the foremost soldiers of a desperate charge, and before the cholera season ended, *seventeen* of them were buried in the City Cemetery." This was a professional mortality never experienced before; only two in three survived this awful inroad of death, and less than one third escaped infection. Although painfully aware of the odds against survival through this ordeal, not a single educated physician turned his back on the city in its distress. After the first of November, the death rate slowly declined and by the fourteenth, was down to twelve per day. On November 17, 1850, the plague was reported to have entirely disappeared.

From the contemporary remarks, it appears that the means by which cholera is transmitted were not clear to the medical profession in 1850. There was no mention of boiling or chemically purifying the water and some surprise that heavy users of ardent spirits were not as likely to be infected. These users drank little water and much of that had been sterilized by alcohol. Sacramento City water in late 1850 was pumped from the river at the foot of I Street or from a competing location on Sutter Lake at 2nd and I Streets, and then distributed by water carts. By the end of a long summer both these sources were low, and undesirable material might have remained near the pump intakes. The first rain of the 1850-1851 season occurred on November 10th, and may have caused the rivers to flow more rapidly and yield cleaner water. There were no more cholera attacks that season in Sacramento after November 17, 1850.

— § —

The people of Sacramento had lived through the first eleven months of 1850 in which they withstood an awesome succession of disasters, and despite the terrible suffering, without the loss of honor, their beliefs, or their wonderful enthusiasm. As the historian Livy[84] wrote of Rome after the battle of Cannae followed other defeats, "No other nation in the world could have suffered so tremendous a

---

84. Livy (Titus Livius, 59 B.C.-A.D. 17), *The War with Hannibal,* Translated by Aubey de Sélincourt, (Baltimore: Penguin Books, 1972) Book XXII, p. 154. In the battle of Cannae, (216 B.C.), the Romans suffered, at the hand of Hannibal, possibly the worst loss in the history of war. In a single afternoon, their whole army of 50,000 men, and the political leader of the country, were destroyed. The rings from the dead Roman officers were said to have filled a bushel basket.

series of disasters, and not been overwhelmed." If one substituted "new city" for "nation," Livy's statement would have described Sacramento during the year 1850.

Almost as if fate had decided Sacramento had suffered enough, the month of December was peaceful as James Culver gathered the data for his coming directory. Even the weather remained very mild and the total rainfall in the 1850-1851 season was reported by Drs. Logan and Hatch in 1880 to have been only 4.71 inches—the lowest recorded by them.[85]

With this short history ending on a quiet note, it is still easy to see why one gold rush observer said of California, "The longest period of time ever thought of was a month; all engagements were made by the month, during which period the changes and contingencies were so great that no one was willing to commit himself for a longer term . . . *People lived more there in a week than they would in a year most other places.*"[86]

— § —

85. According to the United States National Weather Service's Scott Staggs, the corrected rainfall in Sacramento for the 1850-1851 season was 8.26 inches and the lowest rainfall on record was the 1976-1977 season when 7.25 inches fell.

86. John D. Borthwick, *Three years in California*, Edited by Joseph A. Sullivan, (Oakland: Biobooks Publishing, 1948), p. 40.

BIOGRAPHICAL SKETCHES OF SELECTED NAMES IN THE DIRECTORY

The business or trade shown in the directory appears in italics after the names listed.

Names shown here which appear only in the advertisements, historical entries, or appendix at the back of the directory, are followed by a subscript page number.

§

An apology is due the reader for the large number of exact dates appearing here. They are not always needed to follow the stories, but are absolutely invaluable to a researcher who wishes to obtain additional information from old newspapers, court documents, and other contemporary records. They also provide a means of differentiating between persons of similar or identical names.

ARENTS, HIRAM A., *Merchant.* He established this business in November 1849, and later specialized in the cooperage trade. He was appointed chief engineer of the Sacramento Fire Department on January 25, 1851. Arents was born in New York state and was a member of the Sacramento Pioneer Association[87], photographed in 1878 with 109 of the other 250 surviving members, and died July 22,1890.

BECKLEY, LUCIUS RIPLEY, *Boarding House.* In 1844 he moved, with his wife, the former Mary Ann Gorsline of Fort Wayne, Indiana, to Van Buren County, Iowa, where he wholesaled pottery manufactured locally. On April 5, 1850, the family left Boneparte, Iowa with three ox teams in a group of 38 wagons. They crossed the Missouri River about May first, and arrived in Placerville, September 20, 1850. Beckley operated a bakery at Diamond Springs for a few months and then moved to Sacramento in December, where he ran a boarding house. His wife died June 5, 1851, and he married Mrs. Phoebe Shaeffer in 1852. In 1855, Beckley commenced farming in the Franklin area south of Sacramento on 320 acres, to which he later added 1,000 acres.

---

87. The *Sacramento Pioneer Association* was formed in February, 1854 and membership was limited to men who had arrived in the State before January 1, 1850. The name of the organization was changed from time to time to the, *Sacramento Society of California Pioneers, The Sacramento Pioneer Society,* in 1966 to the *Sacramento Pioneer Foundation,* and a few years later returned to the *Sacramento Pioneer Association.* In 1908, the original membership having declined to 14, membership was extended to male and female descendants of pioneers. By 1966 even this group had shrunk to four members, and the qualifications, in addition to those in place earlier, were changed to include persons who contributed to, or had a marked interest in, Sacramento history. The board of directors meets monthly, and activities include contributions to local historical groups, ownership of Pioneer Hall (completed in 1868), local historical trips for members, and publication of information on the history of Sacramento. In addition, a special committee of the Association maintains and improves the Pioneer Grove section of the old Sacramento City Cemetery where Association members and their relatives are buried. The current membership is about 280 [The executive secretary's telephone number (916) 447-7411].

He was elected county supervisor in 1855 and later served as Public Administrator. He died May 15, 1859, leaving three sons and a daughter by his first marriage and a daughter by the second. He is buried with his wife Mary Ann in the Sacramento City Cemetery, plot 452, lot 11.

BENSLEY, JOHN, *Merchant.* He was born in 1812 in Herkimer County, New York, graduated from Columbia University, and came to California in 1849. He and F. R. Starr were partners in the firm of Starr, Bensley & Co., and during the flood of January 1850, it was reported that a small steamer actually came up J Street and unloaded goods directly into their store at 58 J Street (224, new style, which is now under the freeway)[88]. In 1852 Bensley moved to San Francisco where he set up a company to introduce the first regular supply of water.

In 1864 he was living at 708 Mission Street and was president of the San Francisco Water Works. He was on the first board of trustees of the Citizens Gas Company, organized the Pacific Rolling Mills and the Pacific Oil and Lead works, and was one of the organizers of the Electric Light Company. In 1871, using his own money, he incorporated the San Joaquin and Kings River Canal and Irrigation Company and began building the first 40 miles of the canal, which by 1880 was the largest irrigation canal in California. This was accomplished under adverse conditions with all implements, materials and supplies transported over mountainous and difficult country.[89] In the 1880 San Francisco directory he was listed as a capitalist living at Number 9, South Park. John Bensley died at San Francisco in June 1889, at the age of 77, and a lengthy notice appeared in the *San Francisco Call* on June 21, 1889.

BENTON, REV. JOSEPH AUGUSTINE[51], *Pastor of Presbyterian Church.* He was born in Connecticut, graduated from Yale in 1842, was principal of Brainard Academy 1843-1844, studied theology at New Haven from 1844 to 1847, and preached at Winthrop Church, South Malden, Massachusetts from 1847 to 1849. He arrived in California July 6, 1849, and preached his first sermon in Sacramento on July 22. On Monday, October 15, he reopened the first school in Sacramento, which had been taught during August by Charles T. H. Palmer at 307 I Street

---

88. Irving McKee, Editor, *Alonzo Deland's California Correspondence,* (Sacramento: Sacramento Book Collector's Club, 1952) p.42.

89. Hubert H. Bancroft, *History of California,* Vol. VII, pp. 9 &10

(new style). Benton purchased the school furniture from Palmer in September, and started with four pupils. This number rose to nine and included the two daughters of James M. Woodland, the city assessor later murdered by the squatters on July 14, 1850, and three or four children of Barton Lee whose biography appears on page 126. Rev. Benton permanently closed the school "By stress of weather" about December 1, just in time to miss the huge flood of early January 1850, which entered the city at this location. The school building was owned by Professor Forest Shepherd and is described on page 153.

On December 18, 1849, Benton was named a trustee of the foundation of the University California (then called "the College of California"). He was on the committee that assisted Rev. Henry Durant in 1853 in opening the first building of the College of California in Oakland at Broadway and Fifth Streets with three students.[90] In the Declaration of Incorporation of the College of California, signed by Governor John Bigler on April 13, 1855, Benton is named a founding trustee. He was asked to prepare and read a poem at the first commencement literary exercises, held in October 1858. He named it "The Republic of Letters" and two of its many stanzas read:

> But a truce to all this. Be our thanks manifold,
> For the day, and the scene, the light we behold,
> That here on our shores, all prophetic of fates,
> Our College hath lifted her beautiful gates.
>
> Then be honored the realm and its sons of great fame,
> That have filled the whole earth with such joyous acclaim,
> By an old world and new, clasped with thought-flashing
> fetters,
> Yea, live, live forever, Republic of Letters!

While these lines are interesting, they may explain why Rev. Benton is better known as a preacher than a 19th century poet.

---

90. Samuel Willey, D.D. *A History of the College of California*, (San Francisco: Samuel Carson & Co., 1887) p. 9. College administrators were a different breed in early California. On page 11, is a story of a hard time in U.C. history when they had fallen behind in payments to a tough Oakland contractor who was working on their new building at 12th and Harrison Streets. Reverend Durant moved into the partially completed building at night, and with only an ax under his bed for defense, held off the contractor and two burly assistants who were trying to gain possession the next day.

In January 1863, he gave the invocation when Governor Stanford turned the first shovel of earth for the Pacific Railroad at the foot of K Street in Sacramento, and in the fall of 1863, Benton was elected to the California State Senate representing Sacramento County.

As the chairman of a committee to name the streets of Berkeley, the future home of the University of California, Benton proposed on May 7, 1866, that:

> . . .there be scientific streets and literary ways; the streets to run north and south, and the ways east and west. That the streets be called in alphabetical order after the names of American men of science, and the ways in like order, after American men of letters; beginning on the east side with the streets, Audubon, Bowditch, Choate, Dana, Ellsworth, Fulton, Guyot, Henry, etc.; and the ways, beginning on the north side, Allston, Bancroft, Channing, Dwight, Everett, Fulton, etc.

From a modern map, it appears that *Audubon* may have been changed to *College* and *Guyot* to *Shattuck*, while Allston remains to the west of the modern campus. It thus seems that Benton intended the north east corner of Berkeley to be at a point on the campus, a short distance south east of the present location of the Campanile. His proposal was adopted, and a large number of the names he suggested continue in use today. New streets named for people important to Berkeley have been inserted between some of the original east-west "ways."

The Reverend Dr. Benton was an important member of the Sacramento Pioneer Association and died April 8, 1892.

BIGLER, JOHN, *Lawyer.* He was born in 1803, in Cumberland County, Pennsylvania, and came to California in 1849. A political opposite, but honest historian, Dr. John Morse wrote of Bigler's incredible kindness during the Sacramento cholera epidemic of 1850:[91]

> But we will mention one name, our motive for which will be readily acknowledged more as the extortion of truth than the result of partisan partiality. That name is John Bigler, the present Governor of California. This man with strong impulses of sympathy, could be seen in every refuge of distress, that concealed the miseries of the dying and destitute. . . .he braved every scene of danger that presented, and with his own hands administered relief to his suffering and uncared for fellow

---

91. Dr. John F. Morse in Samuel Colville, *Sacramento Directory for the Year 1853-54,* Mead Kibbey , Editor, (Sacramento: California State Library Foundation, 1997) p. 68.

beings. . . .no means of relieving the mind from an instinctive fear that depresses the vital forces, should ever disparage those ennobling impulses of benevolence which conduct a man voluntarily into the haunts of danger and distress.

John Bigler must have been well aware that in those 26 terrible days seventeen of Sacramento's 54 doctors died from cholera. He practiced law in Sacramento in 1849-1850, and was governor of California in 1852-1856. The capitol was moved from Benicia to Sacramento during his term, and Lake Tahoe was, in 1853, named Lake Bigler in his honor. This was the mightiest natural feature of California ever named for a citizen of Sacramento, the Sutter Buttes running a poor second. Bigler was a Democrat, and while he was not from the South, the California proponents of southern sentiments (including slavery), had been politically powerful during his time as governor. During the early years of the Civil War, in 1862, William H. Knight of Los Angeles met with two other Republican newspaper men, including the correspondent of the *Sacramento Union*, at H. H. Bancroft's publishing house in San Francisco. Knight mentioned that Governor Bigler had "not distinguished himself in any way," and induced the group to approve changing the name of the lake to *Tahoe,* on a large map of California he was publishing.

John Bigler's Grave
Sacramento City Cemetery

Knight immediately wrote the Land Office in Washington telling what had been done, and on the next federal map, Lake Bigler became Lake Tahoe.[92] This was not a new problem for former rulers, although some foresaw it. In Egypt there are still dozens of congratulatory inscriptions where the cartouches with the name of Ramses II have been cut six inches deep into granite monuments to inhibit subsequent pharaohs from leaving the remarks, but changing his name to theirs.

---

92. George Wharton James, *The Lake of the Sky, Lake Tahoe,* (Chicago: Charles T. Powner Co., 1956) pp. 60-61. He quotes a letter from Knight on the subject.

Bigler later served as minister to Chile, U.S. inspector of the
Pacific Railroad, and collector of internal revenue. Bigler died in
Sacramento on November 28, 1871. Although he was an active
member of the Sacramento Pioneer Association, he is buried in the
Masonic section, Sacramento City Cemetery, Grave BB37, code H.

*The following short biography of Jacob Binninger was made
possible by the assistance and advice of Binninger's great, great
granddaughter, Mrs. Dolores Hendricks Campbell. A relative, Mrs.
Carolyn M. Degenkolb is preparing to publish a family history and
additional valuable research information from this source is included here.*

BINNINGER, JACOB, *Hotel Proprietor*, was born in Baden, Germany
February 6, 1793, served briefly in the Napoleonic Wars, and in 1816
married Anna Marie Hülin at Nimburg. They had four children, and
with the surviving three, emigrated to New York in the ship *Elizabeth*,
arriving in 1826. Another child was born there on December 25, 1826,
and shortly after the family moved to Cincinnati where Binninger
continued in the trade of master tailor. Their sixth child, William Tell
Binninger, was born in Cincinnati, February 4, 1829, and sadly Mrs.
Binninger died shortly after. In 1830, Binninger had moved to Galena,
Illinois, operated a tailoring business, and owned some mining claims.
He married Miss Margaret Wallace, July 21, 1830, and by 1844 four
children were born to this marriage.

In April 1849, the family left with a party from Wisconsin
overland for California and arrived in Sacramento in October.
Binninger started a hotel here, which was destroyed in the flood of
1849/50, and he promptly rebuilt the "Fourth Street House" at 49
Fourth Street (new style 1017-4th). In 1852, he sold this establishment
to James M. Day, who had also come from Wisconsin and it was
renamed "Mansion House." That same year Binninger bought the
brick hotel owned by George Zins at 151 Front Street near N (new
style 1323, Front), which Binninger named the "Green Tree Hotel."
This structure was completed in October 1849, and was the first brick
building in Sacramento. In 1856 a newspaper mentioned Binninger was
building an addition to his hotel on Front Street. In December 1999, a
modern hotel was being constructed at the site. He also bought
property in 1853 in Birchville, Nevada County, and the Empire Ranch
near Brown's Valley, Yuba County, where he later built the Empire
House Hotel.

He also donated the land for the Peoria Cemetery a mile or two
above Brown's Valley on the La Porte road with the proviso that any of

his descendants could be buried there free of charge. His reason for the name may have been the happy memory of some event which occurred long before in Peoria, Illinois. Jacob Binninger died at the Empire House January 7, 1867, and is buried in the Peoria Cemetery.

BIRCH, JAMES, *Stage [coach] Proprietor.* In September 1849, he founded the first stage line in California from Sacramento to Mormon Island. In 1854 he was president of the California Stage Company which by 1856 had 80 Concord coaches, 125 Concord freight wagons, and 1,100 horses covering 1,474 miles of routes in northern California. On September 29, 1855, Birch bought the finest commercial building in Sacramento, the Adams & Co.'s building (46 & 48, Second St.), after the failure of that company, earlier in 1855. He was a member of the Sacramento Pioneer Association and died September 12, 1857.

BOOTH, LUCIUS, A., *Wholesale Merchant.* His firm was originally established in 1849 as Lindley & Booth, and in May 1850, became Forshee, Booth & Co. In May 1851, it became Smith & Booth, in November 1852, became Booth & Co., in April 1855, became Booth, Carrol & Co., and in March 1856, became Booth & Co. In the 1860 presidential election, Lucius Booth was a representative from Sacramento to the state Union Party convention, backing Bell and Everett. The Republican party prevailed in the election, and all four of California's electorial votes went to Lincoln. By 1863, Lucius Booth was listed as a clerk and Booth & Company was owned by C. T. Wheeler, J. T. Glover, and Newton Booth (later Governor of California and possibly a relative). Lucius Booth was a member of the Sacramento Pioneer Association and died on September 22, 1870.

BROCKWAY, CHARLES V., *Merchant.* He was born in 1807 in New London, Connecticut, in 1822 went to New York where he learned the coach making trade, and in 1828 moved to Washington D.C. In 1837 he had moved to Louisville, where he made coaches and wagons. In April 1849, he started from St. Joseph, Missouri across the plains to Placerville, where he arrived on August 4, 1849, and kept a general store. In November 1849, Brockway moved to 11th & K in Sacramento and built the first residence in that vicinity. At the age of 58 he married Miss M. E. Offett of Georgetown, D.C. and they had one son and four daughters. He was a member of the Sacramento Pioneer

Association, died March 31, 1884, and is buried in the Sacramento City Cemetery, lot 67, code H.

BURNETT, PETER HARDEMAN, *Attorney.* He became the first elected governor of California in 1850, when the Capitol was at San Jose. He was born in Nashville, Tennessee, November 15, 1807, and grew up there and in western Missouri, receiving the rough equivalent of a grammar school education. Although he had worked around the farm and for his relatives since childhood, at nineteen he obtained his first real job—as a hotel clerk for $100 per year in Bolivar Tennessee. While there he met Sam Houston, David Crockett, Newton Cannon and other men important in early western history.

In 1827, Burnett left the hotel to become the sole employee and manager of a small store in Clear Creek, Tennessee at $200 per year plus his laundry, room and board. While living there he married sixteen-year-old Harriet Rogers, on August 20, 1828. With various partners Burnett continued in the mercantile business in Missouri and occasionally studied law. Despite much hardship, great frugality (he and his family rented a log house for $25 a year), and diligent effort, by 1839 he was further in debt than when he left Tennessee. It became obvious that he should change direction and enter the legal profession.

He obtained his license that year and joined a firm defending Mormon leaders who were being expelled from Missouri. In one important case before a fair judge but a most hostile courtroom audience, Burnett whispered to his associate attorney just before his closing argument; "Let yourself out, my good fellow; and I will kill the first man that attacks you." With noble courage, the associate gave an eloquent and withering speech, while Burnett sat six feet away with his hand on his pistol calmly determined to do as he had promised. Despite furious protests from the audience, their client was acquitted and Burnett kept his revolver under the table.[93] Burnett later served as a district attorney in Missouri in 1840-1843.

He had been interested in moving to Oregon for some time, and on May 22, 1843, he and his family started out from Independence, Missouri with two ox wagons and a small two-horse wagon. The first part of the trip was rather uneventful but very tiring, and he mentioned drivers on the road being so drowsy during the day that they fell asleep on the front seat of their wagons. The oxen, being as sleepy, would stop until the driver awakened. The group passed Fort Hall on

---

93. Peter H. Burnett, *An Old California Pioneer,* (Oakland: Biobooks, 1946), p. 33.

August 30, and Salmon Falls on the Snake River on September 7, 1843. At a crossing of the Snake River they secured a 23-pound salmon by running over it with an ox wagon, which might be a record for this unusual means of fishing.

Gov. Peter Hardeman Burnett 1807-1895

Fort Boise (273 miles from Fort Hall) was passed on September 20th, and they reached Fort Walla Walla on October 16, 1843. They had traveled the 1,691 miles from their departure point, twelve miles west of Independence, Missouri in 147 days at an average speed of 11½ miles per day.

The group divided in two at Walla Walla, with the larger part driving their cattle and wagons on to Fort Vancouver, while Burnett's part left their wagons with the others, procured an old 40-foot Hudson's Bay Company boat, and descended the Columbia River with an Indian pilot. After some hair-raising adventures shooting rapids, Burnett reached Vancouver, (Washington) November 7, 1843. In 1844 he helped form a provisional government for Oregon, ownership of the territory then being in contention between the United States and Great Britain. He also became a member of the new legislature and one of the first laws passed forbade the introduction, manufacture, sale, or barter of ardent spirits in the Oregon Territory. On December 4, 1845, he was elected judge of the Supreme Court of Oregon by the Oregon House of Representatives. There being no others, he was in effect chief justice, and was referred to as "Supreme Judge."

By a treaty, signed June 15, 1846, between the United States and Great Britain, Oregon Territory, south of the 49th parallel of latitude, came under the sovereignty of the United States. The Mexican War had been declared on May 13, 1846, and about noon on

July 7, 1846, the flag of the United States was raised on the custom house at Monterey, California. Thus in the 22 day period between June 13, and July 7, 1846, the United States had gained sovereignty of the Pacific Coast from Cape Flattery at the mouth of the Strait of Juan de Fuca to the border with lower California in latitude 32° 40'.[94]

Sometime in July of 1848, news of the gold discovery in California reached Oregon by way of Honolulu, Nesqualy (on Vancouver Island), and finally up the Columbia River to the Hudson's Bay Company at Fort Vancouver. Burnett checked the news carefully, and satisfied himself the mines were as rich as first reported. By mid-September, he had organized a party of 150 men, 50 wagons and ox teams, and an ample supply of provisions for six months. No wagons had ever passed between Oregon and California, but Dr. McLoughlin, chief factor of the Hudson's Bay Company, said that he thought Burnett and his experienced men would succeed, and recommended Thomas McKay as pilot or guide. Burnett was elected captain of the group. Although the party was heavily armed, they treated the Indians they met with kindness, and had no trouble from them. Burnett's party reached the summit of the Sierra Nevada Mountains by October 20, 1848, and after some difficulties got their wagons down to the valley. They made a visit to Sutter's Hock Farm below Marysville, and then started for the mines on the Yuba River.

They arrived at Long's Bar, named for John Long, a friend of Burnett's from Missouri, on November 5; just 46 days after their departure from Oregon City. In his journal, he mentioned that a few days before, near the Yuba River, he had first heard the word "prospecting" used with the sense of "looking for gold." He surmised this meaning was invented in California and he was probably correct.[95]

Burnett, his brother-in-law, John P. Rogers, and his nephew, Horace Burnett, bought a claim the next day, on November 6, and started mining (For more details on John P. Rogers, see his biographical sketch on page 151). During their stay at Long's Bar, Burnett met two surviving members of the Donner Party and obtained a long story from Mrs. William Foster of their sufferings in the California mountains two years before.

---

94. Peter H. Burnett, *ibid*, p. 143.

95. The Oxford English Dictionary gives over a page of meanings and uses of the word "prospect" with citations back to the sixteenth century, but the earliest citation of "prospecting" in connection with mining was in the June 3, 1848 edition of the *New York Literary World,* which read, "Two or three men with a bucket, a rope, a pick-axe, and a portable windless...This... is a prospecting party."

Burnett and his relatives quit mining and went to Sutter's Fort on December 19, 1848, where he soon became young Sutter's attorney and his agent for the sale of lots in Sacramento.[96] Burnett's legal services in all matters and his services as agent were to be paid by a modest 25% share of the gross price of all lots he sold. From these activities he was shortly able to start paying off his creditors, with interest, and in addition became wealthy. He began selling lots early in January 1849, first near the Fort, but by the end of the month business was moving toward the embarcadero or river front, and lots began selling better there.

He made several trips to San Francisco hoping to induce immigrants to come to Sacramento, and also became involved in the formation of a state government. General Bennett Riley, the military governor, who had known Burnett in Missouri, appointed him "Judge or Minister of the Supreme Tribunal of California" on August 15, 1849. At a September session of this tribunal in Monterey, Burnett was elected chief justice by his fellow judges. Even in the wild West, it was most unusual to see a man serve as chief justice in two states in a three year period. The business of the tribunal was completed in a short time and he remained until the end of the month to observe the deliberations of the Constitutional Convention. When the work of the convention was completed, he announced his candidacy for the office of governor. Burnett actively campaigned against four other candidates and on November 13, the election was held with the following result: Peter H. Burnett, of San Jose, 6,716; Winfield Scott Sherwood, of Sacramento, 3,188; John A. Sutter, of Sacramento, 2,201; John W. Geary, of San Francisco, 1,475; William M. Steuart, of San Francisco, 619 – total votes 14,199. Burnett was inaugurated the first governor of California on December 20, 1849.

On January 9, 1851, for reasons that are not perfectly clear he resigned the office of governor. His short letter of resignation said in part:

> Circumstances entirely unexpected and unforeseen by me, and over which I have no control, render it indispensable that I should devote all my time and attention to my private affairs. I therefore tender to both Houses of the Legislature my resignation as Governor of the State.

---

96. Peter Burnett, *ibid*, pp. 164-169

Philetus Watson Burnett, 1808 - 1897

After this he practiced law in San Jose and Sacramento, and he mentioned in his memoirs that he paid off the last of his indebtedness in 1852. Early in 1860 he wrote a book *The Path which led a Protestant Lawyer to the Catholic Church,* and in 1863, moved to San Francisco to become the president of the Pacific Bank, replacing the founder, Sam Brannan. Peter Burnett died May 17, 1895, at San Francisco. The *San Francisco Call* printed a lengthy obituary the next day. Bancroft said of him "Burnett has never been credited with any brilliant abilities, nor charged with any great weakness; lacking force and decision in official positions; an honest, industrious, kind-hearted, diplomatic, lucky man."

BURNETT, PHILETUS WATSON, *Carpenter. Burnett's biography here was kindly researched and edited by a descendent, his great great grandson, Burnett Miller, a former mayor of Sacramento, and president of Burnett & Sons Mill and Lumber Company.*

Philetus Burnett was born March 8, 1808, in Granby Massachusetts and became a skilled carpenter, specializing in cabinets and stair building. He married Abigail Burr October 1, 1829, at Ludlow, Massachusetts where she was born. Their first child, Henry A. Burnett, was born in Belchertown, Massachusetts, October 10, 1832. During the following seventeen years they had five more sons, and three daughters. In addition to raising a family and carrying on his business, Burnett built, for the expanding family, an attractive frame house which is still standing in Belchertown.

He left his pregnant wife in the East and departed for California by ship from Charleston, Massachusetts, June 25, 1849. He landed in the Isthmus, crossed over to Panama, where he took another ship which arrived in San Francisco, October 11. Burnett came almost immediately to Sacramento where he assisted Rev. J. A. Benton of the Congregational Church which had been organized on September 16, 1849. He appeared to have no interest in mining for gold, and by late 1850, he was listed as a carpenter located on M Street between Front and Second Streets. In 1851, he returned to New England to obtain equipment which he intended to bring overland to California. He also booked passage for his wife and assisted her in packing up for moving with their seven surviving children, (two had died in infancy), to California by way of Nicaragua. The youngest had been born November 25, 1849, during Burnett's absence.

Abigail Burnett and the children departed in 1852, on the ship

J. Gold for Nicaragua (most probably on the Vanderbilt line which included a stop at Havana). Their passage was also booked on another ship for the trip from San Juan del Sur, on the Pacific side, to San Francisco, where they expected to be met by Philetus Burnett after his overland trip. When Abigail arrived in Nicaragua, she learned that the ship for San Francisco had been wrecked, and no substitute provided. She was forced to remain in that fever-infested country under terrible conditions. On July 8, 1852, Emma, the baby not yet three years old, was the first to die.

The captain of the *S. S. Lewis,* a large propeller steamer, took pity on the Burnett family and agreed to take them to San Francisco. This ship was new to the coast, but already had sad experience with death from tropical diseases. On its first trip up the coast a few weeks before, it arrived in San Francisco on July 7, 1852, with 636 passengers, of whom 36 had died of cholera, yellow fever, or malaria,[97] and usually more died after landing from the same causes. Either just before or after boarding the ship, Adolphus Burnett who was 20, died on August 28, 1852, and while at sea, seventeen-year-old Sophia died September 5, 1852. On September 15, this awful trip ended in San Francisco with only Abigail and four children remaining, and the captain's kindness to them (and others) was rewarded by the authorities who seized the ship for carrying more passengers than allowed by law.   The family came to Sacramento, and Philetus and Abigail joined the Congregational Church later in 1852. Burnett became a member of the Sacramento Pioneer Association May 31, 1854. He then engaged in farming for a period, and was not listed in the 1853 Sacramento City Directory, but in the 1854-1855 directory he and his son, Henry Ashbel Burnett (1831-1908) are listed as carpenters living on the alley between 7th and 8th and O and P Streets. An 1854 map of Sacramento shows a building at the back of an 80 x 160 lot on the north side of P Street at about 209 P (717, new style). The city directory entries for 1856 mention P. W. Burnett was married and had three children, and H. A. Burnett, drayman, was also living there. Possibly through an oversight, the Burnetts are not listed in the 1857-1858 directory, but return in 1859 and continue on through 1880. About 1860, P. W. Burnett must have built a larger residence at the front of his lot because he is listed afterward as being on the north side of P Street between 7th and 8th Streets, and in 1880 at 717 P Street.

His son, Henry A. Burnett, enlisted as a private in Company F,

---

97. Earnest A. Wiltsee, *Gold Rush Steamers of the Pacific,* (San Francisco: The Grabhorn Press, 1938). pp. 82, 86 and also an illustration of the *S.S. Lewis* at anchor on p.109.

Second Cavalry Regiment of the California State Volunteers on August 29, 1861, and was honorably discharged a first lieutenant in 1865. He married Mary A. Bassett, September 10, 1866, and later moved to 223 (731, new style) P Street, at the north west corner of 8th and P Streets. Both these two-story homes are shown on an 1872 birdseye view of Sacramento. In 1869, P. W. Burnett was working as a finish carpenter on the new State Capitol, and he joined with his son Henry to form the partnership of Burnett & Son which received the contract for the main doors, carved banisters, and a magnificent spiral stair installed in the building. They both were involved with other partners in later years, but the original partnership survived and is carried on today by their descendants at 11th and C Streets.

Philetus Burnett's wife, Abigail, died February 21, 1874, and he later remarried. His second wife died on Christmas Day 1880, and they are both buried with him in the Sacramento City Cemetery lot 113, code H. He was photographed in 1878 with 109 other surviving members of the Sacramento Pioneer Association, and died on March 4, 1897, four days before his eighty-ninth birthday. He was the only man listed in Sacramento in 1850 who founded a business which is still here and wholly owned by his descendants.

CAULFIELD, HENRY A., *Carpenter.* He had a notable career in Sacramento, but not in the ways followed by most of the other entries in this list. He was born in 1827 in Ireland, came to Albany, New York at an early age, and he served there in the Emmet Guards in 1844. In 1849, he came to California by way of Cape Horn and settled in Sacramento, where he was a carpenter and quite active in Democratic politics. In the afternoon of August 14, 1850, at the height of the Squatter Riots, the mayor of Sacramento was shot four times and barely survived, and J. W. Woodland, the former City Assessor was killed. Caulfield and a Doctor Robinson (later Governor of Kansas) were seen aiming guns at the two victims. Dr. Robinson was shot in the leg, escaped to a nearby residence, and was arrested later that day.

The mounted leader of the Squatters, a man named Maloney, had his horse shot from under him, and attempted to escape on foot, but was found in a nearby alley and shot in the head. Caulfield fled on foot and escaped to the eastern part of the city. He was apprehended near Brighton by John Cleal, the city surveyor, and brought back into Sacramento rather inelegantly tied to the back of a horse, from which conveyance he was transferred to the city prison brig *La Grange* on the river front at the foot of H Street. Although indicted for murder and conspiracy to murder by the Grand Jury, Caulfield was eventually released and continued to be active in the Squatter troubles. Early in 1851 Caulfield bought a farm on the high ground north of the mouth of the American River which is now part of Discovery Park. The following year he traded this land for several city lots owned by Patrick Bannon including one at the southeast corner of 6th and R Streets where Caulfield took up residence in a shanty.

On June 19, 1851, Caulfield had a "disagreement" with George Wilson, a justice of the peace and associate judge of the Court of Sessions. Judge Wilson had made an offensive remark about attorney J. H. McKune, and the attorney had come into Wilson's court demanding a retraction, which Wilson refused to give, after which, the attorney struck him. Judge Wilson was busy stabbing the attorney with a sword he had just pulled from his cane, when Caulfield, who may have been drinking, by chance entered the room, saw an opportunity to revenge some past problem with the judge, and fired five shots at Wilson without hitting him. After this new enemy appeared, Wilson stopped the sword-play with the disgruntled attorney, seized Caulfield around the neck, and pressed a large revolver to his head. Before Wilson could pull the trigger, R. P. Jacobs, a policeman, appeared and saved Caulfield's life. The judge in his disappointment about this interference charged Caulfield with attempted murder.

Although Caulfield had no further encounters with heavily armed judges, he did not give up violence, and around 1856 was in a second-floor room of the house of a man named Miller having an active discussion about politics and some mules. Caulfield who was only five feet three inches tall, attempted to convince Miller by striking him with a flat-iron, and Miller countered by breaking a heavy cane into several pieces over Caulfield's head and forcing him partly out of a window. Mr. Miller was holding Caulfield's feet when suddenly Mrs. Miller entered the room, and Mr. Miller let go of Caulfield who then fell to the ground. Miller sent word to the coroner that he had killed Caulfield, but before the dead-wagon arrived, the victim had walked to the county hospital.

Not long after recovering from his visit to the Miller residence, Caulfield engaged in an argument with Frank Nolan on Front Street. Nolan attempted to end the matter with a large knife and damaged Caulfield's pulmonary system so severely that for several days he breathed through a stab wound in his back. Caulfield fiercely objected to this informal surgical procedure and incurred terrible wounds to his hand when he finally wrested the knife from Nolan.

Other such encounters continued and on August 15, 1878, in a lot dispute south of R Street, Caulfield shot William G. English who died two days later. Caulfield was indicted and after a short trial was found guilty of manslaughter and sentenced to prison for six years. While the record does not demonstrate he held any qualifications for the job, other than a possible ability to maintain order in the reading room, he was appointed Prison Librarian.

An interesting summation of the effects of his previous activities on Henry Caulfield himself is contained in the routine physical examination report when he entered San Quentin to serve his term:

> Henry A. Caulfield, native of Ireland, sentenced for manslaughter 6 years, from Sacramento, age 50, carpenter, height 5 feet 3 inches, complexion light, brown eyes, black hair, square features, high forehead, heavy eyebrows, knife wound on right side of stomach, knife wound below left nipple, finger on right hand crooked, 3 fingers on same hand cut, 7 wounds from knife and pistol on back, another cut across left foot, knife wound in right leg, stout build.

In addition to the record he carried on his body, Caulfield had an impressive list of contacts with the Sacramento judicial system:

Year	Court	Charge
1850	District Court	Assault with intent to kill
1851	Court of Sessions	Assault to Murder
1852	Court of Sessions	Assault to Murder
1852	Court of Sessions	Grand Larceny
1852	—	Misdemeanor
1854	Court of Sessions	Assault to Murder
1854	Court of Sessions	Grand Larceny
1854	Court of Sessions	False Imprisonment
1856	Court of Sessions	Assault with intent to kill
1857	Court of Sessions	Assault & Battery (2)
1857	Court of Sessions	Concealing of Public Offense
1857	Court of Sessions	Perjury
1858	Court of Sessions	Assault to Murder
1861	Court of Sessions	Assault with a Deadly Weapon
1864	County Court	Assault & Battery
1867	County Court	Assault & Battery
1870	County Court	Misdemeanor
1870	County Court	Disturbing the Peace

Year	Court	Charge
1872	County Court	Assault to Murder
1878	District Court	Murder (W. English),mis-trial, hung jury
1878	—	Manslaughter (William English), 6 years

This record does not indicate any jail time served, but Caulfield must have had some really exceptional defense attorneys if he only served one six-year-sentence in San Quentin. In the words of biographer W. J. Davis, "besides the foregoing, Caulfield was involved in many other ugly scrapes, nearly killing some one or being killed himself." He hated Judge E. B. Crocker, the Central Pacific Railroad's chief counsel, and had killed William English, a close friend of its president, Leland Stanford. It was ironic that just at the cocktail hour on July 2, 1888, our hero, while walking down the tracks from his home, was run over near Fourth and R Streets by a Central Pacific locomotive pulling the evening train from Folsom. He was buried in an unmarked grave in St. Joseph's Cemetery at a cost of $17.00.[98]

CHAMBERLAIN, W. E., *Merchant.* He was born in Nashua, New Hampshire, October 31, 1801. Daniel Webster was a relative and sometimes made his home in Nashua so that Chamberlain knew him well. He owned or worked in stores in Andover in 1822, in Boston in 1824, and in 1827 Cincinnati and Oxford, Ohio. While living in Cincinnati he was married in Searsport, Maine to Miss Charlotte A. Kidder whose father had been an important merchant in Boston. In 1844 he owned an extensive lard factory in Terre Haute, Indiana under the firm name of Cruft & Chamberlain. On January 1, 1849, the lard works was totally destroyed by fire (imagine trying to fight that conflagration) and at 10 A.M., Chambelain told his wife that despite his age, he was going to California. This he did, by way of St. Joseph, Missouri, and after walking almost the entire way and with many difficulties, reached Sacramento on August 23, 1849. He bought a small store on L Street from Lindley & Booth, and later owned one facing the City Plaza, (Cesar Chavez Park) which was burned out in the great fire of 1852. He then formed the firm of Chamberlain & Kidder, wholesalers. In 1854 he was elected Sacramento City Treasurer, and in 1855, Secretary of the City Council, and later the vice-president and a director of the bank of D. O. Mills. Mrs. Chamberlain came to Sacramento in 1855 by way of

---

98. Mickey Knapp, *A Chronicle of Henry Caulfield, Irishman,* (Sacramento: Sacramento County Historical Society, 1992 Golden Notes Vol.38 Numbers 3 & 4) pp. 23-37. This author has provided a well researched and readable history of the Squatter Riots and Henry Caulfield.

Nicaragua leaving their children for two years in Indiana in the care of Dr. Scott, father-in-law of President (1889-1893) Benjamin Harrison, after which they also came to Sacramento. Mrs. Chamberlain died June 1, 1888, and Mr. Chamberlain on January 9, 1896. He was a member of the Sacramento Pioneer Association, and is buried in section B-125, plot 113 of the Sacramento City Cemetery.

CHESLEY, GEORGE W., *Auctioneer,* Born on February 3, 1822, in Dover, New Hampshire, he moved to Providence, Rhode Island in 1839 and in 1844 married Miss Alice Marie Whipple, a descendent of one of the signers of the Declaration of Independence. He left New York aboard the steamer *Crescent City* February 5, 1849, bound for Chagres. After a few months' stay during which he conducted auctions and brokered tickets, Chesley boarded the steamer *Oregon* at Panama on May 25, 1849, and arrived in San Francisco on June 13. He immediately formed the firm of Johnson, Chesley & Clark in the auction and commission business. The business was dissolved in March of 1850, and Mr. Chesley came to Sacramento. He was elected high constable of Sacramento in October 1851, and served until October 1853. He also had an auction business at the NW corner of 6th & K Streets until its destruction in the great fire of November 1852. Not long after that he moved to San Francisco, subdivided some lots with financial success, and Chesley Street on the south side of Harrison Street between 7th and 8th Streets was named for him. In 1854 Chesley returned to Sacramento and after participating in two partnerships, founded G. W. Chesley & Co, groceries & provisions at 51 Front Street in 1863.

During the Franco-Prussian War (1870-1871), Mrs. Chesley was trapped in Paris during its siege by the Germans, and wrote interesting letters to her friends in Sacramento describing the deprivations suffered by the inhabitants of the French capital. Mr. Chesley may have been missing her too, as in the 1868, 1869, and 1871 directories his residence was listed as "rooms at the Orleans Hotel." He was president in 1887-1890 of the Sacramento Pioneer Association, was photographed in 1878 with 109 other surviving members, died November 23, 1891, and is buried in the Sacramento City Cemetery, Lot 29 code M.

CORNWALL, PIERRE BARLOW, *Land Office,* was born near Andes, Delaware County, New York, November 23, 1821, and remained there until 1826. The family then travelled three weeks by packet boat on the new Erie Canal to Buffalo, then by a small steamer to Portland Harbor, and finally 13 miles by wagon to their new log home near Westfield, New York. At age ten, young Cornwall began helping in his father's general store, and at fifteen he left home for Buffalo to enter the shipping and commission trade. By 1839, he had saved enough capital to begin a fur trading venture in Wisconsin Territory. He left this operation in the fall of 1840 in order to settle the estate of his father, who had died in Mansfield, Ohio where he owned a successful merchandising company. Cornwall operated a similar business there until 1847, but was forced to close by financial reverses. In early 1848, he and his sixteen-year-old brother Arthur decided to go overland to California, inspired by John C. Frémont's *Expedition to California*, and unaware of the discovery of gold.[99]

They hired an experienced guide, Tom Fallon, purchased equipment and trading goods and departed from St. Joseph, Missouri in early April 1848. They travelled first to Council Bluffs and met a party of about 500 emigrants waiting to leave for Oregon. Cornwall saw that it would be a great advantage if they could keep ahead of this crowd, both in feed for their animals and convenient camping and watering locations for themselves. Four other men had similar opinions, and departed immediately with Cornwall's party. They were able to make rapid progress, but the disadvantage of being in a small party became evident when they were captured by a large band of Pawnee Indians. The younger braves wanted to dispatch the seven emigrants immediately, but Cornwall, by signs and a drawing, convinced the chiefs that his little band were "but the advance couriers of an army of warriors to be likened in numbers only to the leaves on the trees."[100]

The party was released, but in a subsequent attack by some of the young Pawnees, Cornwall was wounded severely by an arrow in the leg. They were finally rescued by a larger group of Sioux Indians fortunately headed by Tom Fallon's father-in-law. The Sioux recovered Cornwall's equipment from the Pawnees and accompanied them until the were well clear of the Pawnee territory. Cornwall had convinced some of the original Oregon emigrants to come to California and the party under his command (he was then 26 years old), had grown to about 45 men, with their families, livestock and 30 wagons. As they approached California, Fallon and one other emigrant went on ahead

---

99. Bruce Cornwall, *Life Sketch of Pierre Barlow Cornwall,* (San Francisco: A. M. Robertson, 1906) For private distribution p. 14. Citation by Gary Kurutz.

100. Bruce Cornwall, *ibid* p. 20.

to scout out the route and were killed by Indians. The whole party had been following directions from Fallon, and this sad event left Cornwall with only a copy of Frémont's map as a guide. He followed a route along the Humboldt River and through the Humboldt Sink, across 60 miles of desert to the vicinity of modern Reno, where, possibly because he had heard of the Donner Party's difficulties the year before, he turned south to the Carson Pass. After great difficulty, the group reached Mormon Island on the American River and disbanded. Cornwall tried mining for a day or two, but quickly decided he would be far better off supplying, rather than competing with the miners.

Pierre Barlow Cornwall 1821-1904
City Councilman and Sacramento's Delegate to the State Legislature at the age of 28. He was also a partner in the city's largest banking firm and had extensive land holdings.
From a Daguerreotype taken in 1849

He and his brother travelled by way of the Livermore Pass to San Jose, and there rested a few weeks while they bought supplies for a general merchandise store which they opened at Drytown, Amador County (about four miles south east of Plymouth) in the fall of 1848. Soon thereafter Cornwall bought sailing ships and commenced carrying his own and other's freight between San Francisco and Sacramento. In late 1848, at the age of 27, he joined the firm of Priest, Lee and Company at Sutter's Fort, and became its business manager. On December 11, 1848, he was secretary of a meeting at the alcalde's office in San Jose to set up the government of California, and was a delegate to a similar meeting in Sacramento, July 5, 1849. He also served on the first Sacramento City Council from July to November of 1849, and at a meeting outside the City Hotel on

Front Street, he was nominated for the California Assembly to represent Sacramento. He was elected November 13, and participated in the organization of the legislature December 17, 1849, at San Jose. He had previously been involved in a title dispute which is mentioned on page 78.

At Christmas he returned to Sacramento to see his fiancée, Miss George Anna Cutler, who had recently ridden on horseback across the plains to Sacramento with her stepfather, Daniel Green Whitney. The young couple were married January 5, 1850, and Cornwall and his bride returned to San Jose where he continued his work with the legislature. On January 28, he became temporarily blind from an eye infection, and resigned from the legislature. By March he was able to return to Sacramento, and April 10, 1850, he sold his interest in the business and two thirds of his real estate to Barton Lee for $640,000. Eighteen months before he had entered California a stranger and $8,000 in debt, and was now about to return east with his young wife and well over half a million dollars, largely in Barton Lee's notes paying over 12%. On the evening of April 10, Cornwall and his bride attended a piano concert, after which the artist and many friends were invited to a farewell party for the couple at their Sacramento home on Second Street. They left San Francisco April 20, 1850, on the steamer for Panama and New York. At the old home in Westfield, New York, Cornwall paid off his mother's mortgage and gave her a sum that would provide for her future. He went to New York City and on August 28, signed an agreement with Ward Price & Co, bankers, to set up a banking and exchange business with them upon his return to Sacramento.

Just when everything seemed perfect, the news of Barton Lee's failure in Sacramento on August 5, and the Squatter Riots of the 15th, reached New York. Pierre Cornwall and his wife promptly booked passage for California and arrived on the steamer *Caroline* October 7, 1850. Over 60 of the passengers had died of cholera since leaving Panama and had been buried at sea. The Cornwalls had avoided cholera, but he was seriously ill with yellow fever and was carried ashore. He returned to Sacramento to recuperate, and lay ill in bed as the cholera raged, the town almost emptied, his notes became worthless, and his remaining real estate unsalable. A more perfect example of the vicissitudes of Gold Rush business could hardly be imagined. Cornwall regained his health, and by December, was operating a real estate office at 41 (1009, new style) 2nd Street and living at the corner of 2nd and L Streets. His eighteen-year-old brother, Arthur, lived at the office. By 1856, Pierre Cornwall was listed as a real estate dealer with three children, living at the NE corner of 9th and H Streets.

In 1854, Cornwall and some friends chartered, and bountifully stocked with food and drinks, a fine steamer which they took to Benicia where the State Capital was then located. The legislators had been bitterly complaining about the bad food and accommodations there, and Cornwall's friends hoped to induce them to move to Sacramento. The steamer arrived with flags flying and bands playing, and that night a few legislators dined aboard and stayed all night. The next day most of the members took up permanent quarters aboard. On Friday, February 25, 1854, both houses of the legislature moved to adjourn and to meet in Sacramento on the next Thursday. Some of the enthusiastic immigrants actually moved to Sacramento on Cornwall's chartered steamer. After assisting in this triumph for his adopted city, he briefly took part in the gold adventures on the Fraser River, British Columbia from June to August 1858, and upon his return, sold his remaining Sacramento real estate and moved permanently to San Francisco.

Cornwall opened a business as a notary public and real estate agent. The business prospered, and in 1862, he became a founding member of the San Francisco Stock Exchange and remained an active trader until 1867. Unfortunately his wife of fourteen years died in 1864 after a lingering illness, leaving Cornwall with their three children. By 1867, he was the San Francisco agent of the Black Diamond and Bellingham Bay Coal Company shipping 5,000 tons per month from the Black Diamond Mine near Martinez and a quarter of that amount from Bellingham, Washington. He married Miss Sada Davis at her mother's home in San Diego on June 25, 1871. He later owned the *Great Republic*, the second largest sidewheel steamer in the world after the *Great Eastern*, became the president of the coal company, founded the California Electric Light Company with the first central station electric lighting plant ever built, and controlled a railroad and large sawmill in Washington. He was also a regent of the University of California for ten years, and a director of the San Francisco public schools. Surrounded by his wife and children, Pierre Barlow Cornwall died in San Francisco at the age of 83 in the evening of September 25, 1904.

CULVER, JAMES HORACE, *Auctioneer.* He was born in 1814 and came to California from Pennsylvania in 1849, and was elected in September 1849, to the office of alcalde of Volcano district. He moved to Sacramento in April 1850, where he was a partner in a real estate and auction business. In that same year he became the author and publisher of the 1851 Sacramento directory, which was the first book published in Sacramento and it included an eleven page "historical sketch." In February 1851 he was the proprietor of the Missouri Hotel, and in June 1852, he became a lime dealer. He was a member of the Sacramento Pioneer Association, died in Sacramento May 11, 1864, and is buried in the old Masonic section of the Sacramento City Cemetery, Tier DD, Grave 7B, code H.

DEAL, SAMUEL, *Auctioneer.* He was born March 31, 1822, at Shippensburg, Pennsylvania, learned the trade of harness-making, and in 1846, enlisted as a private in Company D, Second Regiment Pennsylvania Volunteers. The lieutenant-colonel of his regiment was John W. Geary, later alcalde of Yerba Buena and first mayor of San Francisco. In the Mexican War, Deal went to Vera Cruz, arrived at Cerro Gordo the day after the battle, and in September 1847, at Puebla was attached to Steptoe's battery which he accompanied to the Valley of Mexico. On the day of the capture of Mexico City, he was serving in Company H of the Third Regiment of regular Artillery and was wounded in the side. Despite this, he entered the city with his battery of four guns and eighty horses and camped on the plaza. After the war, in March of 1849, at Pittsburgh, Pennsylvania he married Miss Jane Blair, and shortly after went to St. Joseph, Missouri, and from there crossed the plains to Sutter's Fort where he arrived on August 31, 1849. He mined on the south fork of the Yuba River and also engaged in teaming,[101] but returned to Sacramento in 1850, and was Captain of Sacramento Police 1851-1854. He was a member of the Sacramento Pioneer Association photographed in 1878 with 109 other surviving members. He died on June 4, 1895, and is buried in the City Cemetery, Section B-124, Lot 93.

DUNCOMBE, DR. CHARLES, *Physician.* He was born in Connecticut in 1794, lived in Canada for several years, and came to California in 1848. During the war of 1812, he escaped from Canada dressed as a woman, and was transported across a river to the United States by British soldiers to whom he gleefully disclosed his true identity when he was safely ashore. He served on the Sacramento City Council and later in the State Assembly from which he was expelled in 1859. Although re-elected that same year, the Assembly refused to seat him. In 1863/1864 Duncombe was again elected to the California assembly and was allowed to serve, completing his term at the age of 70. He was the second

---

101. *Teaming* was used to describe the business of hauling goods by heavy wagons and teams of horses, oxen, and occasionally mules. He may have owned the wagon or could have been employed to drive a company wagon.

oldest man listed in this 1851 directory, being 56 at the time of its publication (Jacob Binninger was a year older). For comparison, in that year, John Sutter was 53 and Abel Stearns of Los Angles, who had lived there 21 years was 52 years of age. Dr. Duncomb died in Sacramento October 1, 1867, and is buried in the Masonic section of the Sacramento City Cemetery, Lot 19 code H.

EWER, F. C., *Editor of the Transcript.* Ferdinand Cartwright Ewer was born in Nantucket, Massachusetts, May 22, 1826, and graduated from Harvard University in 1848. In September 1849, he arrived in California, and by April 1, 1850, was a founder and co-editor of Sacramento's first tri-weekly newspaper, the *Sacramento Transcript.* The other editor, George Kenyon Fitch, contributed the press and type, and later obtained the State printing business. Ewer was referred to as "literary editor," and therefore was probably editor in the modern sense, while Fitch acted as the business editor.[102] The *Transcript* merged with the *Placer Times* on June 16, 1851, and the resulting newspaper, the *Times and Transcript* closed one year later. Ewer left for San Francisco, and on January 27, 1854, he became founding editor of California's first magazine, the San Francisco *Pioneer*, a highly regarded monthly magazine of 64 pages. He continued in this capacity until the magazine went out of business in the fall of 1855. In September of that year he took a position in the San Francisco Custom House under Milton S. Latham. Ewer became a Protestant Episcopal minister about 1858, and by 1860 was pastor of San Francisco's Grace Church. He was described as having "a sweet voice, ready utterance, and an aggressive manner"—perfect attributes for success in many endeavors.[103] By 1864 he had left for New York where he became rector of St. Ignatius Church. Ferdinand C. Ewer died in Montreal October 10, 1883, at the age of 57, leaving a widow in San Francisco.

FIGG, E. P. *Merchant.* He was born near Danville, Kentucky, April 24, 1819. By 1840, he was engaged in the fur business in St. Louis, and in 1844 was a merchant in Lexington, Missouri. In 1849 he left Lexington

---

102. Edward C. Kemble, *A History of California Newspapers, 1846-1858,* (Reprinted Los Gatos, California: Talisman Press, 1962, Helen Bretnor, Editor) pp. 143, 339.

103. Winfield J. Davis, *Illustrated History of Sacramento County*, (Chicago: Lewis Publishing Co., 1890) p. 807

in a party of sixteen wagons bound for California. After 30 days on the way, he and another wagon separated from the others and by travelling mostly at night reached California in 71 days, setting a record for ox teams.[104]

Figg arrived in Sacramento in September 1849, and put up near the NW corner of 7th and J Streets by the horse market, and took a job clerking for H. E. Robinson on J near Front Street. On September 16, 1849, he became a clerk with Alexander Sibley at $19 per day plus board. After saving $5,000, he bought Sibley's store on J between 2nd and 3rd Streets. He later was very successful in raising and shipping fruit (peaches and Bartlett pears, but no figs) and operated a salt business. In 1855 Mr. Figg married Mrs Hattie McCormack, a widow. They had two children and adopted two more. He was a member of the Sacramento Pioneer Association, died March 27, 1895, and is buried in the Sacramento City Cemetery, Lot 19 code H.

FORMAN, COLONEL FERRIS, *Lawyer*. He came to California from Illinois and was agent for the government for relief of the emigrants crossing the plains. In April 1853, President Pierce appointed him Postmaster of Sacramento. He was active in founding the Democratic Party in California and was a director and on the construction committee of the Sacramento Valley Railroad, completed to Folsom on February 22, 1856. In 1861 and 1862, Col. Forman commanded the 4th Infantry Regiment of the California Volunteers (in Southern California). He was a member of the Sacramento Pioneer Association.

GOODALE, M.D.,[90] *Carpenter*. Probably **Nathaniel D. Goodell** who was born April 18, 1814, at Belchertown, Massachusetts, and learned the trade of carpenter at Amherst. He married Sarah Pease of Granby, Massachusetts on May 2, 1838, and they celebrated their golden wedding anniversary in Sacramento. He became an architect and designed the city hall of Belchertown, three large factories in Ware, and several hundred workers' houses. With eleven other men, he formed a company which set sail from New York in the brig *Everett*, March 29, 1849, and arrived at Panama April 23. After waiting nearly a month,

---

104. This seems quite remarkable as by modern highways it is 1,710 miles from Lexington, Missouri to the California border and Figg's oxen must have averaged 24.1 miles every day. For a sad comparison, the Donner Party went from Independence, Missouri to Truckee Lake (now Donner Lake}, California (1,945 miles) in 166 days averaging 11.7 miles per day. Men could apparently do better without oxen because in the 1860s Edward Peyson Weston is said to have walked from New York City to San Francisco in 70 days, averaging about 42.5 miles per day.

he set sail for San Francisco in the small brig *Copiaco*. The trip took 95 days and was quite difficult, but he finally reached California and went to Mormon Island by way of Sacramento. After a few months of mining on the American River, he returned to Sacramento and was employed as a carpenter starting at $16 per day. As the demand for finer homes and commercial buildings arose, he gradually shifted back to contracting and the practice of architecture. In 1863, he designed and built Wachorst's jewelry store at 61, (now 229) J Street, the site of which is now under the freeway. Among over a hundred of his later commissions in Sacramento, two are still standing, the Governor's Mansion (originally owned by Albert Gallatin) at 16th and H Streets, and Pioneer Hall at 1011 7th street. Goodell was a member and past-president of the Sacramento Pioneer Association, was photographed in 1878 with 109 other surviving members, died November 30, 1895, and is buried in Plot B-124, lot 84 of the City Cemetery.

GREEN, CHARLES E., *Merchant*. In April 1853, he founded the Forest Line of stages which had four Concord coaches, four Concord wagons, 88 horses, and eight drivers. Their main route was to Sonora by way of Jackson and Mokelumne Hill. He is included in the 1878 photograph of surviving members of the Sacramento Pioneer Association, and died on July 10, 1886.

HARDENBERGH, JAMES R(ICHMOND). He came to Sacramento from New Jersey, and started a merchandising business in August 1849. In April of 1850, he was elected to the Sacramento City Council and immediately chosen by his colleagues as president. After the mayor, Hardin Bigelow, suffered serious injuries in the Squatter Riots (August 15, 1850), Demas Strong became acting mayor. He went east, and Hardenbergh was required to assume the office. He continued as acting mayor until December 15, when Horace Smith was elected mayor. Hardenbergh had been appointed chairman of the Levee Committee, and on September 10, 1850, he began building nine miles of levee, about three feet high, six feet wide at the top and twelve feet wide at the base, starting near Brighton and thence along the American River to its mouth. From the mouth of the American along the Sacramento River to R Street, it was three to six feet high, fourteen feet wide on top and 30 feet wide at the base. From the river bank at about 10th Avenue, east to the hills (about 21st Street) it was fifteen to 20 feet high, 20 feet wide at the top and 70 feet wide at the base. It was completed by late December, and required digging, transporting and putting in place 121,000 cubic yards of earth at a cost to the City of about $170,000. While this was being accomplished, the first case of cholera was reported on October 19, 1850, and within a few days became an epidemic. At its inception, the population of the city was about 6,000, and in late November, when the terrible sickness ended, 653 persons or 10.9% of its citizens had died. The difficulties of being mayor and supervising the levee construction under such circumstances seem almost more than one person could bear. But bear it he did, and after the levee was done and the epidemic over, he passed the duties of mayor to Horace Smith. Hardenbergh apparently recovered interest in the job, because in May 1851, and again in 1853 he was elected mayor of Sacramento. In addition, on May 19, 1851, he was a delegate at Benicia to the first state convention of the Democratic Party. In February of 1852, Hardenbergh's company bought the Orleans Hotel, 52 Second Street (1018, new style) only to have it destroyed in the fire of November 2, 1852, with personal losses to him of $102,000.[105]

As soon as the ashes were cold, the owners commenced rebuilding. The words "commenced rebuilding" simply did not have the same meaning as they would have now. Labor and all building materials were in very short supply—virtually the whole city had been destroyed in one night, and everyone wanted to rebuild. Money was also tight and their building was to be all brick, 85 feet by 50 feet, three stories high, containing 40 bedrooms, with parlors and a huge saloon on the first floor. In the very finest Sacramento pioneer tradition, they completed the building in just twenty days and six hours after laying the first brick in the foundation. They later added to the structure, and for many years it was the finest hotel in Sacramento and the office and originating point for a whole net work of stage coach lines. Under various owners it continued as a hotel until 1877, when Whittier, Fuller & Co. (later W. P. Fuller Paint Co.) purchased it for use as a warehouse and office facility. It was finally razed sometime after 1901 according to the Sacramento Union for June 29, 1904, page 10.

Upon the occasion of his 1856 departure for a visit to the east , the citizens of Sacramento presented James R. Hardenburgh with a solid gold medal and a matching gold-mounted cane as a spontaneous tribute to him as a man and a citizen. His name appeared in the 1864

---

105. Samuel Colville, *Sacramento Directory for the year commencing May, 1856,* (San Francisco:, Monson, Valentine & Co. 1856), p. 60. The information on rebuilding is in Colville's 1854/1855 Sacramento directory p.13.

George Kraus discussing Huntington said,[109] "Despite his great wealth and power, innumerable interests and the controversies that constantly revolved about him, Huntington always spoke out strongly for the working man and insisted on a day's pay for a day's work. He also had a high regard for the public. At a gathering for Southern Pacific engineers and conductors at his San Francisco home on May 6, 1897, Huntington said: 'We all serve the same master—the public . . . We exist for their convenience, and we cannot live without them'."

After years of buying railroads, steamship lines to Asia and Latin America, owning Southern California real estate, influencing national and California legislation, and making a massive donation to the New York Metropolitan Museum of Art, Collis Potter Huntington died on August 13, 1900, at Raquett Lake, New York. His altruism was continued by his nephew, Henry E. Huntington who founded the Huntington Library in San Marino, California.

JOHNSON, JOHN NEELY, *Lawyer.* A native of Indiana, Johnson was born on August 2, 1825, practiced law in Keokuk, Iowa, and arrived in Sacramento in July 1849. He first engaged in teaming and mining and then opened a Sacramento law office in a tent. In 1850, he was elected Sacramento city attorney and district attorney, and later was appointed by President Filmore special territorial census agent. He was appointed a colonel on the staff of Governor McDougal in 1851 and sent to the site of the Mariposa Indian troubles. In 1852, he married the daughter of Col. J. C. Zabriskie (see biography on page 171). In 1853 he represented Sacramento in the legislature, and on September 5, 1855, was elected Governor of California. His residence at the NW corner of 11th and F Streets still stands. Johnson moved to Carson City, Nevada in 1860 and became wealthy managing the affairs of Sandy Bowers during the latter's extended absence in Europe. Johnson was active in forming the state government, and was elected to the Nevada Supreme Court in 1867. He was a member of the Sacramento Pioneer Association, and died of sunstroke in Salt Lake City on August 31, 1872.

LATHAM, MILTON SLOCUM, *Lawyer.* He was born May 23, 1827, in

---

109. George Krause, *High Road to Promontory,* (Palo Alto: American West Publishing, 1969) pp 294-295. For a biography of Huntington see: Cerinda W. Evans, *Collis P. Huntington* (Newport News, Va. 1954)

Ohio, and graduated at nineteen from Jefferson College, Pennsylvania. He studied law in Alabama and was appointed clerk of the circuit court of Russell County there. In 1850 he came to Sacramento and later that year was elected District Attorney of the judicial district of Sacramento and El Dorado counties. On November 2, 1852, he was elected a congressional representative, in September of 1855, appointed collector of customs at San Francisco, and September 7, 1859, elected the youngest Governor of California,   For reasons that later became painfully obvious, on January 11, 1860, he was appointed United States senator to fill the remaining three years of David C. Brodericks's term, and three days later resigned from the office of governor. The fascinating details of this political transaction involve forces wishing to separate southern California and possibly allow slavery there, and are covered in Bancroft's *History of California*, (Vol. VI pp. 722-736, and Vol. VII pp. 251-260). While in the U. S. Senate, Latham spoke in favor of the Pacific Railroad, and later became the president of the California Pacific Railroad. He continued in business in San Francisco and died in New York on March 4, 1882.

LEE, BARTON, *Office*. He was a pioneer capitalist, born in Cayuga County, New York in 1813, who came to Sutter's Fort in November 1848, with stops in Iowa, Missouri, and Oregon. At the Fort, he entered into a mercantile business in company with Albert Priest under the firm name of Priest, Lee and Co. In early 1849, they built the second building in Sacramento City, a frame-and-canvas store at 2nd and J Streets. Lee was on the committee to formulate the resolutions to be decided at meetings presided over by Peter H. Burnett to request a Constitutional Convention. The meetings were held in Sacramento on January 6–8, 1849. The convention was convened September 1, 1849, in Monterey, and completed its work on October 13, 1849.

The first lots in Sacramento went on sale January 8, and within a few weeks Sam Brannan and Lee were given 500 lots to keep their businesses in Sacramento. On April 30, 1849, at a meeting on the embarcadero, Lee was elected to an eleven-member legislature to temporarily govern the Sacramento District, stretching from the Sacramento River to the Sierra Nevada and south to the Cosumnes River. The northern boundary seemed to have been near the present site of Redding where the river entered the mountains. In the fall of 1849, to fill a desperate need, Lee and his partner, Albert Priest, quickly built a hospital 35 x 55 feet at 3rd and K Streets, for the use of Doctors John F. Morse and Jacob D. B. Stillman, to whom it was rented at $1500 per month. Considering the huge rents then prevailing, they reckoned that

Lee had set, for charitable reasons, the rate at the lowest in the city. As a comparison; a building about the same size at Front & K Streets was rented in January 1850, to Col. J. B. Starr, an auctioneer, for $24,000 per month. The new building was the largest hospital existing in California at that time.[110] The doctors there charged $10 per day, compared to the $16 per day prevailing elsewhere in the city.

As an indication of his financial activities, Lee paid the most individual taxes ($16,253.12) of any person in Sacramento in its first year, 1849, and on April 10, 1850, he bought out the last of his partners, Pierre B. Cornwall, for $640,000. His income after this transaction was estimated to have been between $55,000 and $80,000 per month, and in July he was said to have represented a capital of $1,500.000, used in his activities as a merchant, banker, and real estate investor.[111] In August of 1850, he suffered serious financial reverses, and as creditors' demands increased, he assigned all his assets August 5, 1850, and closed the doors of his bank.

In 1853 Barton Lee was a salesman for an importer at 40 J Street and by 1854 was listed at a livery stable, without specifying his duties. Suffering from acute rheumatism, he fractured his leg in a fall on the sidewalk of Second Street, died at 43 on December 1, 1856, and was buried with honors the next day by the Sacramento Pioneer Association, of which he was a member. His grave is in the older part of the Sacramento City Cemetery, lot 34.

LIGHT, DR. WILLIAM W., *Dentist*. He was born July 29, 1819 near Bethel, Ohio and attended school there with Ulysses S. Grant. In 1827 Light moved to Cincinnati where he studied medicine, and in 1840, dentistry. On January 1, 1849, he started for California by way of New Orleans and the Isthmus of Panama, where he practiced medicine while waiting for the old whaler *Humboldt*. She loaded 363 passengers, some hard tack, jerked beef, and drinking water in old whale oil barrels and took 102 days to reach San Francisco, finally arriving on August 30, 1849. Dr. Light's total time from Cincinnati was 241 days. He went

---

110. J.D.B. Stillman, MD, *Seeking the Golden Fleece,* (San Francisco: A Roman & Co., 1877) pp. 146-148 describes the building and their assistants. On pages 149-154 he describes life in the flooded hospital during January, 1850, with patients arriving through upstairs windows and the dead stored under water below.

111. Bruce Cornwall, *ibid,* p. 49.

immediately to Sacramento and joined the firm of J. S. Ormsby making private gold five and ten dollar coins.[112]

He next tried mining for a time near Placerville and then moved to Shingle Springs where he met with considerable success. While there, he met a Spanish gentleman who was recommending that Dr. Light and some others should abandon their claims and go with him to an immensely rich mine of his, near Sonora, with the ominous name of *Dark Gulch*. They finally agreed to go, but upon arrival found the mine to be worthless, and when they looked for their Spanish guide, he had vanished. The whole thing was a scam organized by the local store-keeper who used the "guide" to bring in suckers who would buy supplies from his store. Light moved north to mine a short time on the Stanislaus River, and then returned to Sacramento in the summer of 1850. There he became a partner in a drugstore, Light, Ames, & Watts at 66, J Street, and also practiced dentistry at the same address. It was reported that *Light's Cholera Remedy* was both popular and effective during the great epidemic. Knowing that 11% of the population died of cholera in 27 days while Dr. Light's cure was available, how much worse would it have been without it?

He married Mrs. C. M. Weber, a lady of unusual talent as a writer, artist, and botanist. They suffered severe losses during the great Sacramento fire of November 2, 1852. In 1861 he became financially interested, with others including his wife's relative, in a mine at Alamos, Sonora, Mexico. In 1863, he was sent there by his associates to act as metallurgist at the mine. Eventually, the mine proved unprofitable, and it was sold in San Francisco, but Light's $50,000 share never reached him. During his stay in Mexico at the mine, when Maximilian sought to gain control of the country, Dr. Light gave medical aid to the local Mexican soldiers wounded in this war, and thereby gained their friendship. One day a soldier brought him a piece of rock to identify which proved to be ore of almost fabulous richness. Guided by the soldier to the point where he had found the piece, Light saw that the rock was only a fragment of a wonderful body of gold-bearing ore. He named the mine *Dos Hermanos* (probably because his brother had then joined him) set up a smelting works, and began operations with no participation by his crooked ex-partners.

---

112. In 1980, four Ormsby $10 coins were known, and one sold in the Garrett sale for $100,000. See R.S. Yeoman, *A Guide Book of United States Coins,* (Racine, Wis.: Western Publishing Company, 1995) p. 265. "In the sense that no state or territory had authority to coin money, 'private gold' simply refers to those interesting necessity pieces...which were circulated in isolated areas of our country by individual assayers, bankers, etc."

The mine was indeed rich, and Dr. Light took the bullion into Hermosillo and received gold coin in return, which he then secreted about his cabin. At that time, rural Mexico was in a state approaching anarchy, with gangs of bandits, tough Indians, and American army deserters wandering around. One afternoon, when A. A. Light, the doctor's brother, was bathing in a distant stream, Dr. Light and his nephew were sitting at the door. A band of desperados approached and began to speak to him. Suddenly he was grabbed from behind and simultaneously felt the sting of a bullet wound. Possibly because his assailant had taken a hit from the same bullet, Light was able to free himself, and while receiving four more wounds, groped for his rifle on the floor. Although half-blinded by blood, he found the rifle and some cartridges. His brother at the river and his nephew had been killed, and the roof of the adobe cabin was on fire, but Dr. Light's deadly shots killed five of his attackers, and the rest departed without finding the treasure. The burned roof fell in upon the cabin, covering all the valuables, and a heavy rain the next day made a total mess. Despite the painful wounds, he stayed by the cabin with one Indian boy, who helped him dig out the gold coins and wash off the ashes. He somehow made his way back to Sacramento, leaving the mine to be worked by others on commission. He attempted to form a company of men to return to his mine who were dumb enough to go and still smart enough to be of some use when they arrived. These qualifications were not met among his Sacramento acquaintances, and he finally gave up on mining Mexican gold. Although the date is not given, his wife died in Mexico, probably while he was at the partners' mine in Alamos.[113]

In the 1873 Sacramento Directory his name appears again as a dentist and continues each year through 1880 or later. His residence for over 20 years was at 1115-I Street. He appears in the 1878 Sacramento Pioneer Association photograph, and he died on June 14, 1895, and is buried in the Sacramento City Cemetery, Lot 16, code H.

LUCE, ISRAEL, *Marble workman.* He was born on August 14, 1824, near Ithaca, New York, learned the marble-cutter's trade at West Troy, and

---

113, Dr. Light's adventures in Mexico are taken from Winfield J. Davis, *Illustrated History of Sacramento County*, (Chicago: Lewis Publishing Co., 1890) pp. 271-273. The information used was probably taken in one or more interviews with Dr. Light years after the events mentioned. Hubert Howe Bancroft's comments on such sources are most informative, and appear at the bottom of page 175.

later worked at Woonsocket, Rhode Island, Pittsfield, and Worcester, Massachusetts. He married Mary Adeline Nichols of Worcester in 1848, and they had two sons and a daughter. On January 29, 1849, in a company with James McClatchy, he left New York for California, sailing on the *John Castner* for Brazos Santiago, Texas near the mouth of the Rio Grande. After a difficult land trip across Mexico, he boarded a ship at Mazatlán and arrived in San Francisco, May 29, 1849.

In December 1850, after mining near Coloma, clerking in a Sacramento store, and building the Nine Mile House near present-day Rancho Cordova, he bought a load of marble on the wharf in San Francisco, transported it to Sacramento, and on the east side of 7th Street between J and K Streets, opened the city's first marble yard. In 1853 he moved to a location on K Street near 7th and formed the partnership of Luce & Aitken which lasted for 25 years. They obtained most of their marble from a quarry at Indian Diggings, El Dorado County. Luce's first wife died in 1861 and in 1863 he married Mrs. Eliza Elliot, by whom he had a son and a daughter. In 1867, he was the superintendent of the Sacramento City Cemetery, where he was later buried in Lot 40 code H. He was a member of the Sacramento Pioneer Association and died on October 11, 1898.

MCCLATCHY, JAMES, 90 *Placer Times.*

Special thanks are due to James B. McClatchy, James McClatchy's great grandson who contributed most of the data used in preparing this biography and supplied photographs. Most importantly, he used skills learned in over 40 years in the newspaper business, to edit and rewrite parts of the author's original article.

James McClatchy was born June 30, 1824, to Scotch-Irish parents in Lisburn, Ireland and orphaned by the age of sixteen. He sailed for the United States in 1840, and took his first job in New York as an apprentice with a bakery, driving the delivery wagon and making bread. He enjoyed his work, but also became active in causes that fought intolerance and promoted the innate rights of mankind. A few years after his arrival, he met, probably through membership in anti-land monopoly organizations, the founder and editor of the *New York Tribune*, Horace Greeley, who both personally and through his newspaper, shared young McClatchy's beliefs. He began writing for the *Tribune*, and by 1845, the baking business was history; he was and forever would be, a newspaper journalist. The principles to which he remained true through the rest of his life were described by McClatchy a few months before his death with these words:

> My life, my hope, my very self have gone into journalism. I have no regret to offer. Although it is said by many people that they would not, if they had the chance, consent to begin life over again and go through the same routine, yet I am free to say that—seeing what I have seen, knowing what I know and feeling as I feel—I would, if I were young again, begin at the bottom of the same ladder and climb it at every hazard, for there would be no dishonor to repeat.

He obtained United States citizenship by naturalization on November 2, 1846, and continued living in New York. He was still working as a newspaper man late in 1848 when the news of the gold discovery in California was confirmed in a speech on December 5, 1848, by President James K. Polk. There is no evidence that this particular information was the deciding factor in McClatchy's subsequent plan, but a surprising number of California pioneers seemed to have started thinking seriously about taking the trip at that time. He had already made one break with his past in coming to America from Ireland, when he was 16, and he must have viewed California as another land of opportunity. It was understood it would be a long and difficult trip, whose problems he knew better than most young emigrants. At 24, he was young, intelligent, strong, determined to succeed, and unencumbered by a family.

The 83 names of McClatchy's company, with F. Harding as "Captain" or leader, were published in the January 30, 1848, edition of the *New York Herald*. Of these, Alex Clark and Edward Jefferys were to be newspaper printers at the Sacramento *Transcript*, and Israel Luce, a marble carver, Their names are included in this 1851 Sacramento directory. The group's destination on the Pacific was Mazatlán, and they crossed Mexico occasionally on foot, and using mules or horses when available.[114] The Mexican war with the United States had ended a year before with the treaty of Guadalupe Hidalgo under the terms of which California and New Mexico were purchased from Mexico. As one would imagine, while respecting the military ability of their recent invaders, it was hard for the citizens to practice the usual Mexican hospitality toward the Americans. In addition, due to the dislocations of the recent war, many bandits were operating along the route.

---

114. A dispatch from McClatchy, recounting details of this trip and a note about the circumstances of its preparation, appears in Appendix E, page 332.

Later, on April 20, 1849, McClatchy sent a dispatch from
Mazatlán describing the trip which was reprinted in his old paper, the
New York Tribune, where it was characterized as "by far the clearest
and fullest directions for reaching California via Texas and Mexico that
we have seen." The dispatch reflected his sensitive instinct for fair play
when McClatchy advised future travelers who might follow his route
across Mexico. In part he wrote:

> . . .Act like gentlemen, if not for your own sakes, at least
> for the sake of the country to which you belong. Let not the
> good name of America or the fair name of her citizens receive
> injury at your hands. . . .

He also mentions the fate of some of those who started with him:

> Eight out of the 84 persons who came in the same vessel
> with me took the back track before they had traveled three days
> in Mexico. Five others died of cholera, one of dysentery; and
> others who were left sick had since died or returned home. All
> these men left what many called good situations and most of
> them, wives and family, perhaps in no very prosperous condition.
> Take care that their cases may not be yours.

After reading this dispatch, one might have thought that the rest of
McClatchy's trip would be a relatively easy voyage up the coast from
Mazatlán to San Francisco. Actually just reaching San Diego was
agonizing in both duration and difficulties, which included constant fear
their ship would sink, thirst, partial starvation, and walking 300 miles
through a near-desert. At Mazatlán, which is on the coast of Mexico
almost opposite the southern tip of Baja California, he joined the
passengers of the schooner *Dolphin*, a very old ship in poor condition,
which had recently taken 84 days to sail up the coast from Panama to
Mazatlán.[115] On April 23, 1849, she set sail from Mazatlán with 69
people aboard, all of whom took turns as crew members. Due to a
defective compass and possibly a bit of poor navigation, the *Dolphin*
made a wrong turn into the Gulf of California, and was lost for three
days. After going back around Cabo San Lucas, the southern tip of
Baja California, and into the open Pacific, conditions deteriorated with

---

115. The distance from Panama City to Mazatlan by sea following the coast was about
2,135 nautical miles. The poor old *Dolphin* therefore averaged about 27 miles per day, after
allowing 4 days for supply stops. For comparison, the sailing ships carrying steel rails and
locomotives for the Central Pacific Railroad (hardly clipper ships), regularly made the 16,000 mile
trip from Boston around Cape Horn to San Francisco in 120 to 125 days. This would be an
average speed, with no allowance for the stops they had to make, of 130 miles per day.

the prevailing winds requiring them to sail close hauled into heavy seas.

The ship leaked so badly that the pumps had to be manned continuously, and as fast as one leak in the rotting hull was plugged, another developed. They intended to sail due west for almost 1000 miles before turning north, but began to run out of drinking water and took the fastest route back to the forbidding shore of Baja California where they hoped to find a stream. After several attempts which involved rowing to the rocky coast in the ship's boat, no fresh water had been found and the currents had carried them 70 miles back to the south. It was then thirty six days since they left Mazatlán, and they were still 300 miles below San Diego. They realized there remained so little food and water that if the whole group stayed on board the *Dolphin*, all but the healthiest would die before reaching San Diego. A meeting was held on May 28, 1849, and 48 of the strongest, including McClatchy, volunteered to land on the dry and uninhabited shore of Baja California, and walk to San Diego. On each trip from the ship to the beach, the small boat brought four or five of the selected marching party, and during every landing the boat swamped in the surf. The landing was made in the protection of a small rocky point in approximately lat. N 29°-00', long. W 114°-40', about 40 miles north west of the present village of Punta Prieta, and 90 miles south east of Rosario, Mexico. They hoped to find a coastal road shown on a nautical chart they carried, and they desperately needed drinking water, as they only had been able to take with them small bottles of "nauseous fluid" from the schooner. McClatchy's group were all in a weakened condition from the bad food and lack of exercise on the ship; the daytime temperatures were high, and the route lay over sharp loose rocks that looked as if they had been "burned in a kiln."

In the late afternoon of the second day, their constant search for water had led them to the bottom of a steep canyon, where some of the group were licking moisture from damp, muddy rocks. Others saw a bulldog belonging to Mr. Houghton begin pawing the ground about 50 feet away. Following this suggestion, they dug a hole around four feet deep and found a good stream of pure water. Only four days later their gratitude to the bulldog had been so far reduced by agonizing hunger that they were discussing killing and eating the animal. Fortunately for him, and with his assistance, they found and overtook a dying horse which they drove into a canyon, promptly dispatched and roasted. In addition to being a canine water-witch, the bulldog may have been able to understand some ominous overtones of human conversation.

The rest of the trip was even more grueling, and each page of the narrative bears a heading which gives a fair idea of the journey:— LAND ON LOWER CALIFORNIA,— GREAT SUFFERING,— RELIEVED BY INSTINCT OF THEIR DOG,— ABANDON THEIR BAGGAGE,— HUNTING A TRAIL,— EAT RATTLESNAKES,— THE LAST RICE, —THEY EAT A HORSE,— MELVILLE TAKEN SICK,— REACH SAN FERNANDO, —ARRIVE AT EL ROSARIO,— A FEAST,— A DEN OF RATTLESNAKES,— MELVILLE'S SUFFERINGS,— ARRIVE AT SAN DIEGO.[116]

They reached San Diego, June 24, 1849, covering the 300 miles in 26 days. After Rosario, they found mules or horses for those unable to travel on foot. The travelers reported being met everywhere with kindness from the natives, and north of Rosario obtained food from them as required. The ordeal ended with tragedy in San Diego where Melville died and was buried.[117] Their colleagues finally arrived aboard the old *Dolphin,* which was in a sinking condition and had to be condemned and sold. The proceeds were divided among the passengers and crew who then made their way north as best they could. In his letter from Mazatlán on April 20th, McClatchy mentions favoring this route (across northern Mexico) over all others save the Isthmus of Panama. No such letter has come to light from San Diego, but after his walking the three hundred odd miles up the coast, his preferences may have drastically changed.

It is unknown how McClatchy reached San Francisco, but many of the *Dolphin's* passengers walked or rode horseback. He was reported to be trying out mining beyond Sacramento as early as mid-summer of 1849: so he may have covered the 500 miles from San Diego

---

116. Dr. J.D.B. Stillman, *Seeking the Golden Fleece*, (San Francisco: A Roman & Co., 1877) pp. 327-352. Dr. Stillman first heard of the *Dolphin* story from a patient in Sacramento in the winter of 1849, and in 1875 wrote this 26-page, detailed version, by combining information from two manuscripts furnished him by passengers. John W. Griffith provided a journal written during the trip, and Samuel P. Crane of Sacramento wrote later from memory.

117. The extreme difficulties of McClatchy's trip during which they averaged 11.5 miles per day, may be understood from a comparison with the 2,091 mile journey of Edwin Bryant's party from Independence, Missouri to Sutter's Fort, in 1846. Despite innumerable difficulties described in 229 pages of his book *What I Saw in California*, his party covered the distance in 120 days at an average rate of 17.4 miles per day. This trip was accomplished with oxen and wagons to Fort Laramie which were traded for pack mules and ended by crossing the Sierra by Truckee Lake (now called Donner Lake). Even the unfortunate Donner party with great difficulty and keeping their oxen and wagons the whole way, reached Donner Lake later in the same year in 166 days and averaged 11.7 miles per day.

on a favored means of land transportation, a good mule who ate corn and covered 25 miles a day.

By the late summer of 1849, he had finished with prospecting and at the age of 25, had settled in Sacramento working for the *Placer Times,* Sacramento's first newspaper. It had started publishing on April 28, 1849,[118] next to Sutter's Fort in a small building at the corner of present-day 28th & K Streets. In the beginning of July 1849, the *Times,* like so many other early businesses, moved from the Fort to Front Street, and it was probably at that location McClatchy started his newspaper career in Sacramento. About July 12, 1849, Jesse Howard Giles, who had been a printer at the *New York Tribune,* and had known McClatchy there, became the editor and publisher of the *Times.* Giles thought enough of young McClatchy's ability as a journalist to send him to report on the constitutional convention.

From September 1, 1849, to October 13, delegates elected from all the districts of the state, met in Monterey to write the constitution of California—even before it was a State. The importance of Sacramento at that time can be seen from the numbers attending and the cities they represented. Of the 48 delegates, Sacramento and San Francisco each provided eight, San Diego provided two, Los Angeles, 5 and Santa Barbara, one.[119] While he probably did not attend for the whole time, McClatchy had the opportunity of meeting some of the legendary pioneers of California, including Thomas O. Larkin, Abel Stearns, Captain John Sutter, Robert Semple, and Mariano G. Vallejo. On April 1, 1850, the second newspaper in Sacramento was founded, the Sacramento *Transcript.* Also in April of 1850, Giles was replaced as the editor of the *Placer Times,* by J. E. Lawrence as listed in this 1851 directory, page 280, and McClatchy continued at the *Times.*

A problem of land titles to lots in Sacramento City had been brewing since October of 1849 (see pages 74-86). By the summer of 1850, most of the citizens of Sacramento were backing one or the other

---

118. Edward C. Kemble, *A History of California Newspapers, 1846-1858,* (Reprinted Los Gatos, California: Talisman Press, 1962, Helen Bretnor, Editor) p. 137.

119. J. Ross Browne, *The Debates in the Convention of California, on the Formation of the State Constitution,* (Washington: John F. Townes, 1850) pp.478-479. Seven of the delegates were Mexican, born in California. Of the rest, their average time in California was four years and ten months, with the shortest residency being 3 months and the longest, Abel Stearns, 20 years.

of two factions. Property owners who had purchased land in Sacramento which had first been sold by John Sutter, Sr. and their backers formed one faction. They referred to themselves as "landholders" and the other faction as "squatters." The other faction believed John Sutter's original title was invalid, and the land thus was in the public domain of the United States by conquest and purchase, ready for homesteading by settlers.[120] *They* referred to themselves as "settlers" and the other faction as "speculators." In Sacramento in 1850, the settlers were led by Dr. Charles Robinson, later the first governor of Kansas, and a good friend of James McClatchy's. Because of the latter's experiences in Ireland, his support of the Free Soil movement in New York, his loyalty to Robinson, and his lifelong support of the working man, McClatchy actively supported the settlers.

After the trial of a settler, John T. Madden, failed on appeal in favor of a landholder, the settlers began an armed march on August, 15, 1850. This was led by William Maloney on horseback, with Dr. Robinson and Henry Caulfield marching close behind. Although at the time he owned no property in Sacramento, and was not claiming any, McClatchy because of his deep belief in the cause, would probably, if not detained elsewhere, have been with them. He was instead in jail, where he had been placed August 13, upon delivering himself after receiving an arrest warrant on a charge of resisting the authority of the sheriff. McClatchy had refused to leave the house claimed by settler, John Madden. At 4th and J Streets the marchers were met by the city authorities and a large crowd of supporters drawn up in a line diagonally across the intersection. In the battle that followed, the mayor was shot and seriously injured, the city assessor was killed, Maloney was shot in the head and killed, Jessie Morgan, a settler, was killed and four others were injured by gunfire. The next day the sheriff was killed while attempting to arrest a group of settlers, after which 3 of the settlers were shot. Dr. Robinson and Henry Caulfield were arrested as were some other leaders, but while awaiting trial, Robinson

---

120. *Careful readers: This footnote also appears on page 77 with additional information on early California real estate law in the Treaty of Guadalupe Hidalgo.* The Homestead Movement became active in the U.S. about 1830, when western farmers began asking that 160 acre portions of the United States public domain be given to settlers willing to work the land. In 1848 the Free Soil Party included a plank in the party platform urging distribution of public land to settlers free of charge. The southern slave holders, large eastern landowners, and employers opposed this view. As a result no legislation resulted until the southerners were expelled from Congress, and the Republicans passed, and Abraham Lincoln signed, the Homestead Act on May 20, 1862. The act provided 160 acres of public land to any citizen, or citizenship applicant, either 21 years old or head of a family who had lived on and cultivated the land for at least five years.

was elected to the state legislature, and he and the others were later exonerated.[121]

The problem continued for some time, but the United States Board of Land Commissioners for California finally confirmed Sutter's grant. He and his heirs were given a federal (land) patent dated June 26, 1866, and recorded November 28, 1866, as No. 1 of patents page 225. Third persons were exempted because their title problems had apparently been covered by the fifteenth section of the Act of Congress of March 3, 1851,—less than six months after the riot.

McClatchy continued to be active in civic affairs, and later in 1850 was nominated as a Democrat for mayor of Sacramento. In the election which followed in May 1851, he ran third in a field of five. The *Settlers' and Miners' Tribune* espousing the views of the squatters, commenced publishing October 30, 1850, and in addition to his other interests, McClatchy was associate editor with his friend, Dr. C. L. Robinson, as editor. Eight weeks later, this paper, along with many Sacramento citizens, succumbed during the terrible cholera epidemic in the late fall of 1850. By December 1850, McClatchy was shown in the Sacramento City Directory back at the *Placer Times*, probably continuing as a reporter, although the entry listed him as a printer. In 1853, he was editor and part-owner of the *Democratic State Journal,* and the *Californian,* and in 1856, with Cornelius Cole, he founded a Republican paper, the *Sacramento Times.*

He had been courting a young widow, Charlotte McCormack Feeny who was born in Prince Edward Island, Canada in 1830. She had arrived in Sacramento November 3, 1852, and lost her husband in 1854. McClatchy's romantic efforts eventually proved successful, and they were married on election day, November 4, 1856.

On February 3, 1857, the Sacramento newspaper, *California American,* founded June 2, 1856, ceased publication and was replaced by *The Sacramento Daily Bee.*[122] It was a politically independent, morning paper owned by Levi C. Chandler, William H. Tobey, John Church, and Lyman P. Davis with John Rollin Ridge who had held the

---

121. The Settler/Squatter problem in Sacramento was really more complicated and widespread than appears at first glance. For an extensive discussion of the underlying reasons and an explanation of the fervor of well meaning people on both sides, see Bancroft, *History of California,* Volume VI, footnotes, pp. 328 - 335.

122. Kemble, *History of California Newspapers*, p.162.

James McClatchy
Born, Lisburn Ireland, 1824
Died, Monterey, California, 1883

Charlotte McCormack McClatchy
Born, Prince Edward Island, 1830
Died, Sacramento, 1916

same position on the *California American* as editor. Although not on the masthead as a founding editor, McClatchy had written for the *Bee* from its beginning.[123]

The *Bee's* future policy was stated on February 3, 1857, in the salutatory editorial which may have been written by McClatchy:

> The object of this paper is not only independence, but permanence. Relying upon a just, honorable and fearless course of conduct for its support, it expects only to make those men enemies, who are the enemies of the country. Its purpose is whatever may be the measures which it will advocate in future, to owe no thanks to any cliques or factions, but based on the broader foundation of right, to survive the wreck of mere party organizations, and still be supported by good and true men . . . All the hope that a truly independent journal can have is in the encouragement of the intelligent and uncorrupted masses and upon them this paper relies.[124]

Since then, word meanings and writing style have changed, and referring to readers as "masses," even with complimentary adjectives, is no longer considered an effective way to gain circulation. Never the less the meaning is clear, unequivocal, and has been followed for some 141 years. The word "permanence" in the second line is particularly important if one considers the state of newspapers in that day. Edward C. Kemble, an editor of San Francisco's, and later Sacramento's, first newspapers, wrote a history of California newspapers which was initially printed in a supplement to the Sacramento *Union* on December 25, 1858. He mentions that Sacramento, considering its size, was called the graveyard of newspapers, and states that of the 44 distinct newspapers founded up to that date, only four then survived in 1858, including the *Daily Bee, Sacramento Daily Union,* the *Morning Star*, then one month old, and one monthly, the *Baptist Circular.* After listing 30 or 40 defunct publications, he cheerfully wrote of the *Sacramento Daily Bee,*

---

123. There is some confusion as to McClatchy's exact position with the *Bee* at the time of its beginning. The 1857/58 *Sacramento Directory and Gazetteer* by I.N. Irwin lists him as "associate editor," and Kemble, p. 162 states McClatchy became editor in the summer of 1857. Winfield J. Davis, *Illustrated History of Sacramento County,* (Chicago: Lewis Publishing, 1890), p. 87 confirms this fact, gives much information about McClatchy's later life in Sacramento, and mentions that the he bought an interest in the *Bee* on February 12, 1866.

124. *Daily Bee,* February 3, 1857, p. 1, Column 1. Original at California State Library.

After long groping in this newspaper charnel–house, it is a pleasure to come upon the steps of a living and breathing acquaintance. The *Bee* is the only surviving member, beside the *Union*, of the pretty large newspaper family whose remains we have been exploring.

Carrying on the old tradition, the 1998 Sacramento telephone directory listed 64 local area newspapers including, among others, the interesting titles of *The Fish Sniffer, Bingo Bugle, Drum Corps World,* and the *Chinese Community Tribune*, but only one that was in business here in 1857, the *Sacramento Bee.*

On April 6, 1857, McClatchy joined the *Bee* as associate editor, and when Ridge resigned in July, became editor. The record does not explain the coincidence, but also on April 6, the *Bee* changed from a morning to an evening paper and continued as such for 121 years. The change could have been a purely business decision, because there were three other morning papers, or it may have been McClatchy's idea.

During the next few years, McClatchy had some run-ins with local political criminals, won a free speech case, published the names of biased jurors, and generally brought the honor and respect to be expected for a paper whose editor had written in the *Bee's* first year.

It is impossible for the editor of a newspaper to please everybody. It is utterly useless for him to expect that everything he writes will be acceptable to all his readers. He must be a fool who entertains any such ideas. When an editor writes, he is expected to write what he believes to be the truth; if he does not do this, he is unworthy of his calling, and the sooner the paper over which presides dies, the better. [and later that year wrote] The Bee will be hereafter as it has been heretofore–independent in everything, neutral in nothing. It will have a word to say on every subject of local interest or general interest. It will speak the truth at all times.

This had been his policy before he came to the *Bee*, and it continued through the rest of his life. While there was never doubt about where he stood in political matters, McClatchy was not a bully and could use his charm to bring together persons of widely differing opinions.

In a matter of national security at the start of the Civil War, he acted so quietly and effectively in a major political event that his participation remained a secret for almost 20 years. Late in 1860 there was real doubt in California whether the many Southern sympathizers in high political office might cause the state to secede from the Union and join the Confederacy or form a new *Pacific Republic* with the Mexican province of Sonora. South Carolina seceded in December 1860, and in January 1861, many California newspapers were still undecided what course should be followed. Charles L. Scott, California's U.S. Senator in 1860, had written to C. V. Lindley, chairman of the California State Democratic central committee:

> If this union is divided, and two separate confederacies are formed, I will strenuously advocate the secession of California and the establishment of a separate republic on the Pacific slope.[125] . . .

In these turbulent times an added concern to loyal union citizens was the appointment in January 1861, of General Albert Sidney Johnston, a Southern supporter, born in Kentucky, as commander of the Department of the Pacific. He was later appointed a general in the Confederate army, and was killed April 6, 1862, at the battle of Shiloh by troops under the command of General William T. Sherman. McClatchy knew of Johnston's reputation, and probably suspected some plans in favor of secession existed, but he had no hard evidence. Shortly after Johnston's arrival in California, McClatchy made an evening visit to the bedside of Edmund Randolph who was from an important Virginia family, had been a state assemblyman from San Francisco in 1850, and nominated for U.S. Senator in 1860.

Although normally a very rational person, Randolph had been suffering for some time from a mental disorder which resulted in his professing a belief in the union while advocating the assassination of the president. In a feverish condition he informed McClatchy that he believed California to be in grave danger from General Johnston's plans to release government arms to the state's Southern sympathizers. It was late Tuesday evening, but the weekly Pony Express accepted letters until midnight, so McClatchy hurriedly wrote to U.S. Senator E. D. Baker in Washington stating in part:

> . . .You know me and you know Randolph. I fear that what he says is but too true. Be swift to see the president. Tell him this, and if you and he and the war department think that

---

125. Bancroft, *History of California,* Vol. VII p. 277. A section beginning "The People Moving," on page 279 of Vol. VII, and running through page 307 details these wild times including the capture of a newly outfitted pirate ship in San Francisco Bay, described on pp 287-288.

treason is brooding in this quarter, lose not an hour in placing
a trusty soldier in command – and the people of California will
take care of the rest. . . .

As a result on the very day the letter was received, General Edwin
V. Sumner was quietly sent to replace General A. S. Johnston in
California. Despite all the caution observed in this transaction,
Johnston received information by pony express in time to resign before
Sumner arrived and immediately took command. Johnston and several
other secession officers promptly departed by way of Los Angeles for
Texas to join the Confederate Army.[126] These actions proved both the
correctness of McClatchy's information and the respect with which he
was held in Washington.

Two years later in 1863, the Civil War was raging and although
reduced in numbers and influence, the California secessionists or
"copperheads" continued to agitate for separation from the Union.
McClatchy had come to realize that in the event of real trouble from
that quarter, in any given location, the local sheriff wielded critical
power. Under California law as it then existed, in case of riot or
insurrection, the governor could call out troops only if requested by the
sheriff of the area affected. In April of 1862, McClatchy had named
the copperhead newspapers advocating a Pacific Republic and further
observed:

> These journals would have people "do nothing," make
> no expression of their loyalty to the Union lest by so doing they
> give offense to the secessionists among us; or lest they give
> offense to the traitors in the south who are in arms against this
> nation; just as if American citizens who love their country should
> not give expression to that love for fear of offending traitors, or
> those who sympathize with treason. . . .

In that same year McClatchy had enrolled in the California
National Guard as a private, further evidencing he stood with the north
and was ready to fight for the Union.   His position was so well understood that at one point southern sympathizers threatened to burn down
his house.   He also was aware of the problems in 1857, of then Major
General of California Militia, William T. Sherman, in San Francisco in
controlling Vigilantes in 1856 with little help from Sheriff Scanlon.
Major General John E. Wool, commander of the Pacific department at
Benicia had been of even less value, when he first promised arms and

---

126. Bancroft, *History of California*, Vol. VII p. 282.

then refused to release them.[127] With these facts in mind, McClatchy became a candidate for Sacramento County sheriff on the Union State ticket and was elected by a large majority on September 2, 1863. He served his term of two years and received, as he had expected, the verbal and published wrath of the copperheads, but otherwise he kept Sacramento a safe and peaceful city – and no one ignited his residence.

At the end of his service as sheriff in early 1866, McClatchy returned to the editor's desk at the *Bee*, and thereafter he concentrated on expanding the news coverage and widespread distribution of his newspaper while remaining active in the political and social life of Sacramento. Over this same period he gradually bought the interests of the other owners, until by June of 1872, he and Jeremiah O'Leary were the only proprietors, using the name of *James McClatchy & Co.* McClatchy sold a one third interest in August of the same year to John Francis Sheehan, and together they bought O'Leary's share from his estate in 1876. On November 1, 1879, Sheehan & James McClatchy were joined as proprietors by Charles Kenny McClatchy, James's son, with the firm continuing as *James McClatchy & Co.* James McClatchy died while on a trip to Monterey in 1883, and he left his share of the business to his wife and two sons, Charles and Valentine Stuart McClatchy. They

**James McClatchy's small Gravestone
Sacramento City Cemetery**

continued the firm with Charles as editor and Valentine as business manager. On January 29, 1884, the family members purchased the interest of John Sheehan and the business remained with the name of *James McClatchy & Co.* under family ownership.

From its founding in 1854, James McClatchy was a member of the Sacramento Pioneer Association, and was president in 1868 when they completed their new hall at 1011 7th Street. His long and eloquent

---

127. W.T. Sherman, *Memoirs of General William T. Sherman*, (New York: D. Appleton & Co., 1875) pp. 125-132

speech on that occasion was published in the local newspapers.[128]   He
was photographed in 1878 with 109 other surviving Pioneers, died
October 25, 1883, and is buried in Pioneer Grove, Section B-124, lot 95
in the Sacramento City Cemetery.

MCCLEERY, JAMES, *Cabinetmaker with Fitch & McCleery.* He was born
in Beaver County, Pennsylvania on January 11, 1817, and later learned
wagon making at the factory of James Wilson in New Brighton. He
then moved to Warren, Ohio and started a business with his brother,
after which he formed a partnership called McCleery & Pitts in Galena,
Illinois, and in the spring of 1847, McCleery married Miss Sidney
Garritt of St. Louis. In February 1849, he started with a party using ox
teams and traveled by way of the Sublett cut-off and the Truckee route,
to California, where they arrived about 180 days later on August 17,
1849. He promptly set up business making shingles from the redwoods
near the site of modern Oakland and selling them at $40 per thousand
(or possibly per "square" of 100 sq. feet coverage). In February 1850,
this profitable enterprise was devastated by the arrival of 21 shiploads
of lumber and shingles causing the price of the latter to fall to $6.

He decided to try mining and worked in the Oroville area, Big
Bar, on the American River, Todd's Valley, Shirt Tail Canyon, and
Nevada City, finally returning to Sacramento in the fall of 1850. Here,
he set up a cabinet making business with Charles Fitch on Fourth
Street. After a short trip east to Philadelphia in 1852 to get his family,
he returned to start a blacksmith and wagon business in March 1853,
called McCleery & Kimball at Tenth and K Streets which changed to
McCleery & Brown in July 1853. At this time McCleery resided on K
near Tenth Street with his wife and two children. He was later active in
Republican politics, was secretary of the Sacramento Pioneer
Association, died here on October 31, 1890, and is buried in the
Sacramento City Cemetery, lot 66, code H.

MCCULLOCH, BENJAMIN, *Sheriff.* He was born in Rutherford County,
Tennessee in 1814, and later went with David Crockett to Texas where
he joined the Texas Army under General Sam Houston. He was
assigned to the artillery, served in the battle of San Jacinto, and later
worked on the frontier surveying and locating lands in Texas. When
the Mexican War started, he raised a company of Texas Rangers who

---

144

served under General Zachary Taylor at the battles of Monterey and Buena Vista, and participated later in the capture of Mexico City. On August 15, 1850, McCulloch succeeded to the office of sheriff of Sacramento County upon the death, (some said murder) of Sheriff Joseph McKinney at Brighton while attempting to arrest an alleged member of the Squatters Party named Allen. McCulloch served until replaced in 1852, and a short time later was appointed United States Marshall of Texas by President Franklin Pierce. In 1857 he was appointed a commissioner to Utah Territory. When the Civil War started he was appointed a brigadier-general in the Confederate Army assigned the command of the forces of Arkansas. He was killed at the battle of Pea Ridge, Arkansas on March 7, 1862.

MCGUIRE, JAMES B., *Blacksmith*. A native of County Kings, Ireland, he was born August 13, 1824, emigrated with his family to Connecticut in 1827, and moved to Cincinnati in 1832. He came across the plains to Sacramento, leaving St. Joseph, Missouri May 3, 1849, and arriving in Sacramento, 110 days later on August 21, 1849. He mined for two weeks near Spanish Bar on the American River, which seemed to permanently satisfy his desire to prospect for gold, and then returned to Sacramento and entered business as a blacksmith on Third Street between J and K. He specialized in the manufacture of iron shutters and doors for brick buildings. These were of vital importance, not for keeping out burglars, but to protect the contents of a building from the radiant heat of nearby fires. In the fire of November 1852, a new brick building without shutters burned from the inside, while a nearby similar structure with iron shutters closed, was saved. McGuire also made cemetery railings, road-scraper blades, and gratings, and by 1890 was using over 100 tons of iron per year.

In the early days, the blacksmith business was apparently slow in the winter months, because he made trading trips to Marysville by whale-boat. He married Mary Coffee on September 1, 1856, and they had two sons and two daughters. His wife died in 1879. McGuire was a director and president of the Sacramento Pioneer Association, and was photographed in 1878 with 109 other surviving members. He died April 21, 1895, and is buried in the Sacramento City Cemetery, Lot 24 Code H.

MCKUNE, HON. JOHN H.,[90] *Lawyer*. He was born in Sullivan County,

New York on March 22, 1819, and in 1839 he moved to Montrose, Pennsylvania where he read law until 1844 when he was admitted to the bar. In 1848 he moved to Lee Center, Illinois and practiced law there until 1849, when he departed for California. His party left Independence, Missouri on May 7, 1849, and after 117 days crossed the Sierra near Donner Pass on September 1, 1849. He mined for gold at Nevada City until late fall, hunted deer commercially until January 1850, and then came to Sacramento. McKune was elected county attorney on April 5, 1850, appointed agent of the United States Land Commission in March 1854, by the President, and in 1856 he was elected to the state legislature as a Democrat. On February 26, 1855, he married Mary G. Bennett of San Francisco and they had a son and a daughter, Florence, neither of whom ever married. The children died in Sacramento, the son in 1869 and Florence on January 12, 1931.

McKune served as district judge of the Sixth Judicial District from 1858 to December 31, 1869. In 1890 it was said that Judge McKune had been connected with more celebrated lawsuits than any other attorney in Sacramento. He was a member of the Sacramento Pioneer Association, died on March 22, 1905, and is buried with his family, in San Francisco. His widow, Mary B. McKune, died in Sacramento on February 18, 1914.

MORSE, DR. JOHN FREDERICK, *Real Estate*, (with Morse & Mitchell). *His biography here was kindly researched and written by a descendent, Dr. John Morse Erskine, of San Francisco, Dr. Morse's great great grandson.*

John F. Morse was born in 1815 in Essex, Vermont, near Lake Champlain. Both his parents were descendants of Puritans who arrived in Massachusetts in 1635. Young Morse grew up working on his father's farm, had little early formal education, but had great intellectual curiosity and read extensively. He ultimately received a medical degree from the University of New York City in 1844, and then practiced medicine and surgery in Brooklyn, where he had a very successful practice. In 1843, while still a medical student, he married Rebecca Cannon. He participated in community activities which included involvement in the Plymouth Church and the Independent Order of Odd Fellows lodge. In 1848, he was forced to close his office due to poor health, and he thought a change of climate would give him relief.

On February 22, 1849, at the age of 33, he sailed for Panama on the bark *Bogata,* spent some weeks on the Isthmus, and on May 20, 1849, left Panama on the *Alexander von Humboldt.* The ship arrived in San Francisco at the end of August after a very difficult voyage, during which he served as the ship's doctor. After a brief time spent in Coloma, Dr. Morse decided to settle in Sacramento and engage in the practice of medicine and surgery.

On December 22, 1849, a notice announced that Doctors John F. Morse and Jacob Stillman had opened a hospital on the corner of Third and K Streets—and Dr. Morse was appointed by the Odd Fellows and the Masons to be the secretary of the board of trustees to govern a hospital at Sutter's Fort.

Early in 1850, Sacramento was flooded, submerging the first floor of the K Street hospital, and patients were brought by boat to the second story window. That event combined with high expenses and the poor payment by the patients, lead to closure of the hospital in April 1850. Apparently Dr. Morse was the first in California to inaugurate a system of health insurance because in July 1850, an announcement was made that the Masons and Odd Fellows Hospital upon payment of $100 would provide free attendance at the hospital to a subscriber who was sick any time during the year. During the cholera epidemic in the fall of 1850, the hospital admitted all who required care, regardless of their ability to pay, and Dr. Morse gave freely of his time during that trying period. Because the financial rewards of medical practice were poor and the expenses of life in Sacramento high, Dr. Morse was forced into business and real estate activities, but only to be enveloped by the business depression of 1850 that left the doctor with more debts. Consequently in March of 1851, he became the first editor of the *Sacramento Union,* a position which he held until May of 1851. About this time, his wife and two children joined him in Sacramento.

He then resumed the practice of medicine, but his office and all

Dr. John F. Morse 1815-1874

his possessions were destroyed in the huge fire in the night of November 2, 1852. His pregnant wife, Rebecca, was removed from the burning city on the steamer *Camanche*.[129] On the way to the bay, she gave birth to a son who survived, but sadly she died as the ship reached San Francisco. The doctor was left in a burned out city with no wife, three children, and no possessions.

Morse quickly obtained the use of an office above the Stanford Brothers store at 56 K Street (now 222, under the freeway). To care for his three children, he hired Miss Caroline Lowney, who at the age of twenty four, had traveled alone from Belfast, Maine to California by way of Nicaragua. He married her on January 16, 1854, and in the following nine years they had six children, five of whom reached adulthood. The three previous children all died in childhood. Of the children born to his second marriage, the one surviving boy, John F. Morse Jr., became a very well trained and prominent San Francisco surgeon.

Morse continued as a physician, sometimes alone and sometimes with an associate, and he had unique qualities as a doctor to which his patients responded. He was full of human love and sympathy, and had tremendous nervous energy in spite of his continued frail health. He was a very public spirited man, took a lively interest in community activities, and was prominently involved in many social and political activities that shaped the young city of Sacramento. The doctor had an unusual fluency of speech with a rapid, stimulating delivery, and was often asked to speak on public occasions. He also wrote a great deal and became widely known throughout California.

Morse was a truly Renaissance man, and some of his notable accomplishments are mentioned in the following paragraphs. In addition to helping establish the first two hospitals in Sacramento, working ceaselessly during the fearful cholera epidemic of 1850, and in 1851, being the first editor of the *Sacramento Union,* he was a founding member of the Sacramento Mercantile Library Association, and helped found the Sacramento Odd Fellows Lodge. In 1852 he was vice-chairman of the Whig State Central Committee, was made a director of the California State Library, and became a Master Mason. In 1853 Dr. Morse wrote the first extensive history of Sacramento, which appeared

---

129. The *Camanche* was a small sidewheel steamer assembled at Sacramento on the Yolo side of the river. She was shipped in parts from Pennsylvania by sailing ship, and was launched September 18, 1851. On January 5, 1853 she collided with the *J. Bragdon* on Suisun Bay. The *Camanche* sank in ten minutes with the loss of ten lives and all the cargo. She was raised, refitted and returned to service within the same year. McMullen, *ibid,* pp. 25, 50, and 135.

as a forty page foreword to the 1853 *Sacramento City Directory*. In 1854 he founded and edited the *California Farmer and Journal of Useful Sciences*, the first agricultural newspaper on the Pacific Coast, and wrote a 46 page book, *Illustrated Historical Sketches of California*, published by his friend Samuel Colville. His writing of history was both interesting and amusing, with descriptive passages of the highest quality.

He was founding vice-president of the Sacramento Medical Society in 1855, and in 1856, was chairman of the convention to found the Medical Society of California and became proprietor and editor of the California State Medical Journal. In 1858, Dr. Morse was president of the Sacramento Pioneer Association, and in 1861 purchased shares of the original stock of the Central Pacific Railroad. In 1862 he was elected a director of the Central Pacific, and moved to San Francisco to become the first professor of medicine in the newly formed University of the Pacific Medical School which later became Stanford Medical School. On January 8, 1863, he was one of the orators who spoke at the ceremonies on Front Street when Leland Stanford turned the first shovel of earth to commence the building of the Central Pacific, and Dr. Morse spoke again on May 10, 1869, at the driving of the golden spike at Promontory, Utah.

For a period in 1863, he became the editor of the *Pacific Medical and Surgical Journal*. In 1864, he withdrew from the University of the Pacific to join the original faculty as professor of medicine of the Toland Medical College, the forerunner of the University of California Medical School. Also in 1864, he was appointed to the first commission to manage Yosemite Valley, served on the State Prison Commission and as a director of the new state asylum in Napa. In 1868 he was a founding member of the San Francisco Medical Society, and the next year its president. In 1870 he resigned from the Toland medical faculty and took his family to Italy, Germany and Switzerland where he rested and tried to regain his health. While there, he founded Odd Fellows lodges in Germany and Switzerland.

On his return to San Francisco in 1871, Dr. Morse was reappointed to the faculty of the reorganized medical department of the University of the Pacific, and resumed his medical practice. In 1872, he served another term as president of the San Francisco Medical Society. He remained in San Francisco until 1874 when he set out for Australia, but became ill before reaching Honolulu, and returned to San Francisco where he died on December 30, 1874 at the age of 59.

Dr. John F. Morse is buried in the Mount Olivet Cemetery, Lawndale, near Colma, California, where a large base with a lengthy inscription supports a life size marble statue of him, standing with his hand on a book. He had led a very interesting, useful, and productive life, and was indeed a man to match the western mountains.

OSBORN, HOSMER P., [Grocery] *Merchant..* A native of Oswego, New York, he was born in 1803, and was a tailor in New York City from 1824 to 1849, when he came to Sacramento. He opened a grocery business near 9th and J Streets, and in 1858 became a farmer twelve miles from Sacramento. He returned about 1870 and operated a wood and coal yard at various Sacramento locations. He married Jane McArthur of Hudson, New York in 1825, and she died in 1831. In 1832 he married Marrietta Folger who died in 1879. He had six children living at that time. Osborn was a president of the Sacramento Pioneer Association.

READING, MAJ. PIERSON B. He was born in New Jersey, in 1816, and left Independence, Missouri bound for Oregon with the Chiles-Walker party in 1843. At Fort Hall, Chiles and several men, including Reading, turned South and entered California by way of the Pitt River on a route that had not been used before. They reached Sutter's Fort in the latter part of 1843 where Reading became Sutter's clerk and chief of trappers at the Fort, and made wide explorations in that capacity in 1844 and 1845. He was left in command of the Fort while Sutter was campaigning in Southern California in support of Gov. Manuel Micheltorena. Reading was active in the Bear Flag Revolt, and served in 1846-1847 as a paymaster with the rank of major in the California Battalion. In 1848 he mined on the Trinity River and, with Samuel Hensley, ran a store at Sutter's Fort. In January 1849, they moved the store to a small building (said to be the first frame structure in Sacramento City) near the NE corner of Front and I Streets. After a business trip to Vicksburg in 1850, he returned to Sacramento, and was active in politics.

By the fall of 1849 Major Reading was considered the northernmost settler in California, and his ranch supported a small town called "Reading," the county seat of Shasta County. In its earliest days, the county covered a huge area, from which Lassen, Modoc, Siskiyou, and Tehema Counties were later removed. The name of modern Redding evolved from his name. In 1851, Major Reading was nominated for governor of California, and barely missed election. He returned to farming at his Shasta County rancho, married Fanny Washington in 1856, and died in 1868, leaving a widow and five children. Bancroft wrote of him: "Major Reading was a man of well-balanced mind, honorable, energetic, and courteous; one whose California record seems never to have furnished material for adverse criticism."

ROGERS, JOHN P., *Auctioneer with Moss & Co.* He was born in Wilson County, Tennessee and came to California in 1848 from Oregon with his brother-in-law, Peter H. Burnett, later governor of California. On November 5, 1848, Rogers and Burnett in company with Horace Burnett, purchased a claim at Long's Bar, on the Yuba River 25 by 50 feet for $300. They bought on credit, agreeing to make repayment in gold dust at $16 per troy ounce (or 18¾ ounces). The first day they built a rocker and the next day started digging for gold. Within a few days they were getting 3¾ ounces per day and paid for the claim soon after. This work continued until December 19, 1848, when they sold off the wagons brought from Oregon and left Long's Bar for Sutter's Fort, driving in a wagon pulled by oxen. They left Long's Bar at noon and by evening had reached Johnson's Ranch near the Bear River. The oxen developed an affinity for this area and were all missing in the morning. Most of the next day was spent in rounding up these would-be settlers, delaying departure until about two hours before sunset. As darkness fell it started to rain briskly and at midnight the wind came around to the north accompanied by snow which fell to a depth of three inches. They reached the Fort about 10 A.M. the next day, covering the 40 miles in eighteen uncomfortable hours without eating or stopping. The oxen probably didn't enjoy the trip much either. Peter Burnett almost immediately became young Sutter's attorney and land agent selling lots in newly surveyed Sacramento City.[130] It is probable that John Rogers also obtained employment at the fort and bought some of the lots being sold by his brother-in-law. In the summer of 1850, Rogers and DeWitt J. Burnett owned the lot at 34 N Street (200 N new style), at the south east corner of 2nd and N Streets, from which John Madden, who had settled, or "squatted," upon it, was ejected by a successful suit initiated by Rogers. This action inflamed the passion of the other squatters to the point that a few days later, on August 14, 1850, they commenced the Squatter Riots in which the sheriff and the assessor were killed and the mayor severely wounded.

---

130. Peter H. Burnett, *An Old California Pioneer*, (Oakland: Biobooks, 1946), pp.163-164 & 171-172.

ROE, FREDERICK J., *At Reynolds & McLeary's* (saloon). He was a professional gambler born in England in 1830 and had the dubious honor of being the first man lynched in Sacramento.

On January 26, 1851, at 8 P.M. the following verdict of a committee of prominent citizens was read from the balcony of the Orleans Hotel on 2nd Street:

> We, the committee of investigation appointed by our fellow citizens to investigate the circumstances of the unfortunate occurrence that took place this afternoon, report that after a full and impartial examination of the evidence we find that at about 2 o'clock P.M. this day, Frederick J. Roe and some other person, whose name is unknown, were engaged in an altercation which originated [at the monte table] in the Mansion House; and that after said parties had proceeded to the street, and where they were fighting, Charles H. Myers, who was passing in the street, interfered with words requesting them to desist fighting or show fair play; and that immediately thereupon the said Roe called out, "What the devil have you to say?" and drew his pistol and without further provocation shot said Myers through the head.

Within an hour, a huge crowd had assembled and pulled up awning posts to be used as battering rams to enter the jail and gain custody of the prisoner. He was taken to a platform which had been erected under a large oak tree on 6th Street between K & L Streets. The Reverend M. C. Briggs was sent for, and through him, Roe said to the assembled crowd, estimated at 5,000 persons, that he committed the deed in a fit of passion, and had nothing more to say in self defense; that he was an Englishman by birth, was twenty years of age, and had a mother and sister living in the old country. The minister then performed his duties, and the prisoner was hanged without further ceremony at about 10 P.M. Ironically, although Myers' head wound was fatal, immediately after the shooting he had been attended by a physician, and did not die until after the hanging.

SCHOOLCRAFT, HENRY A., 54, *Junior Warden, Sutter Lodge.* He came to California in 1847 in Stevenson's Regiment as a sergeant in Company H which was raised at Albany, New York. In 1848 he was Sutter's agent and at a public meeting in January 1849, was elected First Magistrate and Recorder for the District of Sacramento. Later in the spring of 1849, at the Fort he replaced John S. Fowler as the second alcalde. When the Sacramento District was formally organized in May of 1849, Schoolcraft was chosen alcalde, and A. M. Turner, Sheriff.

Later Schoolcraft went to Washington and obtained an appointment as Collector of Revenue at Sacramento, but on the return trip, he died at sea off Acapulco in 1853.

SHEPHERD, PROF. FOREST, *Office*, a graduate of Yale, who did post graduate studies in both theology and medicine and obtained licenses in both professions. In August 1849, he built the first school building in the Sacramento Valley at 71, I Street (307 new style) beside Sutter Lake. The structure was a one-story house, about 14 by 28 feet, covered at the ends with rough clapboards, and on the roof and sides with old sails from some craft moored to the river bank. Shakes and pickets were nailed over the places not covered by the sails, near the ground. The doorway was covered by a piece of canvas nailed at the top, and the floor was of uneven dirt.[131]

Just to the north of the school was the bank of Sutter Lake and a large sycamore tree. A small oak tree stood at the eastern end near the door. I Street was not passable for wagons at that time, and as a source of entertainment for the students and worry for the teacher, the remains of a pit for burning oak wood to charcoal was in the middle of the street a few yards to the east of the building. Charles T. H. Palmer was the teacher and the student body never exceeded ten in number. After about a month, he gave up teaching, and later operated a very successful express business.[131] In September Reverend Joseph A. Benton, bought the school furniture from Palmer and reopened the school with four pupils on Monday, October 15, 1849. He permanently closed the school "By stress of weather" about December 1, just in time to miss the huge flood of early January 1850, which entered the city at this location. There is some evidence from a flood view of Sacramento that the frame of this structure may have survived the inundation, and at least in December 1850, Prof. Shepherd was listed as being at "I Street between 3rd and 4th." Bancroft (Vol. VII, p.728) mentions that in 1849, Shepherd started a Sunday-school later taught by Rev. Benton.

SMITH, CAPTAIN NAPOLEON B., *Express Hotel*. Nicknamed "old Bony," he came to California with the Lansford Hastings party in 1845 as a

---

131. Robert D. Livingston, *Charles T. H. Palmer*, (*Golden Notes*, Sacramento County Historical Society, 1991) Vol 37 Number 3, p. 4. The detailed description of the building is by Daniel J. Thomas, *History of Sacramento*, in *Sacramento Directory for 1871*, (Sacramento: H.S. Crocker, 1871) pp.31-32.

game hunter and arrived at New Helvetia on Christmas Day. He worked some time for Sutter, became a lumberman in the San Antonio, Monterey County, redwoods, married Margelina Brown, of Benicia and had eight children. Their son Frank, in January 1848, became the first American child born in Contra Costa County. He went mining in 1848-1849, and later in '49 kept a store at Mission San Jose. He was in Sacramento in 1850, later was a trader in Martinez, was elected Contra Costa county assessor, and he represented Contra Costa County in the California assembly in 1852. In 1857 he moved to a ranch in a rural part of the county, where he still lived in 1885.

SMITH, JOEL, *Grocer,* [with Smith & Hines]. Smith was reared in Barcelona, New York, on Lake Erie where he later engaged in a mercantile business. He married Miss Thankful Holmes there in the 1830s and she died a few years later leaving a son, George. Joel Smith left his young son with relatives and came to California by way of Cape Horn, arriving in Sacramento in 1850, where, with William T. Hines, he set up a grocery business at the corner of 3rd and I Streets. Smith bought out his partner after a year or two and continued alone until 1854, when his sixteen year old son, George joined him. George Smith's trip started from New York on February 5, 1854, aboard the steamer *Georgia* carrying 1500 passengers bound for Aspinwall on the Atlantic side of the Isthmus of Panama. Two days out from New York the ship nearly sank in a terrible storm and had to put into Norfolk, Virginia for repairs. The *Empire City* was sent down from New York to carry the passengers on to Aspinwall, where they transferred to the Panama Railroad which was then partly completed to Panama City. George rode the balance of the distance on mule back in a day and one night, transferred to another steamer, and arrived in San Francisco on March 15, 1854, thirty nine days after leaving New York. George Smith continued working with his father until 1856. Joel Smith retired from the grocery business about 1867, died in Sacramento January 18, 1877, and is buried in the Sacramento City Cemetery, Lot 383, code D.

STARR, COL. JAMES BLACKWELL,[65] *Auctioneer.* A native of New York, Born in 1810, he came across the plains from New York to Sacramento in 1849. The trip occupied six months, two months riding a mule and the remainder on foot. Immediately after his arrival he located his business next door to Priest, Lee and Co. at 2nd and J Streets. His first sale, of surplus government horses and mules from the Army Quartermaster, amounted to $35,000. Soon after, he rented a two story building at the SE corner of Front and K Streets where he rapidly expanded his operation until he was selling $60,000 per day.

He lost heavily in the flood of January 1850, but a large loft over his store remained dry and provided shelter for most of the women and children in Sacramento. They remained nearly a month, but Col. Starr positively refused any remuneration stating that he was utterly opposed to benefitting himself from the misfortune of others. At that time he was paying a monthly rental of $24,000 for the whole building. In 1851, he opened a branch in San Francisco under the name of Starr, Minturn & Co. which proved so unprofitable that by 1852, he was forced to give all his possessions to his creditors. He soon resumed business in company with F. McGilvery, but this ended in bankruptcy. By 1855 he was back as an auctioneer at the NE corner of Front and K. He died on a trip to San Francisco, October 18, 1862, and is buried in the Pioneer section of the Sacramento City Cemetery.

SWEETSER, ALBION C., *Carpenter* [also architect and contractor]. A native of Waterville, Maine, born on November 3, 1819, he was the grandson of a revolutionary war veteran who lived to be 94 years old. Sweetser was a house and ship joiner at Belfast, Maine until 1847 after which he was in the shoe trade at Cambridgeport, Massachusetts until 1849 when he joined with 25 others to form the Boston and Newton Joint Stock Association to go to California.[132] They purchased a year's provisions which they sent by ship around Cape Horn to San Francisco while the members of the association left Boston on April 16, 1849, for Buffalo, thence by lake steamer to Sandusky, Ohio, by rail to Cincinnati, by steamer to St. Louis, and finally to Independence, Missouri where they completed their outfit with additional provisions. They left Independence on May 16, 1849, and followed the regular route to Salt Lake City, where they sold their wagons and harness, bought pack saddles, and rested for ten days. Their last night on the road was spent at Shingle Springs. One hundred and sixty four days after leaving Boston and 134 days from Independence, they arrived in Sacramento on September 27, 1849. They sold their horses and mules, sent to San Francisco for their provisions and tools that had come around Cape Horn, and broke up the association. Sweetser later recalled that the trip was rather enjoyable and most of the members of his group had

---

132. Jessie Gould Hannon, *The Boston-Newton Company Venture from Massachusetts to California in 1849*, (Lincoln: University of Nebraska Press, 1969). Citation by Gary Kurutz.

"become in the habit of walking a great deal." He seemed to thrive on adversity, and in the flood of January 1850, with water all around , he set up business on a pile of lumber on the levee making $20 a day producing boats, oars, and bath tubs.

After the flood, he continued in contracting until the fire of November 2, 1852, and then turned to architecture. In December 1853, Sweetser married Miss Sarah S. Pratt of Portland, Maine who came to Sacramento in 1852. Their only child died in 1857. He entered the real estate and insurance business in 1860 and continued in that line for over 30 years. He was active in the Sons of Temperance, the Odd Fellows, the Congregational Church, and the Sacramento Pioneer Association. He was photographed in 1878 with 109 other surviving members, died on August 29, 1910, at the ripe old age of 90, and is buried in the Sacramento City Cemetery, Lot 83, code H.

WARREN, JAMES LLOYD LaFAYETTE FRANKLIN, *Merchant.* Born August 12, 1805, in Brighton, Massachusetts, he came to California in 1849, and ran a store at Mormon Island. He soon moved to Sacramento to open a seed store at No. 3, J Street [agriculturists and seedmen]. On September 20, 1852, his firm, Warren & Son, opened an exposition in Sacramento modestly called the Great Agricultural Fair which offered cups and medals as premiums for outstanding entries from California farms and nurseries. There were also displays of mineral collections and art treasures with lectures on various subjects. The next year in October, they held a similar but larger show in San Francisco. With these successes in mind, the State Agricultural Society was formed May 13, 1854, and held the annual State Agricultural Exhibition for decades afterward. The name was eventually changed to the California State Fair which is held each year at Sacramento. During these years Warren lived in the Oak Hill area, which lay between 40th and 45th, and J and R Streets (the modern "fabulous forties"). In 1853, he was a founding director of the Sacramento Valley Railroad. Completed in 1856, it ran from Sacramento to Folsom, and was the first passenger railroad on the Pacific Coast. In 1854, he also began publishing the *California Farmer* weekly newspaper. He is included in the 1878 photograph of surviving members of the Sacramento Pioneer Association. James L. L. F. Warren died in San Francisco, and an obituary appeared in the *San Francisco Call* of April 24, 1896, page 7, column 3.[133]

133.Helen Bretnor in the index of, *History of California Newspapers* (Los Gatos: Talisman Press, 1962) p. 388, lists Warren's name as James Lloyd LaFayette Warren.

WHEATON, WILLIAM RUFUS,[20] *Grocer,* [partner in Hamilton & Wheaton]
Wheaton's great, great, grandson, John R. Wheaton lives in Sacramento, and has provided copies of early documents (including many gathered by his cousin, Margery Wheaton), and editorial assistance for this biography of William Rufus Wheaton.

W. R. Wheaton was born in New York City, May 7, 1814, and received his early education at Union Hall Academy, then located at the corner of Madison and Oliver Streets. After graduation, he read law with John Leveredge in New York, was admitted to practice in the Court of Chancery, and the Supreme Court of New York. He later formed a law partnership with Ebenezer Griffin.

William Rufus Wheaton, 1814-1888

At the age of 23 Wheaton married Miss Elizabeth A. Jennings on February 1, 1837, and they had seven children of whom five daughters and one son were living at the time of their parent's golden wedding anniversary in 1887. When he was 35, he decided to seek adventure in California, and joined the *New York Mining Company,* a group of 100 men who purchased and fitted out a ship for their trip to San Francisco via Cape Horn. This was no hardship type cruise, and bore absolutely no resemblance to crossing the plains in a covered wagon and making fires with buffalo chips while dodging arrows. They departed on January 28, 1849, in the *Strafford* with Captain W. L. Coffin in command. The *New York Herald* edition for February 2, 1849, reported the departure along with that of many other vessels, but none with so glowing a description of the organization and accommodations of the ship's company. In tiny 4 point type the item read:

SAILING OF THE STRAFFORD — DEPARTURE OF THE NEW YORK MINING COMPANY.— This noble bark, with her precious living freight, got under weigh and stood out to sea at an early hour on Sunday morning [Jan.28, 1849], accompanied by the steaming Samson[134] and a host of friends, who sought this last opportunity of bidding farewell and God-speed to as noble a band of adventurers as ever left their homes for a country "far off and distant." We were particularly excited by a thorough examination of the internal and domestic arrangements of the ship.

The bark, which was purchased and fitted by this company, measures about 400 tons [actually 314 tons], having 'tween decks, the whole length of which on either side is neatly and comfortably fitted up with double tiers of single berths, and from immediately forward of the main hatch, with double berths, giving ample sleeping accommodations to every individual. Abaft the main hatch are arranged the mess tables, yielding comfort and convenience while nourishing the inner man. Away aft is fitted up an admirably selected library, comprising works on every subject, and consisting of fully 3,000 volumes.

These are the individual contributions of the members and generous donations from the Bible and Tract Societies. For the amusement and enlivement of the company, a splendid piano and numerous other musical instruments have been presented to these fine fellows; and, to crown it all, a glee club has been formed, numbering voices of no ordinary sound and sweetness. The police of the ship partakes of the same complete arrangement as the social organization. At the roll of the drum, in the morning, every man is to tumble out; at 10 o'clock the "glim is to be douced," and all must tumble in, except those whose squad have charge of the ship for the day. These squads consist of ten men each, who appoint their own captain, and into whose hands is confided the supreme government of all the affairs of the vessel, save that which pertains to her locomotion. This department was unhesitatingly yielded to the well known and tried ability of Capt. Coffin. God bless him! The main features of this company, are the grand principles which govern them — mutual assistance being the chief, and the cultivation of all those friendly offices one to another, which so tend to make life agreeable. Connected with these features, is a determination to accomplish, if attainable by human means, the great object for which they have been so ready to sacrifice all the sweet endearments of families, friends and firesides. Being personally acquainted with a number of this company, and having, with

---

134. In 1849, "Samson" may have been a generic name for "steam tug" rather than the name of a particular vessel.

some, been long and intimately associated, we do not say too much when we give the assurance, that no other body of men who been induced to leave all behind them, by rumers [sic] of untold wealth, can there be found more mind, more soul, more inflexibility of purpose, more moral worth, more social and harmonious intercourse, than among the members of the *New York Mining Company*. They go amply provided with provisions for two years, and a stock of mining implements, with everything necessary to procure subsistence from the earth, sea or air.

Such has been the eagerness to join this company, that $500 has been repeatedly offered for a share which cost but $350. The steamer went as far as the Hook with the ship, and on the word being given, "let go all!" cheer followed cheer, and old ocean rang again with the hearty and enthusiastic huzzah from one party to the other, and amid them all, not the least hearty was three times three for the *New York Herald*. The "deep, deep sea" never bore on its broad bosom a more cheerful and hilarious company than that which left on Sunday, in the good bark *Strafford* [it was four days before William Rufus Wheaton's 12th wedding anniversary]. Every man's eye glistened with gladness as sail after sail was loosed and sheeted home, to waft them onward to the consummation of that enterprise in which all concerned have evinced an indomitable perseverance, and an untiring energy. The following list of officers and members was kindly furnished by Mr. Freeman, the active and gentlemanly Secretary: . . .

There follows a list, in no particular order, with the exception that the Master, Captain Coffin, is mentioned first of the 101 men departing on the ship. The officers of the company aboard were the five members of the finance committee, which included Wheaton, the president, vice president, treasurer, secretary (mentioned above), surgeon, "Chorister," drummer, assayer and mineralogist, gunner, and last but not least, the Fifer. After reading the almost overly enthusiastic description of the members of the company, it really seems the *Herald*'s reporter should have been added to the roster as "New York Publicist."The trip must have been very interesting, but no letters from Wheaton covering it appear to have survived.

Fortunately, the company's president, Franklin B. Austin wrote a letter on October 20, 1849, from the *Strafford* while it was anchored in the Sacramento River at Sutterville. This letter was printed in the December 27 edition of the *New York Herald* and mentions a little about their trip.

We left New York with 100 men in our company, and after a

voyage of 206 days, (stopping at St. Catharine's and Juan Fernandez) arrived safe without sickness or accident, in good health and spirits at San Francisco on the 29th of August [1849]. We remained there fifteen days and from there we came to this place, it taking us ten days to accomplish the distance of 120 miles. Our bark drew ten feet six inches of water; and from the frequent sand bars that obstruct the channel, we experienced much delay as we constantly grounded and were obliged to drag her over by main strength; however we arrived, and are at the end of our voyage,

Cape Horn from the east on February 28, 1999.
Its Chilean weather station is the southernmost settlement in South America.

St. Catherine's was an island (lat. 27°–38.5' S; long. 48°–30' W) just off the south west coast of Brazil which had an excellent harbor and is now linked to the mainland by the longest bridge in Brazil. Some Argonauts stopped there at the town of Desterro (which was renamed Florianopolis in 1893) because the landing charges and the cost of provisions were less than at Rio de Janeiro. The reduced diversions available to the crew were thought to be another advantage. The *Strafford's* other stop at Juan Fernandez seemed off the beaten track, but actually assisted in gaining the westerly position needed for the long beat against the prevailing north west winds to San Francisco.[135] They probably anchored at Cumberland Bay on Isla Mas a Tierra and obtained supplies by boat. The limited entertainment available can be

---

135. John Bartlett Goodman III, *The Key to the Goodman Encyclopedia to the California Gold Rush Fleet*, (Los Angeles: The Zamorano Club, 1992). Goodman lists concise descriptions of 762 voyages of ships sailing from the east coast of the United States and Canada for San Francisco, December 7, 1848 to December 31, 1849. Of this fleet of ships, 78 (or 10.2%), stopped at St. Catherine's, and 45 (or 5.9%) at Juan Fernandez. Remarkably, about 20% made no stops.

judged by the fact that Daniel Defoe's *Robinson Crusoe* was based on the five years spent on that island by Alexander Selkirk who was finally rescued in 1709. In the ensuing 291 years the population of Mas Tierra and the adjoining Mas Afuera has increased to over 500, and the island can be reached by air from Valparaiso, Chile, 400 miles to the east.

The *Strafford* arrived in San Francisco August 29, 1849, 213 days after leaving New York City. The voyage was long (16,000 miles), but about average in duration for ships carrying 49ers around Cape Horn.[136] As mentioned in F. B. Austin's letter, fifteen days after reaching San Francisco, the company moved the *Strafford* up the Sacramento River to Sutterville, and Wheaton left the ship for Drytown (11 miles NW of Jackson, Amador County). He did some placer mining and became alcalde of the town. Within 3 months, he had returned to Sutterville, joined his shipmates in moving the *Strafford* to the foot of O Street in Sacramento where they sold it for a slight loss. J. B. Starr (see page 154) called the auction in December 1849, and the ship was knocked down to C. C. Hayden for $3,750. Sacramento County was short of accommodations for the numerous inmates being produced by an active criminal element and some busy judges. The *Strafford* was leased in March 1850, and moored in the river opposite the foot of I Street, to become Sacramento's first "prison brig." About the time of his old ship's descent into the criminal justice system, Wheaton had started a successful wholesale grocery business in Sacramento with Alonzo Hamilton under the trade name of Hamilton & Wheaton. Wheaton called him "Alonzo" in a letter home, but later directories up until 1868 when Hamilton was working in a grocery store and Collector of Customs, always use "Lorenzo." While on a business trip to San Francisco, May 31, 1850, Wheaton wrote a long letter to his parents portions of which read — with his parentheses and underlining shown as written and added information in brackets:

. . .My health at this time is tolerably good, although I have

---

136. During the Mexican War Lieutenant (later Civil War General) William T. Sherman traveled in the old navy store ship U.S.S. *Lexington* with a company of troops to protect American interests in California. They left Governor's Island, New York, July 14, 1846, stopped for a week in Rio de Janeiro, were held up 30 days in rounding Cape Horn, spent 10 days in Valparaiso, and still reached Monterey, California January 26, 1847 in 196 days.

Nelson Kingsley who kept a diary of the trip, left New Haven, Connecticut in the *Anna Reynolds,* March 17,1849, stopped 10 days at Isle St. Vincent, 9 days in the Falkland Islands, passed Cape Horn August 21, 1849, spent 17 days at Talcahuano, Chile, rammed another ship off San Francisco and entered the Bay November 22, 1849 — 250 days out of New Haven.

experienced more sickness since the middle of April last than during the whole period of my absence from home. I have had the Piles, Dysentery, and Bronchitis. Looseness of the bowels I am affected with frequently. Medical attendance is very costly in this country; the doctor charged me for calling on him [apparently not the usual arrangement in New York in those days] seven times once a day, $70. So you see it won't answer to be sick. . . .living is very high. I am paying $25 per week for board. You will want to know what I am doing in this place. I am established in business in Sacramento City in connection with Mr. Alonzo Hamilton and Mr. Charles Howlett. We are engaged in two different species or kinds of business viz. A general merchandise business and a wholesale [meat] market and butchering business. The store is carried on by Mr. Hamilton and myself under the firm of Hamilton, Wheaton Co., and the market by Mr. Howlett under the firm of C. Howlett Co. I am an equal partner in both. We have a stock of goods in the store worth upwards of $10,000 and on the ranche upwards of 15,000 head of beef cattle and sheep, besides a monopoly of vegetables from three large ranches. I think that I am in a fair way at last of making money and that without any aid from (so called) friends.

I am in this place [San Francisco] for the purpose of buying goods. The weather is now very dry and warm. The thermometer (at Sacramento) during the day standing at 100 while at sundown it is cool enough to require an overcoat. I wear flannel undershirts, drawers and woolen socks constantly and shall continue to do so notwithstanding I am told that the heat of summer will increase to 120 or 130 in the shade. Money should be made fast here as I am satisfied that there are but a few constitutions that can stand it for many years. People grow old fast in this country, particularly in the mines.

There is a great risk in doing business in this city or in Sacramento which place (the latter I mean) numbers some 8000 inhabitants. One may go to bed at night comparatively well off or rich, and on the succeeding day not have a dollar, having lost all by fire or flood, as no insurance can be effected, . . .I learn that father as well as others have sent me newspapers. It is useless to do so as I have not received one since I have been in this country. I desire letters to be directed to me at Sacramento City. . . .

If any of my friends or acquaintances are disposed to ship goods to this State and to consign them to our house [then, a business firm rather than a residence] at Sacramento City, I will remit the invoice price immediately on receipt, or will sell

for joint account at half profits. We have sufficient cash capital
and buy and sell only for cash. I send by this mail papers to you
. . .You will find therein the Prices Current. You will observe
that articles which are usually sold in the States by measure are
sold in this country by the pound [possibly because freight, which
comprised most of the delivered cost, was charged by the pound
or "hundred-weight"]. I have sent per Adams & Co. Express a
small package to Elizabeth (my wife) [one of Wheaton's sisters
was also named Elizabeth]. They, or rather the members of the
house here, are friends of mine and as a favor they carry this
(the package) for me for only $15; so you see I cannot send
many things at this time. . . .

San Francisco is a dusty, dirty, windy, disagreeable place
and although Sacramento is a much warmer place, I greatly
prefer it. The shipping cannot approach the banks or water's
edge at San Francisco, while at Sacramento they come alongside
the levee. I forgot to say that our store is situated on the Levee
or Front Street between I and J Streets [now 905 Front Street,
very near I] . . .With the prayer that God will bless and protect
you all, and with heartfelt wishes for your welfare, I remain.
Your affectionate Son,
William

P.S. Please send this letter to my dear wife and say to brother
John that although I have not mentioned his name above, yet he
is included and has my love with the rest.

He wrote another letter to his parents, again from San Francisco,
dated August 31, 1850. This was only two weeks after the Squatter
Riots in Sacramento, the three largest banks there had failed, and the
cholera epidemic had begun in Placerville and would reach Sacramento
in 50 days. He planned to remain in San Francisco a few weeks on
business, which may have saved him from infection. At its peak in
Sacramento on November 1, 1850, cholera was killing at an average
rate of one victim per hour. All these factors may have contributed to
the more serious tone of this next letter:

. . .I am doing well, perhaps better than any who came
out in our company, I except none. I have made money, but
whether I shall be able to realize all will depend upon what shall
be the state of affairs in our city for the next few months. We
have had serious times as you will have learned through the
papers. . . . [he may be referring to the bank failures, cholera

epidemic and the Squatter Riots] Matters are not settled with us yet, let the papers say what they may.[137]

Mr. Hamilton and myself have bought out the interest of Mr. Howlett in our business and hereafter there will be but us two interested under the firm of Hamilton & Wheaton. . . .

My absence from home has proven what I often used to attest, that I had no friends (always excepting my own family) — there has not been one that has shown friendship enough to cheer me with one line. If I had been wealthy or my prospects encouraging when I left home, I should have had professions enough. Now I am independent, I suppose matters in that respect will improve. I am now indifferent about it. A few years at my time of life [he was 36] make great changes in feelings and character. Success! coupled with all I have passed through since I left home, together with constant exercise of all the faculties of the mind and body have made a great change in me. You will not be able to recognize any but the outer man. With sincere prayers for your health and happiness and in the hope that another year will enable me to see you all again, I remain, my dear parents,

Your affectionate son,
William R. Wheaton

From information in a letter Wheaton wrote to his parents from Sacramento City, May 30, 1851, it appears he made a voyage to New York in the winter of 1850/51, returning to Sacramento on May 22. He regretted very much that he had not brought his wife, Elizabeth, with him. Wheaton also mentions the terrible San Francisco fire of May 4, 1851, in which 22 city blocks were consumed with a loss of about $12,000,000, and the subsequent very mild earthquake. His grieving for the suffering of the citizens of San Francisco, seemed a little relieved by his knowledge that huge quantities of goods were destroyed in the fire and merchandise stored elsewhere, such as that owned by Hamilton & Wheaton in Sacramento, would rise in price.

He thanks his parents for some peaches when he says, "The peaches arrived a few days before me and have proved very fine. So my friends say who received them and ate them up before my arrival." By this time, Mr. A. D. Brown, formerly of Maine, had joined the partnership of Hamilton and Wheaton, and they had moved the store one block south on Front Street to larger quarters.

---

137. Of the 100 men who came to California with Wheaton in the *Strafford*, 8 stayed in business in Sacramento long enough to be listed in the 1850/51 directory, and 9, including Wheaton, were mentioned in Hubert Howe Bancroft's seven volume *History of California*.

During the trip home in the winter of 1850/51, Wheaton apparently did some buying for the firm. By that time the Panama route was well organized with the Panama Railroad covering part of the trip across the Isthmus, and with steamers available on both sides. The actual travel time round trip could have occupied less than 70 days.

On October 25, 1851, he wrote to his parents from Colusa, which he spelled "Calusi." It was one of the few California gold rush towns with a native Indian name, and liberalities in spelling seemed permissible:

> You will observe on reading the enclosed Handbill that we have extended our business to this place which is located on the west bank of the Sacramento River about 130 miles north of Sacramento City. I am here but temporarily. One of my partners, M. Brown, who has charge of our business at this place being sick. My health continues good. I should much like to be settled down in some one location and have my family about me.
>
> When this will happen, I cannot say at present, but shall endeavor to accomplish it as soon as I possibly can without great detriment to my primary interests. Almost ever since I have been out here, [he had first arrived in California only 2 years and 56 days before] I have been called from post to pillar; having an office in San Francisco, a store at Sacramento, one at Calusi, one at Dry Town, two or three Gold Mines on the middle fork of the American River, and divers other interests which keep my time pretty well occupied in supervising.
>
> I lost so much on account of my absence last winter that I shall not risk another trip home until I am differently situated from what I now am. My desire is to dispose of my interests North and to confine myself exclusively to San Francisco. . . . With love to all
>
> I am your affectionate son
> William

Even considering the modern stories from Silicon Valley, these letters demonstrate the astonishing speed with which a determined person could become financially established in gold rush California (see also P. B. Cornwall's 15-month-profits, page 114). As the gold rush fever subsided in the late 1850s, Wheaton's later letters reflect that it became significantly more difficult to become and remain a financial success. He also devoted himself extensively to governmental and

165

charitable activities so that in his years in the Bay Area he was not rich, but still in comfortable circumstances.

In the late fall of 1851 or early in 1852, Wheaton withdrew from the partnership and opened a similar mercantile house on Battery near Jackson Street in San Francisco. In the 1853 Sacramento directory, his old partners were listed as wholesale merchants on Front Street under the name of Hamilton & Howlett. Wheaton was lucky in that he moved his goods to San Francisco before the great Sacramento fire of November 2, 1852, in which his old store was totally destroyed.

Earlier in 1852, his wife, Elizabeth, traveled to San Francisco to be with her husband for an extended stay, leaving their children with Wheaton's parents in New York. In a closely spaced four-page letter admonishing their 15-year-old son, George Henry Wheaton, for not writing, she shows that some things never change:

> SAN FRANCISCO, DECEMBER 15, '52.
> . . .I fear the trait in your character I have warned you of so often. It is increasing instead of diminishing as you get older. Do you remember how often I warned you not to give way to it—"Procrastinate." . . .No doubt you promised yourself from day to day you would write, and then allowed some frivolous excuse for self to interfere (are you selfish?—examine yourself) and then on the last day in the thirty—in the afternoon and on Sunday—sat down in haste and scribbled us a letter. Your father is much disappointed.

Wheaton added a short note at the bottom which certainly indicated the truth of the last line in his wife's message. He added:

> Read your mother's letter attentively and often, and let it be your guide. When you have studied it well, give it to your Grandmother Wheaton, and tell her it is my request that she will read it to you frequently and endeavor to impress the advice contained in it upon your mind. Let it be preserved that I may see it when I come home.
>
> Your affec. father,
> *W.R.. Wheaton*

The former procrastinator obviously obeyed at least the last two lines of his father's note, because the original letter still exists in the possession of the Wheaton family.

William Wheaton remained another year as a merchant, and then, in 1853 returned to the practice of his earlier profession, opening a law office on Montgomery Street in San Francisco. He continued as an attorney until 1855 and then returned for a visit home in New York (possibly to see if the 1852 letter had been saved). In 1856, he was again in San Francisco where he was deeply involved in the Committee of Vigilance and later lived through the earthquake of October 10, 1856. Economic conditions were chaotic in San Francisco that year as a number of large banks had failed, the city government was corrupt, and real estate values dropped sharply. At the beginning of 1857, Wheaton wrote of his experience as a Vigilante,[138] in a letter to his parents. It was also obvious he was rather depressed by his situation at the time:

SAN FRANCISCO, Jan.y 19, 1857

My Dear Parents;

Attempting to write a letter when you have nothing to communicate is rather a difficult task. Such is the case with me at this time. . . .I was not successful in the matter alluded to in my last letter, for the very reason of my "Vigilant" proclivities. The Vigilance Legislative Ticket was withdrawn in favor of the Republican, which was believed to be sufficiently Vigilant for all purposes and which succeeded in this City alone, the State having gone largely for the Democratic Ticket. . . .I was one of the prime movers in the Vigilance matter. The Executive Committee was organized in my room on the night Jas. King of Wm. was killed [there were 25 members, and they first met May 15, 1856], and I held and still hold a commission as a lieutenant of the 3rd. Company of Infantry, and was in active service during the whole time. The Committee have not disbanded. The organization is still maintained, although it has ceased active

---

138. Bancroft in volume VI, pages 740-754 gives the history of the 1856 San Francisco Committee of Vigilance. Problems with gangs of criminals and easy-going judges had been going on for some time, and all came to a head when James King of William was shot while walking from his office. The gunman, James Casey, was a ballot-stuffer and the proprietor of a small and disreputable newspaper, the *Weekly Sunday Times.* King had been a clerk at Sutter's Fort, a banker in Sacramento, and had recently become editor of a reformist newspaper in San Francisco. The two had entered into an editorial battle, which Casey decided to settle permanently. King was considered a martyr and a committee was immediately formed to try and hang Casey. The shooting occurred on May 14, 1856, and on the 18th, Casey was taken from the jail by the Vigilantes with over 1000 men armed with bayonetted rifles, and most importantly, a loaded 9-pounder cannon aimed at the door of the jail. James King of William died on the 20th and during his funeral, on May 22, 1856, Casey was tried and hung by the Vigilantes.

In the ensuing three months, a Justice of California's Supreme Court stabbed a vigilante-sympathizing police officer and was arrested, three more murderers were hung (the officer survived), and over 800 lesser criminals were banished or voluntarily left San Francisco. On August 21, 1856, the Committee of Vigilance ceased operations, and largely disbanded..

167

operations. There has been and still is, a very bad state of affairs existing here. There are almost daily being discovered gross frauds and peculations in almost every department of the State government. Our State Treasurer, and also the Comptroller of the State have been impeached by the present Legislature, and are soon to be tried by the Senate.

I suppose that you have read in the newspapers accounts of the Earthquakes we have had here [February 15th and October 10, 1856,—which was "steamer day"]. One was very severe, opening the ground from ten to twenty feet in width for forty miles, destroying houses etc. The last one occurred on the last Steamer day. I was asleep at the time, it awakened me, and I with the other inhabitants of Brick buildings, hurried into the Street. This shock was a Vertical one accompanied by a loud noise.

Four buildings next adjoining the one I reside in, were burned down a few days since, doing considerable damage to our house. At one time during the fire, I was apprehensive that I should lose what little I possessed, having escaped into the Street with my Revolver (a very necessary item with us these days) and my wife's Daguerreotype only, but providentially our effects were all saved.

. . .I think it especially hard that brother George does not write to me . . .I have asked him whether his influence or exertions could not procure for me some occupation or subordinate situation whereby I could earn a living for myself & family at home. This was long since and I have not received any reply. . . .Time which worketh a change in all things, may bring about a brighter & better change of circumstances.

Your affectionate son
William

The change of circumstances occurred right in San Francisco as its economy rapidly improved and by 1860 he was secretary of the Society of California Pioneers, and an attorney at 197 Washington Street.

Elizabeth Wheaton and their four daughters moved to San Francisco permanently in 1860. Their son, George Henry, joined them in 1865, after serving in the Civil War as a judge-advocate and reaching the rank of major. William R. Wheaton was elected to represent San Francisco in the California State Legislature in 1862, and in addition, became the assessor of the City and County of San Francisco in 1863. He returned to the legislature in 1871-1873 where he was the chairman of the San Francisco delegation and a member of the ways and means committee. In the latter capacity he actively promoted the funding for the building of the University of California. A nineteenth century biography[139] said "to him more than to any living man is due the building of that seat of learning, which is today an honor to the State and a blessing to its youth," a description of the great university that is as true today as when first written over a century ago.

In 1872-1876 he was the general manager of the California Life Insurance Company, and in 1876, President U. S. Grant appointed him registrar of the General Land Office of the United States for Northern California. His work in this capacity must have been most satisfactory, because he was reappointed by Presidents Hayes, Garfield, and Cleveland, and finally retired in 1886. He and Elizabeth celebrated their golden wedding anniversary on February 1, 1887, at which time her gift was not recorded, but he received an engraved gold-handled cane.

Perhaps because of his early traveling in California, Wheaton moved around the Bay area for many years. San Francisco city directories list the family residence on Eddy Street between Mason and Taylor in 1863, on Varney street in South Park in 1867, and on Capp Street near 16th in 1874. In 1878 they moved to 1060 Poplar Street in Oakland where he remained until his death on September 11, 1888.

WINN, GEN. A. M., *Resident*. Albert Maver Winn was born May 12, 1810, in Pennsylvania, and in 1831 went to Zanesville, Ohio where he married his first wife. About 1834, he and his family moved to Vicksburg, Mississippi, and in 1836 he was appointed a lieutenant in the first regiment of Mississippi Militia. In 1840 he became the quarter-master general with the rank of major on the staff of Governor Charles Lynch of Mississippi, and in 1845, a colonel and drillmaster of the militia. On February 14, 1849, Winn left New Orleans, crossed Mexico and arrived in San Francisco May 28, 1849, his wife and family remaining in Vicksburg. Shortly after his arrival, he came to Sacramento, formed the partnership of Winn & Baker, and set up a store on 3rd Street between J and K Streets. At the formation of the first town council in July, he became a member, and at the meeting of August 25, 1849, was elected president. A few days later, he called a meeting at his store for the purpose of forming a local chapter of the Fraternity of Odd Fellows "to visit the sick, relieve the distressed, and

---

139. An excerpt from a publication of the Society of California Pioneers, pp 143 and 144 headed "William Rufus Wheaton," now in Mr. John Wheaton's collection.

bury the dead."[140] Col. Winn accepted the presidency of the society.

Turning to political matters, the council worked hard to prepare a city charter for the governance of Sacramento, which to their surprise was defeated on September 20, 1849, by 146 votes.[141] Winn and the council then asked the citizens for guidance in a proclamation that was posted in public places. One of these broadsides is preserved in the California State Library, and reads as follows:

PROCLAMATION
To the People of Sacramento City,
by Order of the President and Council

On the first day of August, 1849, we were elected councilmen of this city, and our powers or duties were not defined. On the 13th of September following we presented to you a charter for your consideration, which you have seen fit to reject by a majority of 146 votes. Since then we have been unable to determine what the good people of this city desire us to do; and being republicans in principle, and having every confidence in the ability of the people to govern themselves, we again request the residents of Sacramento City to meet at the St. Louis Exchange [a saloon on 2nd Street], at half-past seven o'clock, on Wednesday Oct. 3rd, 1849, then and there to declare what they wish the City Council to do. If you wish us to act under the Mexican laws now in force, however inapplicable they may be in our condition, then we must do the best we can; if you have objections to particular features of the charter, then strike out the objectional features and insert such as you desire. The health and safety of our city demand immediate action on your part, for in our primitive condition, and in the absence of legislative authority, we can in fact be of no service to you without your confidence and consent.

A. M. Winn, president

This remarkable request is also signed by the other members of the council, and excited the 1,321 voters who assembled to vote in favor of the charter, 808 for, and 513 against. On October 13, 1849, the charter, with a few modifications suggested by the voters, became law, and the design of the city seal, adopted (a facsimile of this first seal of

---

140. John F. Morse in his *History of Sacramento, ibid*, p. 46, adds some details including the fact that a plain pine coffin cost $60 to $150.

141. George Holbrook Baker, *Sacramento Illustrated,* (Sacramento: Barber & Baker, 1855) Reprinted by Sacramento Book Collector's Club, 1950. pp. 30-34.

170

Sacramento City appears on the front cover of this book).

In 1850, he was appointed a brigadier-general in the California State Militia by Governor Peter Burnett, and commanded the force at Sacramento during the Squatter Riots. After 1850, his residence is listed in directories without a business or profession, and one year his son, A. G. Winn, is listed as a surveyor "assisting his father, A. M. Winn." His first wife died in 1862, and in 1865 he moved to San Francisco and married the widow of James King of William.

General Winn founded the *Native Sons of the Golden West*, which became a large organization with many local chapters. He and his wife later moved to Sonoma County, where he died, August 26, 1883. He was a founding member of the Sacramento Pioneers, and is buried in the Pioneer Grove section of the Sacramento City Cemetery.

ZABRISKIE, COL. JAMES C., *Notary Public*. James Carmen Zabriskie was the colonel of a regiment of New Jersey militia which participated in the inaugural ceremonies of President Andrew Jackson. Zabriskie was a friend of Commodore R. F. Stockton, and on February 28, 1844, was aboard the U.S. Steam Frigate *Princeton* along with President John Tyler and his cabinet (and Commander Charles Wilkes mentioned on page 44) on the Potomac River during an evening excursion. The gala occasion was organized to demonstrate a large experimental cannon named *The Peace-Maker* which was fired, and exploded, instantly killing the secretaries of State and Navy together with several dignitaries, and injuring many others, including Senator Thomas Hart Benton. Zabriskie had somehow believed the gun unsafe and had retreated some distance from the firing demonstration. As a result, he was able to give assistance to a number of the wounded.

He arrived in Sacramento in January 1849,[142] and set up an office in a small shanty under an oak tree at 2nd and K Streets. In July 1849, he was elected second magistrate of the city and later employed to write the first city charter which was approved by the voters on October 13, 1849. In 1861, he moved to San Francisco where he

---

142. This date may be incorrect for two reasons: The *New York Herald* of February 2, 1849 listed a J.C. Zabriskie as a passenger on a vessel departing New York a few days earlier. He could have reached Sacramento by May or June, 1849, but not much before.

Secondly, in January, 1849, lot sales (deeds then being the mainstay of the legal profession) were still handled at Sutter's Fort and he would have been more likely to have first opened an office there. By June, the action was all in Sacramento City.

continued to practice law until his death on July 10, 1883. He was a member of the Sacramento Pioneer Association.

ZINS, GEORGE, [92] *Brewer.* A native of Lorraine, born in 1799, he came to California with four emigrants from Switzerland. They left Saint Louis, Missouri, on April 21, 1846, with a wagon, four oxen, two cows, a large supply of meal, a ten-gallon water keg, an assortment of guns, and a chest containing knives, forks and cooking utensils. The first part of their journey was made on a boat up the Missouri River to Independence. Here they joined an emigrant train of eight wagons which travelled about 150 miles due south to the small Mormon town of Indian Creek, Missouri, where a much larger train was forming. They departed from Indian Creek on May 12, 1846.[143] and followed the trail through Kansas and Nebraska, down the north fork of the Platte River to Fort Laramie, Wyoming, over the Rockies through South Pass to Fort Bridger, Wyoming. A short way beyond, the trail divided with one branch going to Oregon, the other southwest to California over the Hastings Cut-Off around Salt Lake and up the Humboldt and Truckee Rivers to what we now call Donner Pass. In those days before the discovery of gold, many of the emigrants were in families expecting to settle in California as farmers. The larger parties were fairly safe from Indians, but almost every day they lost some time due to births, deaths, and sickness. Zins and his bachelor friends, Heinrich Lienhard, Heinrich Thomen, Jacob Rippstein, and Valentine Diehl felt that they could make much better time alone.

They indeed pulled ahead of the main group, and reached the summit of the Sierras on October 4, 1846, 145 days after leaving Missouri. Fortunately for them, this was just 24 days before the Donner Party arrived at the east end of Donner Lake to face impassibly heavy snow. Zins' party proceeded over Emigrant Gap and down the Bear River to Johnson's Ranch in Yuba County. Here they learned that California was no longer under Mexican control and had been United States territory for over 3 months. After a gala welcome and a feast of huge beefsteaks, they rested a few days, and then took the wagon on to Sutter's Fort where they arrived in the latter half of October 1846.[144]

Captain John A. Sutter had come to realize that the flood-free

---

143. According to the *California Star* of February 13, 1847, p.3, Col. 1, the Donner Party departed form Indian Creek the next day—May 13th, 1846.

144. Marguerite E. Wilbur, *A Pioneer at Sutter's Fort, 1846 - 1850, The Adventures of Heinrich Lienhard,* (Los Angeles: Califía Society, 1941) pp. iv-vi.

area around the Fort was too small to accommodate a large settlement and he selected a site to be called *Sutterville* facing on the river and about 5/8 mile below present-day Broadway. On January 28, 1846, Sutter's diary mentions Mr. [Henry] Trow was cutting stakes to be used in laying out a new town. The survey was completed by Hastings and Bidwell about a month later.

On Sunday, June 20, 1847, Alcalde John Sinclair married George Zins and Mrs. Doris Woolfinger, the widow of a member of the Donner Party, at Sutter's Fort. Sutter built the first house in the new town of Sutterville in 1847, and Zins and his wife moved into a tent nearby and set up a brick kiln and burnt 40,000 bricks. Some of his bricks were marked with his initials "G Z" and in the 1960s, Sacramento historian, Newton Cope, dug one from a pile of excavated material near Capitol Avenue and Front Street (it can still be seen, set into the brickwork about 15 inches above the mantel of the fireplace at his Fire House restaurant on Second Street). Zins gave 10,000 of these first bricks to Sutter for an oven at the Fort, and used the remaining 30,000 to build, at Sutterville, the first regular brick house ever erected in California. This structure was completed in 1847, 18 by 35 feet in size, and was floored with tiles.

At Sutterville, in the late fall of 1848, he burned another kiln of 100,000 bricks and from these, in early 1849, he built the second brick structure in Sacramento County, and the first in Sacramento City. It was 60 by 40 feet, two stories high. It was located at 151 (1323 new style) Front Street between M and N Streets, where a hotel building is now under construction. The 60 by 150 foot lot was given to Zins as a wedding present by Captain Sutter.

George Zins' 1848 Brick

The building contained two stores on the ground floor and upstairs was a hotel, first called the Anchor House. It survived both the 1850 flood and, with some damage, the great fire of November 1852. Zins had sold it earlier in 1852 to Jacob Binninger , who enlarged it in 1856, and continued to operate the hotel under the names of *Green Tree Hotel, Empire House*, and last as *Pioneer Hotel*.

In the summer of 1999, a team of archaeologists from Sonoma State University under Dr. Adrian Praetzellis, excavated the site and

Foundation and floor of the first brick building in Sacramento
Built by George Zins on Front near N Street in October 1849. The layer of white ash from the 1852 fire (shoulder level) is about 8 ft. below modern Front Street.(1999 photo)

recovered 40 boxes of artifacts for study and preservation.[145]
Zins also operated a brewery in partnership with a Mr. Weiser on 29th Street between J & K Streets in 1850, and then became a fruit grower. He suffered losses, first from fire, and later from hydraulic mining debris, which killed his orchards. After 1872, Zins was reduced to living on a chicken ranch and died in Oakland in 1885, at the age of 86.

— § —

Unfortunately there are no biographies of women included in the preceding fifty-five entries. This is not a matter of carelessness nor prejudice. It resulted from a total inability to find information of any kind on the sixteen women listed in the directory. This number represents 1.12 percent of the 1425 names in the directory, and must have been well below the percentage of women in the general population of Sacramento, even at that early date. Of the sixteen

---

145. Matthew Barrows, *Sacramento Bee*, November 5, 1999, Section B, p. 1, col. 2.

names, nine used "Mrs.," two used "Miss," and five just listed their names. One owned a hotel, ten owned boarding houses or restaurants, one was shown as "washer" and four, including one "Miss" had no profession listed.

NOTES ON SOURCES

Many sources are mentioned in the footnotes, or were used for verification of data found elsewhere. Some were particularly useful and informative, and more detailed descriptions of these are included here:

Hubert Howe Bancroft, ***History of California, 1542-1890,*** (San Francisco: The History Company, Publishers, 1886-1890) 7 volumes. This history will probably stand forever among the mightiest efforts to chronicle the story of a people in a rather limited section of the world.

Bancroft used a small army of assistants who interviewed over 160 Hispanic and Anglo-Saxon pioneers who were still living in 1860-1885. He collected thousands of manuscripts and even more printed pamphlets, books and articles. His list of authorities, or sources, as of 1856, numbers approximately 4,000, principally in English and Spanish, but he also cites works in Dutch, French, German, Latin, and a translation from Russian. The nature of these references may be seen from the first, "Aa, Pieter van der, *Naaukeurige Versameling.* Leyden, 1737, 30 volumes;" and the last, "Zúñiga, José, Cartas del Comandante de S. Diego, 1781-95, MS." Bancroft also includes as one item 68 volumes of "newspaper scraps" carefully classified under 55 headings from *Academy of Sciences* to *Water Supply,* plus *Miscellaneous.* In Bancroft's own slightly immodest, but true words:

> As it stands the list is more complete than any other within
> my knowledge relating to any state or territory of our union,
> or indeed to any other country in the world.

This list does not include literally thousands of citations appearing in footnotes and a large number of printed publications he gathered after 1856. In the light of the popularity of modern oral histories, his comments on extensive interviews with pioneers like Governor Alvarado, John Bidwell, Governor Bigler, William H. Davis, Captain Sutter, General Vallejo, and hundreds of others are of interest.

> While the personal reminiscences of both natives and
> pioneers, as used in connection with and tested by
> contemporaneous documentary evidence, have been in the
> aggregate of great value to me. . .yet I cannot give them
> unlimited praise as authorities. . . .And in criticizing this material

in bulk, I . . .allude to . . .the general mass of statements from honest and intelligent men. In the statements of past events made by the best of men from memory—will be found a strange and often inexplicable mixture of truth and falsehood. Side by side in the best narratives I find accounts of one event which are models of faithful accuracy and accounts of another event not even remotely founded in fact. . . .There seems to exist a general inability to distinguish between the memory of real occurrences that have been seen and known, and that of idle tales that have been heard in years long past..[146]

To assist in accessing the vast store of information contained in the seven volumes, Bancroft provided a 66 page index at the end of the last volume. This is, of course, helpful but covers only a portion of the names and classifications within the work. In 1985, a complete 759 page index in two volumes was published (see next item below). Under the letter "X" the original index had one entry, while the 1985 index has sixteen entries; under "Z" the respective numbers are 4 and 74.

Bancroft includes a list of over 1700 male inhabitants of California who lived here between 1769 and 1800, with an indication of the decade in which they arrived. Finally at the end of volumes II through V, he placed the alphabetic *Pioneer Register*, a biographical dictionary containing thousands of names and condensed biographies of persons who came to California before the year 1849. Bancroft explained the need to save space and mentions, "Of private individuals, as a rule, no attempt is made to depict the character, to picture them as 'nature's noblemen,' or to point out the fact that they were not members of temperance societies. It is taken for granted that they were more or less good, bad and indifferent citizens according to circumstances." Despite all the cold facts, abbreviated biographies, and concise tables, Bancroft often inserted some rollicking and even quotable passages such as one that described the indifference in 1850 of the miners to the legislative questions in the national capital.
In Volume VI, on page 347, he wrote:
There were men in the mines, whose journey to

---

146. Bancroft's conclusions regarding oral reports of past events have been observed by many others. Even letters reporting recent events should, if possible, be checked against other sources. During World War II, as executive officer of a small minesweeper, the author was required for intelligence purposes to censor letters from members of the ship's company. Descriptions of events and the actions of the letter writers occasionally differed markedly from those entered only days before in the ship's deck log. Such differences were, of course, not censored. Only the rarely appearing names of ships, unit commanders, and exact locations were blacked out.

California, whose digging and delving, whose gambling and whiskey-drinking, whose prospecting, Indian-shooting, and clubbing of foreigners, were all as lenses that enabled them to see how much of self and how little of public weal occupied the ponderous brains of the eight-dollars-a-day law-makers at Washington.

Although Hubert Howe Bancroft's California history was completed over a century ago, there is nothing else like it, and almost certainly never will be.

Everett and Anna Hager, *The Zamorano Index to History of California by Hubert Howe Bancroft,* (Los Angeles: University of Southern California, 1985), in two volumes. Names of people, towns, creeks rivers, mountains, vessels, and notable events are listed giving each location by volume and page where the item is mentioned. For cities, a large chronological list is present with dates inserted before each name. The same treatment is given to recurring events like fires and floods. The section headed "Ranchos" contains a nineteen-page alphabetical list of names of ranchos, but the names also appear elsewhere under the rancho name. For the occasional user of Bancroft's history, this work will save hours of time—partly because an item can be quickly located, and for some, avoiding the hours lost when fascinating unrelated stories are noticed while conducting a general search.

Winfield J. Davis, *An Illustrated History of Sacramento County, California,* (Chicago: The Lewis Publishing Company, 1890). In this work, much of the biographical information seems to come from interviews recorded long after 1850 and some dates and details may vary a little from those available from other sources. Many of the biographies, which are generally limited to persons living in 1890, contain extensive information on the subject's trip to Sacramento. For some reason, few of the biographies give details of a sea voyage around Cape Horn. The table of contents lists 650 "biographical sketches" in alphabetical order, although they are not so arranged in the text covering 557 pages. Many other notable people are also mentioned in chapters devoted to various professions and industries. There is even a chapter on criminals and early ruffians.

Sacramento City and County Directories, 1853 through 1871, and particularly , Samuel Colville, *Sacramento Directory for the year commencing May, 1856,* (San Francisco: Monson, Valentine & Co, 1856) because this work contains over one hundred short biographies of citizens and histories of businesses. The 1871 directory includes a foldout map of the county, an interesting 102-page history of Sacramento, and several full-page engravings of important buildings.

Dr. John F. Morse's 40-page *History of Sacramento* in Samuel Colville, *Sacramento Directory for the Year 1853-54*, Reprinted, (Sacramento: California State Library Foundation, 1997) pp. 33-72. Morse was present in Sacramento during the most interesting part of this history and gives the reader an excellent picture of the main events. His history has few references, but provides the timing and names of participants, so that further research can be started. His writing style is above reproach, if one excuses some of the obvious prejudices of that time, and includes lines such as; "Champagne circulated so freely that identity became jeopardized, and the very illumination of the room converted into a grand magnifying medium, for the revels of fancy and delights of illusion."

J. S. Holliday, *Rush for Riches, Gold Fever and the Making of California,* (Berkeley: Oakland Museum and University of California Press, 1999) 355 pages, a fascinating history of California from 1847 to 1890. One could own this book for years and think of it only as the finest collection of beautifully presented illustrations of the period, yet surrounding these is a masterfully written text which even by itself gives the reader a *feeling* of the times. The author has carefully selected the words and phrases which will convey the desired impression in a minimum of space. He includes 28 pages of end notes, about 320 literary sources on eight pages, five pages of illustration sources, and a nine page index. The index is particularly useful because it refers the reader to both text and illustrations.

— § —

Researching the histories of the Sacramentans in this section has been fascinating, and it became apparent that without regard to their later lives <u>all</u> the people listed in Sacramento in 1850 had experienced incredible adventures in just getting here. As it would have been for a miner in 1848, gold in the form of another great biography was everywhere, and I didn't want to stop looking. I can only hope that my readers will enjoy at least a few of the nuggets that were found.

— § —

CONVERTING OLD AND NEW SACRAMENTO ADDRESSES

The City of Sacramento was laid out (and probably the numbering system planned) by U.S. Army Topographical Engineer, Captain William H. Warner (1812-1849), in 1848 under contract to Sam Brannon and John A. Sutter Jr.   Captain Warner was paid $16.00 per day, which was large by army standards, but little in 1848 in California, where you could still pick that much gold out of some streams in a day, using only your fingers. He was assisted by Lieutenants (later Generals) William Tecumseh Sherman and Edward Oliver Cresap Ord. They camped on the south bank of the American River at about 28th Street where Sutter first landed.

The blocks of Sacramento City, with the exception of those lying between 12th and 13th Streets, were 320 x 320 feet net size. Because of the 20-foot-wide, east-west alley, the actual blocks measured 340 feet from north to south and 320 feet from east to west. The streets were 80 feet wide, with the exception of M Street, (later Capitol Avenue) which was 100 feet wide. Although not shown on the original map 32 house numbers were assigned to each block; 16 even numbers on the south and west sides of the street, and odd numbers to the other sides. This provided 20 feet between succeeding even numbers on the south and west sides of the streets, and the same interval between odd numbers on the north and east sides of the streets. Probably because of the early building in 1848 before the survey, the alleys between Front and 2nd Streets run parallel to the river or north-south, all other alleys run east-west between the lettered streets.

The blocks between 12th and 13th Streets had 400 feet in the east-west direction and 40 numbers were assigned. Streets running east and west were given letters from A to Y and the north-south streets were numbered from 1 to 31 starting at the west or Sacramento River side of the city. The lettered streets began with A at the north on the American River levee. As a practical matter the main part of the city contained uniform square blocks, with the exception noted, but the river boundaries curved and short streets with names were inserted to fill out the areas inside the curves. Possibly because it was on the original road from the Sacramento River to Sutter's Fort, the alley between J and K Streets was wider than usual from 4th to 8th Streets and was named "Oak Street" (in 1999 one block of it remains, called "Merchant Street," because of the Merchant's National Bank located at its west end since 1921).

Culver's directory reproduced here was the first on the Pacific Coast to use street address numbers. Four months before, on

September 1, 1850, Charles P. Kimball published his *San Francisco City Directory* without address numbers, and in his conclusion (page 129) wrote,

> In conclusion, we shall touch upon but two things, about which little has been said by others but which we think are of importance, and first, the one brought more particularly to our notice as connected with this work that of numbering the Streets.
>
> Under the present [un]settled state of change it is very plain that all plans of numbering the buildings will very soon become defective from the building-up and tearing-down process continually going on, nor will it be likely to be better for some time to come. If then a plan could be adopted giving the location quite accurate, and still independent of the buildings. We think it worthy the consideration of the public. Now we enjoy the opinion that we have one of that nature, which, for all business operations, would answer every purpose. It is this: to have the streets, commencing at Bay street, on the north, and Front st., on the east marked off by posts, or otherwise into spaces of fifteen or twenty feet, more or less, [Sacramento used 20] as would seem to be most convenient. By having these spaces numbered, you have your streets marked off perfectly independent of any change which may occur in the building. This could be done by the city government wholly, or they could merely designate the number of feet to each space, and any one by means of a map, could easily tell what the number should be, and put them up accordingly. [The second problem concerned confusion between church and fire bells]

In this instance Sacramento was ahead of San Francisco because this city had been using street address numbers since early in 1849. As far as is known, Sacramento used a system that followed Kimball's second suggestion of setting the feet between succeeding numbers and letting the owners figure out where they were by using a map and measuring from the street corner.

The old numbering system for Sacramento started at the intersection of Front and I Streets, where the first frame store had been built. Under this system number 1, I Street was at the north-east corner of the intersection (now an entrance to the California State Railroad Museum), and number 1, Front Street was on the east side of Front at

I Street. House numbers on the lettered (east-west) streets commenced at Front Street on the Sacramento River, with even numbers on the south side and odd numbers on the north side of the lettered streets. Thus the address for the *north* east corner of front and J Streets was No. 1, J Street and for the *south* east corner No. 2, J Street, and so on eastward to number 32 J Street at the intersection of second and J Streets. At this point the system differed from that in use after 1880 because the addresses continued onward with no break, and the address at the south east corner of 2nd and J was No. 34, J Street. Unless one had memorized the multiples of 32 up to 31 times 32 it was difficult to figure the cross Street nearest to the address being sought. The citizens of those days obviously had the same problem, because a majority of the advertisements listing a numbered address also listed the cross streets between which it lay. For an army officer used to navigating the trackless wastes of the west with a topographic map in hand, the system was easy, but for a stranger or a new postman—a nightmare.

More confusion occurred in the house numbers on the numbered streets running north and south because of a geographic problem facing the surveyors in 1848. In the few months between the gold discovery and the start of the survey a number of structures had been erected along Front Street, but nothing could be built north of I street because of Sutter Lake which in 1848 connected to the Sacramento River at that point.

The owners probably did not want their street addresses referenced to some mythical point across a lake and often under water. Numbers on Front Street (and all parallel numbered streets running north-south) therefore commenced at I street increasing to the south at 32 numbers to the block. East of 6th Street Sutter Lake ended, and the city was extended north to A street. By 1851 houses were being built north of I Street and rather than re-number the houses on Front to 6th streets, it was just decided that the houses would be numbered *both north and south beginning at I Street.* Thus 161-8th Street would be either at the south-east corner of 8th and N Streets (Leland Stanford's residence) or at the north-east corner of 8th and D Streets. For some reason advertisers seldom used "north" or "south" with their number street addresses, just the usual "between D and E Streets", or "corner of D".

With the introduction of local delivery of mail, the old address system was changed, and by 1880, the modern system was in use. After 1880, for *lettered* streets each block started at its west edge with 100 times the number of the cross street on the south side of the street and one number higher on the north side.[147]

The old "20 feet per number" continued so that at the east end of each block the address was 30 numbers higher than that at the west end. As an example, on the north side of K Street the address for the north east corner of 9th and K is 901 K Street (old style, 257 K Street) and at the east end of the same block, the address for the north west corner of 10th and K Streets is 931 K Street (old style 287 K Street). The system for the *numbered* streets running north-south was greatly simplified, (the American River having been diverted to north of A Street and Sutter Lake filled in) by having the numbers start at A street with the odd numbers on the east side and the even numbers on the west. The new address for the south west corner of 7th and I streets (old style number 2 Seventh Street) became 900 Seventh Street.

This material has been included so the reader can, with the aid of the following table, convert a modern address to its old 1848-1880 equivalent and vice-versa. Remembering the "20 feet per number" rule gives the location even if nothing remains.

Unfortunately there are some modern exceptions to the numbering system in the blocks bounded by Front, Alhambra, A, and Broadway. Although an old city ordinance specifies that the <u>city</u> shall determine street address numbers, some building owners have been allowed to ignore the original and eminently sensible system; changing 515 to 555 Capitol Mall being a notable example.

---

147. Since in the early system, "0" L Street was not used as an address for the first house on the south east corner of Front and L Streets (Stanford's store), that point was assigned the number "2" L Street. Thus all the way to the east end of all lettered streets the numbers at the start of each block were one higher on the south side. Under the *new* system (after 1880), addresses on the south side of the street started with "100" and the numbers at the start of each block were one *lower* on the south side.

SACRAMENTO STREET NUMBERS BEFORE & AFTER 1880
House numbering   **LETTERED Streets**
EVEN (South Side), ODD (North Side)

old	new	old	new	old	new	old	new
1	101	2	100	3	103	4	102
5	105	6	104	7	107	8	106
9	109	10	108	11	111	12	110
13	113	14	112	15	115	16	114
17	117	18	116	19	119	20	118
21	121	22	120	23	123	24	122
25	125	26	124	27	127	28	126
29	129	30	128	31	131	32	130
33	201	34	200	35	203	36	202
37	205	38	204	39	207	40	206
41	209	42	208	43	211	44	210
45	213	46	212	47	215	48	214
49	217	50	216	51	219	52	218
53	221	54	220	55	223	56	222
57	225	58	224	59	227	60	226
61	229	62	228	63	231	64	230
65	301	66	300	67	303	68	302
69	305	70	304	71	307	72	306
73	309	74	308	75	311	76	310
77	313	78	312	79	315	80	314
81	317	82	316	83	319	84	318
85	321	86	320	87	323	88	322
89	325	90	324	91	327	92	326
93	329	94	328	95	331	96	330
97	401	98	400	99	403	100	402
101	405	102	404	103	407	104	406
105	409	106	408	107	411	108	410
109	413	110	412	111	415	112	414
113	417	114	416	115	419	116	418
117	421	118	420	119	423	120	422
121	425	122	424	123	427	124	426
125	429	126	428	127	431	128	430
129	501	130	500	131	503	132	502
133	505	134	504	135	507	136	506
137	509	138	508	139	511	140	510
141	513	142	512	143	515	144	514
145	517	146	516	147	519	148	518
149	521	150	520	151	523	152	522
153	525	154	524	155	527	156	526
157	529	158	528	159	531	160	530

SACRAMENTO STREET NUMBERS BEFORE & AFTER 1880
House numbering **LETTERED Streets**
EVEN (South Side), ODD (North Side)

old	new	old	new	old	new	old	new
161	601	162	600	163	603	164	602
165	605	166	604	167	607	168	606
169	609	170	608	171	611	172	610
173	613	174	612	175	615	176	614
177	617	178	616	179	619	180	618
181	621	182	620	183	623	184	622
185	625	186	624	187	627	188	626
189	629	190	628	191	631	192	630
193	701	194	700	195	703	196	702
197	705	198	704	199	707	200	706
201	709	202	708	203	711	204	710
205	713	206	712	207	715	208	714
209	717	210	716	211	719	212	718
213	721	214	720	215	723	216	722
217	725	218	724	219	727	220	726
221	729	222	728	223	731	224	730
225	801	226	800	227	803	228	802
229	805	230	804	231	807	232	806
233	809	234	808	235	811	236	810
237	813	238	812	239	815	240	814
241	817	242	816	243	819	244	818
245	821	246	820	247	823	248	822
249	825	250	824	251	827	252	826
253	829	254	828	255	831	256	830
257	901	258	900	259	903	260	902
261	905	262	904	263	907	264	906
265	909	266	908	267	911	268	910
269	913	270	912	271	915	272	914
273	917	274	916	275	919	276	918
277	921	278	920	279	923	280	922
281	925	282	924	283	927	284	926
285	929	286	928	287	931	288	930
289	1001	290	1000	291	1003	292	1002
293	1005	294	1004	295	1007	296	1006
297	1009	298	1008	299	1011	300	1010
301	1013	302	1012	303	1015	304	1014
305	1017	306	1016	307	1019	308	1018
309	1021	310	1020	311	1023	312	1022
313	1025	314	1024	315	1027	316	1026
317	1029	318	1028	319	1031	320	1030

SACRAMENTO STREET NUMBERS BEFORE & AFTER 1880
House numbering **LETTERED Streets**
EVEN (South Side), ODD (North Side)

old	new	old	new	old	new	old	new
321	1101	322	1100	323	1103	324	1102
325	1105	326	1104	327	1107	328	1106
329	1109	330	1108	331	1111	332	1110
333	1113	334	1112	335	1115	336	1114
337	1117	338	1116	339	1119	340	1118
341	1121	342	1120	343	1123	344	1122
345	1125	346	1124	347	1127	348	1126
349	1129	350	1128	351	1131	352	1130
353	1201	354	1200	355	1203	356	1202
357	1205	358	1204	359	1207	360	1206
361	1209	362	1208	363	1211	364	1210
365	1213	366	1212	367	1215	368	1214
369	1217	370	1216	371	1219	372	1218
373	1221	374	1220	375	1223	376	1222
377	1225	378	1224	379	1227	380	1226
381	1229	382	1228	383	1231	384	1230
385	1233	386	1232	387	1235	388	1234
389	1237	390	1236	391	1239	392	1238
393	1301	394	1300	395	1303	396	1302
397	1305	398	1304	399	1307	400	1306
401	1309	402	1308	403	1311	404	1310
405	1313	406	1312	407	1315	408	1314
409	1317	410	1316	411	1319	412	1318
413	1321	414	1320	415	1323	416	1322
417	1325	418	1324	419	1327	420	1326
421	1329	422	1328	423	1331	424	1330
425	1401	426	1400	427	1403	428	1402
429	1405	430	1404	431	1407	432	1406
433	1409	434	1408	435	1411	436	1410
437	1413	438	1412	439	1415	440	1414
441	1417	442	1416	443	1419	444	1418
445	1421	446	1420	447	1423	448	1422
449	1425	450	1424	451	1427	452	1426
453	1429	454	1428	455	1431	456	1430
457	1501	458	1500	459	1503	460	1502
461	1505	462	1504	463	1507	464	1506
465	1509	466	1508	467	1511	468	1510
469	1513	470	1512	471	1515	472	1514
473	1517	474	1516	475	1519	476	1518
477	1521	478	1520	479	1523	480	1522

SACRAMENTO STREET NUMBERS BEFORE & AFTER 1880
House numbering **LETTERED Streets**
EVEN (South Side), ODD (North Side)

old	new	old	new	old	new	old	new
481	1525	482	1524	483	1527	484	1526
485	1529	486	1528	487	1531	488	1530
489	1601	490	1600	491	1603	492	1602
493	1605	494	1604	495	1607	496	1606
497	1609	498	1608	499	1611	500	1610
501	1613	502	1612	503	1615	504	1614
505	1617	506	1616	507	1619	508	1618
509	1621	510	1620	511	1623	512	1622
513	1625	514	1624	515	1627	516	1626
517	1629	518	1628	519	1631	520	1630
521	1701	522	1700	523	1703	524	1702
525	1705	526	1704	527	1707	528	1706
529	1709	530	1708	531	1711	532	1710
533	1713	534	1712	535	1715	536	1714
537	1717	538	1716	539	1719	540	1718
541	1721	542	1720	543	1723	544	1722
545	1725	546	1724	547	1727	548	1726
549	1729	550	1728	551	1731	552	1730
553	1801	554	1800	555	1803	556	1802
557	1805	558	1804	559	1807	560	1806
561	1809	562	1808	563	1811	564	1810
565	1813	566	1812	567	1815	568	1814
569	1817	570	1816	571	1819	572	1818
573	1821	574	1820	575	1823	576	1822
577	1825	578	1824	579	1827	580	1826
581	1829	582	1828	583	1831	584	1830
585	1901	586	1900	587	1903	588	1902
589	1905	590	1904	591	1907	592	1906
593	1909	594	1908	595	1911	596	1910
597	1913	598	1912	599	1915	600	1914
601	1917	602	1916	603	1919	604	1918
605	1921	606	1920	607	1923	608	1922
609	1925	610	1924	611	1927	612	1926
613	1929	614	1928	615	1931	616	1930
617	2001	618	2000	619	2003	620	2002
621	2005	622	2004	623	2007	624	2006
625	2009	626	2008	627	2011	628	2010
629	2013	630	2012	631	2015	632	2014
633	2017	634	2016	635	2019	636	2018
637	2021	638	2020	639	2023	640	2022

SACRAMENTO STREET NUMBERS BEFORE & AFTER 1880
House numbering **LETTERED Streets**
EVEN (South Side), ODD (North Side)

old	new	old	new	old	new	old	new
641	2025	642	2024	643	2027	644	2026
645	2029	646	2028	647	2031	648	2030
649	2101	650	2100	651	2103	652	2102
653	2105	654	2104	655	2107	656	2106
657	2109	658	2108	659	2111	660	2110
661	2113	662	2112	663	2115	664	2114
665	2117	666	2116	667	2119	668	2118
669	2121	670	2120	671	2123	672	2122
673	2125	674	2124	675	2127	676	2126
677	2129	678	2128	679	2131	680	2130
681	2201	682	2200	683	2203	684	2202
685	2205	686	2204	687	2207	688	2206
689	2209	690	2208	691	2211	692	2210
693	2213	694	2212	695	2215	696	2214
697	2217	698	2216	699	2219	700	2218
701	2221	702	2220	703	2223	704	2222
705	2225	706	2224	707	2227	708	2226
709	2229	710	2228	711	2231	712	2230
713	2301	714	2300	715	2303	716	2302
717	2305	718	2304	719	2307	720	2306
721	2309	722	2308	723	2311	724	2310
725	2313	726	2312	727	2315	728	2314
729	2317	730	2316	731	2319	732	2318
733	2321	734	2320	735	2323	736	2322
737	2325	738	2324	739	2327	740	2326
741	2329	742	2328	743	2331	744	2330
745	2401	746	2400	747	2403	748	2402
749	2405	750	2404	751	2407	752	2406
753	2409	754	2408	755	2411	756	2410
757	2413	758	2412	759	2415	760	2414
761	2417	762	2416	763	2519	764	2418
765	2421	766	2420	767	2523	768	2422
769	2425	770	2424	771	2527	772	2426
773	2429	774	2428	775	2531	776	2430
777	2501	778	2500	779	2503	780	2502
781	2505	782	2504	783	2507	784	2506
785	2509	786	2508	787	2511	788	2510
789	2513	790	2512	791	2515	792	2514
793	2517	794	2516	795	2519	796	2518
797	2521	798	2520	799	2523	800	2522

SACRAMENTO STREET NUMBERS BEFORE & AFTER 1880
House numbering   **LETTERED Streets**
EVEN (South Side), ODD (North Side)

old	new	old	new	old	new	old	new
801	2525	802	2524	803	2527	804	2526
805	2529	806	2528	807	2531	808	2530
809	2601	810	2600	811	2603	812	2602
813	2605	814	2604	815	2607	816	2606
817	2609	818	2608	819	2611	820	2610
821	2613	822	2612	823	2615	824	2614
825	2617	826	2616	827	2619	828	2618
829	2621	830	2620	831	2623	832	2622
833	2625	834	2624	835	2627	836	2626
837	2629	838	2628	839	2631	840	2630
841	2701	842	2700	843	2703	844	2702
845	2705	846	2704	847	2707	848	2706
849	2709	850	2708	851	2711	852	2710
853	2713	854	2712	855	2715	856	2714
857	2717	858	2716	859	2719	860	2718
861	2721	862	2720	863	2723	864	2722
865	2725	866	2724	867	2727	868	2726
869	2729	870	2728	871	2731	872	2730
873	2801	874	2800	875	2803	876	2802
877	2805	878	2804	879	2807	880	2806
881	2809	882	2808	883	2811	884	2810
885	2813	886	2812	887	2815	888	2814
889	2817	890	2816	891	2819	892	2818
893	2821	894	2820	895	2823	896	2822
897	2825	898	2824	899	2827	900	2826
901	2829	902	2828	903	2831	904	2830
905	2901	906	2900	907	2903	908	2902
909	2905	910	2904	911	2907	912	2906
913	2909	914	2908	915	2911	916	2910
917	2913	918	2912	919	2915	920	2914
921	2917	922	2916	923	2919	924	2918
925	2921	926	2920	927	2923	928	2922
929	2925	930	2924	931	2927	932	2926
933	2929	934	2928	935	2931	936	2930
937	3001	938	3000	939	3003	940	3002
941	3005	942	3004	943	3007	944	3006
945	3009	946	3008	947	3011	948	3010
949	3013	950	3012	951	3015	952	3014
953	3017	954	3016	955	3019	956	3018
957	3021	958	3020	959	3023	960	3022

House numbering, **NUMBERED Streets**

SOUTH of I St., ODD (East Side) EVEN (West Side)

old	new	old	new	old	new	old	new	old	new
				I Street					
1	**901**	2	**900**	3	**903**	4	**902**	5	**905**
6	**904**	7	**907**	8	**906**	9	**909**	10	**908**
11	**911**	12	**910**	13	**913**	14	**912**	15	**915**
16	**914**	17	**917**	18	**916**	19	**919**	20	**918**
21	**921**	22	**920**	23	**923**	24	**922**	25	**925**
26	**924**	27	**927**	28	**926**	29	**929**	30	**928**
31	**931**	32	**930**	**J Street**					
33	**1001**	34	**1000**	35	**1003**	36	**1002**	37	**1005**
38	**1004**	39	**1007**	40	**1006**	41	**1009**	42	**1008**
43	**1011**	44	**1010**	45	**1013**	46	**1012**	47	**1015**
48	**1014**	49	**1017**	50	**1016**	51	**1019**	52	**1018**
53	**1021**	54	**1020**	55	**1023**	56	**1022**	57	**1025**
58	**1024**	59	**1027**	60	**1026**	61	**1029**	62	**1028**
63	**1031**	64	**1030**	**K Street**					
65	**1101**	66	**1100**	67	**1103**	68	**1102**	69	**1105**
70	**1104**	71	**1107**	72	**1106**	73	**1109**	74	**1108**
75	**1111**	76	**1110**	77	**1113**	78	**1112**	79	**1115**
80	**1114**	81	**1117**	82	**1116**	83	**1119**	84	**1118**
85	**1121**	86	**1120**	87	**1123**	88	**1122**	89	**1125**
90	**1124**	91	**1127**	92	**1126**	93	**1129**	94	**1128**
95	**1131**	96	**1130**	**L Street**					
97	**1201**	98	**1200**	99	**1203**	100	**1202**	101	**1205**
102	**1204**	103	**1207**	104	**1206**	105	**1209**	106	**1208**
107	**1211**	108	**1210**	109	**1213**	110	**1212**	111	**1215**
112	**1214**	113	**1217**	114	**1216**	115	**1219**	116	**1218**
117	**1221**	118	**1220**	119	**1223**	120	**1222**	121	**1225**
122	**1224**	123	**1227**	124	**1226**	125	**1229**	126	**1228**
127	**1231**	128	**1230**	**M Street** (Now Capitol Ave.)					
129	**1301**	130	**1300**	131	**1303**	132	**1302**	133	**1305**
134	**1304**	135	**1307**	136	**1306**	137	**1309**	138	**1308**
139	**1311**	140	**1310**	141	**1313**	142	**1312**	143	**1315**
144	**1314**	145	**1317**	146	**1316**	147	**1319**	148	**1318**
149	**1321**	150	**1320**	151	**1323**	152	**1322**	153	**1325**
154	**1324**	155	**1327**	156	**1326**	157	**1329**	158	**1328**
159	**1331**	160	**1330**	**N Street**					
161	**1401**	162	**1400**	163	**1403**	164	**1402**	165	**1405**
166	**1404**	167	**1407**	168	**1406**	169	**1409**	170	**1408**
171	**1411**	172	**1410**	173	**1413**	174	**1412**	175	**1415**
176	**1414**	177	**1417**	178	**1416**	179	**1419**	180	**1418**

SACRAMENTO STREET NUMBERS BEFORE & AFTER 1880
House numbering, **NUMBERED Streets**
SOUTH of I St., ODD (East Side) EVEN (West Side)

old	new	old	new	old	new	old	new	old	new
				N Street (Continued)					
181	**1421**	182	**1420**	183	**1423**	184	**1422**	185	**1425**
186	**1424**	187	**1427**	188	**1426**	189	**1429**	190	**1428**
191	**1431**	192	**1430**	**O Street**					
193	**1501**	194	**1500**	195	**1503**	196	**1502**	197	**1505**
198	**1504**	199	**1507**	200	**1506**	201	**1509**	202	**1508**
203	**1511**	204	**1510**	205	**1513**	206	**1512**	207	**1515**
208	**1514**	209	**1517**	210	**1516**	211	**1519**	212	**1518**
213	**1521**	214	**1520**	215	**1523**	216	**1522**	217	**1525**
218	**1524**	219	**1527**	220	**1526**	221	**1529**	222	**1528**
223	**1531**	224	**1530**	**P Street**					
225	**1601**	226	**1600**	227	**1603**	228	**1602**	229	**1605**
230	**1604**	231	**1607**	232	**1606**	233	**1609**	234	**1608**
235	**1611**	236	**1610**	237	**1613**	238	**1612**	239	**1615**
240	**1614**	241	**1617**	242	**1616**	243	**1619**	244	**1618**
245	**1621**	246	**1620**	247	**1623**	248	**1622**	249	**1625**
250	**1624**	251	**1627**	252	**1626**	253	**1629**	254	**1628**
255	**1631**	256	**1630**	**Q Street**					
257	**1701**	258	**1700**	259	**1703**	260	**1702**	261	**1705**
262	**1704**	263	**1707**	264	**1706**	265	**1709**	266	**1708**
267	**1711**	268	**1710**	269	**1713**	270	**1712**	271	**1715**
272	**1714**	273	**1717**	274	**1716**	275	**1719**	276	**1718**
277	**1721**	278	**1720**	279	**1723**	280	**1722**	281	**1725**
282	**1724**	283	**1727**	284	**1726**	285	**1729**	286	**1728**
287	**1731**	288	**1730**	**R Street**					
289	**1801**	290	**1800**	291	**1803**	292	**1804**	293	**1805**
294	**1804**	295	**1807**	296	**1806**	297	**1811**	298	**1808**
299	**1811**	300	**1810**	301	**1813**	302	**1814**	303	**1815**
304	**1814**	305	**1817**	306	**1816**	307	**1821**	308	**1818**
309	**1821**	310	**1820**	311	**1823**	312	**1824**	313	**1825**
314	**1824**	315	**1827**	316	**1826**	317	**1831**	318	**1828**
319	**1831**	320	**1830**	**S Street**					
321	**1901**	322	**1900**	323	**1903**	324	**1902**	325	**1905**
326	**1904**	327	**1907**	328	**1906**	329	**1909**	330	**1908**
331	**1911**	332	**1910**	333	**1913**	334	**1912**	335	**1915**
336	**1914**	337	**1917**	338	**1916**	339	**1919**	340	**1918**
341	**1921**	342	**1920**	343	**1923**	344	**1922**	345	**1925**
346	**1924**	347	**1927**	348	**1926**	349	**1929**	350	**1928**
351	**1931**	352	**1930**	**T Street**					

old	new	old	new	old	new	old	new	old	new
				T Street					
353	**2001**	354	**2000**	355	**2003**	356	**2002**	357	**2005**
358	**2004**	359	**2007**	360	**2006**	361	**2009**	362	**2008**
363	**2011**	364	**2010**	365	**2013**	366	**2012**	367	**2015**
368	**2014**	369	**2017**	370	**2016**	371	**2019**	372	**2018**
373	**2021**	374	**2020**	375	**2023**	376	**2022**	377	**2025**
378	**2024**	379	**2027**	380	**2026**	381	**2029**	382	**2028**
383	**2031**	384	**2030**	**U Street**					
385	**2101**	386	**2100**	387	**2103**	388	**2102**	389	**2105**
390	**2104**	391	**2107**	392	**2106**	393	**2109**	394	**2108**
395	**2111**	396	**2110**	397	**2113**	398	**2112**	399	**2115**
400	**2114**	401	**2117**	402	**2116**	403	**2119**	404	**2118**
405	**2121**	406	**2120**	407	**2123**	408	**2122**	409	**2125**
410	**2124**	411	**2127**	412	**2126**	413	**2129**	414	**2128**
415	**2131**	416	**2130**	**V Street**					
417	**2201**	418	**2200**	419	**2203**	420	**2202**	421	**2205**
422	**2204**	423	**2207**	424	**2206**	425	**2209**	426	**2208**
427	**2211**	428	**2210**	429	**2213**	430	**2212**	431	**2215**
432	**2214**	433	**2217**	434	**2216**	435	**2219**	436	**2218**
437	**2221**	438	**2220**	439	**2223**	440	**2222**	441	**2225**
442	**2224**	443	**2227**	444	**2226**	445	**2229**	446	**2228**
447	**2231**	448	**2230**	**W Street**					
449	**2301**	450	**2300**	451	**2303**	452	**2302**	453	**2305**
454	**2304**	455	**2307**	456	**2306**	457	**2309**	458	**2308**
459	**2311**	460	**2310**	461	**2313**	462	**2312**	463	**2315**
464	**2314**	465	**2317**	466	**2316**	467	**2319**	468	**2318**
469	**2321**	470	**2320**	471	**2323**	472	**2322**	473	**2325**
474	**2324**	475	**2327**	476	**2326**	477	**2329**	478	**2328**
479	**2331**	480	**2330**	**X Street**					
481	**2401**	482	**2400**	483	**2403**	484	**2402**	485	**2405**
486	**2404**	487	**2407**	488	**2406**	489	**2409**	490	**2408**
491	**2411**	492	**2410**	493	**2413**	494	**2412**	495	**2415**
496	**2414**	497	**2417**	498	**2416**	499	**2419**	500	**2418**
501	**2421**	502	**2420**	503	**2423**	504	**2422**	505	**2425**
506	**2424**	507	**2427**	508	**2426**	509	**2429**	510	**2428**
511	**2431**	512	**2430**						

Y Street (Now Broadway)

SACRAMENTO STREET NUMBERS BEFORE & AFTER 1880
House numbering, **NUMBERED Streets**
NORTH of I St., ODD (East Side) EVEN (West Side)

old	new	old	new	old	new	old	new	old	new
				| **I Street**					
1	831	2	830	3	829	4	828	5	827
6	826	7	825	8	824	9	823	10	822
11	821	12	820	13	819	14	818	15	817
16	816	17	815	18	814	19	813	20	812
21	811	22	810	23	809	24	808	25	807
26	806	27	805	28	804	29	803	30	802
31	801	32	800	**H Street**					
33	731	34	730	35	729	36	728	37	727
38	726	39	725	40	724	41	723	42	722
43	721	44	720	45	719	46	718	47	717
48	716	49	715	50	714	51	713	52	712
53	711	54	710	55	709	56	708	57	707
58	706	59	705	60	704	61	703	62	702
63	701	64	700	**G Street**					
65	631	66	630	67	629	68	628	69	627
70	626	71	625	72	624	73	623	74	622
75	621	76	620	77	619	78	618	79	617
80	616	81	615	82	614	83	613	84	612
85	611	86	610	87	609	88	608	89	607
90	606	91	605	92	604	93	603	94	602
95	601	96	600	**F Street**					
97	531	98	530	99	529	100	528	101	527
102	526	103	525	104	524	105	523	106	522
107	521	108	520	109	519	110	518	111	517
112	516	113	515	114	514	115	513	116	512
117	511	118	510	119	509	120	508	121	507
122	506	123	505	124	504	125	503	126	502
127	501	128	500	**E Street**					
129	431	130	430	131	429	132	428	133	427
134	426	135	425	136	424	137	423	138	422
139	421	140	420	141	419	142	418	143	417
144	416	145	415	146	414	147	413	148	412
149	411	150	410	151	409	152	408	153	407
154	406	155	405	156	404	157	403	158	402
159	401	160	400	**D Street**					

Since no old addresses north of D Street are in the 1851 Sacramento Directory, conversions for such address numbers are not listed here.

REPRODUCTION OF CULVER'S 1851 DIRECTORY

As mentioned earlier, Culver's small work measuring 4 x 6 inches, and containing 96 pages is the first book printed in Sacramento, as well as the first city directory on the Pacific Coast to use street address numbers. It was issued in a paper wrapper imprinted on the outside of the front and back. The eight-page signatures were folded, and sewn through two holes in the face of the pages near the gutter (inner fold) with a single strand of thread, tied off with a bow knot. The first page of each signature (excepting the first which was easily identified by the title page) was imprinted with an upper case letter at the bottom. These appear as *B* on page 9, *C* on page 17 and so forth. These allowed the binder to re-assemble the pages in proper order without looking at individual page numbers and were particularly important in a book with blank, unnumbered pages. The printer probably used paper measuring about 10 x 19 inches to produce the book and they regularly published a newspaper 18 x 22 inches. If the news print were an inch over size, half-sheets would have been just right for the book, or it could have been printed two signatures at a time and cut afterward.

The buyer could have it bound in a better cover which involved sewing with multiple stitches through the gutters of all the 12 signatures and gluing on the spine and cover. The single strand of cross-sewn thread and the wrappers would normally be discarded. The fold at the top of each signature could be neatly trimmed at the bindery or left for the owner to slit with a knife. If the binding were done later when the book was already a historical treasure, it was common to save the wrapper and either bind it in, or paste the front part inside the front cover and the back part inside the back cover.

No record has been found of the number of copies originally sold, but the directory's great rarity (4 copies known, all in major libraries) may well be due to it's instant popularity and use as issued, in the fragile paper wrapper held together with a single thread. Losses in Sacramento fires and floods during the 1850s also reduced the supply. The printer of this work was the Sacramento *Transcript*, established on April 1, 1850, where Ferdinand Cartwright Ewer was the literary editor. He apparently realized the importance of the directory because he saved a copy and donated it to Harvard University, August 30, 1859. F. C. Ewer's biography appears on page 117.

The directory has been reproduced by photographing the original pages with an enlargement of 42%, making them much easier to read. In seeking a name in this directory, the reader should realize

that Culver was rather casual about alphabetical order after the first
two letters of a name. It appears that he kept cards or a book arranged
alphabetically and then entered names in the proper sections when he
visited an area of the city. He probably meant to later sort them out
within each section, but was prohibited by the press of time. Culver
also made a great effort to use street addresses, but as he moved away
from the center of the city, this became difficult. He was after all, an
author and an auctioneer — not a mathematician and surveyor.

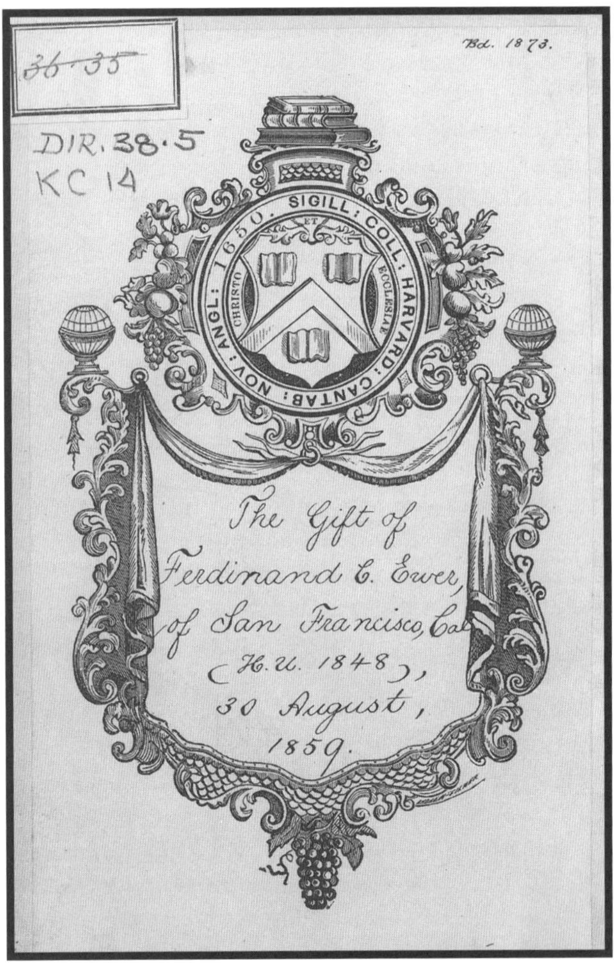

Bookplate in Harvard copy of Horace Culver's
1851 Sacramento Directory
Courtesy Houghton Library, Harvard University

THE

SACRAMENTO

CITY DIRECTORY:

BY

J. HORACE CULVER.

JANUARY 1, 1851.

SACRAMENTO CITY:

TRANSCRIPT PRESS, K ST., BETWEEN SECOND AND THIRD.

1851.

195

COUNTING-HOUSE ALMANAC:

FOR THE YEAR

1851.

	Sund'y	Mond.	Tuesd.	Wedn.	Thurs.	Frid'y.	Sat'r.	SUN rises	SUN sets
JAN'Y.	..	..	..	1	2	3	4	7 20	4 40
	5	6	7	8	9	10	11	7 16	4 44
	12	13	14	15	16	17	18	7 11	4 49
	19	20	21	22	23	24	25	7 5	4 55
	26	27	28	29	30	31	..	6 59	5 1
FEB'Y.	..	..	..	..	..	..	1	6 58	5 2
	2	3	4	5	6	7	8	6 51	5 9
	9	10	11	12	13	14	15	6 42	5 18
	16	17	18	19	20	21	22	6 35	5 25
	23	24	25	26	27	28	..	6 27	5 33
MARCH.	..	..	..	..	..	..	1	6 25	5 35
	2	3	4	5	6	7	8	6 16	5 44
	9	10	11	12	13	14	15	6 7	5 53
	16	17	18	19	20	21	22	5 58	6 2
	23	24	25	26	27	28	29	5 49	6 11
	30	31	..	..	..	..	..	5 47	6 13
APRIL.	..	..	1	2	3	4	5	5 41	6 19
	6	7	8	9	10	11	12	5 32	6 28
	13	14	15	16	17	18	19	5 23	6 27
	20	21	22	23	24	25	26	5 15	6 45
	27	28	29	30	..	..	..	5 11	6 49
MAY.	..	..	..	..	1	2	3	5 8	6 52
	4	5	6	7	8	9	10	5 0	7 0
	11	12	13	14	15	16	17	4 54	7 6
	18	19	20	21	22	23	24	4 48	7 12
	25	26	27	28	29	30	31	4 44	7 16
JUNE.	1	2	3	4	5	6	7	4 40	7 20
	8	9	10	11	12	13	14	4 38	7 22
	15	16	17	18	19	20	21	4 37	7 23
	22	23	24	25	26	27	28	4 39	7 21
	29	30	..	..	..	..	..	4 39	7 21

	Sund'y	Mond.	Tuesd.	Wedn.	Thurs.	Frid'y.	Sat'r.	SUN rises	SUN sets
JULY.	..	..	1	2	3	4	5	4 40	7 20
	6	7	8	9	10	11	12	4 43	7 17
	13	14	15	16	17	18	19	4 48	7 12
	20	21	22	23	24	25	26	4 53	7 7
	27	28	29	30	31	..	..	4 57	7 3
AUG.	..	..	..	..	..	1	2	4 59	7 1
	3	4	5	6	7	8	9	5 6	6 54
	10	11	12	13	14	15	16	5 14	6 46
	17	18	19	20	21	22	23	5 22	6 38
	24	25	26	27	28	29	30	5 30	6 30
	31	..	..	..	..	..	..	5 31	6 29
SEPT.	..	1	2	3	4	5	6	5 38	6 22
	7	8	9	10	11	12	13	5 47	6 13
	14	15	16	17	18	19	20	5 56	6 4
	21	22	23	24	25	26	27	6 5	5 55
	28	29	30	..	..	..	..	6 9	5 51
OCT.	..	..	..	1	2	3	4	6 14	5 46
	5	6	7	8	9	10	11	6 23	5 37
	12	13	14	15	16	17	18	6 31	5 29
	19	20	21	22	23	24	25	6 40	5 20
	26	27	28	29	30	31	..	6 47	5 13
NOV.	..	..	..	..	..	..	1	6 48	5 12
	2	3	4	5	6	7	8	6 56	5 4
	9	10	11	12	13	14	15	7 3	4 57
	16	17	18	19	20	21	22	7 9	4 51
	23	24	25	26	27	28	29	7 14	4 46
	30	..	..	..	..	..	..	7 15	4 45
DEC.	..	1	2	3	4	5	6	7 19	4 41
	7	8	9	10	11	12	13	7 22	4 38
	14	15	16	17	18	19	20	7 23	4 37
	21	22	23	24	25	26	27	7 22	4 38
	28	29	30	31	..	..	..	7 21	4 39

PREFACE.

The "Directory of Sacramento" is a work that has been prepared for the press with the hope that it will be a source of valuable information, from which all may glean something of profit. The utmost care and attention have been paid in its compilation, in order that it may be made as correct as possible. In a City like Sacramento, where whole blocks of buildings are erected in the course of a single week, and where Merchants change their location monthly, it cannot be expected that the same degree of accuracy will prevail as marks works of a like character in old and established cities.

The publisher has devoted much time and feels conscious of having done his duty, as far as the work goes, but he does not claim that completeness which is so necessary for a work of this nature.

With the conviction that it will be a useful book of reference to our own citizens as well as strangers, the author sends it forth, depending alone on the merits of the work for a compensation for his labor.

Note.—There are but few abbreviations but that will be easily understood. As b for between, &c. Where a firm follows a single name, it is understood that the person named either composes a part of the firm or is engaged in the house.

DIRECTORY

ABBEY, RUSSELL, at Buckley & Co's.
Abrams, Lewis, Burnett House.
Adams, W R, at Wolf, Gallop & Co's.
Albarez, Manuel, Bar-keeper, Orleans House.
Alderman, White, Whitman & Co., Auction and Commission Merchants, 136 J street.
Alderman, Geo., at Alderman, White, Whitman & Co's.
Alderman, E G,   do   do   do   do
Alexandria, James, No 11, 2d st.
Aldrich, Lewis, Lawyer, Tweed, A & Peden.
Alexander, A W, Fancy store, 138 J st.
Alderman & White, Merchants, 150 J st.
Alderman & Whitman, Merchants, 152 J st.
Allen & Redding, Hotel, 245 J st.
Allison, R, Boarding house, J b 14 and 15 st.
Allison, Wm, Blacksmith, 24, 4th st.
Allen, Wm, Carman, 44, 4th st.
Aldrich, David W, 78, J st. up stairs.
Alswite, Coorier & Jillett, Coffee-house, 32 front st.
Ames, Dr F W, office, 66 J st.
Amberg, M, at J Chenoweth's·
Ames, C M, Lumber merchant corner M and 2d.
Ames, A C, at C M Ames'.
Anderson & Co, J G, Tinner, 78 J st.
Andariese, Dr, office 93 J st.
Andrew & Carpenter, Blacksmiths 58, 4th.
Appleman & Brother, merchants 139 K st.

Appleman, H, at A & Brother.
Appleman, R B,   do
Arents & Co, H, merchants 229 J st.
Arents, Wm, at H Arents & co's·
Arnold, Wm, boarding house I b 10th and 11th.
Armstrong, Ed J, Columbia Hotel 21, 2d.
Arbaugh, Peter, at J W Pugh's.
Arnold & Pennybaker, Hawk-Eye house 148 K st.
Arnold, Geo W, at A & Pennybaker's.
Ashley & Howes, Blacksmiths 205 J st.
Ashley, Wm, at Siles A & co's.
Atkins, H B, No 9 J st.
Atkins, Rob't, boarding house 70 front st.
Angur, Jas S, Restaurant 19 K st.
Ault, Dr A T, at Williams & A.
Avery, Jno W, at J B Silsby & co's.
Avery & Grows, Lumber merchants 257 J st.
BARNEY, BLOSSOM & Co, Merchants 41, 2d st.
Barney, B B, at B. Blossom & co's.
Baker, S, clothier 22 J st.
Baker, J P, at Flint & Baker's.
Ball, Dr J, Dentist 105 J st.
Bankhead, S P, Lawyer 80 J st.
Baker, Farr & Co, Merchants 118 J st.
Baker, M A, at B, Farr & co's.
Baker, J S, at   do   do
Batters & Creegan, Tinners 133 J st.
Bailie, Dr Thos B, Druggist 157 J st.
Baker, E G, Tinner 180 J st.
Ball & Wells, Missouri house 252 J st.
Barns & Spotts, boarding house 324 J st.
Bailey, Peter, boarding house K b 9th and 10th.
Ball, Martin, boarding house 44, 5th st.
Barber, E L, Engineer 57 J st.
Bartels, F, boarding house 36 K st.
Ballou, Almanda, at White & B's.
Barker, Dr R D, office Galt house.

Barton & Boulden, Commission merchants No 40 front st.
Balchelder, D F, at Smith & B's.
Bay, Dr J W, office 3d b L and M.
Babson, Seth, blind manufactory b 2d and 3d, L and M.
Barker & Long, Galt house K b 3d and 4th.
Ben, Oppenheimer, Zinser & Kremer, clothiers 32 & 94 J st.
Benneson, W H, Lawyer 105 J st.
Bewley, C W, Cal Trading co. 129 J st.
Bensti, E, Clothier 130 J st.
Bennsee, A, Orleans house 181 J st.
Bercaw, Wm M, Cooper 221 J st.
Beckley, L R, boarding house J b 17th and 18th.
Benson, H, Chicago house 7th b J and K.
Beatson, D, laborer 15 I st.
Benett, E L, boarding house cor I and 10th.
Beals, Dr H H, office 96 J st.
Bell, Dr R, office 55 J st.
Bensley, Jno, at Starr, B & co.
Bearns & Co, merchants 5 K st.
Bearns, F J, at Bearns & co.
Bearns, H M, at Bearns & co.
Bell, G W, Land agent cor K and 3d.
Beaumdrain, Dr J G, office 28, 3d st.
Bernes & Dinsmore, Atlantic house 82 J st.
Birdsall & Co, S B, merchants cor J and 3d.
Birdsall, Dr L A, county Recorder and Auditor office 34, 2d.
Biscoe, W F, at Watson & B.
Binninger, J, 4th st house 49, 4th st.
Birch, J, stage proprietor 36 front st.
Billings, Dr E J, Columbia Hotel.
Binney, A J, Engineer 51, 2d st.
Bigler, Jno, Lawyer 3d b L and M.
Bilengs, Stephen, at Wick & Spink's.
Bliss, D H, Gregory's Express No 1 J st.
Bloom, Herman, No 14 J st.
Blumenthal, M A, Fancy store 124 J st.
Black, Jno, at Jaqua & B.
B

Blossom, J H, Barney, B & co.
Blanchard, Jas, Carpenter front above sycamore.
Blackway, C H, Tinner at Canon & Kempt.
Blair, J D, Ward & B.
Blair, Henry, Ringold hotel 42, 3d st.
Blunt, L, Moreland, B & Smith.
Booth, L A, Forshee & Reynolds.
Booth, L M, Lawyer 105 J st.
Bond & Co, E, Boston bakery, 9, 4th st.
Bogart, S B, Trader I b 4th and 5th.
Booz, Mrs M A. between J and K and 4th and 5th.
Boyington, C C. Grocer, Front street, b I and Broad.
Boller, Geo. Baker, 79 Front street.
Bowers, S L. Meat Market, 108 K street.
Boone, Dr J T. office 187 J street.
Bornholt, C. Butcher, 154 K street.
Brannon, M. No. 2, J street.
Bricker, Myers & Co., Winslow's Exchange, 50 J street.
Bray, J G. at Bullard, Figg & Co.'s.
Bradley, John, Clothier, 88 J street.
Browder, Thos. Jenny Lind House, 77 J street,
Brown, Henry & Co., Merchants, 89 J street.
Brown, Robert T., at Brown, Henry & Co.'s.
Bramsky, M A. Clothier, 126 J street.
Brown, Edward J. at A J Downer & Co.
Brown, Samuel, Grocer, 253 J street.
Bradley, Wm. at Proctor & B's.
Brugier, Adolpha Restaurant, 270 J street.
Brock, J M. at Terhune, Edwards & Co.'s.
Breitenstein, Wm. at Ochsner & Co's.
Briggs, Blacksmith, 293 J street.
Brockway, Chas. Merchant, cor K and 11th street.
Brown, Edward, Maine House, K b 9th and 10th.
Briggs, Rev M C., cor L and 7th.
Brown, W G., residence 6th, between H and I.
Brown, Dr. residence H street, b 8th and 9th.
Brothers, Hort, Importers, 6 Front street.

Brown, P J. Grocer, 25 Front street.
Brigham, S. Otis, Commission Merchant, 38 Front st.
Brooks, & Co. J W. Merchants, 39 Front street.
Brown, William, at Jennings & co's.
Brownell, Romer & Roller, Butchers, 40 2d street.
Brownell, Stephen, at B. R. and co's.
Brastow & Co., Lumber Dealers, 2d street, b M and N.
Brastow H B. at B. and co's.
Breen, R. Wagon Maker, 42 6th street.
Brown, J K. cleik, at J B Milliken's.
Burns, A. butcher, 20 J street.
Burnam Dr A J. at Price and B's.
Bullard, Figg & co., Merchants, 64 J street.
Butcher, Robert H. at James Haworth's.
Burnett, Edwards & Gass, Lawyers, 115 J street.
Burnett, P H. at B. Edwards & Gass, 115 J street.
Burton, G R. California Trading co., 129 J street.
Burton C H. at Whitfield, Venable & co's.
Buckley & co., merchants, 130 J street.
Budget & co., A. clothiers, 155 J street.
Butler, John O. Tremont House, 184 J street.
Burrell, Dr Charles, office 175 J street.
Burdick & Lawrence, merchants, 202 J street.
Burdick, H J. at B. & Lawrence's.
Burk, Seth, at H A Fairman & Co's.
Butterfield, R. residence I street, b 8th and 9th.
Burk, Margaret, washer, 21 5th street.
Burge, R K. foreman at Orton & Hoy's.
Burk & co., S W. grocers, 24 Front street.
Buckley & Dodd, painters, 58 2d street.
Buckley, D. at B. & Dodd's.
Buffum, John W. b 3d and 4th, and L and M.
Bullock, D D. Magistrate, 134 K street.
Burnett, P W, carpenter M street, b 1st and 2d.
Byers, John, Abbey, 170 J street.
Campbell, Barber, 24 J st.
Carpenter, A D, Titcomb, Sampson & co.

California Trading Co, No 129 J st.
Carrall & Staring, merchants 116 J st.
Caskel, Jos, clothier 157 J st.
Caswell, Harvey, Caswell, Ingalls & co.
Canfield, W C, Crane & co.
Cadwalader, Geo, J W Foard & co.
Campbell & Hay, Bakers, 295 J st.
Carman, T, Milwaukie house J b 15th and 16th.
Cannon & Kempt, Tinners 98 J st.
Casada, M, Penola house 7 b I and J.
Camfield & Co, W D, Soda manufactory front b I & Broad.
Cary, R D, Sac Steam Mills corner of union and front sts.
Cavert, Hill & Co, Merchants 53 front.
Carswell, Priscilla, Flor de la Mar.
Carpenter, Dr W M, office 49. 2d st.
Carter, Wm, clerk for J B Milliken.
Chapman, W O, N York Lunch 16 J st.
Chrysup, W L, McGowan & co Oregon saloon.
Churchman, J, Lawyer 72 J st.
Chatburn, Richard, Daguerrean 139 J st.
Chedic, G W, at H Arents & co.
Chenoworth, J, Grocer 303 J st.
Chaffey, M, boarding house 134 K st.
Chamberlain, W E, Merchant L b 7th and 8th.
Chappell, M, silk and cloth dyer I b 3d and 4th.
Chandler, Josiah, Lawyer I b 5th and 6th.
Chenery, Richard, cor M and front sts.
Childs, S B, carpenter 39 K st.
Chesley, W, mason 59 K st.
Chapman, S at Wibans, Jacobs & co.
Chaoltier, Jno, Eating house 29 front st.
Chatterton, Jno, at Smith Ells.
Chase, R H, Engineer 51, 2d st.
Chesley, G W Auctioneer 150 K st.
Chesebrough, A, Grocer 49, 6th st.
Chesebrough, H D, Grocer 49, 6th st.
Clark, Geo E, agent for Gregory's express office No 1 J st.

Clover & Winchell, Lawyers 118 J st.
Clark, J D, barber 144 J st.
Clift, Amos, Folger & Clift.
Clark, G W, merchant 210 J st.
Clark, Lewis, Hotel 314 J st.
Clark, Henry, boarding house K b 10th and 11th.
Cleal, Jno G, County surveyor 44, 5th st.
Clark, Lyman, Restaurant 15 K st
Clark, Alex, Printer Transcript office.
Clark, Horace, carpenter J March.
Clark & Milne, Auction and com merchants 34 front st.
Clark, J H, C & Milne.
Clement, Andrew, blacksmith 3d b K and L.
Clarke, Henry A, Interpreter 123 K st.
Cone, Robert, tinner 60, 2d st.
Cover & Green, blacksmiths 58, 6th st.
Cook, Jos, Restaurant 187 K st.
Cochran, Chas, jeweler 150 K st.
Collins, Dr M G, Crescent city hotel.
Conradi, A H, Hole in the Wall.
Cogswell, J A, Missouri hotel.
Cohan & Green, clothiers 95 J st.
Cook & Pomeroy, Jenny Lind 113 J st.
Cook, L D, at C & Pomeroy.
Courtois & Co, B, Fancy Store 121 J st.
Coonrod & Gillig, tinners 154 J st.
Coffin, Mark, cooper 141 J st.
Cole, Jno, at Fulkerson, Cole & co's.
Cole, N W, carpenter 192 J st.
Cooledge & Co, W S, merchants 169 J st.
Conley, Jno A, Union hotel.
Conrad, S, boarding house 230 J st.
Comstock, W, Mansfield house.
Conger, Thos, Conger house cor K and 10th.
Coulter, A, Laundryman 5th b K and L.
Coody, Mrs S, boarding house 72, 4th st.
Collins, George, cooper 21 I st.

Cook, John, market 1 b 3d and 4th.
Comstock, Geo, trader I b 4th and 5th.
Conduitte, Dr Thos J, merchant 10th b I and J.
Cotting & Co, H P, grocer 11 K st.
Coleman, Jas W, merchant 3d b J and K.
Cochran, Jno L, confectioner 40 K st.
Cook, Lyman, at Pugh, C & co's.
Conklin, Geo W, Florence restaurant.
Court, Job, Printer Transcript office.
Comins, P B, gunsmith 57 K st.
Coleman, S T, at Sisson & co's.   [ramento sts.
Cook, Thos E, Sacramento house front b Broad and Sac.
Cornwall, P B, land office 41, 2d ; residence cor L and 2d.
Cornwall, Arthur, 41, 2d st.
Conner & Forrest, booksellers 49, 2d st.
Conner, J W, at C & Forrest.
Coleman & Nelson, restaurant 56, 2d st.
Coleman, T C, at C & Nelson.
Creegan, Jas, at Batters & co.
Craw, A, carman at J Downer & co's.
Crowley, Daniel, Florence restaurant.   [front st.
Crane, L P and S S, druggists 176 J st, 96 K st, and 30
Cronin, Dr E, office 40, 3d st.
Creig & Rayner, N Y hotel 99 K st.
Creig, J B, at C & Rayner.
Cushing, H, Woodcock 15 J st.
Cushing, Edwin, at Jas Hayworth's.
Cummings, Wm, at Hastings & co's.
Curwood, Jos, at 36, 4th st.
Cummin, Geo, blacksmith 46, 5th st.
Cunningham, Noble C, city marshal No 1, 2d st.
Custer, Jno, 21, 3d st.
Cunningham, Theodore, Lawyer, 3, 2d st.
Culver, J H, auctioneer 43, 4th st.
DANIEL, W H, No 3 Eldorado building.
Dangerfield, W P, Lawyer 88 J st.
Daval, J F, Daguerrean 139 J st.

Daval & Chatburn, Daguerreans 139 J st.
Davis, Jas E, Chicago house.
Dannels, Jas, cabinet maker 45, 4th st.
Daniels, S, at E S Youmans & co.
Davis & Jaynes, blacksmiths 7th b I and J.
David, Jno S, at Prugh, Cook & co's.
Dougherty, E C, Fulwiler & D.
Davis, N H, Robinson, D & Ryerson.
Dayley, Jas, 69, 3d st.
Davis, V H, Fleming house 137 K st.
Davis & Co, hay yard 56, 6th st.
Davis, A J, Davis & co.
Dashiell, W A, auctioneer 148 K st.
Defrees, W C, N York Lunch 16 J st.
Dennis, Samuel J, barkeeper Jenny Lind house.
Desrosiers & Co, clothiers 145 J st.
Dennison, B F, Kendall and D.
Denniston, Chas, Restaurant 233 J st.
Deal, Dr W Grove, office 47, 4th st.
Derham & Eaton, Eagle bakery 55, 4th st.
Derham, Jas, D and Eaton.
Demarst, Dr J D office 59 J st.
Deming, Jno F, at H F Labau and co's.
Dewey & Smith, Sutter hotel 37 front st.
Denckis, Chas, barkeeper at Chas Henrich's.
Dickson & Denny, Western market 183 J st.
Deitz & Molenoar, 4th st market 44, 4th st.
Dickey, Maj E, Orleans hotel.
Dlugn, Francis, candle and beer factory 2d b Q and R.
Dozier, Richard, at Pearis and Brockway.
Downer & Co, A J, merchants 188 J st.
Dodson, Dr W B H, office 196 J street.
Doswell, Thos O, Jones and Doswell.
Dupont, J H, boarding house J b 12th and 13th streets.
Dodson, Mrs H, residence H b 6th and 7th streets.
Dosh, Samuel H, Printer Transcript office.
Dodd, W, Buckley and Dodd.

Doward, Geo, corner P and 2d streets.
Dodge, S F, Buckeye house.
Drake & Co, J H, merchants 156 J street.
Deyfuse, Benjamin, Florence restaurant.
Dubroski, A, No 10 J street.
Dunbar, R, Tailor, 74 J street.
Duncombe, Dr C, office 206 J street.
Duncan, M D Chas, residence J b 13th and 14th streets.
Duke, M, residence I b 9th and 10th streets.
Dudley, Charles, Kinney and D.
Dugart, John, Rice and D.
Dunn, Patrick, carpenter, front b R and S.
Duryee, Dr Wm, office 63, 2d street.
Dyer, Samuel, butcher 250 J street.
EATON, FREEMAN, Durham and co.
Eakins, W H, livery stable b I and J, 3d and 4th streets.
Earl, Thomas, 21 3d street.
Eckley, L. at the Pocahontas, 73 J street.
Edwards, P L. lawyer, 115 J street.
Edwards, R D. at Terhune, E. & co's.
Edwards, John, at Haines, Lyon & co's.
Edwards, Mrs. Front street, between Q and R.
Edwards, E R. Tremont Market, 51 3d street.
Ells, Rufus, at Smith & E's.
Ellison, Wm S. Oak Tree Bakery, 113 J street.
Elsbury, Thos. at Sowter & E's.
Emmons & Mann, Buckeye House, 161 K street.
Emmons, H. at E. & Mann's.
English, James L. lawyer, 102 J street.
Easse, Theodore, boarding house, 8 4th street.
Ettling & Pinchowar, clothiers, 20 Front street.
Eveans & Thomas, blacksmiths, J st., b 14th and 15th.
Evens & Hart, painters, 23 3d street.
Evens, Elisha, at E. & Hart's.
Evens, Wm.   do   do
Ewing, Wm. Hay Yatd, J street, b 16th and 17th.
Ewer, F. C. editor of the Transcript, 49 K street.

Ewer, P. F. coroner and port warden, office at the Central Warehouse, Front st., b M and N.
Ewer, W. B. printer, boards at 89, 2d st.
Ewer, C. B.   do   do   do.
Eyre & Wood, stock auction, 162 K street.
Eyre, Ed. E. at E. & Wood's.
FAKE, GEORGE S, Lawyer, 77 J street.
Farr, Volney A, at Baker & co's.
Fairchild, E, at Fulkerson, Cole & co's.
Fairman & Co., H A, merchants, 297 J street.
Faulk, H. at E Wait & Co's.
Farrar & Jones, carpenters, 17 K street.
Farrar, Alexander, at F. & Jones'.
Fay, Pierce & Willis, com merchants, 39 Front street.
Falls, Dr James R. Columbia Hotel, 2d street.
Fash & Co., butchers, 62 2d street.
Feathers, David, boarding house, 7th street, b J and K.
Ferry, W R. clerk, Freeman's Express.
Feris, Dr L. office 34 2d street.
Fella, Plasitos, 2d street, b M and N.
Feidler, Jacob, at Williams & F's.
Feeney, Capt E J. at the Bull's Head.
Feeney & Co Bull's Head Hotel, 127 K street.
Figg, E P. at Bullard, Figg & Co's.
Fish, E N. at R A Knox & Co's.
Fifield & Hoyt, painters, 219 J street.
Fuller & Waldron, paper hangers, 219 J street.
Fitch & McCleery, cabinet makers, 46 4th street.
Fitch, Charles B. at F & McCleery's.
Fitch G K. editor Transcript, 49 K street.
Fisher, Eugene, Cafe de Paris, 31 3d street.
Fitch & Luckett, grocers, 59 2d street.
Fitch, P G. at F & Luckett's.
Flint & Baker, merchants, 41 J street.
Flint, J W. at F & Bakers.
Flagg, C C. commission merchant, 45 6th street.
Floyd, G. blacksmith, M b 1st and 2d.

C

Forshee & Reynolds, merchants, 80 J street.
Foley, James J. Missouri Hotel.
Fogg & Green, merchants, 107 J street.
Foard & Co. J W. merchants, 182 J street.
Folger & Clift, merchants, 222 J street.
Folger R M. at F & Clift's.
Fox, Anthony, at Marsh's boarding house.
Forsyth, Robert, upholsterer, 45 4th street.
Fox, J A. blacksmith, 5th street b I and J.
Ford & Jakes, barbers, 96 J street.
Foote, C A. saddle and harness manufactory, 24 3d street.
Forman, Col F. at Johnson & F's.
Fowler, John S. general agent, 6 2d street.
Forrest, J O. at Conner & F's.
Foote, Arthur W. banker, 55 2d street.
Freeman, Dr E N. office K street, b 5th and 6th.
Freeman, O D. at Reed & Co's.
Fry, G W. at Steele & Co's., 141 J street.
Frisby, William, baker, 145 J street.
Fry, D B. lawyer and notary public, 65 2d street.
Francis, Augustus, & Pierson, Gem, 40 3d street.
Fremont & Phelps, stock yard, 48 6th street.
Fremont, James, at F & Phelps'.
Fulkerson, Cole & Co., merchants, 178 J street.
Fulkerson, J D. at F Cole & Co's.
Fulwiler & Daugherty, butchers, 60 K street.
Fulwiler, Abram, at F & Daugherty's.
GALANT, W. Merchant, 29 J street.
Gass, John H. notary public, 115 J street.
Gaster, John, Wabash House, 199 J street.
Galant, Benjamin, clothier, 149 J street.
Gates, jr., Dr Justin, botanico, 68 K street.
Gay, E. b 2d and 3d and L and M.
Gandy, J. at Rightmire & G's., 164 K street.
Gallop, Josiah, at Woolf, G & Co's.
Garrard, Capt W. at Smith & G's.
Geeseka & Mathewson, Pacific Eating House, 24 J st.

Geiger, Vincent E. trader, Missouri Hotel.
Gillig, John, at Coonrod & G's.
Gibson, Josephine, restaurant, 46 K street.
Glen & Bruce, steam boat agents, corner J and front sts.
Gregory, J W. Express office, 1 J street.
Green, P. at Fogg & G's. 107 J street.
Grosh, Samuel, at J H Drake & Co's.
Grows, W W. at J B Silsby & Co's.
Greenman, Dr M. office 286 J street.
Green, C E. at Hutchinson, G & Co's.
Grow, A. blacksmith, J b 12th and 13th.
Grant, Joseph, auctioneer, J street, b Front and 2d.
Grisse, Joseph, washer, b 2d and 3d, and K and L.
Griffin, J R. Albion House, 157 K street.
Green, T J. at Cover & G's.
Griswell, G. at Wright & G's.
Graden, Thomas, clerk, at O Ludington's.
Gridley George W. auctioneer, 144 K street.
Gregor, William, trader, 144 K street.
Greeley, G W. ship carpenter, 57 K street.
Gulick & Warner, commission merchants, 14 Front st.
HATCH, JOHN, jeweler, 10 J st, resid b 3d and 4th, L and M.
Hatch, John B. clerk, 10 J street.
Hadles, T, silver smith, 10 J street.
Hastings & Co B F. bankers and merchants, 51 J street.
Haswell, D B. at Titcomb, Sampson & Co's.
Harkleroads William, at Lee H & Co's.
Hamelin, Joseph Peter, at Lee, H & Co's.
Harris & Rice, merchants, 96 J street.
Hall, G B. at G W Goodall's.
Haworth, James, tinner, 101 J street.
Harris, L B. at Mrs Warner's.
Hatch, H A. Oak Tree bakery, 113 J street.
Hastings & Co. jewelers, 110 J street.
Hastings, B B. at Hastings & Co's.
Hall, Dr R B. office 164 J street.
Haskell, White & Co. merchants, 231 J street.

Haskell, W L. at H., White & Co's.
Hapnes, Lyon & Co. merchants, corner J and 11th sts.
Hacker, J C. blacksmith, J street, b 13th and 14th.
Harvey, H C. at Hunt & H's.
Hamilton, David, blacksmith, K street, b 9th and 10th.
Hall, P R. Chicago House.
Hahn, J. carpenter, b I and J and 3d and 4th.
Hagan, L. b J and K and 4th and 5th streets.
Hazeltine, C B. corner M and Front streets.
Hammond, Daniel, at Huntington H & Co's.
Hartnett, Michael J. printer, Transcript office, K street.
Hansicker, Charles L.   do   do   do   do
Haines & Stevens, merchants, 55 K street.
Haines, Joseph A. at H & Stevens'.
Hall & Sweet, boarding house, 91 K street.
Hall, James, at H & Sweet's.
Hamilton & Wheaton, grocers, 5 Front street.
Hanna & Bowman, Brannan Hotel, 47 Front street.
Harris, S T. at W Taylor's.
Hart, Thomas, at Evens & H's.
Haywood & Warring, butchers, 30 2d street.
Hagin, J B. at Hill & Smith's.
Haskell, D H. at C M Ames'.
Hanner & Jennings, 3d street, b K and L.
Hayden, D S. lumberman, b 2d and 3d and K and L sts.
Harris & Co, variety store, 107 K street.
Harris, J., at Harris & co's.
Hall, Pierre, grocer, 111 K street.
Hall, M. S., at Davis & co's.
Hammond, W. P., saddle tree manufactory, 79, 6th street.
Hayden, C. C., commission merchant, 2d street, b L & M,
Hardenbergh, J. R., N street, b 1st and 2d.
Herman, M., clothier, 18 J street.
Heyman & Sanford, clothiers, 40 J street.
Heard, John, lawyer, 74 J street.
Henderson, J., lawyer, 73 J street.
Hermance, L., auctioneer, 99 J street.

Hedges, S. N., at G. P. Post & co's., 109 J street.
Henrickson, Dr. A. M. D·, office 255 J street,
Herrings, G. H., hay yard, J street, b 12th and 13th.
Heermann, Dr., office, 102 J street.
Hensley & Merrill, bankers, 47, 2d street.
Hellinghause, F., gunsmith, 38, 5th street.
Helm, A. F., restaurant, 19, K street.
Herrick, Jr., Joseph, carpenter, 59 K street.
Heek, Phil., baker, front, b Broad and Sacramento streets.
Hedenberg, Walker & Co., liquor store, 57 front street.
Heslep A. M., lawyer, No. 3, 2d street.
Hein, Mrs., dress maker, 67, 3d street.
Heinrich, Charles, boarding house, cor L and 3d streets.
Henarie & Co., grocers and com. mer., front st., b H & I.
Henarie, D. W., at Henarie & co's.
Herrick, Dr. J., office at the Crescent City hotel.
Henley, Thomas J. lawyer, Sutter hotel.
Higgins, M S. merchant. 75 J street.
Hirsfelter, A. clothier, 97 J street.
Hinks. John W., at Titcomb, Sampson & co's.
Himrod, O. W., at James Mills & co's.
Highton, Edward, Tremont house, 184 J street.
Hirshfeld, P., at S Wand & co's.
Hite, Edmund, residence, H street, b 6th and 7th.
Hihn, F. A, at Wibans, Jacobs & co's.
Hines, William, at Smith & H.
Hill & Smith, St Charles, 65 2d street.
Hill, S. G., at Hill & Smith's.
High, William, auctioneer, 148 K street.
Hopkins, B. F., grocer, No. 1 J street.
Hopkins & Miller, merchants, 160 J street.
Howell, Dr. C. W., Howell's hospital, 151 J street.
How, Richard, Wheeler, How & co.
Holton, ——, Burnett house.
Hoope & L'Amoureux, merchants, 191 J street.
Hoope, A. J., Hoope & L'Amoureux.
Holt, Robert, Gordon & Holt.

Holbrook, W. H., at Gore, Wilder & co's.
Hoyt, B. F., Mansfield house, J street, b 12th and 13th.
Holman, F., 4th street house.
Hopkins, Mrs. H A., restaurant, I street, b 5th and 6th.
Hoy, William, Orton & Hoy.
Hope, Thomas B., Florence restaurant.
Homer & Wright, lumber merchants, cor L & 2d streets.
Homer, Charles, Homer & Wright.
Howard, M. J., Trumbo hotel, 133 K street.
Hoy & Orton, blacksmiths 42 K street.
Hughes, Thomas. Crescent City hotel.
Huerstel, Bilay & Albrecht, harness man'f., 131 J. street.
Hughes & Co, confectioners and lemon syrup manufac-
    turers, 148 J street.
Hulburd, M. O., Wisconsin house, 137 J street.
Hunter, Dr. Thomas, office, 139 J street.
Hughes, Joseph, American hotel, 166 J street.
Hutchinson, Green & Co., merchants, 316 J street.
Hutchinson, C. J., Hutchinson, Green & co.
Hunt & Harvey, merchants, cor J and 13th streets.
Hunt, Philander, Hunt & Harvey.
Hunt, W. B., drayman, I street, b 5th and 6th.
Humphrey, John H., painter, 40 5th street.
Huntington, Hammond & Co., merchants, 34 K street.
Huntington, C., Huntington, Hammond & co.
Hyslop, James, Empire saloon, 6 J street.
Isaacs, Lewis, clothier, 78 J street.
Ingalls, John, at Caswell Ingalls & co's.
Illinski, A. X., Tremont house.
Isaacs, J., clothier, 171 J street.
Ihmels, C., Lady Adams company, 12 K street.
Irvin, A., 3d street, b N and O.
Janes, James, No. 2 J street.
Jaretsky, Lewis, clothier, 98 J street.
Jaynes, S., at S. Wand & co's.
Jackson & Johnson, hay yard, J street, b 12th and 13th.
Jackson, T. H., L street, b 8th and 9th.

Jaqua & Black, livery stable, 50, 4th street.
Jarrot, V., blacksmith, 5th street, b I and J.
Jacobs, J. B., Wibans, Jacobs & co.
Jacobs, L., clothier, 27 front street.
Jackson, John, grocer, front street, b Q and R.
Jackson, George C., at Smith & Eells.
Jacobs, John, at Coleman & Nelson's.
Jacobs, R P., auctioneer, 148 K street.
Jefferis, E. G., printer, Transcript office.
Jelly, Samuel, watchmaker, 33 front street.
Jennings & Brown, Julep house, 38 2d street.
Jennings, J. H., Jennings & Brown.
Jones & Doswell, merchants, 254 J street.
Johnson, Henry, boarding house, 319 J street.
Johnson, B. F., Magnolia, 23 J street.
Johnson, C. A., lawyer, 96 J street.
Johnson, G. H., daguerrean, 81 J street.
Johnson, Josiah, broker, 164 J street.
Johnson & Forman, lawyers, 28, 3d street.
Johnson, J Neely, Johnson & Forman.
Johnson, W. N., Johnson & Forman.
Johnson, Richard, 52, 3d street.
Josephi & Co., Robert, jeweler, 125 J street.
Joseph & Co., E., clothiers, 110 J street.
Jordan, John, restaurant, 36, 4th street.
Job, Jeremiah, livery stable, 17, 5th street.
Jordon, Dr., office, 42, 5th street.
Jorss, F., merchant tailor, 16 K street.
Jones, John, Ferrar & Jones.
Jones, Thomas, Williams & Jones.
KALKMANN, P., merchant, 119 J street.
Kennedy, E. D. & W. T., merchants, 74 J street.
Kenney, D. M., tobacconist and cutler, 88 J street.
Kendall & Dennison, grocers, 219 J street.
Kellogg, Leonard, tinner, 249 J street.
Kendal, Dr., office, 255 J street.
Kellar, Francis, butcher, 264 J street.

Kerns, Henry, tailor, 51 K street.
Kelly, Maj. J. Harrison, Transcript office.
Kewen & Morrison, lawyers, 34 2d street.
Kewen, E. J. C., Kewen & Morrison.
Kenyons, E. B., Wood & Kenyons.
Kenyons, John A., Wood & Kenyons.
King, James L., at James Mills & co.'s.
Kibbe, Henry. Youngs, Kibbe & co.
Kimbail, John B., E. Bond & Co.
Kinsey, Jesse, jeweler, 25 J street.
Kinne & Dudley, restaurant, 3 K street.
Kinne, A. S., Kinne & Dudley.
Kirkley & Liness, restaurant, 13 K street,
Kirkley, M. A., Kirley & Liness.
Klopenstine & Co., merchants, 151 J street.
Knox & Co., R. A., tinners, 203 J street.
Knight, Francis P., clerk for Joseph Grant.
Kohlmann & Brieger, clothiers, 36 and 54 J street.
Kohen & Co., clothiers, 134 J street.
Kohner, John, front street. b I and Broad.
Kraener, P. H., at E. D. & W. T. Kennedy's.
Kuhlan, William, jeweler, 13 J street.
Lardner, F. S., dairyman, American fork.
Lacroze, John, at Hastings & Co.
Lamar, J. B., lawyer, 73 J street.
Langfelt & Co., merchants, 85 J street.
Lathrop, B. G., Southern house, 91 J street.
Lane, C. B., City saloon, 142 J street.
L'Amoreux, George W., Hoope & L'Amoreux.
Lawrence. jr., B., Burdick & Lawrence.
Laing, William, Roberts & Laing.
Lake & Co., Z., merchants, 308 J street.
Lanagan, Daniel, Marsh's boarding house.
Lawson, James, Herkimer hotel, 41, 4th street.
Langley, Henry G. merchant, 19 J street.
Lady Adams Company, mercantile house, 12 K street.
Labau & Co H F. merchants, 92 K street.

Latham, M S. lawyer, 65 2d street.
Larned, William, at Brastow & co's.
Lansing, James, 52 3d street.
Lewis, A. tailor, 74 J street.
Lee, Harklerodes & Co. merchants, 92 J street.
Lee, Preston H. at L Harklerodes & Co's.
Leonard, E W. 92 J street.
Lewis & Bailey, merchants, 93 J street.
Lewis & Co., A. clothiers, 112 J street.
Lewis, J H. at Hutchinson Green & co's.
Lee, Mrs Mary Ann, K street, b 8th and 9th.
Leke, R M. at the Louisville house, cor I and 6th sts.
Leiholt, Henry, shoemaker, 83, 3d street.
Leman, F. grocer, 165 K street.
Lewis, M. trader, 144 K street.
Lee, Barton, office 41 2d street.
Lindsey, L E. New York Lunch, 16 J street.
Light, Ames & Watts, druggists, 66 J street.
Light, Dr W W. dentist, 66 J street.
Lillis, J P. at Fogg & Green's.
Lippencott & Co. J street house, 206 J street.
Liness, John, at Kirkley & L's.
Livingston, D. Trumbo hotel.
Lockitt, Joseph, clothier, 27 J street.
Long & Co. W S. Missouri hotel, 86 J street.
Logan, Dr Thomas M. office 286 J street.
Lord, Joseph A. salesman for Haines & Stevens.
Lolor, Miss Margarett, front b Q and R.
Lovegrove, George, bookseller, 63, 2d street.
Low, jr. F. G., lumber dealer, 2d street, b L and M.
Long, J. R., Barker & Long.
Luce, Israel, marble workman, 7th street, b J and K.
Lucas, A. J., E. Wait & Co.
Luckett, J. A., Fitch, Luckett & Co.
Luco, M. & L., merchants, 123 K street.
Ludington, O., auctioneer, 258 K street.
Lucken, J. F., druggist, 20 J street.

D

Lyon, Robert, barkeeper, Jenny Lind house.
Lyon, George A., *Haynes*, Lyon & Co.
Lynde, W. C., Smith & Lynde.
McBRAYER, J. M., lawyer, 43, 4th street.
McCall, W. R., merchant, 60 J street.
McCrellis, E., tailor, 74 J street.
McConaha, G. N., lawyer, 123 J street.
McCarty, Edward, Oliver, Nunes & McCarty.
McCullough, S·, hotel, 224 J street.
McCleery, James, Fitch & McCleery.
McCord, J. S., cooper, 23 I street.
McCullock, Benjamen, sheriff, office in court house.
McCalpin, T., Indiana house, 16, 5th street.
McCoy, Thomas, Taylor & McCoy.
McClure, Thomas J., at Smith & Eells,
McCracken, M. C., No 6, 2d street.
McCloy, Robert, shoemaker, 90 3d street.
McCloy, John, '   do   do   do
McDonald, Dr. R. H., druggist 143 J street.
McDonough, W. S., tinner, 280 J street.
McDonald, John, H. P. Cotting & Co.
McDivitt, William, painter, Bull's head hotel.
McFerren, Dr. L. A., office, 105 J street.
McFarland, Dr., office, 37 front street.
McGowan & Chrysup, Oregon saloon, 37 J street.
McGowan, L.,   do   do
McGrew, William H., lawyer, 134 K street.
McGrew & Robinson, lawyers, 134 K street.
McGuire, James, blacksmiths, 42, 6th street.
McIlroy, R. H., grocer, cor K and 10th streets.
McIntere & Co., laundryman, 89, 2d street.
McIntire, E., McIntire & Co.
McKamey, Glenn & Co. livery stable, 185 J street.
McKee, S. Finley, deputy cierk, court house.
McKean, Charles P., Bull's head.
McKee, John, trader, 67, 6th street.
McLaren, D., Reynolds & McLaren.

McLeish, Dr. John, office, 63 2d street.
McLeish & Duryee, physicians, 63, 2d street.
McNulty, W., merchant, 43 J street.
McNeir, Dr. M. C., office, 61, 2d street.
McNulty, J., Ohio house, 145 K street.
Mackenzie & Ames, Drs., office, 216 K street.
Mackenzie, Dr. J. M., No 3, 2d street.
Mann, C., Emmons & Mann.
Mason, J. L., 69, 2d street.
Main, Dr. John, office, 60, 2d street.
May, William, cabinet maker, at William Taylor's.
Mattison, D. W., book keeper, J. S. Sprague & Co.
Marsh, Robert, at Hatch's, No 10 J street.
May, Dr. S. J., druggist, 25 J street.
May, Samuel, Rayns & May, Eldorado.
Marshall & Stanley, lawyers, 62 J street.
Maxey, J M., Missouri hotel.
Mason, G., tailor, 85 J street.
Marks & Freidman, merchants, 105 J street.
Mather, W. T., Wheeler, How & Co.
Martin & Wells, merchants, 194 J street.
Martin, Dr. Robert, office, 309 J street.
Marsh, E. A., boarding house, J street, b 11th & 12th.
Magoon, B. F., Mansfield house.
Martin & Well, blacksmiths, K street, b 10th and 11th.
Marz, Henry, Chicago nouse.
Matard, Auguste, baker, 18, 5th street.
May, Albert D., lemon syrup manufactory, 37, 5th street.
Martin, Dr. James S., office, 43 K street.
March, Ichabod, builder, 56 K street.
Martin, Addison, Spaulding & Martin.
Marsh, Dr. L. C., office, 96 K street.
Mallen, H., Allens hotel, J street, b 8th and 9th.
Martin, E. H., artist, 2d street, b J and K.
Merry, S. H., saloon, No 2 J street.
Merritt & Co., Empire mills, 111 J street.
Merritt, Henry, Merritt & Co.

Mead & Smith, merchants, 108 J street.
Mead, Rufus G., Mead & Smith.
Metzinger, A., barber, 145 J street.
Mensingheimer, J. saddler, 189 J street.
Merrill, Mrs., Antartic house, K street, b 10th and 11th.
Mercure, F. D., North American house, L st., b 8th & 9th.
Meredith, H., lawyer, 15 front street.
Mead, R. P. & W. B., Express hotel, 54 front street.
Meeker & Co., grocers and com. merchants, 60 front street.
Merritt, W., grocer, 36, 2d street.
Meire, George, butcher, 221 K street.
Mitchell, T. S., shoe store, No 11 J street.
Miller, R. F., tinner, at Hastings & Co.
Mills & Co., James, merchants, 62 J street.
Mills. D. O., at James Mills & Co.
Mitchell, T. S., shoe store, 87 J street.
Miller, jr., E. H., Hopkins & Miller.
Miller, C. H., merchant, 168 J street.
Mitchell, C., merchant, 194 J street.
Miller, John E.. livery stable, 7 4th street
Mills & Co., J, W., carpenters, 16, 4th street.
Mitchell, J. B., Morse & Mitchell.
Mingued, R., Hotel de France, 7 front street.
Milne, D. B., Clark & Milne.
Milliken, John B., Steam boat agent, front street.
Morton, C. B., No 11 J street.
Moore, James, 13 J street.
Morrill & Whittier, druggists, 49 J street.
Morse, S. R., at James Mills & Co's.
Montgomery, George E., lawyer, 72 J street.
Montgomery, Dr., office, 88 J street.
Morey, David, Southern house.
Moss & Co., H. H., auctioneers, 123 J street.
Morgan, J. R., California Trading Company, 129 J street.
Moris & Co., clothiers, 149 J street.
Moore, T., United States Hotel, 278 J street.
Moore, W. H., carpenter, cor 9th and K streets.

Mooney & Wheelwright, livery stable, I street b 5th & 6th.
Morse & Mitchell, Real estate agents, 35 K street.
Morse. Dr. J. F., Morse & Mitchell.
Moore, P. R , salesman, J. S. Sprague & Co.
Morris, T. Y., tinner, Canon & Kempt.
Morrison, Murray, Kewen & Morrison.
Morrison, John C., merchant, 57, 2d street.
Monson, A. C., lawyer, 65, 2d street.
Mosee, William, trader, 118 K street.
Moore, Dr. Jessee, office, 136 K street.
Moreland, Blunt & Smith, auctioneers, 164 K street.
Moreland, A , Moreland, Blunt & Co.
Murray, D., auctioneer, 7th street, b K and L.
Mulvany, Dr. P. H., office, No 40, 3d street.
Nash, George, Patridge & Nash.
Nail, R., at J. H. Pugh.
Neubauer, Hollub & Co, dry goods store, 31 & 100, J st.
Newman & Brother, clothiers, 106 J street.
Nevett & Co, stoves and hardware, 102 K street.]
Nevett, Joseph H, Nevett & Co.
Nelson, George, grocer, front street, b I and Broad.
Nelson, E E, Coleman & Nelson.
Niman, Truman, bohrding house, I street, b 4th and 5th.
Norman, Joseph, boarding house, I street, b 12th & 13th.
Nolan, F, carpenter, 50, 5th street.
Nuckols, J A, boarding house, 150 K street.
Oberdorfar, S, American hotel, 166 J street.
Obrien, John, washer, 4th street, b L and M,
Obrien, Dr J C, office, 28, 3d street.
Ochsner & Co., grocer and blacksmith, 290 J street.
O'Callaghan, H H, lawyer, Crescent City hotel.
Ogden, F, at Barney, Blossom & Co's.
Oneill, William, Florence restaurant, 43 K street.
Olmstead, T C D, merchant, 111 J street.
Oliver, Nunes & McCarty, merchants, 139 J street.
Oliver, David, Oliver, Nunes & McCarty.
Overshiner & Cochran, carriage makers, J st, b 12th & 13th.

Ormsby & Culver, real estate agents, 45, 4th street.
Ormsby, Maj W M, stock auction, 140 K street.
Ormsby, L P, trader, 140 K street.
Orton & Hoy, blacksmiths, 42 K street.
Orton, Oliver, Ortan & Hoy.
Osborn & Co, H P, merchants, 253 J street.
Otero, Manuel, 70, 4th street.
Overton, J P, lawyer, 65, 2d street.
Owing, W C, at J W Mills & Co's.
Passenand, barber, 28 J street.
Parks, J W, Missouri hotel.
Patterson, Dr E M, American hotel, 166 J street.
Patchin, L B, merchant, 246 J street
Patridge & Nash boarding house, 255 J street.
Parsons, S H, livery stable, J street, b 11th and 12th.
Packer, H B, grocer, J street, b 12th and 13th.
Pawlett, Joseph, joiner, K street, b 8th and 9th.
Parks, Edward, saloon, No 5 K street.
Park, Dr H, rail-road hotel,
Parker, C W, commission merchant, cor M and 2d streets.
Parker, J, restaurant, 75, 6th street.
Paris, D H, trader, 140 K street.
Pearlman & Co, clothiers, No 26 J street.
Pearis, Beirne & Co, druggists, 69 J street.
Pearis & Brockway, grocers, 70 J street.
Peacock, George H, Missouri hotel.
Pellow, J P, merchant, 99 J street.
Pearis & Brockway, druggists, 117 J street.
Pettes, jr. John, Caswell, Ingalls & Co.
Peirce & Miller, merchants, 215 J street.
Petit, A P, office 65, 3d street; residence, cor H and 8th.
Perkins & Powers, merchants, 32 K street.
Perkins, Edward S, Perkins & Powers.
Persian, J D, sadler, at C A Foot.
Pennibaker, George F, Arnold & Pennibaker.
Perkins, Joseph, clerk on bark Eliza.   [dence 7th, b j &'k.
Penman, Rev John, Pastor of the M E Church, South, resi-

Phillips, H, Winslow's Exchange, 50 J street.
Pheiffer, W A, office 40, 4th street.
Phinneys, Dr, office, 52, 3d street.
Pierce, Burns & Co, City market, 20 J street.
Pierce, E, Pierce, Burns & Co.
Prince, W R, merchant 63 J street.
Pettibone, M H, Winsinger, Pettibone & Co·
Pinkham, E, at M Seaman & Co.
Peirson, J H, carpenter, 96 K street.
Pixley, Frank M, lawyer, No 1, 2d street.
Pearce, Henry, at Low's lumber yard.
Pickard, F, merchant, 55, 3d street.
Pitts, A W, trader, 45, 6th street.
Plaisted, E, boarding house, 272 J street.
Plotner & McCormick, taylors, 44, 2d street.
Potter, A H, & Co, merchants, 9 J street.
Polhemus, J L, druggist, 196 J street.
Post & Co, G P, merchants, 109 J street.
Pomeroy, F C, Jenny Lind, 113 J street.
Poage, James F, blacksmith, J street, b 11th and 12th.
Powers, jr, L, Perkins & Powers.
Politz, J, boarding house, 36 K street.
Pond, B F, cashier, A W Foote.
Porter, Col, clerk on Steamboat New World.
Price & Burnam, Physicians, No 3. Eldorado buildings.
Price, Dr Johnson, Price & Burnam.
Proctor, Dr W G, at Hustings & Co.
Pritchard & Gaster, Wabash house, 199 J street.
Prockter & Bradley, Kentucky house, 259 J street.
Prentiss, Dr W, office, 42, 5th street.
Prader, Joseph, blacksmith, 46, 5th street.
Prader, William,   do   do
Prugh, Cook & Co, merchants, 41 K street.
Prugh, John, Prugh, Cook & Co.
Prettyman & Barroll, auctioners, 31 front street.
Prieto, M J, at M & L Luco's, 164 K street.
Provines, John, clerk for M & L Luco.

Prentiss, John, trader, 150 K street.
Purdin, Mathew, gold washer manufactory, 6th, b I & J.
Pujh, J W, tinner, 60, 3d street.
QUIN, JAMES R, grocer, J street, b 12th and 13th.
Quinby, E, carpenter, at Saywood & Weston's.
RAYNS & MAY, Eldorado, 33 J street.
Ralston & Sunderland, lawyers, 107 J street.
Rancietz, Martin, grocer, 135 J street.
Randolph, Dr P, American hotel, 166 J street.
Ramsdell, Joseph, Herkimer hotel, 41, 4th street.
Ransom, W A, deputy clark, court house.
Rawlings, T H, Illinois house, 20, 5th street.
Rayner, William, Craig & Rayner.
Rave, I, gunsmith, 56, 6th street.
Randall, H C, boarding house, 73, 6th street.
Reynolds & McLaren, saloon, No 2 J street.
Reynolds, Joseph R, 2 J street.
Reed, Henry, Woodcock, 15 J street.
Read, John A, at B F Hastings & Co.
Reed, Freeman & Co. merchants, 162 J street.
Reed, L F, Reed, Freeman & Co.
Redding, J L, Allen & Redding.
Reading, Maj P B, No 7 I street.
Rhodes, Sturges & Co, bankers, 53, 2d street.
Rich, Samuel, Our home, 175 J street.
Richart, John, Wm Tell hotel, 262 J street.
Richards, C L, deputy clerk, court house.
Riley, Michael, drayman, I street, b 5th and 6th.
Riggs, S W, front street, north of Sycamore.
Reiux, A, clerk for S Weil.
Richartt, William, Dawsey house, 74 front street.
Rice & Dugart, butchers, 80 front street.
Rice, Charles, Rice & Dugart.
Rice, W A, lumber dealer, cor 2d and M streets.
Rightmire, A D, auctioneer, 164 K street.
Rightmire & Gandy, auctioneers, 164 K street.
Richardson, M, Allen's hotel.

Roe, F J, at Reynolds & McLeary's.
Rosenfield & Mayers, furnishing store, 56 J street.
Rogers, John P, Moss & Co; residence, 13, 4th street.
Roberts & Laing, stock yard, 212 J street.
Roberts, H E, Roberts & Laing.
Roberts, Sutherland & Conley, Union hotel, 217 J street.
Roberts, John, Union hotel.
Robinson, Josiah, blacksmith, J street, b 11th and 12th.
Roberts & Turner, candle factory, 11th street, b J and K.
Rousier, N, at Martin & Wells'.
Rodgers, James, teacher, cor L and 7th streets.
Robinson, John, carpenter, J street, b 8th and 9th.
Rowan, D, laborer, I street, b 3d and 4th.
Rocheblave, P P, merchant, 16 K street.
Rogers, Jacob, Florence restaurant.
Rowland, George, Nevett & Co.
Rowe & Gamans, grocers, 29 front street.
Robertson, A, grocer, 95 front street.
Romer, Jacob, Brownell, Romer & Roller.
Roller, Charles, Brownell, Romer & Roller.
Robinson, Davis & Ryerson, lawyers, 42, 2d street.
Robinson, Todd, Robinson, Davis & Ryerson.
Robinson, Robert, McGrew & Robinson.
Robison, D H, carpenter, at Saywood & Weston's.
Ruff & Co, C F, Illinois hotel, 307 J street.
Ruffin, Dr, William H, office 102 J street.
Ryan, E B, Missouri hotel.
Ryan & Co, tinners, 158 J street.
Ryder, George W, Abbey, 170 J street.
Ryerson, H O, Robinson, Davis & Ryerson.
SAMPSON, F W, Titcomb & Co.
Sackett, C C, justice of the peace, 77 J street.
Salter, Dr John, office, 3d street, b J and K.
Salzer, Charles, grocer, K street, b 10th and 11th.
Sarch, William, residence b I and J streets, 3d and 4th.
Sabin, Stephen C, carpenter, K street, b 3d and 4th.
Sawyear, Clark & Co, merchants, 59 J street.
E

Sawyear, H W, Sawyear, Clark & Co.
Salsbury, Joseph, restaurant, 24 K street.
Saywood & Thorndyke, merchants, 61 K street.
Saywood, William T. Saywood & Thorndyke.
Salasar, Salvadore, 96 K street.
Salasar, Jose Maria, 96 K street.
Salvasar, Jesus, 96 K street.
Satterfield, J F, boards at 91 K street.
Sailly, Myers & Co, grocers, 62 front street.
Sanborn, F C, lumber dealer, 100 front street.
Salter, Dr, office 50, 3d street.
Salbatierra, Julian, grocer, 47, 6th street.
Saywood & Weston, bakers, 152 K street.
Saywood, W P, Saywood & Weston.
Schnider, John, grocer, 165 K street.
Schaffer, Henry, gunsmith, 48 3d street.
Schade, John, gunsmith, 18 3d street.
Schafer & Co, hotel, 26 front street.
Schildknecht & Koester, brewers, front street, above Broad.
Schwarz, M, merchant, 65 J street.
Scranton & Smith, merchants, 79 J street.
Schmidt, C J, ranche, 128 J street.
Scrivner, William, at J W Mills & Co's.
Schrouder, H R, washer, b I and J, 4th and 5th streets.
Schultz, Edward, Huntington, Hammond & Co.
Schantz, J P, at Stiles, Ashley & Co's.
Seaman & Co, W, merchants, 140 J street.
Segar & Co, merchants, 186 J street.
Sedam & Galaway, anctioneers, 220 J street.
Sels, C M, Illinois hotel, 307 J street.
Shafer, George, baker, 223 K street.
Simmons & Curtis, Orleans house, 48, 2d street.
Shed, Charles D, at Martin & Wells.
Shubart, J, Chicago house.
Shepherd, Professor F, office, I street, b 3d and 4th.
Shaw, H N, Harris & Co.
Shields, James P, sadler, 38 4th street.

Simons & Co, clothiers, 76 J street.
Silsby & Co, J B, merchants, 257 J street.
Simonds, F S, drayman, I street, b 5th and 6th.
Sizer, Samuel, clerk at I March's.
Sizer, Daniel,   do   do
Sisson & Coleman, boarding house, 89 K street.
Sisson, Nathan, Sisson & Coleman.
Sidgreaves, William, boarding house, 142 K street.
Skaggs, Thomas, Jenny Lind house, 77 J street.
Skinner, Robert, 69 2d street.
Slomowsky & Co, clothiers, 124 J street.
Sloss & Co, L, clothiers, 214 J street.
Sloper, Albert, Boston restaurant, 39 2d street.
Smith, Capt Napoleon, express hotel, front st., b K & L.
Smith, Horace, lawyer, No 3, Eldorado building.
Smith, Ira G, constable, 105 J st, residence H, b 6th & 7th.
Smith, Charles, Mead & Smith.
Smith & Peterson, merchants, 161 J street.
Smith, E, Elk house, and gold washer manufactory, 51
     and 53, 4th street.
Small, Dr William E, at Crane's, 96 K street.
Smith & Kelly, city hotel, 9 front street.
Smith & Hines, grocers, No 3, 3d street.
Smith, Joel, Smith & Hines.
Smith, George, Wheeler & Smith.
Smith & Eells, blacksmiths, 16, 3d street.
Smith, E, Smith & Eells.
Smith, Fanny, Palace, No 9, 2d street.
Smith & Batchelder, Waverly, 24, 2d street.
Smith, Thomas, Smith & Batchelder.
Smith, T D, Hill & Smith.
Smith, J C, real estate agent, 69, 2d street.
Smith, C H, lumber dealer, cor L and 2d streets.
Smith, John C, blacksmith, 48, 3d street.
Smith, W M, Harris & Co.
Smith & Lynde, bakers, 50, 6th street.
Smith, E M, Smith & Lynde.

Smith, F C, Moreland, Blunt & Co.
Smith & Garrard, lawyers, Eldorado building.
Solomon & Co, clothiers, 72 J street.
Solomon & Co, L, clothiers, 167 J street.
Sowter & Elsbury, City bakery, 6th street, b I and J.
Somes & Co, G W, lumber merchants, 65 front street.
Spencer, B B, at A H Potter & Co's, No 9 J street.
Speeks, R R, tailor, 74 J street.
Spotts, William, Barnes & Spotts.
Spalding, Dr V, office, 25 J street.
Spaulding & Martin, merchants, 84 K street.
Sprague & Co, J S Grocers, 58 front street.
Spink, Peter, Wick & Spink.
Stone & Bloom, clothiers, 14 J street.
Stone, Solomon, Stone & Bloom.
Starr, Bensley & Co, merchants, 58 J street.
Stephens, N T, notary public, 99 J street.
Stark, William, at Mrs Warren's boarding house.
Starring, A L, Carrall & Starring.
Steel & Co, merchants, 141 J street.
Stickler, E, tailor, 155 J street.
Stevens, N M, boarding house, 7th street, b J and K.
Stemmermann, C, Chicago house.
Stingle, A, grocer, 12 I street.
Staffelbach, X, boarding house, I street, b 5th and 6th.
Steinagal, Mrs Sarah M, Quincy house, 6th st., b H & I.
Stocking, Dr D C, dentist, 59 J street.
Starr, F R, Starr, Bensley & Co.
Starr, Henry, do do do
Stevens, Mrs M J, boarding house, 78 J street.
Storkfeth, P, Lady Adams company, 12 K street.
Stiles, Ashby & Co, tinners, 36 K street.
Stiles, C W, Stiles, Ashby & Co.
Stevens, W H, Haines & Stevens.
Storkwell, Joseph P, gunsmith, 57 K street.
Stow, ——, foundryman, cor front and sycamore streets.
Starr, J B, auctioneer, cor of front and K streets.

St John, P D, lumber dealer, 97 front street.
Stoddard, Dr H, office, 179 K street.
Sutherland, James D, Union hotel.
Suydam, J & L, merchants, No 7 I street.
Sutton, George, eating house, 49 front street.
Susias, Pablo, billiard saloon, Orleans hotel.
Swift, C H, justice of the peace, 105 J street.
Swinerton, G H, R A Knox & Co.
Sweetser, A C, carpenter, b J and K, 4th and 5th streets.
Sweet, James, Hall & Sweet.
Sylvester, E, Crescent City hotel.
TANNATT, GEORGE F, watchmaker, 92 J street.
Taylor, Dr G, office, 81 J street.
Taylor, James, Tremont house.
Tarr, B F, lawyer, 102 J street.
Taylor & McCoy, livery stable, b J and K, 4th and 5th.
Taylor, John C, eating house, 85 front street.
Taylor, W P, oabinet maker, 22 3d street.
Taylor, James, 2d street, b M and N.
Tarbox, William, carpenter, at P W Burnett's.
Teagarden, Dr, office, 72 J street.
Temple, Dr J T, office, 76 J street.
Terhune, Edwards & Co, merchants, 282 J street.
Teel, William, turner, at Seth Bason's.
Thom, C E, lawyer, 78 J street.
Thayer, F W, lawyer, 75 J street.
Thomas, Luther, Jenny Lind house.
Thorpe, D W, county assessor, 77 J street.
Thomas, Dr W H, dentist, 81 J street.
Tweed, Aldrich & Pedan, lawyers, 108 J street.
Tweed, Charles A, Tweed, Aldrich & Pedan.
Thomas, Michael, at Ochsner & Co.
Thorndyke, Josiah K, Saywood & Thorndyke.
Thrall, Charles, restaurant, 181 K street.
Tidball, A P, at Hastings & Co.
Titcomb, Sampson & Co, merchants, 53 J street.
Tingman, John, at Brown, Henry & Co's.

Timmons, S W, Tremont house.
Tift, S O, carpenter, Saywood & Weston's.
Torrey, Midian, boarding house, I street, b 4th and 5th.
Tracey, John N, Captain of the watch, market house.
Tutt, John A, constable, 77 J street.
Tuley, John W, carpenter, 137 J street.
Tucker, jr, Charles, coffee and spice mill, 8 I street.
UNGER, JULIUS, cigar store, 38 J street.
Uptegraph & Harris, stock yard, cor K and 10th streets.
Uptegraph, J H, Uptegraph & Harris.
Urian, Samuel, blacksmith, at J C Smith's.
VANDERBERG, L V, No 30 J street.
Vines, Miss Julietta, Jenny Lind house.
Vale & Co, merchants, 175 J street.
Vanorden, John, grocer, 209 J street.
Valentine, Bradford, Herkimer Hotel.
Valentine, Daniel, livery stable, b I and J, 3d and 4th.
Vangardner & Co, butchers, No 1 front street.
Vanpelt, John, cor of O and 2d streets.
WAGNER, W H, clerk for J B Milliken.
Wadsworth, F, clerk at Gregory's Express.
Warren & Co, merchants, 3 J street.
Warren, J L L F, Warren & Co.
Winters, W W, No 2 J street.
Watchorst & Co, jewelers, 13 J street.
Watts, Dr Stephen, physician, 66 J street.
Wallace, W C, lawyer, 74 J street.
Wallace, Dr, office, 74 J street.
Wales, T P, at Forshee & Reynolds.
Ward, T E,   do   do
Warner, Mrs, boarding house, 103 J street.
Whalley, C, merchant, 120 J street.
Whetston, H S, at Buckley & Co's.
Watson & Biscoe, hardware merchants, 159 J street.
Wand & Co. S, merchants, 197 J street.
Watson, N A, stock yard, 238 J street.
Wait, Robert, blacksmith, 24, 4th street.

Watson, Dr Wilkins, office, 102 J street.
Wait & Co, E, Hawkeye house, 72 4th street.
Waddelove, H, cooper b J and K, 4th and 5th.
Warren, H S, Transcript office.
Wade, Robert E, clerk Haines & Webster.
Wadsworth, Dr J A, office 58 K street.
Wadsworth, J Leon, 58 K street.
Washington, B F, City recorder, No 1 2d street.
Walthall, Madison, lawyer, 34, 2d street.
Warrill, A C, Fruit store, 44, 2d street.
Ward & Blair, lawyers, 59, 2d street.
Ward, A F, Ward & Blair.
Wainwright, Charles, Henarie & Co.
Walker, A W, restaurant, 164 K street,
Warner, William, clerk, bark Eliza.
Waters, Capt W C, agent for Senator and New World.
West, L, merchant, 114 J street.
Wensinger, Pettibone & Co. merchants, 132 J street.
Wells, M H, Martin & Wells.
Wells, William, Missouri house, 252 J street.
Webster, A W, Haynes, Lyon & Co.
Webster & Cowper, shoemakers, 21, 4th street.
Westenhaver, baker, 40 K street ; residence, 47, 4th st.
Wetzlar, Julias, front street, b I and Broad.
Welton, Merritt, grocer, 28 front street.
Weil, S, clothier, 35 front street.
Welch, George R, Varandah, 72 front street.
Weston, W, Saywood & Weston.
Welch, Dr Thomas, office, 2d street, b L and M.
Whiteside, N E, lawyer, 72 J street.
Whitfield, Venable & Co, merchants, 129 J street.
White & Co, clothiers, 104 J street.
White, O H P, Alderman, White, Whitman & Co.
White, James R, clerk at   do   do   do
Whitman, B F,   do   do   do   do
Wheeler, How & Co, merchants, 190 J street.
White, Caleb E, Haskell, White & Co.

Whiting, B F, cabinet maker, 45, 4th street.
White, Dr T J, office, cor 3d & J ; residence, I, b 5th & 6th.
Wheelright, Joseph H, Mooney & Wheelright.
White & Ballou, shoe store, 47 K street.
White, William, residence, H street, b 6th and 7th.
White, Danford, White & Ballou.
Wheeler & Smith, livery stable, 7, 3d street.
Wheeler, George, Wheeler & Smith.
Whiteherst, Thomas, at Smith & Eells.
Wilson, James, at Pearis & Brockway.
Wilcoxson & Co, merchants, 81 J street.
Wickersham, Dr R R, 143 J street.
Williams, J, American hotel, 166 J street.
Wilder, L J, Gore, Wilder & Co.
Wilson & Mathews, blacksmiths, J street, b 14th & 15th.
Wilkinson, Thomas, Indiana hotel, J street, b 12th & 13th.
Willis, Hon E J, residence, H street, b 6th and 7th.
Winson, Edmond, residence, H street, b 6th and 7th.
Winkle, H, bakery, 16 K street.
Williams & Ault, hotel, 39 K street.
Williams, John N, Williams & Ault.
Wingate, C D, blacksmith, 3d street, b K and L.
Wibans, Jacobs & Co, hotel, 95 K street.
Wilson, George Rail-road hotel, cor sycamore and front.
Wilson & Spaulding, book-sellers, 21 front street.
Wiley, S R, salesman for W Merrett.
Williams, W F, eating house, 46, 2d street.
Wilber, Wheeler, cor P and 2d streets.
Williams & Feider, Diadem, 38, 3d street.
Williams, W F, Williams & Feider.
Winn, Gen A M, residence, 3d street, b M and N.
Wick & Spink, blacksmiths, 41, 6th street.
Wick, R K, Wick & Spink.
Williams & Jones, painters, cor J and 5th streets.
Williams, John Caner, Williams & Jones.
Wolf, Holton & Abrams, Burnett house, 165 J street.
Wolf, Dr Charles L,   do   do   do

Woods & Brother, W R, stockyard, J st, b 14th and 15th.
Wooodman, C B, H P Cotting & Co.
Wort, Henry, carpenter at J Marsh's.
Woodruff & Co, G W, hardware merchants, 55 front st.
Wood, Charles B, lumber dealer, 88 front street.
Wood & Kenyons, merchants, 105 K street.
Wood, John, Wood & Kenyons.
Wood, N B, Eyre & Wood.
Wolf, Gallop & Co, bakers, 74 6th street.
Wolf, John A, Wolf, Gallop & Co.
Woodward, A, trader, Winslow's Exchange.
Wright, J A, jeweler, 30 J street.
Wright, E M,   do   do
Weay, Charles,   do   do
Wright, G G, Homer & Wright.
Wright & Griswell, blacksmiths, 180 K street.
Wright, J C, Wright & Griswell.
Winans & Hyer, lawyers, 93 J street.
Youngs, Kibbee & Co, merchants, 174 J street.
Youngs, Samuel, Youngs, Kibbee & Co.
Yost, M, stock yard, K street, b 9th and 10th.
Yates, Chapman, boarding house, L street, b 7th and 8th.
Youmans & Co, E S, undertaker, 56 4th street.
Young, Isaac, land agent, 61 2d street.
Zeira & Freedlander, clothiers, 146 J street.
Zabriskie, Col J C, notary public, 6 2d street.
Zabriskie, Dr C B, office, 6 2d street.
Zabriskie, W M, lawyer, 6 2d street.
F

PHYSICIANS.

DR. JOHNSON PRICE.   DR. A. J. BURNAM.

PRICE & BURNAM,

PHYSICIANS AND SURGEONS:

OFFICE:

" El Dorado Buildings," cor. J and Second Streets.

Dr. Wm. H. Ruffen,

PHYSICIAN AND SURGEON.

OFFICE—Corner of J and Fourth Streets.

Drs. McLeish & Duryee,

PHYSICIANS AND SURGEONS:

No. 63, Second Street, in Post Office Building.

[PHYSICIANS—CONTINUED.]

F W Ames,
Andariese,
A T Ault,
J Ball,
Thomas B Bailie,
R D Barker,
J W Bay,
H H Bealls,
R Bell,
J G Baumdrain,
L A Birdsall,
E J Billings,
J T Boone,
B B Brown,
Charles Burrell,
W M Carpenter,
M G Collins,
Thomas J Conduitte,
L P Crane,
S S Crane,
E Cronin,
Curtis & Cowan,
W Grove Deal,
J D Demarst,
W B H Dodson,
C Duncombe,
Aaron Dow,
James R Falls,
L Ferris,
E N Freeman,
M Greenman,
Hardenstein,
A G Hart,
A M D Henrickson.
Heerman,
J Henrick.

C W Howell,
Thomas Hunter,
Jordon,
Kendal,
W Light,
Thomas M Logan,
J F Lucken,
R H McDonald,
L A McFerren,
McFarland,
M C McNeir,
J M McKenzie,
John Main,
S J May,
Robert Martin,
James S Martin,
L C Marsh,
Montgomery,
J F Moore,
Jesse Moore,
P H Mulvany,
J C O'Brien,
E M Patterson,
H Park,
Phinney,
W Prentiss,
P Randolph,
John Salter,
Salter,
W E Small,
V Spalding,
D C Stocking,
G Taylor,
Teegarden,
C H Swift,
W H Thomas,

[PHYSICIANS—CONCLUDED.]

S T Watts,	T Welch,
Wallace,	T J White,
W Watson,	R R Wickersham,
J A Wadsworth.	C B Zabriskie.

L A W Y E R S .

J. H. RALSTON,	THOMAS SUNDERLAND,
Late of Quincy, Ill.	Late of Hannibal, Mo.

Ralston & Sunderland,

Attorneys and Counsellors at Law.

—OFFICE—

Whitney's Brick Buildings, 107 J St., N side, near 4th St.

J. M. McBrayer,

ATTORNEY AND COUNSELLOR AT LAW,

Office—No. 43, 4th St., bet. J and K.

[LAWYERS—CONCLUDED.]

Lewis Aldrich,
Smith P Bankhead,
C W Benneson,
John Bigler,
L M Booth,
P H Burnett,
J Churchman,
Josiah Chandler,
Clover & Winchell,
T Cunningham,
W P Dangerfield,
N H Davis,
P L Edwards,
James L English,
George S Fake,
Col F Forman,
B D Fry,
John H Gass,
Capt William Garrard,
John Heard,
J Henderson,
A M Heslep,
John G Hyer,
C A Johnson,
J N Johnson,
E J C Kewen,
J B Lamar,

M S Latham,
G N McConaha,
W H McGrew,
I B Marshall,
H Meredith,
Washington Meeks,
George E Montgomer
A C Monson,
H H O'Callahan,
J P Overton,
F M Pixley,
J H Ralston,
Todd Robinson,
H O Ryerson,
Horace Smith,
N T Stephens,
R H Stanley,
T Sunderland,
B F Tarr,
C E Thom,
C A Tweed,
W C Wallace,
Madison Walthall,
Joseph W Winans,
Ward & Blair
N E Whiteside,
William M Zabriskie.

HOTELS.

MISSOURI HOTEL,

No. 86 J Street, between Third and Fourth Streets.

WM. S. LONG & CO., Proprietors.

W. S. LONG.   J. A. COGSWELL.   G. H. PEACOCK.

CRESCENT CITY HOTEL,

No. 90 J Street, between 3d and 4th.

PACIFIC HOUSE,

No. 24, J Street,

GEESEKA & MATHEWSON.

R. GEESEKA.   T. D. MATHEWSON.

RINGGOLD HOUSE,

Mrs. JANE A. SHURR, Proprietress.

No. 44, Third Street, between J and K Streets.

[HOTELS—CONTINUED.]

Albion house, J R Griffin, 159 K street.
Allen's hotel, Allen & Redding, 245 J street.
American hotel, Patterson, Hughes & Williams, 166 J st.
Abbey, Ryder & Byers, 170 J street.
Antartic house, Mrs Merrill, K street, b 10th and 11th.
Burnett house, Wolf, Holton & Abrams, 165 J street.
Brannan hotel, Hanna & Bowman, 47 front street.
Bulls' Head hotel, E J Feeney & Co, 127 K street.
Buckeye house, Emmons & Mann, 161 K street.
City hotel, Smith & Kelly, 9 front street.
Cafe de Paris, Eugene Fisher, 31 3d street.
Columbia hotel, E J Armstrong, 21 2d street.
Clarke's hotel, Lewis Clarke, 314 J street.
Conger house, Thomas Conger, cor K and 10th streets.
Chicago house, H Benson, 7th street, b J and K.
Express hotel, R P & W B Mead, 54 front street.
Elk house, E Smith, 53 4th street.
4th Street house, J Binninger, 49 4th street.
Fleming house, O H Davis, 137 K street.
Gait house, Barker & Long, K street, b 3d and 4th.
Globe Hotel, No 10 K street.
Herkimer hotel, Lawson & Ramsdell, 41 4th street.
Hotel, Coleman & Co, 224 J street.
Hotel de France, R Wingued, 7 front street.
Hawkeye & Sucker hotel, Arnold & Pennibaker, 148 K st.
Indiana hotel, T McCalpin, 16 5th street.
Illinois house, T H Rawlings, 20 5th street.
Illinois hotel, Ruff & Co, 305 J street.
Indiana hotel, T Wilkinson, J street, b 12th and 13th.
J Street house, Lippencott & Co, 206 J street.
Kentucky house, Proctor & Bradley, 259 J street.
Louisville house, M Casada, 7th street, b I and J.
Maine house, Edward Brown, K street, b 9th and 10th.
Milwaukie house, T Carman, J street, b 15th and 16th
Missouri house, Ball & Wells, 252 J street.
Massasoit, Baker, 208 J street.

[HOTELS—CONCLUDED.]

Mansfield house, B F Hoyt, J street, b 12th and 13th.
North American hotel, F D Mercure, L street, b 8th & 9th.
Orleans house, Simmons & Curtis, 48 2d street.
Ohio house, J McNulty, 145 K street.
Penola house, M Casada, 7th street, b I and J.
Rail Road hotel, George Wilson, cor front and Sycamore.
St Charles, Hill & Smith, 65 2d street.
Star, S & L Lockhart, 56 5th street.
Sutter hotel, Dewey & Smith, 37 front street.
Southern house, B G Lathrop, 91 J street.
Tremont house, Highten & Butler, 184 J street.
Trumbo house, M J Howard, 132 K street.
United States hotel, T Moore, 278 J street.
Union hotel, Roberts, Sutherland & Conley, 217 J street.
Verandah, George R Welch, 72 front street.
Waverly, Smith & Batchelder, 24 2d street.
Wisconsin house, M O Hubbard, 137 J street.
Wm Tell, John Richart, 262 J street.

BOARDING HOUSES.

Pacific Club house, Masonic Hall, 126 J street.
Our Home, Samuel Rich, 175 J street.
Hawkeye house, E Wait & Co, 72 4th street.
Gust Haus Zur, Switz Staffelbach, I street b 5th and 6th.
Quincy house, Mrs Sarah M Steinagel, 6th st, b H and I.
Wabash house, John Gaster, 199 J street.
Dawsey house, William Richart, 74 front street.

Mrs Warner's 102 J st.	Mrs M A Booz, J&K, 4th&5th.
S Conrad, 230 J st.	Mrs S Coody, 72 4th st.
Patridge & Nash, 255 J st.	J H Dupont, J, b 12th & 13th.
E Plaisted, 272 J st.	Theodore Esse, 8 4th st.
Henry Johnson, 319 J st.	Hall & Sweet, 91 K st.

G

Barns & Spotts, 324 J st.
E A Marsh, J st, 10th & 12th.
J Norman, J st, 12th & 13th.
R Allison, J st, 14th & 15th.
L R Beckley J, 17th & 18th.
H Clark, K st, b 10th & 11th.
M Chaffey, 134 K st.
W Arnold, I st, 10th & 11th.
Robert Atkins, 70 front st.
Martin Ball, 44 5th st.
F Bartell's, 36 K st.
E L Bennett, c I & 10th st's.

J A Nuckols, 150 K st.
Chas Herich, cor L and 3d.
Truman Niman, I, b 4th & 5th
E Plaister, 272 J st.
J Politz, 36 K st.
H C Randall, 73 6th st.
W Sidgreaves, 142 K st.
N M Stevens, 7th st, b J & K.
Mrs M J Stevens, 78 J st.
Mrs Mary Theilhaver, 21 3d.
Midian Torrey, I, b 5th & 6th.

RESTAURANTS.

New York Lunch, W C Defrees, 16 J street.
Woodcock, Reed & Cushing, 15 J street.
Pacific Eating house, Geeseka & Mathewson, 24 J street.
Winslow's Exchange, Bricker, Myers & Co, 50 J street.
Hole in the Wall, A H Conradi, 52 J street.
Jenny Lind, Cook & Pomeroy, 113 J street.
Ranche, C J Schmidt, 128 J street.
City Saloon, C B Lane, 142 J street.
Orleans house, A Bennusse, 181 J street.
Hermitage, Mrs H A Hopkins, I street, b 5th and 6th.
Florence Restaurant, William O'Neill, 43 K street.
Flor de la Mar, P Carswell, 12 2d street.
Cafe de Paris, Eugene Fisher, 31 3d street.
Magnet, Josephine Gibson, 46 K street.
Abbey, George R Ryder, 170 J street.
Diadem, Williams & Feider, 38 3d street.
Gem, Francis, Augustus & Pierson, 40 3d street.

SALOONS.

Eldorado, Rayns & May, 33 J street,
Magnolia, Johnson, 23 J street.
Lee's Exchange, 46 J street.
Humboldt, Gordon, Willburn & Co, 42 J street.
Oregon, McGowan & Chrysup, 37 J street.
St Louis Exchange, 84 J street.
Pocahontas, L Eckey, 73 J street.
Jenny Lind house, Thomas Browder, 77 J street.
Billiard Saloon, Susias Pablo, Orleans Hotel.

CHURCHES.

Methodist Episcopal Church, South,
REV. JOHN PENMAN, PASTOR,
7th street, between J and K streets.
Hours of Service,—Every Sunday at 10 1-2 o'clock, A M,
and 6 1-2, P M.

Methodist Episcopal Church,
REV. M. C. BRIGGS, PASTOR,
7th street, between L and M streets.
Religious Service every Sabbath 10 1-2 o'clock, A M,
3 and 6 1-2 P M.
Sabbath School at 9 1-2 o'clock, A M.

Presbyterian Church,
REV. J. A. BENTON, PASTOR,
6th street, between I and J.
Public Service every Sabbath, at 10 1-2 o'clock A M,
3 and 6 1-2, P M. Sabbath School, at 1 1-2, P. M.

First Baptist Church,

REV. JOHN W. CAPEN, PASTOR,

Public Worship every Sunday, at 10 1-2 o'clock, A M, and 3 o'clock, P M.; at the Court house, corner of 5th and I streets.

Roman Catholic Church,

REV. FATHER INGLESBY,

Corner of K and 7th streets.

Divine Worship every morning at 7 o'clock, A M.; Sundays and Holy Days at 10 o'clock, A M, and 4 o'clock, P M.

Episcopal Congregation,

REV. ORLANDO HARRIMAN, PASTOR,

Public Service every Sabbath, at 11 o'clock, A M, and 4 o'clock, P M, at the old court house, 4th street, between J and K.

African Church,

7th street, between F and G.

Preaching every Sabbath, at 11 o'clock, A M, and 6 1-2 o'clock, P M.

PRINTING OFFICES.

SACRAMENTO TRANSCRIPT,
No. 49, K St., between 2d and 3d,
Published daily by

G. K. FITCH, F. C. EWER, AND H. S. WARREN.

Steamer editions published on the 14th and last day of each month.

DAILY PLACER TIMES,
Published by

PICKERING & LAWRENCE.

El Dorado Building, corner of J and Second Streets.

WEEKLY PLACER TIMES,
Published every Saturday Morning.

L. PICKERING.   J. E. LAWRENCE.

THE EVENING INDEX,
Published Daily

BY H. B. LIVINGSTON & CO.,

El Dorado Building, corner J and Second Streets.

H. B. LIVINGSTON,   JOS. W. WINANS.

BENEVOLENT INSTITUTIONS.

Masonic Hall,
126 J street, between 4th and 5th.
GRAND LODGE.
J D Stevenson, M W G M,   J A Tutt, D G M & G L.
Times of meeting, first Tuesdays of May and November.

TEHAMA LODGE.
T A Thomas, W M.   L Straws, Sec'y.
L J Wilder, S W.   S W Tutt, S D.
R H McDonald, J W.   —— ——, J D.
Samuel Konlman, Treas.   A C Harrison, Tyler.
Times of meeting, first and third Mondays of each month.

JENNING'S LODGE, NO. 4.
B Jennings, W M.   Moitz Schwartz, Sec'y.
J H Ralston, S W.   A Greenwalt, S D.
P Dunlap, J W.   —— ——, J D.
S S May, Treas.   A C Harrison, Tyler.
Times of meetings, first and third Fridays of each month.

SUTTER LODGE, NO. 6.
Hon E J Willis, W M.   F W Ames, S D.
Addison Martin, S W.   Thomas Ellsbury, J D.
H A Schoolcraft, J W.   J A McKinney, } Stew-
N O Hinman, Treas.   W Davenport, } ards.
F W Thayer, Sec'y.   A C Harrison, Tyler,
Times of meeting, first and third Wednesdays of each Mo.

Independent Order of Odd Fellows,

Meeting at the Masonic Hall, every Tuesday at 7 o'clock, P M.

Sons of Temperance,

PACIFIC STAR DIVISION.
J H McKune, R S.
Weekly meetings on Thursday evenings at Judge Swifts' court room, 105 J street, between 4th and 5th.

Sacramento City Hospital,

At the Fort. Established in May, 1850, Dr J R Riggs, Presiding Physician; Dr J W H Stetinius, Assistant Physician.

PLACES OF PUBLIC UTILITY.

MERCANTILE LIBRARY ASSOCIATION,
At Judge Sackett's office, J street, between 3d and 4th.

MASONIC HALL.
126 J street, between 4th and 5th.

PLACES OF AMUSEMENT.

LEE'S THEATRE HALL,
J street, between 2d and 3d,

NATIONAL ARENA,
Front street, between K and L.

PACIFIC THEATRE,
M street, between Front and 2d streets.

TEHAMA THEATRE,
No 3, Second street, between I and J streets.

SCHOOLS.

BOARDING AND DAY SCHOOL,
James Rogers, Teacher.
At the Methodist Church, corner of L and 7th streets.

UNITED STATES OFFICERS.

NORTHERN DISTRICT.

———— ————, District Judge.
Calhoun Benham, of San Francisco, District Attorney.
D F Douglass, of Stockton, Marshal.

SOUTHERN DISTRICT.

———— ————, District Judge.
J M Jones, of San Jose, District Attorney.
Pablo D La Geurray Noriega, Marshal.

Augustus Humbert, Assayer.

J A Cott, Naval officer for San Francisco.

Abram Kintzing, jr., Appraiser for San Francisco.

Hart Fellows, San Francisco,   } Surveyors.
J B Stevens, San Pedro,   }

COLLECTORS.

W M Gallser, of Sonoma, at the port of Benecia.
Madison Walthall, of San Joaquin, at Stockton.
H E Robinson, of Sacramento, at Sacramento.
W C Ferrell, of San Diego, at San Diego.
T B King, of Georgia, at San Francisco.
Alexander Randall, of Monterey, at Monterey.

Major James M Goggin, Mail Agent.

G

STATE OFFICERS.

Peter H Burnett, Gov.   John McDougal, Lieut. Gov.
William Van Voorhies, Secretary of State.
John S Houston, Comptroller of State.
———— Whiting, Surveyor General.
J G Marvin, Superintendent of Public Instruction.
S C Hastings, Chief Justice of the Supreme Court.
Nathaniel Bennett & H A Lyons, Associate Judges.
E F Tharp, Clerk of tho Supeme Court.
J A McDougal, Attorney General.

COURTS.

SIXTH JUDICIAL DISTRICT.
Hon Todd Robinson, Judge.
M S Latham, District Attorney.
First Monday of January, March, May, July and October.

COUNTY COURTS.
Hon E J Willis, Judge.
Third Monday of January, April, July and October.

COURT OF SESSION, FOR THE TRIAL OF CRIMINAL CASES.
Hon E J Willis, Presiding Judge.
C C Sackett, Associate Judge.

Second Monday of each month. For the trial of all matters connected with County business. Third Monday of February, May, August, and November.

PROBATE COURT.

Hon E J Willis, Ex-officio Probate Judge.
First Monday of every month.

COUNTY OFFICERS.

Hon E J Willis, County Judge.
Ben. McCulloch, Sheriff.
Presley Dunlap, Clerk, and ex-officio clerk of the District, Probate and Court of Sessions.
L A Birdsall, County Recorder, and ex-officio Auditor.
D. W. Thorpe, County Assessor.
C H Swift, County Treasurer.
P F Ewer, Coroner.
J H Mackune, County Attorney.
John G Cleal, County Surveyor.

JUSTICES.

FIRST DISTRICT.	SECOND DISTRICT.
George S Fake.	C H Swift.
C C Sackett.	D D Bullock.

Constables, John A Tutt, and Ira B Smith.

CITY OFFICERS.

Mayor--Horace Smith.   Recorder—B. F. Washington.

> J. R. Hardenbergh, Pres't.
> J. M. Mackenzie,
> Jesse Moore,
> V. Spalding,
> Charles A. Tweed,
> Seth Kneeland,
> John Watson,
> J. A. Cogswell,

} Common Council.

Marshal—Noble C. Cunningham.
Attorney—J. Neely Johnson.
Assessor— ——— ———
Treasurer—Barton Lee.
Clerk to the Common Council—Thomas H. Pyatt.
Collector—Wm. Rowland.
Harbor Master—George W. Hammersley.
Port Warden—Peter F. Ewer.
Captain of the Watch—John N. Tracy.

POST OFFICE.

Richard A. Edes, P. M.   E. M. Arsqueth, Ass't P. M.
R. M. French, Box Delivery Clerk.
A. Steck, Mailing Clerk.
N. G. Curtis, General Delivery Clerk.
J. H. Wickizer,   "   "   "
N. G. Holland,   "   "   "
J. Thorne,   "   "   "
Thos. A. Russell, Advertised Letter Clerk.
Wm. N. Johnson Newspaper Delivery Clerk.

Office hours from 8 A. M., to 5 P. M., in winter, and in summer, from 7 A. M., to 6 P. M.

Mails for the Atlantic States and Europe, close on the 14th and last day of each month. Arrives on or about 7th and 22d of each month.

Mail for San Francisco, and all points South and East of this, closes daily, (Sundays excepted,) at 1 P M. Arrives at 7 A. M.

Mail for Marysville, and all offices on the Sacramento, Feather and Yuba Rivers—also, Nevada City and Rough and Ready, closes on Tuesdays and Saturdays at 8 A. M. Arrives on Wednesdays and Sundays, at 7 P. M.

Mail for Coloma, Placerville and Louisville, closes on Thursday of each week, at 9 A. M.

Mail for Oregon closes on the 5th and 20th of each month, at 1 P. M.

RATES OF POSTAGE.
[On letters not exceeding half an ounce.]

Atlantic States, - - -	40	cents.
California and Oregon, - - -	12 1-2	"
England, Ireland and Scotland, -	59	"
Germany, - - - - -	64	"
France and Switzerland, (pre-paid,)	56	"
Mexico, Panama & S Amer., do	30	"
Sandwich Islands, do	13 1-2	"

Newspapers pre-praid.

To Atlantic States & Foreign ports,	5	"
California and Oregon, - -	1 1-2	"

ADVERTISEMENTS.

FREEMAN & CO.'S EXPRESS.

THE only firm in Sacramento connecting with the well known house of Adams & Co. to the Atlantic States.

Gold Dust, Coin, &c., insured against all risks, and forwarded to all the principal cities and towns of the Union.

Bills of Exchange drawn on Adams & Co. Having by contract secured the sole right of an Express on the splendid steamers Senator and New World, we will forward daily, (as heretofore,) between Sacramento and San Francisco.

We have a safe on each of the above steamers, for the security of treasure, which is always accompanied by our own messenger. FREEMAN & CO.

☞ Offices—Sacramento City, 2d street, near J, between J and K. San Francisco, with Adams & Co.

PALMER & CO.'S UNITED STATES SEMI-MONTHLY EXPRESS.
THROUGH WITHOUT DETENTION.

THE subscribers having now completely organized their Express through to the United States, will receive and forward Gold Dust promptly, by steamers every two weeks, Freights Packages, Parcels, Jewelry, Specie, Letters and Valuable Articles, of every description, from San Francisco direct to New York, via Panama, in about thirty-five days, in charge of special messengers. Our arrangements are complete for sending direct from Panama on the arrival of the steamer there ; and as our agents are residents at Panama, Cruces, Gorgona and Chagres, we have uninterrupted dispatch at all times to and from those places.

Our Express leaves New York immediately upon the arrival of the steamers there, with all goods directed to Boston, Philadelphia, Washington, Baltimore, New Orleans, and to all the principal places in the United States.

New York Policies, to the amount of $100,000 on Gold Dust from San Francisco, are in the office here.

Office on Second Street, between J and K, with Hensley & Merrill, Bankers.

☞ We forward daily to San Francisco. Also, to Marysville, Coloma, Georgetown, and Louisville.

J. H. MUMBY, Sacramento City.

C. S. PALMER, Office in N. Y., 159 Broadway.

B. W. PALMER, Office in San Francisco, Miners' Building, Washington street.

☞ We have a safe on the steamers to San Francisco for the security of valuables entrusted to us.

PALMER & CO.

GEORGE E. CLARK,

AGENT OF GREGORY'S U. S. AND CALIFORNIA EXPRESS,

Corner of Front and J streets.

ALL the latest Papers from the East, on the steamers' arrival. Also, a general stock of Merchandize, Miners Clothing, India Rubber Goods, Gold Scales, Stationery, &c., &c., for sale at the lowest market price.

J. H. CLARK.   D. B. MILNE

CLARK & MILNE,

AUCTION AND COMMISSION MERCHANTS,
No. 40, Front street, between K and L.

☞ Regular Sales every morning.

SAMUEL J. HENSLEY,   ROBERT D. MERRILL.

HENSLEY & MERRILL,

BANKERS AND EXCHANGE BROKERS,

No 47, Second street, between J and K,

SACRAMENTO CITY, CAL.

GOLD DUST, Coin, Bank Notes, Certificates of Deposit, City, County, and State Scrip, &c., bought and sold.

Exchange on the United States and Europe.
Checks on San Francisco.
Notes, Bills, &c., collected on reasonable terms.

———

SACRAMENTO CITY BANK,

No 53, Second street, between J and K, a few doors north

of the Post Office.

RHODES, STURGES, & CO., BANKERS,

WILL sell Drafts in sums to suit purchasers—
On Messrs. Corning & Co.,   New York.
Branch of the State Bank of Ohio, Mansfield.
City Bank,   Cincinnati, O.
And receive deposits, make collections, foward Gold Dust, and transact, promptly, all business intrusted to them, of the nature of Banking.

REFER TO—
W. Merritt, Esq., Sacramento City,
P. B. Cornwall, Esq.,   "   "
Barton & Boulden,   "   "
S. B. Birdsall & Co.,   "   "
Turnbull & Walton, San Francisco.
A. Bartol, Esq.,   "
Shaffer & Hall, Marysville.
Foster, Barrett & Co., Nevada City.
J. Foster & Co., Coloma.

B. F. HASTINGS & CO.,
BANKERS & COMMISSION MERCHANTS,
No 51 J street, between 2d and 3d.

EXCHANGE for sale on the principal Cities of the United States. Gold Dust and Coin purchased and sold.

JAMES B. STARR,   JOSEPH R. BEARD.
J. B. STARR, & CO., Auctioneers,
Corner of K and Front streets.

JOSEPH GRANT, Auctioneer,
No 9, J street.

REAL Estate Agent, and sole Agent in California for the True Delta published in New Orleans, on the day of sailing of each mail steamer.

W. M. ORMSBY,
140 K street,
AUCTIONEER, AND

DEALER in Horses, Mules, Cattle and every description of Live Stock. Also, Wagons, Carriages, Harness bought and sold. Auction sales every day.

PEARIS, BEIRNE & CO.,
DRUGGISTS AND CHEMISTS,
N. E. corner of J and 3d streets.

MORRILL & WHITTIER,
DRUGGISTS,
No. 48, J street, between Second and Third streets.
II

SAMUEL DEAL,
AUCTION AND COMMISSION MERCHANT,
No 214 K street.
Live Stock and Merchandise.   Sales every day.

John S. Fowler,
REAL ESTATE AND GENERAL AGENT,
And Special Agent for Capt. J. A. Sutter.
Office—Second street, between I and J, near I street.

Ormsby & Culver,
AUCTION AND COMMISSION MERCHANTS,
AND REAL ESTATE AGENTS.
Office --- No. 43, Fourth street, between J and K.

DRS. L. P. & S. S. CRANE,
NEW YORK DRUG STORE,
Front street, between J and K---J street, between
6th and 7th --- K street, corner of Fourth.

HAVE constantly on hand a full assortment of Drugs,
Medicines, Paints, Oils, Books, Stationery, Choice
Liquors, &c., &c., &c.

BOOKS AND STATIONERY!
GEO. H. LOVEGROVE,
No. 63, 2d street, Post Office Building,
WHOLESALE and Retail Dealer in Books and Stationery.   The latest novels received by every steamer.   Cheap publications and Atlantic and Pacific newspapers for sale.

JOHN W. CONNER.   JAMES O. FORREST.

CONNER & FORREST,

WHOLESALE AND RETAIL DEALERS IN BOOKS AND STATIONERY,

Sacramento City, on 2d st., between J and K.

☞ CONSIGNMENTS ARE RESPECTFULLY SOLICITED.

REFER TO:

Messrs. F. Argenti & Co., E. Gilbert & Co., and De-witt & Harrison, San Francisco; Messrs. Alfred Edwards & Co., Persse & Brooks, and Halsted, Haines & Co., New York.

———

W. H. WATSON.   WALTER BISCOE.

WATSON & BISCOE,

HARDWARE MERCHANTS, AND DEALERS IN BUILD-ING MATERIALS, IRON, STEEL, ETC., ETC.

159 J street, between 5th and 6th sts., Sacramento City.

———

NEVETT & CO.,

No. 102 K street, between Fourth and Fifth streets, DEALERS in Stoves, Hardware, Tinware, sheet iron, Tin plate, Miners' Tools, &c. Metalic Roofing and Job Work done to order.

———

ROBERT FORSYTH,

No 43, 4th street, between J and K.

MATTRASSES, Pillows, &c., made to order; and a general stock of Bedding for sale at low rates.

———

B. F. WHITING,

CABINET MAKER, 45 4th Street, bet. J and K Streets.

CHAIRS, Tables, Bedsteads, and a general stock of Furniture always on hand, and made to order.

HOY & ORTON, Blacksmiths,
42 K street.

AT their shop Ploughs are manufactured after the most approved plan, and all kinds of ship and machine work done to order. Miners' Tools for sale, wholesale and retail.

P. B. COMINS,
57 K street.

A GENERAL supply of Rifles, Shot Guns and Pistols for sale. Fire arms, Locks, &c., repaired and made to order.

C. H. SMITH,
LUMBER YARD,
Corner of L and 2d streets.

EVERY description of Building Material for sale at the lowest market rates.

The Bee Hive Bakery.
GRIFFITHS & HUGHS.
FANCY BAKERY, CONFECTIONERY AND LEMON SYRUP MANUFACTORY.
No 148 J street, between 5th and 6th.

NOTICE.—At the Hive Bakery, 148 J street, Merchants and Miners can be supplied with the best Lemon Syrup and Candies at short notice.

Also—all kinds of Iced and Ornamented Cakes and Confectioneries for Wedding parties.

A variety of small fancy Cakes, Rusks, Tea Biscuit, Pies, &c., fresh every day.

N. B.   All kinds of crackers manufactured here.

C. B. FITCH,   JAMES McCLEERY.

FITCH & McCLEERY,
No 46, 4th street, between J and K.

DEALERS in Furniture, Chairs, &c. Repairing furniture and Cabinet work done to order.

———

JULIUS UNGER,
No 38 J street,

IMPORTER and Wholesale and Retail dealer in Havanah Cigars, and all kind of Tobacco.

———

HISTORICAL SKETCH.

TOPOGRAPHY.

SACRAMENTO CITY is situated on the east bank of the Sacramento River, at the junction of the American River, and on the southern side of the latter. It stands in about 83 deg., 35 min., North Latitude, and 121 deg., 21 min., West Longitude. It is about seventy miles above the mouth of the river Sacramento; and one hundred and twenty-five miles from San Francisco.

The territory on which the City is located, was settled by John A. Sutter, in March, 1839. The Fort erected by him, was commenced the same year. The main wall sand buildings of the Fort are still standing within the City limits; but the walls of the adjoining enclosures have all been removed and most of the ditches filled up.

The gold was discovered by Marshall, on the South Fork of the American River, at what is now Coloma, in the month of February, 1848. In January, 1849—Capt. Warner surveyed and laid off the city plot. The streets run at right angles, and are all eighty feet wide, except M street, the centre street of the plot, which is one hundred feet. The alleys which divide the blocks are all 20 feet wide. The streets which run east and west, or at right angles with the Sacramento river, are designated by the letters of the Alphabet, street A beginning at a point on the American river, and the others coming in order through the alphabet. The streets that run north and south, or parallel with the Sacramento river, are designated by numbers, beginning with First, or Front street, along the bank of the river Sacramento, and extending back to Thirty-first street, beyond the Fort. The blocks are 320 by 400 feet, divided by 20 feet alleys running east and west.

BUILDINGS.

The first building in the city was erected by Samuel Brannan, and completed on the first of January, 1849. This building still stands on the corner of Front and J streets, and is now two years old. In the Spring of 1849, the warehouse of Hensley, Redding & Co., was built on the corner of Front and I street, where it still remains. The store of Priest, Lee & Co., was erected about the same time, and is still left in the block on the corner of Second and J streets, opposite the Eldorado. These are the only wood buildings of any size, built before August, 1849, and still standing. The City Hotel was quite a notability in its day. The frame of it is that which was to have been erected for a Flouring-mill on the American river, near what is now Brighton---which was brought here after that project was abandoned, and put up on what was once a corn-field. It was finished in September, 1849; and is still to be found flourishing on Front street, between I and J. Till the completion of the City Hotel, the St Louis Exchange, situated on Second street, between I and J, a rough board building, had been the principal Hotel of the city. Later, McKnight's American Hotel, on K street, between 2d and 3d, where now appears the sign of "Rest for the Weary and Storage for Trunks," did a very thriving business. During the months of September, October and November, 1849, the number of buildings erected was quite large. Among the largest were the Zinc Warehouse, near the outlet of Lake Sutter; the Zinc house and the Empire in J street, between Front and Second; Merritt's brick building on the corner of J and Second streets; the Sutter House on Front street, between K and L; the brick block on Front street between N and O; the Irving House, now the Missouri Hotel, in J street, between 3d and 4th; and Haycock's building on the corner of J and 5th streets, then quite out of town.

The principal streets now occupied with buildings, are, Front street, from D to P; Second street, from 1 to P; Third street, from I to M; Fourth street, from I to L; Fifth street, from I to L; Sixth street, from H to L; Seventh street, from H to M; Eighth street, from H to M; Ninth street, from I to M; Tenth street, from I to M; Eleventh street, from I to M; Twelfth, street from I to M; and Thirteenth to Eighteenth streets, from J to K and L. I street, from Front to 9th; J street, from Front to 19th; K street, from Front to 13th; L street, from Front to 12th; M, N, O and P streets, from Front to 4th.

MUNICIPAL AFFAIRS.

During the first few months of its existence, there was no organized government in the town.

On the first of August, 1849, the people of the city, in common with all in the region, voted for delegates to the Convention, which had been called to meet in Monterey, and which framed the State Constitution. On the same day they chose a Town Council, and other officers, as follows:

Councilmen — J. P. ROGERS, H. E. ROBINSON, P. B. CORNWALL, WM. STOUT, R. GILLESPIE, T. C. CHAPMAN, A. M. WINN, W. T. McCLELLAND, B. JENNINGS.

J. H. HARPER, Clerk.   J. A. THOMAS, First Magistrate.
B. HANNAH, Sheriff.   J. C. ZABRISKIE, Second do.

The city was chartered by the people, on the 13th of October, 1849. A charter previously presented had been voted down. On the 18th of March, 1850, the city was duly incorporated by an Act of the State Legislature.—The first election under the new charter, was held on the 1st of April, 1850, and resulted in the choice of the following persons:

I

Mayor—HARDIN BIGELOW, formerly of Michigan.
Recorder—B. F. WASHINGTON,   "   "   Virginia.
Marshal—N. C. CUNNINGHAM,   "   "   Missouri.
Assessor—J. W. WOODLAND,   "   "   Louisiana.

JESSE MOORE, of Wisconsin,
D. STRONG, of New York,
C. A. TWEED, of Florida,
THOMAS McDOWELL, of N. J.,
V. SPALDING, of Louisiana,   }   Councilmen.
J. M. MACKENZIE, of Ohio,
CHARLES MILLER, of Conn.,
A. P. PETIT, of Kentucky,
J. R. HARDENBERGH, of N. J.,

VESSELS AND STEAMERS.

Prior to the founding of the city, schooners and other small craft had visited these parts, mainly for the purpose of procuring hides. At high water they have passed through the outlet and tied up on the bank of Lake Sutter.

The first square-rigged vessel that ever came up to the city was the "Eliodora," which arrived in March, 1849. Capt. R Gelston here moored his bark, the Whiton, about the first of May, this was the first cargo of merchandize direct from the Atlantic coast.

Ere mid-summer there were as many as twenty vessels lying constantly at the levee.

From June to September there was a regular line of schooners running to and from San Francisco; and on these the U. S. Mail was carried once a week. The times of arrival and departure were about as uncertain as the payment of debts now is in California.

From September till the rains began, the mail was carried on horseback to Benecia, where it took to the water again. By December the steamers were employed in the mail transportation—but the expresses had all the business.

The first craft that came up the river propelled by steam, was a small flat-bottomed affair, built at Benecia, by the company that came out in the "Edward Everett." She had no particular name but was usually called the Washington. As she came up, ripling the bosom of the placid waters as they slept in their beauty, she was hailed with cheers at every place where there was a tent or shanty; and having sent back a response, on she went puffing and wheezing with all her might at her little high-pressure engine. She reached this place on the 11th of August, a day and a half from Benecia—having "tied up" over night. She was immediately sold ; and ran, during the rest of the season, between this city and Vernon, when at last she was used up.

The "Sacramento" was put on the river in September. She ran as far as New York and there transferred her passengers to sail-vessels, the James L. Day and others. The Sacramento is now plying as a ferry-boat between this city and Washington.

The "Mint," also made several trips on this river in September and October ; as did also some other steamers, of diminutive proportions, about which we cannot be precise. It was a great day when about the 20th of Oct., the McKim first touched at our landing. Speeches were made, cannon boomed, and shouts rent the air. A month later came the "Senator," with all her speed, pride and magnificence, and the hearts of the people were satisfied. Steam-craft of all sorts from that time have continued to multiply till their name is Legion.

WEATHER.

The months of August and September, 1849, were excessively hot ; the thermometer usually rising above 100° in the shade. There was a slight sprinkle of rain one morning about the last of August. It rained nearly the whole of the afternoon of the 10th of October, 1849.

The rainy season began on the 2d of November, and during the three days following, there fell five inches of water.

From the 10th of November onward, for six days, there fell seven inches of water.

From November 20th to December 2d, there were several bright days — nights frosty — some ice formed.

On the 18th of December, there came on a very heavy blow, which prostrated many tents and buildings ; among the rest, the frame of what is now the Tehama Block, corner of J and Front streets.

During the month of December, rain fell to the depth of fifteen inches, and the rivers all ran full.

Dec. 20th. Thermometer, at noon, 55°.

By Christmas, the water was over the lower portions of the city. And on Sunday, the 30th of December, there were ferries arranged for crossing the sloughs in several of the streets ; and the year 1849 closed gloomily.

After the first of January, 1850, the rains ceased a few days, and the water receded a few inches. But in the evening of the 8th of January, it commenced storming again. The winds and rains were exceedingly violent. The waters began to rise rapidly. The River and Lake overflowed their banks. Ere night of Wednesday, the 9th, four-fifths of the city were under water, and boats were seen all about the streets.

On Thursday, there was no dry land in town, except at the knoll on the public square, near Tenth street.— The water continued rising till Saturday, the 12th of January, 1850, when it came to a stand. That evening, there was a clear and beautiful sunset, succeeded by a night of stars. The Thermometer, at sundown, 54°, and turning colder.

The water commenced receding on the 14th, Monday, and continued to abate slowly until Sunday, the 20th, when portions of the city were getting dry. Thermometer down to 42°.

Feb. 1st. Pleasant weather, clear and mild. Thermometer standing at 66° at noon. Nearly the whole month warm and dry.

Sunday, April 7th, was rainy—the second flood came on—the water began to run into town.

Monday, the 8th. The Council voted money for a temporary Levee ; and the work went on vigorously, under the personal superintendence of Mayor Bigelow. By constant watching and repairing, day and night, for a week, the water was kept out of the city, except that which backed up from below.

The last rain fell on the 8th of April, when there were both thunder and hail. During the whole rainy season, water fell to the depth of 42 inches.

On Wednesday, June 12th, there was a shower of rain, with thunder and lightning.

Most of the summer was pleasant and agreeable ; a fresh cool breeze springing up every afternoon.

Friday and Saturday, 29th and 30th of August, 1850, were about the hottest days — the Thermometer at 98° and 100° in the shade, and 130° in the sun.

During the first two weeks of September, there were many cool days. A heavy shower of rain occurred on Sunday evening, the 15th of September, 1850.

Tuesday night, Nov. 19th, 1850, the rainy season began. The storm very violent. Several buildings blown down, and considerable damage done.

About 1 1-2 inches of rain fell in November ; and about 1 3-4 inches fell during the month of December, now gone by. Weather for the last three weeks most delightful.

FORMATION OF CHURCHES.

The "First Church of Christ," (Presbyterian, &c.,) was organized on the 16th of September, 1849.

Grace Church, (Episcopal,) was organized about the 25th of Sept., 1849.

The first Baptist Church was organized in November, 1849.

The M. E. Church was formed in the month of October, 1849.

The M. E. Church, South, was begun about the month of July, 1850.

The first M. E. Church, for the colored race, was started in August, 1850.

The Roman Catholic Church was organized in the month of October, 1850.

There was no church-building erected till November, 1849. Previous to that time there was but one Congregation in the city. Stated preaching was commenced as early as June, 1849. The meetings were sometimes held under cover and in new buildings, but more commonly beneath the shades of the lofty oaks and sycamores that then graced our city with their venerable presence, but have now disappeared forever. At these meetings Rev. Messrs. Deal, Cook, Benton, Owen, and others officiated in turn until November, when the Methodist people went into their church; there were then two meetings kept up until the flood---when there was again but one. As Spring opened all the Churches then in existence began to hold separate meetings, each having its own clergyman; and they have so continued till the present time.

MISCELLANEOUS.

Oct. 1st, 1849,---the population of the city was about 2000. Wood buildings 45; cloth houses and tents 300, and about 300 camp-fires, &c., in the open air and under trees.

The motality in the city was very great during November, 1849, reaching some days to the number of 20.

By the first of December, 1849, the population was about 3500.

The Fourth of July, 1850, was celebrated by the Sons of Temperance, out in their regalia.

On the 14th of August, 1850, there was a conflict between a body of the "Settlers" under arms and the authorities of the city, also armed---during which four persons were killed. Of this number one was Maloney, the leader of the band of "Settler's;" and another, J. W. Woodland, the City Assessor, who was a most estimable citizen. Mayor Bigelow was most dangerously wounded.

On Wednesday, Sept. 4th, 1850, occurred the ceremony of laying the Corner-stone of the "First Church of Christ," in Sixth street.

On Thursday, Sept. 5th, 1850, took place the Funeral ceremonies in grief for the death of Zachary Taylor, President of the United States.

On Sunday, Oct. 14th, 1850, was laid the Corner stone of the Roman Catholic Church.

The ravages of the Cholera began in the city about the 15th of Oct.,---the epidemic increased in malignity till the first of November, when it was at its height, there were 60 persons buried on that day. After the 5th of November the pestilence rapidly abated, and by the 15th had nearly disappeared. Within our limits about 500 fell victims to its rage; not all of them our citizens.

Hon. Hardin Bigelow, Mayor of the city, having died of Cholera, while sojourning at San Francisco, was buried in this city with public honors, on the 28th of Nov. 1850.

The present population of the city consists of about 7000 permanent, and 3000 transient people. No place could be more healthy than ours has been the last six weeks.

PUBLIC IMPROVEMENTS.

There are only two, as undertaken by the city in its corporate capacity; The Levee and the Market House.

Two years have past since Sacramento City was surveyed and laid off. A portion of the city plot had been previously under cultivation, but the greater part was still in its native wildness and beauty. Majestic oaks and sycamores flourished upon it, now throwing their shadows on the green turf of open parks, and now towering like giants above dense, dark thickets and rank undergrowths.

A close observer, even in the dry season, could not fail to notice the evidence of former overflows, as exhibited by the marks on the bark of trees, the character of the low shrubbery, and the conformation of the ground. There were stories, too, afloat of men having sailed over the city plot, and the whole valley having been like a lake.---- There were wooden pins shown, also, driven into trees, five, eight and ten feet from the ground, said to indicate the height of previous floods.

But the great mass were still incredulous. They would not believe such floods possible. Yet the demonstration came. In January, 1850, the water rose to the highest marks any where found of other floods, and the city was suddenly inundated. The early and copious rains of Nov. and Dec., '49, the unprecedented falls of snow in the mountains, combined with the warm weather and violent storms of January, hurried a deluge of water upon the city and over the whole valley. It was no doubt an extraordinary flood, as the season was a most unusual one.

Yet it may have been well for Sacramento that it was such. For it impelled them to a work of vast moment at once, when an ordinary season might not have convinced them of the necessity of protecting the city from overflow; and then when the disaster in its worst form came, it would have been destructive to the last degree.

To the flood of 1850, in part; we owe it that we have now a Levee. Vigorous measures were adopted last Spring for carrying forward the work; but it was not finally commenced until about the tenth of September, 1850. Labor at that time was comparatively cheap, otherwise the circumstances were unfavorable. Many of the people had grown indifferent. Some refused to give the right of way. There was no money in the Treasury. Loans were hard to obtain. Yet, the work went ahead, as few such works have ever gone.

To the untiring industry and energy of Irwin, Gay & Co., the Contractors; to the scientific skill of Mr. Binney, the Engineer, and to the very able and skilful management of J. R. Hardenbergh, Esq., chairman of the Levee Committee, who superintended the work ; are the people indebted for the rearing of this wall of defence around their homes and marts of trade. To all human appearance another inundation is impossible.

The Levee thus completed is nine miles in length. Beginning at the highlands near Brighton, and thence along the American River to its mouth, the Levee is about three feet in height, six feet broad on the top and twelve at the base. From the mouth of the American river along the Sacramento, and in front of the city, the embankment is raised from three to six feet, being fourteen feet broad on the top and thirty at the base. From the river bank to the heights back of Sutter, the most expensive section, the embankment is seventy feet wide at the base, and twenty at the top, and is raised from fifteen to twenty feet above the natural surface of the country. In the construction of the work there have been 37 acres of land cleared off, and 4,000 square rods grubbed. There have been 750 cubic yards of earth puddled, 4,800 cubic yards excavated, and 121,000 cubic yards made into embankment. The whole cost of the work can not fall much short of one hundred and seventy thousand dollars.

Long may it remain as the monument of our enterprize ! No other city of its population has ever completed so grand a work within the first two years of its existence as Sacramento.

The Market House is situated in the centre of M street, between 2d and 3d. It is built of brick, of the following dimensions : 30x110 feet.

The building commenced in the month of October, and is now completed. The upper story will be used for Municipal purposes.

CHURCH BUILDINGS.

The Methodist Episcopal Church, North, and Parson-

K

age were built in autumn of 1849, at an expense of about $8,000. The Church is 24 by 36 feet, with 14 feet posts.

The Methodist Episcopal Church, South, and Parsonage, were built in Sept., 1850, costing about $5,000. The church is 24 by 40 feet, with 16 feet posts.

The Methodist Episcopal Church, for the colored race, and Parsonage, were built in Sept., 1850, costing about $3,000. The church is 20 by 30, 12 feet posts.

The "First Church of Christ," and Parsonage, in sixth street, were completed in October, 1850, at an expense of about $9,000. The Church is 36 by 60 feet, with 20 feet posts, and tower of 20 feet.

The Roman Catholic Church, now nearly completed, will cost about $8,000. The church is 30 by 50 feet, with 16 feet posts. The style is gothic.

TAXES PAID IN SACRAMENTO.

The first taxes assessed for City, County and State purposes, amounted to four and a half per cent. Below is a list of the largest amounts paid :

	City.	Co. and State.	Aggregate.
Barton Lee, - -	$16,253 12	$6,000	$22,253
J. A. Sutter, jr., sold to S. Brannan & Co. - -	14,605 85	5,200	19,805
S. Brannan, - - -	5,354 12	2,000	7,354
P. H. Burnett, - -	1,571 50	5,000	15,467
Burnett, Ferguson & Co.,	8,896 12		
Beezer, Simmons - -	3,573 50	2,000	5,573
Mellus, Howard & Co., -	3,657 50	1,600	5,257
W. M. Carpenter, - -	3,104 50	800	3,904
Maynard, Peachy & Co.,	4,048 25	1,300	5,348
H. E. Robinson, - -	3,144 75	1,000	4,144
E. F. Gillespie, - -	2,014 24	1,000	3,014
R. J. Watson, - -	1,820 00	800	2,620
J. R. Snyder, - - -	1,808 97	700	2,508
Manuel Preto, - -	1,680 00	475	2,655
Hanner, Jennings & Co.,	1,575 00	700	2,275
P. B. Reading, - -	1,660 75	370	2,030
Roland Gelston, - -	1,232 00	600	1,832
S. J. Hensley, - -	1,172 50	450	1,622
Jesse Haycock, - -	1,190 00	325	1,515
Jesse S. Hambleton, -	1,085 00	300	1,385
E. Scott, - - -	1,067 50	300	1,367
L. Maynard, - - -	1,020 25	400	1,420
Isaac T. Mott, - -	971 25	300	1,271
C. H. Soule, - - -	927 50	275	1,202
Starr, Bensley & Co., -	910 00	475	1,385
R. A. Pearis, - - -	808 50	500	1,308
Paul, White & Co., -	1,050 00	350	1,400
Samuel Norris, (country)	892 50	1,800	2,692
Demas Strong, - -	717 50	300	1,017
C. W. Coote, - - -	624 75	350	974
James Queen, - - -	682 50	300	982

STEAMBOATS AND PILOTS.

STEAMBOATS.

Boats.	Tons.	Captain.	Where Plying.
New Orleans,	800,	Wakeman,	Between San Francisco and Sacramento.
Confidence,			
Senator,	755,	Van Pelt,	do do do
New World,	700,		do do do
McKim,	326,	Brenham,	do do do
Hartford,	251,	Averell,	do do do
West Point,	239,	Wright,	do do do
H. T. Clay,	154,	Murray,	do do do
Maj. Tompkins,	151½	Moseby,	do do do
Jenny Lind,	61	Le Fevre,	do do Marysville do
Mariposa,	60	Porter,	do do do do
Gov. Dana,	67	Barroll,	do Sacramento and Marysville.
Linda,	52½		do do do
Lawrence,	36	Chadwick,	do do do
Jack Hays,	42	Moseby,	do do do
Fashion,	81½	Vail,	do do do
Yuba,	32	Spear,	do do Up. Sacramento.
Missouri,	27½	Little,	do do Marysville.
California,	63		do do S. Fr'isco., do

GEO W. HAMERSLEY, Harbor Master.

Licensed Board of Pilots for the San Joaquin and Sacramento Rivers.

W. A. FAUNTLEROY,	H. VAN NESS,
W. NEAL,	L. GAMAGE,
W. BURGES,	H. VAN PELT,
E. PALMER,	W. H. JOLIFFE,
P. HOWARD,	C. CLARKE,

W. SANDEZNISS.

U. S. GOVERNMENT.

THE EXECUTIVE.

MILLARD FILLMORE, of New York, President.
WILLIAM R. KING, of Alabama, Vice President.

THE CABINET.

DANIEL WEBSTER, of Massachusetts, Secretary of State.
THOMAS CORWIN, of Ohio, Sec. of the Treas.
WILLIAM A. GRAHAM, of N. C., Sec. of the Navy.
CHARLES M. CONRAD, of Louisiana, Sec. of War.
A. H. H. STUART, of Pennsylvania, Sec. of Interior.
NATHAN K. HALL, of New York, P. M. General.
JOHN J. CRITTENDEN, of Kentucky, Attorney General.

THE JUDICIARY.

SUPREME COURT OF THE UNITED STATES.

ROGER B. TANEY, of Maryland, - Chief Justice.
JOHN McLEAN, of Ohio, - - - Associate.
JAMES M. WANE, of Georgia, - "
JOHN CATRON, of Tennessee, - - "
JOHN McKINLEY, of Kentucky, - "
PETER V. DANIEL, of Virginia, - "
SAMUEL NELSON, of New York, - "
LEVI WOODBURY, of New Hampshire, "
ROBERT C. GRIER, of Pennsylvania, "

THIRTY-FIRST CONGRESS.

Term commenced March, 4, 1849, and will end March 4, 1851.

SENATE.

Number of States represented, - - 31
President, - - - WILLIAM R. KING.
Secretary, - - - ASHBURY DICKENS.

THE SENATE IN FIGURES.

Democrats,	32
Whigs,	25
Free Soilers,	3
Total number of members,	60
Democratic majority,	7

HOUSE OF REPRESENTATIVES.

Speaker,	HOWELL COBB.
Clerk,	WM. L. YOUNG.

ASPECT OF CONGRESS.

	Whig.	Dem.
Exclusive of Free Soilers,	102	111
Free-soilers,	9	5
Vacancies,	3	1
Total,	114	117
Actual Democratic majority,		3

FREE AND SLAVE STATE CLASSIFICATION.

	Whig.	Dem.	Free-soil.
Free States,	75	51	14
Slaves States,	30	61	—
Total,	105	112	14

CALIFORNIA LEGISLATURE.

SENATE.

Districts.			Members.			Politics.
1st District			Warner	-	-	Democrat.
2d	do	-	Hope	-	-	Whig.
3d	do	-	De la Guerra	-		do
4th	do	-	Woodworth			do
5th	do	-	Tingley	-	-	do
6th	do	-	{ Heydenfeldt	-		do
			Broderick	-	-	Democrat.
7th	do	-	Van Buren	-	-	do
8th	do	-	Douglass	-	-	Whig.
9th	do	-	Lippencott	-	-	do
10th	do	-	Miller	-	-	Democrat.
11th	do	-	Cook	-	-	do
12th	do	-	Robinson	-	-	do
13th	do	-	Green	-	-	do
14th	do	-	Crosby	-	-	do
15th	do	-	Adams	-	-	do

ASSEMBLY.

Counties.		Members.			Politics.
San Diego	-	Cook	-	-	———
Los Angelos	-	{ ———	-	-	Democrat.
		———	-	-	Whig.
Santa Barbara,		{ Covarrubias,	-		Democrat.
		Pico	-	-	Whig.
San Luis Obispo,		———	-	-	Democrat.
Monterey	-	Randall	-	-	do
Santa Cruz	-	Kellogg	-	-	Indep'dt.
Santa Clara	-	{ Campbell	-	-	Whig.
		Bodley	-	-	do

County	Name			Party
Contra Costa -	Brown	-	-	do.
	Carr	-	-	do
	Wethered	-	-	do.
San Francisco -	Bennett	-	-	do
	Thorne	-	-	do
	Hoff	-	-	Democrat.
San Joaquin, -	McDougall	-	-	do
	Yeiser	-	-	do.
Calaveras -	Lynd	-	-	do
	Mann	-	-	do.
	Moore	-	-	Whig.
Tuolumne -	Baldwin	-	-	do
	Wilkins	-	-	do
Mariposa -	Taylor	-	-	Democrat.
	Ormsby	-	-	————
	Bigler	-	-	Democrat.
Sacramento -	Lisle	-	-	Whig.
	Robinson	-	-	Democrat.
El Dorado -	Kendrick	-	-	do
	Hall	-	-	do.
Marin -				
Sonoma -				
Napa -	Bradford	-	-	do.
Solano -				
Mendocino -				
Yolo -				
Colusi -	Crane	-	-	Whig.
Trinity -				
Sutter -	McCorkle	-	-	Democrat.
Yuba -	Field	-	-	do
Butte -	Saunders	-	-	do
Shasta -	McCandless	-	-	————

APPENDIX.

L

Freeman, J M. Express office, 42 Second street.
Gilmore, James, Merchant, 198 J street.
Glen & Bruce, Land Agents, 16 Front street.
Gossag, Z. Fleming House.
Goodrich, A. Pianist, 13 Second street.
Goodall, T. H. Merchant, 71 J street.
Golton. George, Blacksmith, 319 J street.
Goodale, M D. Carpenter, Allen's Hotel.
Gordon, John H. at Gordon & Holt's.
Golstein, M. 18 J street.
Gorden & Holt, Merchants, 200 J street.
Gorden, Willburn & Co., Humboldt, 42 J street.
Gore, Benjamin B. at Gore, Wilder & Co's.
Goodrich & Raymond, Centre Market, 144 J street.
Gohram, J H. Trader, 144 K street.
Gore, Wilder & Co., Merchants, 204 J street.
Golstein & Co., E. Merchants, 83 J street.
Hamersley, George W. Harbor Master, on board the
    storeship Tecumseh, foot of L street.
Hoyt, David, Am. Riv. Ferry, cor B and 28th streets.
Hardenstein, Dr. Homœopathist, 12 K street.
Hutchinson, John J. Transcript Office.
Hyer, John J. Lawyer, J st, between 3d and 4th.
Jackson, W S. K street, between 3d and 4th.
Jaquith & Smith, cabinet makers, 91 K street.
Jaquith, Wm T. at Jaquith & Smith's.
Kendall, W W. tinner, 249 J street.
Kelsey, D M. Transcript office.
Kendall & Dennison, tinners, 249 J street.
Kneeland, Seth, office at Lewis & Bailey's.
Livingston, H B. Editor of the Evening Index.
Lovett, Orestes H. at Brook & Lovett's.
Lawrence, J E. Editor of the Placer Times.
Lynch, P. Printer, Placer Times.
McClatchey, James, do   do
McKune, J H. Lawyer, at the Tribune office.
Marshall, I B. Lawyer, 62 J street.

Martin & Wells, Merchants, No. 194 J street.
Magoon, B F. at the Mansfield House.
Marsh, E A, Boarding House, J st. bet 11th and 12th.
Martin, Dr Robert, office 309 J street.
Meeks, Washington, Lawyer, 15 Front street.
Mumby, J H. Ag't for Palmer's Express, 47 2d street.
Nægle, George D. Bricklayer, cor I and 14th streets.
Norton & Terrell, stock yard, K st. bet 9th and 10th.
Nunes, Ralph at Oliver, Nunes & McCarty's.
Pyatt, Thos H. clerk of Com. Council, N st. b 1st & 2d.
Pomeroy & Peebels, Merchants, 102 J street.
Peebels, Cary, at Pomeroy & Peebels'.
Peyton, R. K street, bet Third and Fourth streets.
Pickering, Loring, Editor of the Placer Times.
Queen, James, at the Columbia Hotel.
Reynolds, George O. at Dupont's Boarding House.
Reynolds, W W. at Forshee & Reynolds'.
Ruth, J A. Engineer, 2d street, bet J and K.
Rowland, Wm. City Collector, N st. bet 1st and 2d.

Saville & Goodall, Merchants, 71 J street.
Scranton J H. at Scranton & Smith's.
Smith, Simeon, at Jaquith and Smith's.
Solomon & Williamson, Carpenters, N st. bet 1st & 2d.
Solomon, A T. at Solomon & Smith's.
Stanley, R H. Lawyer, 62 J street.
Springer, T A. Printer, at the Times office.
Sunderland, T. Lawyer, 107 J street.
Shortridge, Dr A L. K street, between 3d and 4th.
Theilhares, Mrs Mary, Boarding House, 21 3d street.
Van Gelden, A A. clerk at Palmer's Express.

Watson, W H. at Watson & Biscoe's.
Wibens, Jacob, at Wibans, Jacobs & Co.'s.
Watson John, 197 J street.
Watson, R. J. & Co., Land Agents, 244 J street.
Williamson, A. at Solomon & Williamson's.
Williams, John L. at the Pacific Eating House. J st.

Winans & Hyer, Lawyers, J st., between 3d and 4th.
Weiser, George, at Zins & Weiser's.
Wright, W. C. Printer, Placer Times office.
Winans, Joseph W. Editor of Evening Index.
Yates, Chapman, L street, bet 7th and 8th.
Zins & Weiser, Brewers, 29th st., bet J and K.
Zins, George, at Zins & Weiser's.

BUSINESS CARDS.

E. S. YOUMANS.   SENEKA DANIELS.

E. S. YOUMANS & CO., 56 Fourth Street,
UNDERTAKERS AND SEXTONS. Mahogany and Pine Coffins constantly on hand. Lead Coffins furnished to order.

PETER F. EWER,
PORT WARDEN AND CORONER.—Office at the Central Warehouse, on the Levee, between M and N streets.

HENRY A. CLARKE,
INTERPRETER and Translator of the Spanish and English Languages, and Real Estate Agent, No. 123 K street.

HOYT & FIFIELD,

PAINTERS, J street, between 7th and 8th. House and Sign Painting, Gilding, Graining, Imitations of Wood and Marble, and every variety of business in their line executed with dispatch and in the very best manner.

Always in store, a full stock of Paints, Oils and Glass, including White, Red, and Black Lead, Chrome Green, Paris Green, Chrome Yellow, Umber, Venetian Red, Ultramarine Blue, Prussian Blue, Serra de Sienna, Vandyke Brown, Lampblack, French, English and Chinese Vermillion, Gold and Yellow Bronzes, English, French and American Window Glass, Varnishes, Point and Varnish Brushes, &c.; boiled Linseed Oil and Turpentine.

PAPER HANGINGS.

4,000 ROLLS of every description, quality and pattern, being the largest assortment in the city, and comprising the most gorgeous patterns, suitable for parlor decorations.

Messrs. FULLER & JONES, Upholsterers and Paper Hangers, attend to finishing interiors ; lining and papering walls, ceilings, &c., and keep constantly on hand a large supply of Tacks and other material required in their business. They can always be found at the store of Messrs. Fifield & Hoyt.

LIVERY STABLE.

JOHN K. MILLER, No. 7 Fourth street, between I and J, keeps on hand to hire, Horses, Buggies, Carriages, &c., &c.

SIGN PAINTING.

JOHN WILSON, No. 45, Fourth street. House, Sign, and Ornamental Painting done with neatness and dispatch. Houses numbered.

BERRY, BLISS & CO.,

AUCTION AND COMMISSION MERCHANTS, No. 41, Front Street, between K and L. RICHARD N. BERRY, Auctioneer.

HENRY G. LANGLEY,

COMMISSION MERCHANT, and General Dealer. Brick Building, No. 19 J street, bet. Front and 2d.

WINKLE'S BAKERY, Of Pickwick Memory.

A DAILY supply of Fresh Bread, Pies and Cakes, for Hotels and Families. Fancy and Iced Cakes and Confectionery, always an hand.

ALSO—Hot Coffee and Tea, Oysters, Ducks, Ham, &c., furnished at short notice. Call and judge for yourselves, at No. 16, K street, between Front and 2d.

THE CONCLUSION.

THE DIRECTORY is now completed. It is issued to a generous public, with the confident belief that it will be received with that kind partiality and favor which are so essential to the future success of publications of a like character.

Few are aware of the labor incident to a collection of the facts and references necessary to this publication ; and it must of course contain inaccuracies, which another edition can only rectify. This has been an experiment, and its success will determine whether the publisher will again engage, on a future occasion, in rendering a work more worthy of the Queen City of the Pacific, and better entitled to the confidence and regard of the public.

It will be observed that especial regard has been paid to numbering the different residences and places of business, which may be easily understood. No. 1 commences in each street at the left corner, in passing down the river ; the odd numbers occur on the left hand side in passing up the streets, and even numbers on the right. The cross streets are similarly arranged.

By dint of diligence, we have probably been the means of preserving some of the early and unwritten historical events connected with our young and gigantic city, which otherwise would soon have passed away from the minds of all, and been lost to posterity.

For the valuable aid extended us by Rev. J. A. Benton, S. Brannan, Esq., J. R. Hardenbergh, Esq., and Dr. J. M. Mackenzie, they have our sincere thanks; and we trust that in future publications we may have like aid extended from the early settlers, and those familiar with the detail of our early history as a City and State.

In consequence of the late hour at which some names and business cards were handed in, the work is not arranged as systematically as originally designed. Manufactories are springing up with such rapidity that it has been impossible to give them a fair representation. The different branches of the mechanic art are to be found in almost every quarter of the city — blacksmiths, tinners, cabinet makers, carpenters, &c., &c. There are two Flouring Mills, one Foundry, and Candle and Soap Factories, besides other strong evidences which mark the growth of this city as one of permanence and stability.

ERRATUM.—Under the head of "City Government," the name of RICHARD N. BERRY, as a member of the Common Council, was accidentally omitted.

PALMER & CO.'S
United States Semi-Monthly EXPRESS !
THROUGH WITHOUT DETENTION!

WE forward GOLD DUST promptly by steamers, every two weeks, Freights, Packages, Parcels, Jewelry, Letters, and Valuable Articles of every description, from San Francisco direct to New York via Panama, in about 35 days, in charge of special messengers.

ALSO--Daily Express to San Francisco, Marysville, Coloma, Georgetown and Louisville. Office, 47 2d St., between J and K.　　　　J. H. MUMBY, Agent.

GEORGE E. CLARKE,
AGENT OF
GREGORY'S U. S. AND CALIFORNIA EXPRESS,
Corner of J and Front Streets.

WE forward GOLD DUST and PACKAGES of every description promptly, to San Francisco, daily, at 2 o'clock, P. M.　To the up river towns daily, at 9 o'clock, A. M.; and to the Atlantic States with every Mail Steamer.　A general assortment of Miners Goods for sale.

SACRAMENTO TRANSCRIPT
JOB
PRINTING ESTABLISHMENT
K ST., BETWEEN SECOND AND THIRD.

JOB PRINTING, such as Bill Heads, Circulars, Posters, Blanks, Bills Lading, &c., &c., executed with neatness and dispatch, and on the most reasonable terms.

APPENDIX A

THE 1851 SACRAMENTO CITY DIRECTORY
ARRANGED BY STREET ADDRESSES

STREET DIRECTORY

SUPPLEMENT TO THE 1851 SACRAMENTO DIRECTORY
CONVERTED TO NEW STYLE NUMBERING (AFTER 1880)

Names marked with asterisk are mentioned in "Biographies" section

ARCHAIC WORDS APPEARING IN THIS DIRECTORY

Botanico: Not in the largest Oxford English Dictionary. Possibly a vegetarian or herbalist derived from "Botanist"

Carman: A man who drives a delivery wagon or cart. Also might carry small packages by hand.

Merchant: From the advertisements at the back, they seemed to be street-level general stores selling to the public.

Daguerrian: Early name for a professional photographer.

Rusks: (bakery 148 J) A twisted roll or such a roll crisped.

Trader: Seemed to traffic in livestock, but not certain.

Numbers of Businesses Listed Here
Number listed in classified section shown in parentheses

Auctioneers, 28	Express Companies, 3
Bakers 22	Grocers, 36
Bankers 5	Gunsmiths 5
Barbers 5	Hospitals (1)
Blacksmiths, 41	Hotels 58 (57)
Boarding houses 36 (40)	Interpreter, Spanish/English (1)
Book Stores (2)	Jewelers 8
Butchers, 11	Lawyers 47 (55)
Carpenters 22	Library (1)
Churches (7)	Lumbermen 13
Clothiers 45	Merchants 106
Coopers 4	Painters 6
Daguerrean Photographers, 3	Physicians (80) (classified, page 234)
Dentists 4	Printers (3)
Doctors 63	Restaurants 29 (17)
"Dr." 15, some not practicing	Schools (1)
Druggists 10	Saloons 14 (9)
Eating Houses (with Boarding houses)	Shoe Makers & Sellers, 6
Engineers, 4	Steamboat Pilots (11)

STREET DIRECTORY

SUPPLEMENT TO THE 1851 SACRAMENTO DIRECTORY
NEW STYLE NUMBERING (AFTER 1880)
Names marked with asterisk are mentioned in "Biographies" section

B Street:

cor 28th, American River Ferry, James Dexter

cor 28th Hoyt, David, Am. Riv. Ferry

H Street:

[In 1851 Sutter Lake occupied H Street west of 6th]

6th to 7th Streets

Dodson, Mrs. H., residence

Hite, Edmund, residence

Smith, Constable Ira G., residence

White, William, residence

Willis, Hon. E.J., residence

Winson, Edmund, residence

8th to 9th Streets

cor 8th, Petit, A.P., residence

Brown, Doctor, residence

I Street:

Front to 2nd Street

106, Tucker, Chas.,Jr.,coffee & spices

107, Reading, Maj. Pierson*-came to Cal. in 1843 and was Sutter's chief of trappers and later his clerk at Fort

107, Suydam, J & L., merchants

110, Stingle, A., grocer

115, Beatson, D., laborer

121, Collins, George, cooper

123, McCord, J.S., cooper

3rd to 4th Street

305, Sheperd, Professor F.* office [and site of first school in Sacranento]

Chapell,M., silk & cloth dyer

Cook, John, [meat] market

Rowan, D., laborer

4th to 5th Street

Comstock, George, trader

Niman, Truman, boarding house

Torrey, Midian, boarding house

5th to 6th Street

cor 5th, New Court House

First Baptist Church at New Court House, Rev. John W. Green, pastor

Gast Haus Zur Switz, Staffelbach

Hermitage [restaurant] Mrs. Hopkins

Hopkins, Mrs. H.A., restaurant

Hunt, W.B., drayman

Mooney & Wheelwright, livery stable

Riley, Michael, drayman

Simonds, F.S., drayman

Staffelbach, X., boarding house

White, Doctor T.J., residence

cor 6th Louisville House, R.M. Leke

9th to 10th Street

Duke, M., residence

10th to 11th Street

cor 10th, Bennett, E.L., boarding hse.

Arnold, Wm. boarding house

11th to 12th Street

12th to 13th Street

Norman, Joseph, boarding house

13th to 14th Street

1330, Naegle, Geo. D., bricklayer

[this address from other source.]

J Street:

100, Brannan, M, second building in Sacramento, built by Sam Brannan and completed on Jan 1, 1849

100, Janes, James

100, Merry, S.H., saloon

100, Reynolds & McLaren, saloon

100, Roe, Fred. J.*, gambler

100, Winters, W.W.,

101, Clark, G., general store

101, Gregory, J.W., express office

101. Glen & Bruce, steam boat agents

101. Hopkins, B.F., grocer

103, Warren[JLF]* & Co., merchants

104, Empire Saloon, James Hyslop

108, Dubroski, A.

108, Hadles, T., silversmith

108, Hatch, John, jeweler

108, Marsh, Robert, at Hatch's

109, Atkins, H.B.

109, Grant, Joseph, auctioneer & real estate agent

J Street:

109, Potter, A.H.., merchant
111, Mitchell, T.S., shoe store
111, Morton, C.B.
112, Stone & Bloom, clothiers
113, Kuhlan, William, jeweler
113, Moore, James
113, Watchorst, & Co., jewelers
114, New York Lunch, W.C. Defrees
115, Cushing, H., Woodcock's
115, Reed & Henry & Woodcock
116, Herman, M. clothier
116, Golstein, M.
118, City [meat] Market, E. Pierce
118, Burns, A., butcher
118, Lucken, J.F., druggist
119, Langley, Henry G., merchant
120, Baker, S., clothier
122, Campbell, barber
122, Pacific Eating House, Restaurant
122, Pacific House [hotel]
123, Magnolia [saloon], Johnson
124, Pearlman & Co., clothiers
125, Kinsey, Jesse, jeweler
125, May, Dr. S.J., druggist
125, Spaulding, Doctor Volney, office
126, Passenand, barber
127, Lockitt, Joseph, clothier
128, Vanderberg, L.V.,
128, Wright, J.A., jeweler
129, Galant, W., merchant
130, Ben, O Z & K, clothiers
131, Neubauer & Hollub, dry goods
     2nd to 3rd Street
201, *Evening Index,* H.B. Livingston,
 Editor
201, *Placer Times,* J.E. Lawrence,
 Editor
201, *Placer Times,* L. Pickering, Editor
201, Lynch, P., printer at Placer Times
201, McClatchy, James*, Placer Times
201, Eldorado [saloon], Rayns & May
201, Price & Burnham, doctors
201, Smith, Horace, lawyer & Mayor
 of Sacramento
203. Site of "Stinking Tent", first

gambling house in Sacramento,
 James Lee, proprietor
202, Kohlmann & Brieger, clothiers
204, Unger, Julius, cigar store
 Lee's Theatre Hall
205, Oregon [saloon], McGowan & C.
206, Heyman & Sanford, clothiers
208, Humboldt [saloon], Gordon & W.
209, Flint & Baker, merchants
211, McNulty, W., merchant
212, Lee's Exchange [saloon]
214, Morrill & Whittier, druggists
216, Winslow's Exchange, restaurant.
218, Hole in the Wall,. restaurant, A.
  Conradi, proprietor.
219, Hastings, B.F., bankers & merch.
  gold dust and coin
220, Kohlmann & Brieger, clothiers
221, Titcomb & Sampson, merchants
222, Rosenfield & Mayers, furniture
223, Bell, Doctor R.
224, Starr & Bensley*, merchants
225, Barber, E.L. engineer
226, McCall, W.R., merchant
227, Demarst, Doctor J.D.
227, Sawyear & Clark, merchants
227, Stocking, Dr. D.C., dentist
228, Marshall & Stanley, lawyers
228, Mills, James, merchant
228, Stanley, R.H., lawyer
229, Bullard, Figg* & Co., merchants
231, Prince, W.R., merchant
     3rd to 4th Street
300, Ames, Dr. F.W.
300, Light*, Ames & Watts, druggists
300, Light, Dr. W.W.*, dentist
300, Watts, Doctor Stephen, physician
300, White, Doctor T.J., office
301, Schwarz, M., merchant
304, Pearis & Brockway*, grocers
305, Pearis & Beirne, druggists
306, Churchman, J., lawyer
306, Montgomery, George E., lawyer
306, Solomon & Co. clothiers
306, Teagarden, Doctor, office
306, Whiteside, N.E., lawyer

J Street:

307, Edwards & Caldwell, doctors
307, Goodall, T.H., merchant
307, Saville & Goodall, merchants
308, Dunbar, R., tailor
308, McCrellis, E., tailor
308, Heard, John, lawyer
308, Kennedy, E.D. & W.T., merchants
308, Lewis, A., tailor
308, Speeks, R.R., tailor
308, Wallace, W.C., lawyer
308, Wallace, Doctor, office
309, Pocahontas [saloon], L. Eckey
309, Henderson, J., lawyer
309, Lamar, J.B., lawyer
310, Simons & Co., clothiers
310, Temple, Doctor J.T., office
311, Higgins, M.S., merchant
311, Thayer, F.W., lawyer
312, upstairs, Aldrich, David
312, Stevens, Mrs. M.J., boarding hse.
312, Anderson, J.G., tinner
312, Isaacs, Lewis, clothier
312, Thom, C.E., lawyer
313, Jenny Lind House, T. Browder
313, Dennis, barkeeper, Jenny Lind H.
313, Fake, Geo. S., lawyer
313, Lyon, R., barkeep, Jenny Lind H.
313, Sackett, C.C., justice of peace
313, Skaggs, Tom., Jenny Lind House
313, Thorpe, D.W., county assessor
313, Tutt, John A., constable
313, Vines, Miss Julietta, at Jenny Lind
314, Bankhead, S.P., lawyer
314, Forshee & Reynolds, merchants
314, Booth, L. A.*, at F.&R.
315, Scranton & Smith, merchants
316, Atlantic Hse, Barnes & Dinsmore
317, Johnson, G.H., daguerrean
317, Taylor, Doctor, G., office
317, Thomas, Dr. W.H., dentist
317, Wilcoxon & Co., merchants
318, St. Louis Exchange [saloon]
319, Golstein, E. & Co., merchants
320, Missouri Hotel, W.S. Long
320, Maxey, J.M.

321, Langfelt & Co., merchants
321, Mason, G., tailor
322, Bradley, John, clothier
322, Dangerfield, W.P., lawyer
322, Kenny, D.M., tobacconist & cutler
322, Montgomery, Doctor, office
323, Mitchell, T.S., shoe store
324, Crescent City Hotel
325, Henry Brown & Co, merchants
326, Lee & Harklerodes, merchants
326, Tannatt, George F., watchmaker
327, Southern House [hotl], B. Lathrop
327, Morey, David
328, Ben, O Z & K, clothiers
329, Anderiese, doctor
329, Lewis & Bailey, merchants
329, Winans & Hyer, lawyers
330, Beals, Doctor H.H.
330, Ford & Jakes, barbers
330, Harris & Rice, merchants
330, Johnson, C.A., lawyer
331, Cohan & Green, clothiers
Winans & Hyer,, lawyers

4th to 5th Street

400, Cannon & Kempt, tinners
400, Jaretsky, Lewis, clothier
401, Hirsfelter, A., clothier
402, Neubauer & Hollub, dry goods
403, Hermance, L., auctioneer
403, Pellow, J.P., merchant
403, Stephens, N.T., notary public
404, Warner, Mrs., boarding house
404, English, James L., lawyer
404, Harris,Lewis B.*, under-sheriff
404, Heerman, doctor
404, Pomeroy & Peebels, merchants
404, Ruffin, Doctor William H.
404, Tarr, B.F., lawyer
404, Watson, Doctor Wilkins, office
405, Haworth, James, tinner
406, White & Co., clothiers
408, Newman & Bro., clothiers
409, Ball, J. dentist
409, Beuneson, W.H.,. lawyer
409, Booth, L.M., lawyer
409, McFerren, Doctor L.A.

J Street:

409, Marks & Freidman, merchant
409, Smith, Ira G. constable
409, Swift, C.H., justice of peace
409, Sons of Temperance, J.H.
   McCune, R.S., meet Thursdays
410, Mead & Smith, merchants
410, Tweed-Aldrich & Pedan, lawyers
411, Whitney's Brick Buildings
411, Fogg & Gren, merchants
411, Ralston & Sunderland, lawyers
412, Hastings, B.R. & Co., jewelers
412, Joseph, E., clothiers
413, Post, G.P., merchant
414, Lewis, A. & Co., clothiers
415, Empire Mills [flour], H. Merritt
415, Olmstead, T.C.D., merchant
416, West, L., merchant
417, Cook & Pom., Jenny Lind rest.
417, Oak Tree Bakery, W.S. Ellison
417, Pomeroy, F.C., at Jenny Lind
418, Carroll & Strong, merchants
419, Burnett*, Edwards, & Gass, atty.
* 419, Burnett, P.H, lawyer*
419, Edwards, P.L., lawyer
419, Gass, John H,, notary public
420, Baker, Farr & Co., merchants
420, Clover & Winchell, lawyers
421, Pearis & Brockway*, druggists
422, Whalley, C., merchant
423, Kalkmann, P., merchant
425, Courtois, B. fancy store
426, Blumenthal, M.A., fancy store
426, Slomowsky & Co., clothiers
427, McConalin, G.N., lawyer
427, Moss, H.H., auctioneers
428, Masonic Hall
428, Bramsky, M.A., clothier
428, Independent Order of Odd
Fellows meet Tuesdays at Masonic H.
428 Pacific Club, boarding house
429, Josephi, Robert, jeweler
430, Ranche [restaurant], C. Schmidt
                    5th to 6th Street
500, Bensti, E., clothier
500, Buckley & Co., merchants

501, Calif. Trading Co, C.W..Bewley
501, Whitfield & Venable, merchants
502, Wensinger & Pettibone, merchs.
503, Huerstel, Bilay & A., harness mfg
504, Kohen & Co., clothiers
505, Batters & Creegan, tinners
506, Alderman, White & Whitman
507, Rancitz, Martin, grocer
508, Alexander, A.W., fancy store
509, Wisconsin House [hotel], Hubbard
509, Tuley, John W., carpenter
510, Seaman, W. & Co., merchants
511, Chatburn, R. daguerrean [photos]
511, Daval, J.F., daguerrean [photos]
511, Hunter, Doctor Thomas
511, Oliver, Nunes, & M., merchants
512, City Saloon, C. Lane [restaurant]
513, Coffin, Mark, cooper
513, Fry, G.W.
513, Steel & Co. merchants
514, Centre Market, Gordon & R.
514, Gohram, J.H., trader
515, McDonald, Dr. R.H., druggist
515, Wickersham, Doctor R.R.
516, Zeira & Freedlander, clothiers
517, Desrosiers & Co., clothiers
517, Frisby, William, baker
517, Metzinger, A., barber
518, Bee Hive Bakery, Grifffiths &
           Hughes
518, Hughes Co., cakes & lemon syrup
520, Alderman & White, merchants
521, Galant, Benjamin, clothier
521, Moris & Co. clothiers
522, Alderman & Whitman, merch.
523, Howell's Hospital
523, Howell, Doctor C.W.
523, Klopenstine & Co., merchants
524, Coonrod & Gillig, tinners
525, Curtis & Cowan, druggists
526, Drake, J.H., merchants
527, Budget, A., clothiers
527, Stickler, E., tailor
528, Ryan & Co., tinners
529, Bailie, Dr. T., druggist
529, Caskell, Jos., clothier

J Street:

530, Hopkins* & Miller, merchants
531, Watson & Biscoe, hardware mer.
                    6th to 7th Street
600, Reed & Freeman, merchants
601, Smith & Peterson, merchants
602, Hall, Doctor R.B., office
602, Johnson, Josiah, broker
603, Caswell & Ingalls, merchants
604, American Hotel, Patterson et al
604, Patterson, Doctor E.M.
604, Randolph, Doctor P.
604, Williams, J., at Am. Hotel
605, Burnett House, [Hotel], W, H &J
605, Wolf, Holton, & Abrams
606, Miller, C.H,, merchant
607, Solomon, L. clothiers
608, Abbey Hotel, Ryder &Byers
608, Abbey [restaurant] Geo. R. Ryder
609, Cooledge, W.S., merchants
611, Isaacs, J., clothier
612, Youngs & Kibbee, merchants
614, New York Drug Store, Dr. Crane
615, Burrill, Doctor Charles
615, Our Home, boarding house
615, Rich, Samuel, owner of Our home
615, Vale & Co., merchants
616, Fulkerson & Cole, merchants
618, Baker, E.G., tinner
620, Foard, J.W., merchant
621, Orleans House, A. Bennesee
622, Illinski, A.X.
622, Tremont House, [hotel] H. & B
623, Western [meat] Market, D. & D.
624, Segar & Co., merchants
625, McKamey, Glenn, livery stable
626, Craw, A., carman
626, Downer, A.J., merchant
627, Boone, Doctor J.T.
628, Wheeler & How, merchants
629, Mensingheimer, J. saddler
630, Cole, N.W., carpenter
631, Hoope & L'Amoureux, merchants
                    7th to 8th Street
700, Martin & Wells, merchants
700, Miller, C., merchant

702, Dodson, Doctor W.H.B.
703, Polhemus, J.L., druggist
704, Gilmore, James, merchant
705, Wand, S. & Co., merchants
705, Watson, John
706, Gordon & Holt, merchants
707, Wabash House, boarding house,
707, Pritchard & Gaster at Wabash H.
708, Burdick & Lawrence, merchants
710, Gore & Wilder, merchants
711, Knox, R.A., tinner
712, J Street House [hotel]
* 712, Duncombe, Doctor C., office
713, Ashley & Hawes, blacksmiths
714, Massasoit Hotel, Mr. Baker
716, Clark, G.W., merchant
717, Vanorden, John, grocers
718, Roberts & Laing, stockyard
720, Sloss, L., clothier
723, Peirce & Miller, merchants
725, Union Hotel, Roberts, Sutherland
        & Conley
726, Sedam & Galaway, auctioneers
727, Fifield & Hoyt, painters
727, Fuller & Waldron, paper hangers
727, Kendall & Dennison, grocers
728, Folger & Clift, merchants
729, Bercaw, Wm., cooper
730, Coleman Hotel, S. McCullough
731, Shafer, George, baker
                    8th to 9th Street
804, Conrad, S., boarding house
* 805, Arents & Co., merchants
807, Haskell & White, merchants
809, Denniston, Chas., Restaurant
812, Watson, N.A., stock yard
818, Watson, R.J., land agents
820, Patchin, L.B., merchant
821, Allen's Hotel, Allen & Redding
821, Goodale, M. D.*, carpenter
823, Union Hotel, Roberts, S., & C.
824, Dyer, Samuel, butcher
825, Kellogg, Leonard, tinner
825, Kendall & Dennison, tinners
826, Ball & Wells, Missouri House
828, Jones & Doswell, merchants

J Street:

829, Samuel Brown, grocer
829, Osborn, H.P.*, merchants
831, Patridge & Nash, boarding house
831, Henrickson, A., MD, doctor
831, Kendal, Doctor, office
Allen's Hotel, H. Mallen
Robinson, John, carpenter
9th to 10th Street

901, Avery & Grows, lumber
901, Silsby & Co., merchants
903, Kentucky House, Proctor & B.
904, William Tell [hotel] J. Richart
906, Keller, Francis, butcher
912, Brugier, Adolpha, restaurant
914, Plaisted, E., boarding house
920, United States Hotel, T. Moore
922, McDonough, W.S., tinner
924, Terhune & Edwards, merchants
928, Greenman, Doctor M.
928, Logan, Dr. Thomas, office
10th to 11th Street

1000, Oschner Co., grocer & blacksmth
1005, Briggs, blacksmith
1007, Campbell & Hay, bakers
1009, Fairman, H.A., merchants
1015, Chenoworth, J., grocer
1017, Illinois Hotel, Ruff & Co.
1018, Lake, Z. & Co., merchants
1019, Sels, C.M., at Illinois hotel
1021, Martin, Doctor Robert
1024, Clark's Hotel, Lewis Clarke
1026, Hutchinson & Green* merchants
1031, Johnson, Henry, boarding house
1031, Golton, George, blacksmith
Caulfield, Henry,* carpenter
11th to 12th Street

1102, Barnes & Spotts, boarding house
Marsh, E.A., boarding house
Parsons, S.H., livery stable
Poage, James F., blacksmith
Robinson, Josiah, blacksmith
12th to 13th Street

Dupont, J.H., boarding house
Grow, A., blacksmith
Herrings, G.H., hay yard

Indiana Hotel, T. Wilkinson
Jackson & Johnson, hay yard
Mansfield House [hotel], B. Hoyt
Norman, J., boarding house
Overshiner & Cochran, carriage makrs
Packer, H.B. grocer
Quin, James R., grocer
13th to 14th Street

Cor 13th, Hunt & Harvey, merchants
Duncan, Chas., MD, residence
Duncombe, Doctor Charles*,
Hacker, J.C., blacksmith
14th to 15th Street

Allison, R., boarding house
Eveans & Thomas, blacksmiths
Wilson & Mathews, blacksmiths
Woods, W.R.& Brother, stockyard
15th to 16th Street

Milwaukee House, T. carman
16th to 17th Street

Ewing, William, hay yard
17th to 18th Street

* Beckley, L.R., boarding house
29th to 30th Street

* Zins & Weiser, brewers

K Street:

Perkins, J., clerk on bark *ELIZA*
Warner, Wm., clerk on bark *ELIZA*
Porter, Col., clerk on *NEW WORLD*
Front to 2nd Street

100, Starr, J.B.*, auctioneers
103, Kinne & Dudley, restaurant
105, Bearns & Co., merchants
105, Parks, Edward, saloon
108, Globe Hotel
111, Cotting, H.P., grocer
110, Lady Adams Co., mercantile hse.
110, Hardenstein, Doctor,
    homeopathist
110, Storkfeth, P., at Lady Adams
113, Kirkley & Liness, restaurant
114, Jorss, F., merchant tailor
114, Rocheblave, P.P., merchant
114, Winkle, H., bakery & oysters
115, Clark, Lyman, restaurant
117, Farrar & Jones, carpenters

K Street:

119, Angur, J.S., restaurant
119, Helm, A.F., restaurant
122, Salsbury, Joseph, restaurant
131, Clark & Milne, auctions & coins
130, Perkins & Powers, merchants
2nd to 3rd Street

200, Huntington* & Hammond, merch.
202, Bartels, F., boarding house
202, Politz, J., boarding house
202, Stiles & Ashby, tinners
203, Morse* & Mitchell, real estate
203, Morse, Dr. J.F.*, real estate agent
206, Cochran, Jno. L., confectioner
206, Westenhaver, baker
207, Williams & Ault, hotel
207, Childs, S.B., carpenter
208, Hoy & Orton, blacksmiths &
     plough factory
209, Prugh & Cook, merchants
211, Florence Restaurant, Wm. O'Neill
211, Martin, Doctor James, office
212, Magnet [rstrnt] Josephine Gibson
215, White & Ballon, shoe store
217, *Sacramento Transcript*,F.C. Ewer*,
editor. Printed Sacramento's first book,
the 1851 directory reproduced here.
217, Warren, H.S., *Transcript* office
217, Hutchinson, John J.* *Transcript*
219, Kerns, Henry, tailor
222, March, Ichabod, builder
223, Haines & Stevens, merchants
224, Wadsworth, Doctor J.A., office
225, Comins, P.B., retail guns, & fire
     arms made to order
225, Greeley, G.W., ship carpenter
225, Storkwell, Joseph P., gunsmith
226, Fulwiler & Doughterty, butchers
227, Chesley, W., mason
227, Herrick, Joseph, Jr., carpenter
2nd to 3rd Street

229, Saywood & Thorndyke, merchants
3rd to 4th Street

302, Gates, Dr. Justin, botanico
318, Spaulding & Martin, merchants
325, Sisson & Coleman, bording house

326, Laban, H.F., merchants
327, Hall & Sweet, boarding house
327, Jaquith & Smith, cabinet makers
330, New York Drug Store, Crane
330, Marsh, Doctor L.C.
330, Pierson, J.H., carpenter
330, Salasar, Salvadore
330, Salasar, Jose Maria
330, Salasar, Jesus
330, Small, Dr. Wm. E. at NY Drug S.
331, Wibans & Jacobs, hotel
Barker & Long, Gait House
Sabin, Stephen C., carpenter
Shortridge, Doctor A.L.
4th to 5th Street

403, New York Hotel, Creig & R.
404, Nevett J.H., stoves, hardware,
     tinware, & metallic roofing
409, Wood & Kenyons, merchants
410, Bowers, S.L., meat market
411, Harris & Co., variety store
415, Hall, Pierre, grocer
420, Mosee, William, trader
427, Clarke, Henry A., interpreter
427, Luco, M. & L., merchants
431, Bull's Head Hotel, E.J. Feeney
431, McDivitt, William, painter
431, McKean, Chas. P.
5th to 6th Street

502, Trumbo House [hotel] M. Howard
504, Chaffey, M., boarding house
504, Bullock, D.D., magistrate
504, McGrew, Wm. H., lawyer
504, McGrew & Robinson, lawyers
506, Moore, Doctor Jesse, office
509, Fleming House [hotel], O. Davis
510, Ormsby, Maj. W.M., auctioneer,
     horses, mules, cattle, & wagons
     Auction sales every day
510, Ormsby, L.P., trader
510. Paris, D.H., trader
511, Appleman & Bro., merchants
512, Sidgreaves, Wm., boarding house
514, Gregor, William, trader
514, Gridley, George W., auctioneer
514, Lewis, M., trader

297

K Street:

517, Ohio House [hotel], J. McNulty
518, Hawkeye & Sucker Hotel, A.& P.
518, Dashell, W.A., auctioneer
518, High, William, auctioneer
518, Jacobs R.P., auctioneer
520, Cochran, Chas., jeweler
520, Nukols, J.A., boarding house
520, Prentiss, John, trader
522, Saywood & Weston, bakers
524, Bornholt, C., butcher
529, Albion House [hotel] J. Griffen
531, Albion House [hotel] J. Griffen
531, Chesley, G.W.*, auctioneer
6th to 7th Street

600, Eyer & Wood, stock auction
601, Buckeye House [hotel], E. & M.
601, Walker, A.W., restaurant
602, Moreland, Blunt & S., auctioneers
602, Luco, M. & L., merchants
602, Rightmire & Gandy, auctioneers
605, Leman, F., grocer
605, Schnider, John, grocer
618, Wright & Griswell, blacksmiths
619, Stoddard, Doctor H., office
621, Thrall, Charles, restaurant
627, Cook, Jos., restaurant
7th to 8th Street

701, Roman Catholic Church,
Rev. Father Inglesby
720, Deal, Samuel*, livestock auctions
Sales every day.
722, McKenaie & Ames, doctors
729, Meire, George, butcher
8th to 9th Street

Lee, Mrs. Mary Ann
Pawlett, Joseph, joiner
9th to 10th Street

cor 9th, Moore, W.H., carpenter
900, Ludington, O., auctioneer
Bailey, Peter, boarding house
Hamilton, David, blacksmith
Maine House, Edward Brown
Norton & Terrell, stock yard
Yost, M. stock yard
10th to 11th Street

cor 10th, McIlroy, R.H., grocer
cor 10th, Uptegraph & H., stock yard
Antartic House [hotel] Mrs. Merrill
Clark, Henry, boarding house
Martin & Well, blacksmiths
Salzer, Charles, grocer
13th to 14th Street

1331, Clarke, Henry A. interpreter
Spanish/English & real estate sales

L Street:

foot of L, Hamersley, Geo. W., harbor
master on board the storeship
TECUMSEH

Front to 2nd Street
2nd to 3rd Street

cor 2nd, Homer & Wright, lumber mer
cor 2nd, Smith, C.H, lumber dealer
7th to 8th Street

cor 7th, Rogers, James, teacher
Chamberlain, W.E.*, merchant
Yates, Chapman, boarding house
8th to 9th Street

Jackson, T.H.
North American Hotel, F. Mercure
27th to 28th Street

Sutter's Fort

M Street:

Front to 2nd Street

* Burnett, Philetus W.*, carpenter
Tarbox, Wm., carpenter at Burnett's
131, Ames, C.M., lumber
Floyd, G., blacksmith
Pacific Theatre
2nd to 3rd Street

Market House [brick, 30 x 100 ft.]
owned by city and located in the
middle of M Street.
cor 2nd, Rice, W.A., lumber dealer

N Street:

Front to 2nd Street

Hardenbergh, J.R.*
Pyatt, T.H., clerk of Com. Council
Rowland, Wm., City Collector
Solomon & Williamson, carpenters

O Street:

2nd to 3rd Street
200-Rodgers lot where squatter was
evicted, starting "squatters' riot"
cor 2nd Vanpelt, John

Front Street:

[Because there were no structures on
the west side of Front Street between I
and M, the house numbers in that area
were not always consistent with the
regular numbering system.]

Sycamore to Union Street
cor Syc., Stow,___, foundryman
Railroad Hotel, Geo. Wilson
Park, Dr. H., at Railroad Hotel

Union to Sacramento Street
Cary, R.D., Sac. Steam Mills [flour]

Sacramento to Broad Street
Heek, Phil., baker
Sacramento House, Thos. E. Cook
Schildknecht & Koester, brewers

Broad to H Street
Boyington, C.C., grocer
Camfield, W.D., soda factory
Nelson, George, grocer
Wetzlar, Julias

H to I Street
Henarie, D.W. & Co., grocers

I to J Street
901, Vangardner & Co, butchers
904? Brothers, Hort, importers
905, Hamilton & Wheaton*, grocers
905, Wheaton*, William Rufus
907, Hotel de France, R. Wingued
909, City Hotel, Smith & Kelly, built in
         September 1849
912?, Gulick & Warner, com. merch.
915, Meeks, Washington, lawyer
915, Meredith, H., lawyer
916?, Glen & Bruce, land agents

921, Wilson & Spaulding, book sellers
922?, Alswite, Coorier, coffee house
924?, Burk, S.W., grocers
925, Brown, P.J. grocer
926?, Schafer & Co., hotel
927, Jacobs, L., clothier
928?, Welton, Merritt, grocer
929, Chaoltier, John, eating house
929, Rowe & Gamans, grocers
930?, New York Drug Store, Crane
931, Prettyman & Barroll, auctioneers
933, Jelly, Samuel, watchmaker
935, Weil, S. clothier

J to K Street

1002?, Birch, J*, stage proprietor
1005, Sutter Hotel, Dewey & Smith
1005, Henley, T.J., lawyer, Sutter Hotel
1005, McFarland, Doctor, office
1006?, Brigham, S. Otis, comm. merch.
1007, Brooks, J.W. merchants
1007, Fay, Pierce & Wallace,
         commission merchants
1008?, Barton & Boulden, commission
         merchant, auction every morning
1008, Clark & Milne, commission
         merchant, auction every morning
1009, Berry, Bliss & Co. auctioneers
1011, Brannan, D.K., agent of
         Samuel Brannan
1015, Brannan Hotel, Hanna &
         Bowman
1017, Sutton, George, eating house
1021. Cavert & Hill, merchants
1021?, Express Hotel, R.P.& W. Mead
1021?, Smith, Captain Napoleon*, at
         Express Hotel. Came to Cal in
         1845, worked for Sutter, later
         lumberman.
1023, Woodruff, G.W., hardware
         merchant
1025, Hedenberg & Walker, liquors
1026?, Mattison, D.W. bookkeeper,
1026, Meeker & Co. grocers &
         commission merchants
1026?, Sprague, J.S., grocers

Front Street:

K to L Street
1101. J.B. Starr*, auctioneer
1101, Somes, G.W., lumber merchants
1103, Atkins, R., boarding house
1106, Verandah Hotel, George Welch
1111, Dawsey House, [bdg. house]
1115, Boller, Geo., baker
1117, Rice & Dugart, butchers
1121, Taylor, John C., eating house
1125, Wood, Chas. B., lumber dealer
1131, Robertson, A., grocer
 National Arena
L to M Street
1201, St. John, P.D., lumber dealer
M to N Street
1323 George Zins'* Anchor House
[Built 1849, Sac'to's first brick building]
 Central Warehouse [on levee]
 Ewer, P. Coroner & Port Warden at
 Central Warehouse
Q to R Streets
Edwards, Mrs.
Jackson, John, grocer
Lolor, Miss Margarett
R to S Street
Dunn, Patrick, carpenter

Second Street:

I to J Street
901, Cunningham, Noble, city marshall
901, Pixley, Frank M., lawyer
901, Washington, B.F., City recorder
903, Cunningham, Theo., lawyer
903, Heslip, A.M., lawyer
903, McKenzie, Doctor J.M.
903, Tehama Theatre
904, Fowler, J. S., special agent for
 Capt. J.A. Sutter & real estate agent
904, McCracken, M.
*904, Zabriskie, Col. J.C., notary public
904, Zabriskie, Doctor C.B., office
904, Zabriskie, W.M., lawyer
909, Smith, Fanny, Palace [saloon?]
910, Flor de la Mar, Priscilla
911 Alexandria, James Carswell
913, Goodrich, A., pianist

918, Ettling & Pinchowar, clothiers
921, Armstrong, Columbia Hotel
921, Young, Isaac, land agent
922, Waverly [hotel], Smith & B.
928, Haywood & Warring, butchers
J to K Street
1000, Birdsall, Doctor, county recorder
1000, Feris, Doctor L.
1000, Kewen & Morrison, lawyers
1000, Walthall, Madison, lawyer
1002, Merritt, W., grocer
1004, Julep House, Jennings & Brown
1006, Brownell, Romer & R. butchers
1007, Boston Restaurant, Albert Sloper
1008, Freeman, J.M., express office
1008, Robinson, Davis & Ryerson, law.
1009, Barney, Blossom & Co., merch.
* 1009, Cornwall, P.B.*, land office
1009, Cornwall, Arthur
* 1009, Lee, Barton*, office
1010, Plotner & McCormick, tailors
1010, Warrill, A.C., fruit store
1012, Williams, W.F., eating house
1014, Orleans Hotel, Simmons & Curt.
1014, Billiard Saloon, Pablo Susias
1015, Hensley* & Merrill, bankers
 City, County, and State script
1015, Mumby, J.H., agt. Palmer Exp.
1017, Carpenter, Doctor W.M.
1017, Conner & Forrest, booksellers
1019, Chase, R.H., engineer
1020, Binney, A.J., engineer
1021, Sacramento City Bank
 gold dust bought and sold
1021, Rohdes & Sturgis, bankers
1022, Coleman & Nelson, restaurant
1023, Foote, Arthur W., banker
1024, Buckley & Dodd, painters
1025, Morrison, John C., merchant
1026, Cone, Robert, tinner
1026, Main, Doctor John
1027, Fitch & Luckett, grocers
1027, Ward & Blair, lawyers
1029, McNeir, Doctor M.C., office

Second Street:

1028, Fash & Co. butchers

1028, Sailly & Myers, grocers
1031, U.S. Post Office Building
1031, Duryee, Doctor William
1031, Lovegrove, George, bookseller
1031, McLeish, Doctor John
Martin, E.H., artist
Ruth, J.A., engineer

K to L Street
1101, St. Charles Hotel, Hill & Smith
1101, Fry, D.B., lawyer & notary public
1101, Latham, M.S.*, lawyer
1101, Monson, A.C., lawyer
1101, Overton, J.P., lawyer
1105, Mason, J.L.
1105, Skinner, Robert
1105, Smith, J.C., real estate agent
1125, Ewer, W.B., boarded here
1125, McIntire, E., laundryman

L to M Street
1202, Sanborn, F.C., lumber dealer
Hayden, C.C., commission merchant
Low, F.G.,Jr., lumber dealer
Welch, Doctor Thomas, office

M to N Street
Brastow & Co. lumber dealers
Fella, Piasitos
Taylor, James

Q to R Street
Dlugn, candle & beer factory

Third Street:
903, Smith, Joel*& Hines, grocers
907, Wheeler & Smith, livery stable
914, Smith & Eells, blacksmiths
916, Schade, John, grocer
920, Taylor, W.P., cabinet maker
921, Theilhares, Mrs. Mary,brding. hse.
921, Custer, Jno.
921, Earl, Thomas
922, Foote, C.A., saddle & harness mfg
922, Persian, J.D., sadler
923, Evans & Hart, painters
926, Beaumdrain, Doctor J.G.
926, Johnson* & Forman*, lawyers
926, Johnson, J. Neely*, lawyer
926, Obrien, Doctor J.C., office
928, Cronin, Dr. E.

931, Cafe de Paris, Eugene Fisher
931, Cafe de Paris [hotel]

J to K Street
1002, Curwood, Jos.
1004, Diadem [rest],Williams & Feider
1006, Gem [rest], Francis, Augustus&P
1006, Mulvany, Doctor P.H., office
1008, Ringold Hotel, Henry Blair
1010, Ringgold Hse, Mrs. Jane Shurr
1014, Schaffer, Henry, gunsmith
1014. Smith, John C., blacksmith
1016, Salter, Doctor, office
1018, Coleman, Jas. W., merchant
1018, Johnson. Richard
1018, Lansing, James
1018, Phinneys, Doctor, office
1019, Tremont [meat]Market, Edwards
1023, Pickard, F., merchant
1026, Pujh, J.W., tinner
Salter, Doctor John, office

K to L Street
1101, Petit, A.P., office
1103, Hein, Mrs., dressmaker
1105, Dayley, Jas.
1119, Leiholt, Henry, shoemaker
1124, McCloy, Robert, shoemaker
Brook & Lovett, carpenters
Clement, Andrew, blacksmith
Hayden, D.S., lumberman
Wingate, C.D., blacksmith

L to M Street
Bigler, John*, lawyer

M to N Street
Winn, Gen. A.M.*, residence

N to O Street
Irvin, A.

Fourth Street:
I to J Street
906, Esse, Theodore, boarding house
907, Miller, John K., livery stable
909, Boston bakery, E. Bond
913, Rogers, John P.*, residence
914, Mills, J.W., carpenter

Fourth Street:
917, Deal, Doctor W. Grove*

921, Webster & Cowper, shoemakers
922, Allison, Wm., blacksmith
922, Wait, Robert, blacksmith
　　　　　　　　　J to K Street
1002, Jordan, John, restaurant
1004, Shields, James P., sadler
1006, Pheiffer, W.A., office
1009, Herkimer Hotel, Lawson & R.
1009, Ramsdell, Joseph
1010, Allen, Wm., carman
1010, 4th Street [meat] Market
* 1011, Culver, J.H., auctioneer [and
　　　publisher of this directory]
1011, Forsythe, R., mattresses &
　　　bedding.
1011, McBrayer, J.M., lawyer
1011, Ormsby & Culver*, real estate
　　　agents and auctioneers
1012, Fitch & McCleery*, furniture
　　　sales and cabinet makers
1013, Daniels, Jas., cabinet maker
1013, Ormsby & Culver*, real est.
　　　　　　agents
1013, Whiting, B.F., cabinet maker &
　　　furniture sales
1013, Wilson, John, sign painter &
　　　house numbering
1015, Westenhaver, residence
1016, Jaqua & Black, livery stable
1017, Fourth St. House, J. Binninger*
1019/21, Smith, E, gold washer factory
1021, Elk House [hotel], E. Smith
1022, Youmans, E.S., undertaker &
　　　sexton, pine & lead coffins.
1023, Eagle Bakery, Durham & Eaton
1024, Andrew & Carpenter,
　　　blacksmiths
　　　Old Court House
Episcopal Congregation meets at Old
　Court House. Rev. Orlando
　Harriman, pastor
　　　　　　　　　K to L Street
1104, Otero, Manuel
1106, Coody, Mrs. S., boarding house
1106, Hawkeye House, E. Wait
　　　　　　　　　L to M Street

Obrien, John, washer
Fifth Street:
　　　　　　　　　I to J Street
914, Indiana Hotel, T. McAlpine
917, Job, Jeremiah, livery stable
916, Matard, Auguste, baker
918, Illinois House, [hotel], T.H.
　　　Rawlings
921, Burk, Margaret, washer
Fox, J.A., blacksmith
Jarrot, V., blacksmith
　　　　　　　　　J to K Street
1004, Hellinghause, F., gunsmith
1005, May, A.D., lemon syrup factory
1006, Cunnell, George L., painter
1006, Humphrey, John H., painter
1008, Jordon, Doctor, office
1008, Prentiss, Doctor W. office
1010, Ball Martin, boarding house
1010, Cleal, J.G., county surveyor
1012, Cummin, Geo., blacksmith
1012, Prader, Joseph, blacksmith
1016, Nolan, F., carpenter
1022, Star Hotel, S. & L. Lockhart

Fifth Street:
　　　　　　　　　K to L Street
Coulter, A. laundryman
Sixth Street:
　　　　　　　　　H to I Street
Brown, W.G., residence
Quincy House, Mrs. Sarah Steinagal
　　　　　　　　　I to J Street
City Bakery, Sowter & Elsbury
Presbyterian Church, J.A. Benton*
Purdin, Mathew, gold washer factory
　　　　　　　　　J to K Street
1006, ??
1008, Breen, R., wagon maker
1008, McGuire*, James, blacksmith
1009, Wick & Spink, blacksmiths
1013, Flagg, C.C,, commission
　　　merchant
1013, Pitts, A.W., trader
1014, Fremont & Phelps, stock yard
Sixth Street:

1015, Salbatierra, Julian, grocer
1016, Smith & Lynde, bakers
1017, Chesebrough, H.D., grocer
1022, Davis & Co., hay yard
1022, Rave, I., gunsmith
1024, Cover & Green, blacksmiths
K to L Street
1103, McKee, John, trader
1108, Wolf & Gallop, bakers
1109, Randall, H.C. boarding house
1111, Parker, J., restaurant
1115, Hammond, W.P. saddle tree mfg.

Seventh Street:

F to G Street
African Church, open Sundays
I to J Street
Davis & Jaynes, blacksmiths
Louisville House, M. Casada
Penola House, M. Casada
J to K Street
Chicago House, H, Benson
Feathers, David, boarding house
Luce, Israel*, marble workman

Methodist Episcopal Church, South,
Rev. John Penman, pastor
Penman, Rev. John, pastor M.E.Ch.
Stevens, N.M., boarding house
K to L Street
Murray, D., auctioneer
L to M Street
Methodist Episcopal Church,
Rev, M.C. Briggs pastor

Eighth Street:

Ninth Street:

Tenth Street:

I to J Street
Conduitte, Dr. Thos. J., merchant

Eleventh Street:

J to K Street
Roberts & Turner, candle factory

Twenty Ninth Street:

J to K Street
Zins* & Weiser, brewers

Commander Charles Wilkes, U.S.N.
Born in New York, 1798 — Died in Washington 1875
Engraved from a painting done in 1843

APPENDIX B

Charles Wilkes' United States Exploring Expedition 1841 Visits to New Helvetia and the future site of Sacramento City

COMMANDER CHARLES WILKES' REPORT

Charles Wilkes (also mentioned on pages 44 and 46) described an expedition led by Lt. Commander Cadwalader Ringgold up the Sacramento River commencing on August 20, 1841. They visited New Helvetia (Sacramento), and excerpts from this narrative are included here. Wilkes' monumental work, *Narrative of the United States Exploring Expedition,* chronicles the discoveries and observations of skilled explorers who were sent out by the United States Navy in 1838.[148] In his words, written in November 1844, "The Expedition,. . . was the first, and still is the only one fitted out by national munificence for scientific objects, that has ever left our shores."

During the expedition there would be no means of prompt communication from Washington with the squadron, and on August 11, 1838, J. K. Paulding, secretary of the Navy, issued very detailed instructions, from which a few lines (and a Herculean first sentence) are included below:

Sir,—

The Congress of the United States, having in view the important interests of our commerce embarked in the whale-fisheries, and other adventures in the great Southern Ocean, by an act of the 18th of May, 1836, authorized an Expedition to be fitted out for the purpose of exploring and surveying that sea, as well as to determine the existence of all doubtful islands and shoals, as to discover and accurately fix the position of those which lie in or near the track of our vessels in that quarter, and may have escaped the observation of scientific navigators.Liberal appropriations have been made for the attainment of these objects, and the President [Martin Van Buren], reposing great confidence in your courage, capacity, and zeal, has appointed you to the command of the Expedition, requiring you to proceed to the performance of the duties of that station with the vessels placed under your orders, consisting of the sloops of war Vincennes and Peacock, the ship Relief, the brig Porpoise, and tenders Sea-Gull and Flying-Fish.

---

148. Charles Wilkes, U.S.N., Commander of the Expedition, *Narrative of the United States Exploring Expedition during the years 1838, 1839, 1840, 1841, 1842*, (Philadelphia: Lea & Blanchard, 1845.), in six volumes, five of text and one of maps. Chapter 5 of Volume V deals with their stay in California (pp. 151-214), and the description of the trip to the Sacramento Valley occupies pp. 177-194. Another short passage is devoted to the lower Sacramento Valley and New Helvetia on pp. 245-246 of the next chapter.

The following paragraphs are included here to indicate the conduct expected of the members of the Expedition.

> In the prosecution of these long and devious voyages, you will necessarily be placed in situations which cannot be anticipated, and in which, sometimes your own judgement and discretion, at others, necessity, must be your guide. . . You will permit no trade to be carried on by the squadron, with the countries you may visit, . . . except for necessaries or curiosities, and that under express regulations established by yourself, in which the rights of the natives must be scrupulously respected and carefully guarded.

> You will neither interfere, nor permit any wanton interference with the customs, habits, manners, or prejudices of the natives of such countries or islands you may visit; nor take part in their disputes, except as a mediator; nor commit any act of hostility, unless in self defense, or to protect or secure the property of those under your command, or whom circumstances may have placed within reach of your protection. . . You will carefully inculcate on all the officers and men under your command, that courtesy and kindness towards the natives, which is understood and felt by all classes of mankind; to display neither arrogance nor contempt, and to appeal to their good-will rather than their fears.

Returning to the regular order of the instructions:

> . . . you will proceed to a safe port or ports in Tierra del Fuego, where the members of the scientific corps may have favorable opportunities of prosecuting their researches. Leaving the larger vessels securely moored, and the officers and crews occupied in their respective duties, you will proceed with the brig Porpoise, and the tenders, to explore the southern Antarctic. . . [A vast area of Antarctica, extending from longitude 70° E. through longitude 160° E. was later named Wilkes Land as a result of this foray.]

> . . . You will then, on rejoining your vessels at Tierra del Fuego, with all your squadron. . . return Northward to Valpariso, where a store-ship will meet you in the month of March 1839.

> . . . From the Isle of Desolation you will proceed to the Sandwich Islands by such route as you deem best from the information you may acquire from such sources as fall in your

way. A store-ship from the United States will meet you there, with a supply of provisions, in the month of April 1840.

Thence you will direct your course to the Northwest Coast of America, making such surveys and examinations, first of the territory of the United States on the seaboard [ownership of Oregon was then in contention between England and the United States, while California was not under U.S. sovereignty until 1846], and of the Columbia river, and afterwards along coast of California, with special reference to the Bay of St. Francisco, as you can accomplish by the month of October following your arrival.

Due to a series of events in the Fiji Islands, the squadron did not reach Honolulu until September 24, 1840. Because repairs were needed and an opportunity arose for explorations of the Mauna Loa and Kilauea craters, the departure from the Hawaiian Islands was delayed until April 5, 1841. Shortly after arriving in Oregon, further trouble, including the loss of the *Peacock* by grounding at the mouth of the Columbia River, resulted in the squadron's division into three groups. Commander Charles Wilkes temporarily left his flagship, the *Vincennes* and remained in charge of exploring the Columbia. Lieutenant-Commander Cadwalader Ringgold took command of the *Vincennes* and sailed to San Francisco Bay where it anchored on August 14, 1841. The third group under Lieutenant George F. Emmons, formerly commander of the *Peacock,* proceeded by land from the Columbia River south to the Sacramento River and then down to New Helvetia. Here they were met by a ship's boat which later came up the Sacramento River from the *Vincennes* anchored in the Bay.

Six days after the *Vincennes* first arrived in San Francisco Bay, Commander Ringgold took charge of a group of boats to explore the upper part of the bay and the Sacramento River at least as far north as the Sutter Buttes. The following lines are from Volume V of the *Narrative* starting on page 177:

On the 20th of August [1841], Lieutenant-Commander Ringgold left the Vincennes with six boats, accompanied by Dr. Pickering [naturalist], Lieutenants Alden and Budd, Passed-Midshipman Sandford, Midshipmen Hammersley and Elliot, and Gunner Williamson, with provisions for thirty days, accompanied by an Indian pilot. [The sailors involved were not listed, but Captain

William Phelps said there were over 60 officers and men in the party]. . . . on the 23rd, they reached the residence of Captain Suter and encamped on the opposite bank. Captain Suter is a Swiss by birth, and informed them that he had been a lieutenant in the Swiss guards during the time of Charles X. Soon after the revolution of July, he came to the United States and passed several years in the state of Missouri. He has but recently removed to California, where he has obtained from the government a conditional grant of thirty leagues square, bounded by the Sacramento on the west, and extending as far up the river as the Prairie Buttes. The spot he has chosen for his dwelling and fortification, he has called New Helvetia: it is situated on the summit of a small knoll, rising from the level prairie, two miles from the east bank of the Sacramento and fifty miles from its mouth. New Helvetia is bounded on the north by the American Fork, *a small serpentine stream which has a course of but a few miles.*[Italics added]

If Lt.-Commander Ringgold had known the true length of the American River, had ascended only 25 miles to Morman Island or almost anywhere above, and examined the geology with the care applied three weeks later to the Prairie or Sutter Buttes by Lt. Emmons' party, their discovery of gold in 1841 might have changed the whole history of the West. Ringgold described the area:

This river [the American] having a bar near its mouth, no vessels larger than boats can enter it. At this place the Sacramento is eight hundred feet wide, and this may be termed the head of its navigation during the dry season, or the stage of low water.

Mr. Geiger, a young American from Newport, is now attached to Captain Suter's [Sutter's] establishment; but he informed me that he intended to settle higher up the Sacramento, on the banks of the Feather river. When Captain Suter first settled here in 1839, he was surrounded by some of the most hostile tribes of Indians on the river; but by his energy and management, with the aid of a small party of trappers, has thus far prevented opposition to his plans. He has even succeeded in winning the good-will of the Indians, who are now laboring for him in building houses, and a line of wall, to protect him against the inroads or attacks that he apprehends, more from the present authorities of the land, than from the tribes about him, who are now working in his employ. He holds, by appointment of the government, the office of administrador, and has, according to his own belief, supreme power in his own district, condemning, acquitting, and punishing, as well as marrying and burying those who are under him. He treats the Indians very kindly, and pays them well for their services in trapping and working for him. His object is to attach them, as much as possible, to his interests, that in case of need he may rely on their chiefs for assistance.

Although Captain Suter is, in general, in the habit of treating the Indians with kindness, yet he related to our gentlemen instances in which he had been obliged to fusillade nine of them; indeed, he does not seem to stand upon much ceremony with those who oppose him in any way. His buildings consist of extensive currals and dwelling-houses, for himself and people, all built of adobes. Labor is paid for in goods. [Captain Phelps, who visited a month before, reported their rate of pay to be the equivalent of 25¢ per day] The extent of his stock amounts to about one thousand horses, two thousand cattle, and about one thousand sheep, many of which are now to be seen around his premises, giving them the appearance of civilization.

Captain Suter has commenced extensive operations in farming; but in the year of our visit the drought had affected him, as well as others, and ruined all his crops. About forty Indians were at work for him, whom he had taught to make adobes. The agreement for their services is usually made with their chiefs, and in this way, as many as are wanted are readily obtained. These chiefs have far more authority over their tribes than those we had seen in the north; and in the opinion of an intelligent American, they have more power over and are more respected by their tribes than those of any other North American Indians. Connected with the establishment, Captain Suter has erected a distillery, in which he makes a kind of pisco [A brandy made near Pisco, a seaport in Peru] from the wild grape of the country.

Captain Phelps, mentioned on page 41, was a merchant captain and temperance advocate, not bound by the rules of the Exploring Expedition regarding respecting the customs of the natives. He wrote that during his July visit, he thought he had convinced Sutter that making ardent spirits was an evil enterprise, and should be stopped.

Ringgold then added his observations:

> . . . During our stay, there was much apprehension on the part
> of some that the present governor of the district next west of
> New Helvetia, felt jealous of the power and influence that
> Captain Suter was obtaining in the country; and it was thought
> that had it not been for the force which the latter could bring to
> oppose any attempt to dislodge him, it would have been tried.
> In the mean time Captain Suter is using all his energies to
> render himself impregnable. . . . New Helvetia was found to be
> in latitude 38° 33' 45" N, and longitude 121° 20' 05" W.

From a 1967 USGS topographic map of Sacramento, the central building of Sutter's Fort appears to have the coordinates 38° 34' 21" N latitude and 121° 28' 12" W longitude. Ringgold's latitude which was probably obtained by taking a noon sun sight (using a bowl of mercury for an artificial horizon), was quite accurate, being 36 seconds or about six tenths of a mile too far south. That is the Fort would have been in the block between U and V Streets of modern Sacramento instead of between K and L Streets as it actually is. The Longitude is another matter, since it was determined using a chronometer or very accurate clock. The spot on the surface of the earth exactly under a fixed star is moving over 13 miles a minute at the latitude of Sacramento, and Lieutenant-Commander Ringgold's time would have been kept on a boat trip by a secondary chronometer carefully compared to the main one on the *Vincennes* just before departure. Unfortunately the last place where they had access to another master chronometer was at Honolulu several months before. In any event the longitude of the Fort given by their observations was eight minutes and six seconds of longitude to the east of the actual location (indicating a slow chronometer), or about 7.4 statute miles. This placed the Fort near the intersection of Folsom Boulevard and Bradshaw Road on a modern map instead of its actual location between 26th and 28th Streets.

A longitudinal error of nine miles is not bad considering that in 1714 the British Government offered a prize of £20,000 to any person who could make a chronometer accurate enough to allow computation of longitude with an error of 34 statute miles after having been at sea for six weeks.[149] Ringgold's chronometer had been cruising for over two years. Returning to the narrative on page 180 of Volume V:

> According to this gentleman [Captain Sutter], there are nine different tribes of Indians that are now in his neighborhood, and within a short distance of his territory.
>
> In the evening our party was favored with a dance by Indian boys, who, before they began, ornamented themselves with white masks and decked their bodies each according to his own taste. The music was vocal and several joined in the song. Their motions were thought to resemble the Pawnees' mode of dancing. Their music was more in harmony than the other tribes we had seen; neither has their language any of the harsh guttural sounds found in those of the Oregon Indians. Every word of their language appears to terminate with a vowel, after the manner of the Polynesians dialects, which gives their voices much more softness than the tribes to the north, to whom they have no resemblance whatever, though they are said to be somewhat like the Shoshones.
>
> They wear fillets of leaves around their heads, and often tie on them a piece of cotton, after the manner of the Polynesians. These Indians do not build canoes, although they admire and prize them highly; they are excellent swimmers, and in consequence of it do not need them in their narrow streams; they, however, make use of simple rafts, composed of one or two logs, generally split.
>
> The venereal disease is said to prevail to a great extent among them; and whole tribes have been swept off by the small-pox. The former is said to have been communicated by the Indians who have been discharged by the missions. All agree that the Indians have been unjustly treated by the Governor [Alvarado]. Cattle that had been given to them by the padres of the mission when they left it, have been taken away from them by this functionary, and added to his own stock—whence a saying has been derived that the governor's cows produce three times a year. The Spanish laws do not recognize the Indian title to lands, but consider them and the Indians also in the light of public property. . . .The scenery was very much admired, and

---

149. Dava Sobel, *Longitude,* (New York: Penguin Books USA Inc., 1996), p. 53.

> Mount Diavolo [Diablo], near the mouth of the San Joachim [San Joaquin River], adds to its beauty. The mountains to the east are visible from Captain Suter's settlement, it is said that during some portions of the year they are covered with snow [This was August of a drought year]. . .

After staying two days at New Helvetia, the six boats continued northward on the Sacramento River, hoping to explore at least as far as the Sutter Buttes. Lt. Emmons' party coming down from the Columbia expected to explore and survey to that point or a bit beyond:

> . . . On the 25th, the boats left New Helvetia. It was discovered previous to starting, that four men had deserted from their party. This is a common circumstance in this port, and very few vessels visit it without losing some portion of their crews [Even though it was seven years before the gold discovery]. The dissolute habits of the people form such strong temptations for the sailors, that few can resist them. A number of men who were deserters were continually around us. Among others, the sergeant and marine guard that had deserted from H.B.M. [Her Britannic Majesty's] ship Sulphur were the most troublesome. Their appearance did not prove that they had changed their situation for the better.

H.M.S. *Sulphur* had visited San Francisco in 1827, but the desertion mentioned here probably referred to the later visit in which she anchored at Yerba Buena on October 19, 1837 (see page 35). The captain, Sir Edward Belcher, R.N. accompanied a group in five boats which he ordered to explore up the Sacramento from San Francisco Bay. The boats left on October 24th and returned on November 24, 1837, and the northern most point they reached was reported to be in latitude N 38° 46' 47" at a branch "beyond which there was not enough water in either channel for the lightest boats." They named the promontory *Point Victoria*. It seems unlikely that any of the members of the crew of the *Sulphur* would have deserted on this trip up the river, in the total absence of distilled spirits and European or American settlers. Bancroft IV, p. 145, reported that six members of the crew deserted, and it seems probable that they did so in San Francisco Bay and then joined Sutter at New Helvetia after 1839. In a letter dated November 30, 1837 Captain Belcher wrote to Vallejo complaining of the desertion, and on December 26, 1837, Vallejo issued orders for the

the capture of the deserters. Wilkes' narrative continues:

> . . . On the 26th, they reached the mouth of Feather river, which is fifteen miles [actually 21 miles] above New Helvetia. It appeared nearly as broad as the main stream, but there is a bar extending the whole distance across it, on which the boats grounded. On the point of the fork, [possibly Captain Belcher's *Point Victoria*] the ground was strewed with the skulls and bones of an Indian tribe, all of whom are said to have died, within a few years, of the tertian fever [A malarial fever characterized by paroxysms every alternate day] and to have nearly become extinct in consequence. . .They [the exploring party] encamped at a late hour, on a spot where the prairie had been burnt over, and were much disturbed during the night by the bears, wolves, and owls. . . Bears were also in great numbers. It is reported that they will sometimes attack and eat the Indians. . . . Their [The Indians] rancheria, or village, of no more than five or six huts, built around a larger one, which appeared somewhat like the "tamascals"— sweating houses.
>
> All their houses were formed in the following manner: a round pit is dug, three or four feet deep and from ten to twenty feet in diameter; over this a framework of sticks raised, woven together, upon which is laid dried grass and reeds; the whole is then covered with earth. They have one small opening, into which it is necessary to creep on all fours; another is left at the top, which is extended upward with bundles of grass, to serve as a chimney; in some of the houses there was a kind of hanging shelf, apparently for the purpose of drying fish. The tamascal differed in no respect from the others, except in its size, and appeared sufficiently large to contain half the inhabitants of the rancheria; but, unlike the rest, it had several instead of one opening; all of these had coverings, which are intended for the purpose of retaining the heat as long as possible. The Indians are particularly fond of these baths, and make constant use of them. The roofs of their houses are strong enough to bear the weight of several persons, and the Indians are usually seen sitting on top of them. . .

On the return trip down the Sacramento River, the group camped about ten miles below the junction of the Sacramento and Feather Rivers, and thus only 10 miles from New Helvetia.

The narrative continues:

Whilst the men were employed in pitching the tents, Dr. Pickering strolled up the bank, to see what he could find in the botanical way, without arms. On his approaching the bushes, a huge grisly bear made for him, and so close was he that it was necessary for him to make all the exertion he could to effect his escape from so dangerous an adversary. He gave the alarm, and everyone was running for his arms, but before these could be prepared, this inhabitant of the forest made a precipitate retreat, and was soon beyond the reach of the rifle. On the 4th [of September, 1841], they had returned to Captain Suter, where they found that a small Russian schooner had arrived from Bodega, bringing the governor of that establishment, who was about delivering it up to Captain Suter. The vessel [later named by Sutter, *Sacramento*], was understood to have been built at Sitka, and was of only thirty tons burden, very much resembling an English vessel of the same class.

For a boat they [the Russians] use a skin "badaka," that is admirably adapted for the seas and weather they have to contend with. When the persons are seated, and the opening closed, with a skin dress they more resemble an aquatic animal than anything else. . . Several Americans from the United States are beginning to settle in this part of the country, and it will not be long before it becomes in some respects, an American Colony. . . . The Indians have several rancherias around New Helvetia. Their lodges are somewhat like low haycocks, being composed of a framework of sticks, thatched with the bulrush. In these there was no excavation, neither were they covered with earth;. . . . In the preparation of acorn-bread all assist. The acorns are gathered in very large quantities, piled in heaps, and spread in the sun to dry. Both men and women are to be seen employed shelling, pounding, and baking them into bread: the pounding is preformed upon a plank that has been hollowed out, with a stone pestle. To reduce the large quantity to a fine powder, requires great labour.

Around New Helvetia, although but a few days had elapsed since their former visit [Lt-Commander Ringgold's exploring party had left on August 25th and returned on September 4th], the country, if possible, appeared to be more arid; it by no means justified the high encomiums that we had heard bestowed upon the far-famed valley. Our expectations probably had been so much raised as scarcely to allow us to give it that credit it really deserves. . . On the 6th, the survey being finished down to this point, they descended the river on their return to the ship. On the 8th, they had arrived at the mouth of the river, and the Straits of Kaquines [Carquinez]. On the 9th [of October, 1841], at midnight, they reached the Vincennes, after an absence of twenty days.

The land exploration party under Lt. George Emmons arrived at New Helvetia on October 19, after many adventures with the Sacramento Valley Indians. They then divided into two parties; one, under Lt. Emmons, taking the *Vincennes'* launch which met them just below New Helvetia and reached the squadron at San Francisco Bay, October 24th. The other party under Passed Midshipman Henry Eld, proceeded by land to San Jose and finally Yerba Buena (San Francisco), where they boarded the ship in the afternoon of October 28, 1841.

On the afternoon November 1, 1841 the squadron left San Francisco Bay for Honolulu, arriving at 10 A.M. November 17, 1841. They later proceeded to New York with stops at Manila, Singapore, Capetown, and Saint Helena. The *Vincennes* entered the New York navy yard in the afternoon of June 10, 1842, having completed a cruise of 1,392 days during which the circumnavigation of the earth was but a small part.

In February or March of 1849 Wilkes produced a book about California and the West,[150]. Most of data upon which it is based were collected during his visits in 1841, and unfortunately his names of places, tribes, lakes, rivers, and even Captain "Suter" were often incorrect or misspelled. Although Sacramento City had been surveyed in 1848 and houses built there in 1849, he makes no mention of it. He had apparently seen some of the gold samples sent to Washington, and incorrectly deduced that mercury was present in the gold deposits of the Coloma region. Despite these problems, he made some interesting conjectures about future routes to California, and provided an early set of maps of the region.

---

150. Charles Wilkes, *Western America, including California and Oregon with Maps of those Regions and of "The Sacramento Valley,"* (Philadelphia: Lea & Blanchard, 1849), 130 pages and 3 folding maps. Kurutz 679(a)

APPENDIX C

Thomas O. Larkin's letter to James Buchanan,
United States Secretary of State
reporting a June, 1848 trip to the mines
on the American River

Consul Thomas O. Larkin's Report

This letter[151] was written by Thomas Oliver Larkin who was the United States confidential agent and Consul to California stationed at Monterey from 1843 until May of 1848. Larkin was born in 1802 at Charlestown, Massachusetts, came to California in 1832, and married, at Santa Barbara in 1833, Mrs. Rachel Hobson Holmes, the first American woman who was a U.S. citizen to live in California. Their son, born in April 1834, was the first child of American parents born in California. The historian, Hubert Howe Bancroft characterized Larkin as "a man of slight education, but of much tact and practical good sense." In 1849 Larkin was a member of the California Convention which gathered at Monterey to write the first California State Constitution. In 1850 to 1853 he lived in New York, but returned to San Francisco and died there in 1858.

Within the letter, "Americans" were persons who were U.S. citizens, or had lived there since childhood, "Californians" were persons of Hispanic or European background who were long-term residents of the state (usually since birth), and "Indians" were native Americans born in California. For the modern reader, an ounce of gold was worth in 1848 about sixteen dollars in the foothills, seventeen dollars at San Francisco, and eighteen dollars on the Atlantic Coast. Occasionally questions regarding the purity (of the gold or the seller's character), or unseemly eagerness on the part of the seller could depress the price paid. Considering that Larkin only spent a few days at the mines, and most of the miners had worked 60 days or less, his predictions as to the richness and extent of the gold fields and their effect on immigration were remarkably accurate. Words placed in brackets within the letter are explanatory in nature and do not appear in the original:

Mr Larkin to Mr Buchanan:

MONTEREY, CALIFORNIA
June 28, 1848

SIR: My last dispatch to the State Department was written in San Francisco, the first of this month. In that I had the honor to give some information respecting the new "placer," or gold regions lately discovered on the branches of the Sacramento River. Since the writing

---

151. House Executive Document 1, pp. 53-56, for 34th Congress, 2nd Session, 1848-49. Reproduced in, Elisabeth Eganhoff, *The Elephant as they Saw It*, (Cal. Division of Mines, 1949)

of that dispatch, I have visited a part of the gold regions, and found it all that I had heard, and much more than I anticipated. The part that I visited was upon a fork of the American River, a branch of the Sacramento, joining the main river at Sutter's Fort. The place in which I found the people digging was about twenty-five miles from the fort by land.

I have reason to believe that gold will be found on many branches of the Sacramento and the Joaquim rivers. People are already scattered over one hundred miles of land, and it is supposed that the "placer' extends from river to river. At present the workmen are employed within ten or twenty yards of the river, that they may be convenient to water. On Feather River, there are several branches upon which the people are digging for gold. This is two or three days ride from the place I visited.

At my camping place I found, on a surface of two or three miles on the banks of the river, some fifty tents, mostly owned by Americans. These had their families. There are no Californians who have taken their families as yet to the gold regions; but few or none will ever do it. Some from New Mexico may do it next year , but no Californians. I was two nights at a tent occupied by eight Americans, viz: two sailors, one clerk, two carpenters, and three daily workmen. These men were in company; had two machines, each made from one hundred feet of boards (worth there one hundred and fifty dollars; in Monterey, fifteen dollars-- being one day's work), made similar to a child's cradle, ten feet long, without ends.

The two evenings I saw these eight men bring to their tents the labor of the day. I suppose they made each fifty dollars per day; their own calculation was two pounds of gold a day - four ounces to a man - sixty four dollars.[152] I saw two brothers that worked together, and only worked by washing the dirt in a tin pan, weigh the gold they obtained in one day; the result was, seven dollars to one and eighty-two to the other. There were two reasons for this difference; one man worked less hours than the other, and by chance had ground less impregnated with gold. I give this statement as an extreme case. During my visit I was an interpreter for a native of Monterey, who was purchasing a machine or canoe. I first tried to purchase boards and

---

152. Larkin may not have known that gold is normally weighed in Troy pounds which contain 12 Troy ounces, then selling for $16.00 per ounce . If the eight miners were speaking of Troy pounds, their estimate was $48.00 and his, $50.00 — only two dollars apart.

hire a carpenter for him. There were but a few hundred feet of boards to be had; for these the owner asked me fifty dollars per hundred ($500 per M), and a carpenter washing gold dust demanded fifty dollars per day for working. I at last purchased a log dug out, with a riddle and sieve made of willow-boughs on it, for one hundred and twenty dollars, payable in gold dust at fourteen dollars per ounce. The owner excused himself for the price, by saying that he was two days in making it, and even then demanded the use of it until sunset. My Californian has told me since that himself, a partner and two Indians obtained with this canoe eight ounces the first and five ounces the second day.

I am of the opinion that, on the American Fork, Feather River, and Copimes [modern Cosumnes] river, there are over two thousand people, nine tenths of them foreigners. Perhaps there are one hundred families, that have their teams, wagons, and tents. Many persons are waiting to see whether the months of July and August will be sickly, before they leave their present business to go to the "placer." The discovery of this gold was made by some Mormons, in January or February, who for a time kept it secret; the majority of those who are working there began in May. In most every instance the men, after digging a few days, have been compelled to leave for the purpose of returning home to see their families, arrange their business, and purchase provisions. I feel confident in saying there are fifty men in this "placer" who have, of an average one thousand dollars each, obtained in May or June. I have not met with any person who had been fully employed in washing gold one month; most however, appear to have averaged an ounce per day. I think there must be at this time be over one thousand men at work upon the different branches of the Sacramento; putting their gains at ten thousand per day, for six days in the week, appears to me not overrated.

Should this news reach the emigration of California and Oregon, now on the road, connected with the Indian wars, now impoverishing the latter country, we should have a large addition to our population; and should the richness of the gold regions continue, our emigration in 1849 will be many thousand, and in 1850 still more. If our countrymen in California as clerks, mechanics, and workmen will forsake employment at from two to six dollars per day, how many more of the same class in the Atlantic States, earning much less, will leave for this country under such prospects? It is the opinion of many who have visited the gold regions the past and present months, that the ground will afford gold for many years, perhaps for a century. From my own examination of the rivers and their banks, I am of the opinion that, at least for a few years, the golden products will equal the present year. However, as neither men of science, nor laborers now at work, have made any explorations of consequence, it is a matter of impossibility to give any opinion as to the extent and richness of this part of California.

Every Mexican who has seen the place says throughout their republic there has never been any "placer" like this one.

Could Mr. [President] Polk and yourself see California as we now see it, you would think that a few thousand people, on one hundred miles square of the Sacramento Valley, would yearly turn out of this river the whole price our country pays [$15,000,000.00] for all the acquired territory. When I finished my first letter I doubted my own writing, and, to be better satisfied, showed it to one of the principal merchants of San Francisco, and to Captain Folsom, of the quartermaster's department, who decided at once I was far below reality. You certainly will suppose, from my two letters, that I am, like others, led away by the excitement of the day. I think I am not.

In my last, I enclosed a small sample of the gold dust, and I find my only error was in putting a value to the sand. At that time I was not aware how the gold was found; I can now describe the mode of collecting it. A person without a machine, after digging off one or two feet of the upper ground, near the water (in some cases they take the top earth), throws into a tin pan or wooden bowl a shovelful of loose dirt and stones; then, placing the basin an inch under water, continues to stir up the dirt with his hand in such a manner that the running water will carry off the light earth, occasionally, with his hand throwing out the stones; after an operation of this kind for twenty or thirty minutes, a spoonful of small black sand remains; this is on a handker-chief or cloth dried in the sun, the emerge is blown off, leaving the pure gold. I have the pleasure of enclosing a paper of this sand and gold which I, from a bucket of dirt and stones, in half an hour, standing at the edge of the water, washed out myself. The value of it may be two or three dollars.

The size of the gold depends in some measure upon the river from which it is taken, the banks of one river having larger grains of gold than another. I presume more than one-half of the gold put into pans or machines is washed out and goes down the stream; this is of no consequence to the washers, who care only for the present time. Some have formed companies of four or five men, and have a rough made machine put together in a day, which worked to much advantage, yet many prefer to work alone, with a wooden bowl or tin pan, worth fifteen or twenty cents in the States, but eight to sixteen dollars at the gold region. As the workmen continue and materials can be obtained, improvements will take place in the mode of obtaining gold; at present it is obtained by standing in the water, and with much severe labor, or such as is called here severe labor.

How long this gathering of gold by the handful will continue here, or the future effect it will have on California, I cannot say. Three-fourths of the houses in the town [then called Yerba Buena] on the bay of San Francisco are deserted. Houses are sold at the price of the ground lots. The effects are this week showing themselves in Monterey. Almost every house I had hired out is given up. Every blacksmith, carpenter and lawyer is leaving; brick yards, saw mills, and ranches are left perfectly alone. A large number of the volunteers at San Francisco and Sonoma have deserted; some have been retaken and brought back; public and private vessels are losing their crews; my clerks have had one hundred percent advance offered them on their wages to accept employment. A complete revolution in the ordinary state of affairs is taking place; both of our newspapers are discontinued from want of workmen and the loss of their agencies; the alcaldes have left San Francisco, and I believe Sonoma likewise; the former place has not a justice of the peace left. The second alcalde of Monterey today joins the keepers of our principal hotel, who has closed their office and house, and will leave tomorrow for the golden rivers. I saw on the ground a lawyer who last year was attorney general of the king of the Sandwich Islands, digging and washing out his ounce and a half per day; near him can be found most of his brethren of the long robe, working in the same occupation.

To conclude; my letter is long, but I could not well describe what I have seen in less words, and now can believe that my account may well be doubted; if the affair proves a bubble, a mere excitement; I know not how we can all be deceived, as we are situated. Governor Mason and his staff [including Lieutenant William Tecumseh Sherman] have left Monterey to visit the place in question, and will, I suppose, soon forward to his department his views and opinions on the subject. Most of the land where gold has been discovered is public land; there are on different rivers some private grants. I have three such purchased in 1846 and '47, but have not learned that any private lands have produced gold, though they may hereafter do so.

I have the honor, dear sir, to be, very respectfully,
    Your obedient servant,
                    THOMAS O. LARKIN

Hon. James Buchanan, Secretary of State, Washington City.

APPENDIX D

Captain Joseph L. Folsom's Report

Joseph Libbey Folsom was born in New Hampshire in 1817 and graduated from West Point in 1840, and later served as an instructor there. In 1847, he had attained the rank of captain in the United States Army, and came to California in the sailing ship "Thomas H. Perkins" with Col. Jonathan D. Stevenson's First Regiment of New York Volunteers as assistant quartermaster. He also served as Collector of Customs for the port of San Francisco in 1847-49. He invested all the money he could raise in San Francisco lots, and within a few years became a rich man. In 1849, on a trip to the east, he was smart and lucky enough to locate the heirs of William A. Leidesdorff, and to cheaply buy from them their title to his immense California estates. Folsom thus became one of California's wealthiest men with extensive holdings in San Francisco and the large Leidesdorff Rancho along the American River containing the future site of the city of Folsom. He was described as being a most enterprising man of business, an honorable gentleman of superior education and refinement, somewhat formal and haughty in manner. Joseph L. Folsom died in San Jose, California in 1855 at the age of 38.[153]

QUARTERMASTER'S OFFICE, SAN FRANCISCO,
CALIFORNIA, SEPTEMBER 18, 1848

"Sir, -- In compliance with an intimation in my monthly report of June 30, [1848] I proceed to give you a hasty account of California as it is seen under the influence of the gold excitement now prevailing throughout the country. I shall proceed my remarks upon the mines by a few observations upon the situation of the country prior to their discovery. Up to the time the American flag was raised in California by Commodore Sloat, in July, 1846, the country may be said to have slumbered on from its first settlement without enterprise or activity on the part of the inhabitants. . .[there follow 16 lines in this vein].[154]

There were many Americans and foreigners in the country prior to the change of flags, [in 1846] but no regular emigration had taken place; and the unsettled conditions of politics, and constant revolutions,

---

153. Hubert Howe Bancroft, *History of California,* (San Francisco: The History Company, 1886) Vol. III, in Pioneer Register section, p. 742.

154 Edwin Bryant, (Late Alcalde of San Francisco), *What I Saw in California*, (New York: D. Appleton, 1849) Fifth edition, pp. 468-476. The first edition of this work was published in late 1848 and helped start the rush of 1849.

prevented any thing like the systematic enterprise which might otherwise have been expected from citizens of Anglo–American origin. The herds of cattle which covered the ranches were slaughtered for their hides and tallow, to be exchanged for merchandise as before, and the people continued to cherish their indolence as much as in former days; but the change of flags brought a corresponding revolution in the various occupations of life. After the first call for volunteers was answered, and the foreigners residing in the country were at leisure to enter upon the improvement of their property, all became activity.

Confidence was inspired by the introduction of American authority, and all believed they were virtually upon United States soil. Crowds came thronging in . . .to seek their fortunes in a new country, under their own flag. Things were assuming a better aspect, and both agricultural and mechanical improvements were going forward rapidly under new auspices. Farmers were introducing the agriculture and horticulture of their own country upon California soil, and mechanical labor knew no respite from its toils. The interminable clatter of the hammer and the saw was heard in every quarter; and frequently the mechanic, in his eagerness to succeed, did not recollect to divide Sunday from the rest of the week. Many little villages sprang up, as if by magic, in various parts of the country; and all promised fair for an indefinite continuance of every type of employment.

But a change came over the face of affairs. In the latter part of February, 1848, [actually January 24, 1848] a mechanic, named James Marshall, was employed in building a saw–mill for John A. Sutter, Esq., on the south branch of a river known in California as the American Fork, some fifty miles from New Helvetia, or Sutter's Fort. While employed in cutting a mill–race or canal for this improvement, Mr. Marshall discovered the pieces of gold as they glistened in the sunlight at the bottom of the sluices. . . . Examinations were prosecuted at other points along the stream, and almost everywhere with success. Reports of a most marvelous nature soon reached the coast touching these mines. Their apparent extravagance created incredulity, and the public attention was not fully called to the subject until gold dust or grain gold was bought into the market in considerable quantities, for sale. Doubt soon became belief, and a change, almost magical in its nature, pervaded the whole population. Lawyers, doctors, clergymen, farmers, mechanics, merchants, sailors, and soldiers, left their legitimate occupations to embark on a business where fortunes were to be made in a few weeks. Villages and districts, where all had been bustle, industry, and improvement, were soon left without male population. Mechanics, merchants, and magistrates, were alike off to the mines, and all kinds of useful occupation, except gold–digging, were here apparently at an end.

In most cases, the crops were remarkably good; but they are generally lost for want of laborers to secure them. In some parts of the country, hundreds of acres of fine wheat will rot in the fields from the impossibility of getting laborers. Vessels are left swinging idly at their anchors, while both captains and crews are at the mines; and the most essential private and public improvements are arrested in their progress. The wages of clerks have advanced at least two hundred per cent., and those of common laborers at least four or five hundred. At the time the excitement broke out, I was repairing the U.S. barque "Anita." The workmen were receiving $3 per day, and lived on board the vessel. They struck for higher wages, and one man finally left and forfeited all his former earnings, rather than continue at work a few days more at $6 per day. Common sailors demanded $100 per month for work in schooners on the bay. Freight from this port to Sutter's is from $3 to $4 per barrel. The distance is little more than one hundred miles. Common four–ox wagons are hired at $50 per day. In one case I have known a Negro cook to be employed at $25 per day for his professional services among the pots and kettles in the gold region.

This was the condition about three months since, and under its influence this village was almost absolutely deserted. It had been one of the most bustling little places I ever saw, and in a few days it became deserted. Two or three merchants and a few soldiers constituted the male population. Recently, however, there has been a reaction, which brings many back from the mines, and an active emigration is flowing from abroad. Sickness has broken out among the miners, and many have returned prostrated with fevers, while others have come to avoid being so. There is now a large number of laborers here, but many of them refuse to work on any terms, while those who labor, do so at exorbitant prices. The ordinary compensation for white laborers is from $6 to $10 per day. I am now paying these prices for men I am forced to employ for repairing the government lighter, and for discharging the ship Huntress, now in this port. At the same time everything is high in proportion. Butter sells by the barrel at $1 per pound, and hams at the same price; flour $25 per barrel, and pilot bread forty cents per pound. For the last three pairs of boots I have had, I have paid, respectively, $18, $14, and $12 per pair. Other things are at corresponding prices in this place, but at the mines everything is much higher. Flour and pork vary in the mines from $40 to $200 per barrel. Common shoes, worth in Boston about 75 cents per pair, sell at $8, or even $12 per pair. There is a kind of recklessness about these prices which would be sought after in vain in any other part of the world. I saw a box of Seidlitz powders [a mild cathartic], worth 50 cents in San Francisco, sold in the mines for $24 in grain gold; and was credibly informed that brandy had been sold for $48 per bottle.

From this very imperfect *price current,* you can infer the cost of other articles in California. With the prices in the mines, however, the cost of almost every thing in California has increased from one to several hundred percent. Rents have advanced in some sections of the country to an incredible extent. Store houses of the most fragile and insecure character, rent for more than the best warehouses of similar dimensions in Boston or New York.

I was in the mines about the 1st of July [1848]; at that time the weather there was insufferably hot.[155] I think it by far the most oppressive climate I was ever in. It is much more uncomfortable than the climate of Brazil at the warmest season of the year, and every thing was literally parched up, after a drought which had then continued for near three months, and which had five months more to run to the rainy season. . . .I then foresaw (what has since happened) that there would be much sickness among the miners. . . .Their diet was bad, their labors were severe, and they were exposed completely without shelter, in the daytime to a burning sun, and at night to the chilly atmosphere of the mountains. Many of them worked with their feet in the water, and inflamed their blood in a feverish climate by a free use of ardent spirits. The natural consequences followed. . . . Most of the streams upon which gold is found, are mountain torrents, flowing through rocky and precipitous channels, and a yellowish soil [in later years, gold was found at higher altitudes to 6000 feet]. There is apparently much iron in the earth, and where most of the gold is obtained, the bed and banks of the rivers are composed of coarse gravel intermingled with sand and a yellowish earth. So far as I have observed, or can ascertain from others, the gold is always found in the stratum of "drift" or "diluvium," unless it has been displaced

---

155. In July of 1850, Nelson Kingsley was working on the Yuba River (about the elevation of Coloma), where Folsom visited. Kingsley kept a careful record of the temperature each day, and reported morning lows of 62 to 68 degrees, noon highs in the shade of 95 to 99 degrees, and highs in the sun up to 117 degrees. Dr. Frederick Teggart, Editor, *Diary of Nelson Kingsley,* (Berkeley: Academy of Pacific Coast History, 1914) Vol. 3, No.3. pp.164, 165.

by mountain torrents, or through other comparatively modern agencies. The fine gold is found in the lower portions of the streams, and is extracted from the earth by means of washing in common tin pans, and vessels of every kind which can be substituted for them. The finest portions of the earth are removed by washing, and a kind of gyratory motion of the pan; the gravel is taken out with the hand, and the gold is left in the vessels, with a kind of black, ferruginous sand, not unlike that used in writing. The residue (gold and sand) is then left upon a board or cloth to dry, when the sand is blown off with a common bellows or the mouth, while the greater specific gravity of the old causes it to remain behind. Much of the finest gold is thus blown off with the sand and lost.

Vast numbers of machines resembling nursery cradles are used in this business. The rocking of the cradle answers to the gyratory motion of the pan; the water, mud, and fine sand escaping from the foot of the machine over a series of small cross-bats on its bottom, which are sufficient impediments to stop the more coarse particles of gold. Over the head of the cradle is a coarse sieve, upon which the auriferous earth is placed, and the machine being in motion, water is poured on the sieve, and the gold, sand, and fine earthy matter is thus taken into the body of the machine, while the gravel is rejected. All these methods are more or less imperfect, and the process by amalgamation with quicksilver has not been adopted up to this date. It is supposed that at least one-half the gold contained in a given quantity of earth is lost, by the imperfect measures taken for cleaning it.

As the workmen ascend the streams into the mountains, the gold becomes coarser and more massive. On the lower portions of the streams, it is found in thin flat particles, resembling small golden fish scales. Higher in the mountains it is found varying in size, from the finest particles to pieces of five or six ounces in weight, and all conceivable forms. Many of the largest pieces contain small portions of quartz and other granite rock imbedded in them. The coarse gold is dug out of the crevices among the rocks, in the dry beds of mountain torrents, with pickaxes, small iron bars, spades, butcher knives, sticks, &c. &c. In many places the streams flow over strata of coarse slate standing vertically, and between the different layers the gold is deposited by the water.

As no one has yet found gold in its native matrix, a question often suggest itself as to its origin. I believe the coarse gold is found near the spots where it originally lay in its native bed, and much of the fine gold has been swept down from the mountains by torrents of water. Almost all the rocks in Upper California ar imperfectly organized, being soft and friable, and incapable of resisting the action of the weather [Folsom had not seen the vast areas of granite in the summits of the Sierra.] In the process of time the mountains have gradually crumbled away into fine dust, and the gold has been liberated. The coarse gold from its massiveness and great specific gravity, was not removed from the mountain sides, whereas the fine gold was swept off to the plains below.

The extent of these golden deposits it is impossible to conjecture. Gold has been found one hundred and forty miles above Sutter's Fort. It is dug in great quantities at almost all points along Feather, Juba and Bear Rivers, and upon the American Fork and all its tributaries, upon the Cosumnes and Stanislaus rivers, and upon both sides of the San Joaquin river. It has been found at Bodega, on the sea–coast, at various points in the chain of mountains which separates the waters flowing into the San Joaquin from those which enter the Pacific as far as Ciudad de los Angeles. It has also been found in considerable quantities in the earth of the plains near the Mission of Santa Clara. It is thus known to exist throughout a region of country of more than six hundred miles in extent, and probably extends into Oregon. There are subjects upon which one cannot write the truth without exciting incredulity, and it is with great diffidence that I shall attempt to speak of the richness of the mines.
I went to them in the most skeptical frame of mind, and came away a *believer*.

From all that I can learn as to similar deposits of gold elsewhere, I believe these to be the richest *placer* mine in the world. I am satisfied, from personal observation, that active workmen can get from $25 to $40 per day, estimating the gold at $16 per ounce, troy [1.09714 avoirdupois ounce]. Many instances are known of persons having obtained from $800 to $1,000 in a day for each man. I am meeting persons daily in this place who have been absent less than three months and have returned with from $2,000 to $5,000 in gold dust.

While among the mines I collected a large number of facts, from which the following are taken at random as a specimen: On the most southern tributary of the American Fork, sixteen miles from the main stream, I saw where Messrs. Neilly and Crowly got, with six men, in six days, ten and a half pounds of gold avoirdupois weight. In the bottom of a dry ravine of the same stream, Messrs. Daly and McCooms removed, with a party of Indians and white men, $17,000 in two days, and within two hundred yards of the main stream. From another dry ravine, within a few rods of the last mentioned, it is said that $30,000 were collected in three days. Mr. C. S. Lyman, a clergyman, unaccustomed to labor, informed me that he got $50 for about five hours labor each day. Mr. Vaca, a New Mexican, who resides about thirty miles from Sutter's, told me, he, with four other men, got seventeen pounds of gold, avoirdupois weight in seven days [an avoirdupois pound is 14.85 ounces, troy, so this amounted to 252.45 troy ounces, then worth $4,039, and now $75,735]. I saw the gold. Major Cooper, late of Mississippi, with two men and one boy, got $1,000 in two days.

Mr. Sinclar [John Sinclair, Sutter's neighbor, just to the north of the American River] had been employed in digging gold about five weeks, with a party of Indians, numbering about forty, sometimes more and sometimes less. He gave his indians meat, sugar, coffee, flour and rice, and they ate three times per day. They were mostly wild Indians, and worked together with pans. In five weeks, after paying all his Indians and the current expenses of the party, he had $17,000, or upwards of ninety pounds, troy weight of gold dust [a troy pound was 12 troy ounces]. The gold was shown [to me?]. Mr. Norris and one companion took from a dry ravine, not far from those already mentioned, 3,000 in two days, and the dirt was packed on horses more than two hundred yards to the water. Mr. Aaron Angland got from his own labor, in twenty consecutive days after his arrival in the mines, $2,200. But I might go on stating facts like these until I should tire your patience.

You will be anxious to know where this will end. I see no prospect of exhausting the mines.

J. L. Folsom, Captain, Asst. Quartermaster

This report in the form of a letter was written to United States Quartermaster General Thomas Sydney Jessup in Washington D.C. It was published in the Washington Globe, *and reproduced in Edwin Bryant's 1848* What I Saw in California. *See footnote 154, page 324.*

APPENDIX E

JAMES MCCLATCHY'S DISPATCH ON CROSSING MEXICO
DATED APRIL 20, 1849

JAMES MCCLATCHY'S DISPATCH

A DISPATCH TO GEORGE HENRY EVANS IN NEW YORK FROM JAMES MCCLATCHY WHILE WAITING FOR A SHIP IN MAZATLÁN , MEXICO [156]

Before McClatchy left New York for California he promised the editor of Young America, *an early day New York newspaper dedicated to fighting land monopoly and to protecting the right of free settlement, that he would write describing his travels. George Henry Evans was distinguished in New York's early history for his fights to protect constitutional rights. This letter was also reprinted in the* New York Tribune.

MAZATLÁN , MEX., APRIL 20, 1849

FRIEND EVANS:

As I promised you and others in New York, to write of California as I might see it, I commenced thus early with a few words to those about to go there by the land route through Mexico. If you think of going to California, be sure you are in earnest before you attempt to start. Do not give up any employment worth having until you are positive you have nerve enough to go through a land of journey. And if you have soft hands and are unused to outdoor life or indoor hardship and are still bound to go, take shipping round the Horn, or go by way of the Isthmus.— Eight out of eighty four persons who came to Brazos in the same vessel with me, took the back track before they had traveled three days in Mexico. Five others died of cholera, and one of dysentery: and others who were left sick had since died, or returned home, if they had any home to go to.

All of these men left what many called good situations, and most of them wives and family, perhaps in no very prosperous condition. Take care that their case may not be yours. And I have met others who had gone as far as Parras; full half way, returning homewards. If you will go through Mexico, (and if I had to start again and could not get by the Isthmus, I would go the same route,) provide yourself with a gun and one or more pistols, and if you want side arms, bring a sword if you can use it, or are desirous of carrying one; if not, get a slung shot or "Billy." You need not think of a knife except to carve your food with, for the Mexicans can come the knife game as well as you, and perhaps a leetle better, and

---

156. The above letter is taken from page cc-6 of the *Sacramento Bee* published February 3, 1958. The *Bee* writer mentions that this is "the majority" of McClatchy's letter, but it is not clear if the deletions were made in 1958, or by another person at some earlier date.

every Mexican carries one. Bring only a change of clothing, and let them be strong Summer ones, for you will find that your animal, be he horse or mule, will have enough to carry you through even though you be a small man. At Matamoros and Monterey [near the start of the crossing], I have seen much new clothing actually thrown away.

After you near Monterey and are beyond, you will find a double blanket more comfortable than a single one. (The article should be white in order that you will kill the fleas easy). If you will have a tent bring one, but let it be light and cheap for you will be very likely to pitch it to the dogs before you have been a week in Mexico. I have not seen a tent pitched between Monterey and this place [Mazatlán on the Pacific Coast], but the weather was dry; had it been otherwise, a tent might have been acceptable. If convenient you might bring a little brandy and laudanum [a tincture of opium], but be sure to bring a pint bottle of No. 6. If you should have stomach cramps, which you may expect, a mixture of these will cure you.

When these are provided, count your money and see that you have $200 in your pocket. This, with care, will carry you through. You need not bring any passport from the American Consul or other protection paper from your own Government. When you land in Mexico go to the U. S. Consul, and for three dollars he will get your passport and provide you with a copy which will answer in place of a protection paper. Now a mule is a mule the world over, but never-theless, when you go to purchase an animal to carry you through, buy a mule that will eat corn, if not, do not have him at any price. Never mind his age, or ill looks, or chaffed back, provided he is healed. Any old mule in fair condition that will eat corn will be sure to carry you through at the rate of 25 miles per diem. The less you have to do with horses the better. I have known one man to use up three horses on the way, many others two, and those who have been lucky enough to bring a horse through have been obliged to walk half the way, and lick the animal the other half. And I have not known one mule to fail. Before you pay for your animal, go before an alcalde or some respectable known person, and get a bill of sale containing a description of him from the vendor. If you purchase at a rancho or hacienda, the selling brand of the owner will be sufficient. Tom says to Dick, "Take my mules and sell them for what you can get to those Americans." Tom overhauls you one hundred miles farther and says, "These mules are mine, and they have been stolen." If you refuse to give them up, he brings you before the authorities, and how, unless you have taken the proper precaution, are you to establish your innocence?

Saddles and bridles can be had in Mexico cheaper and better than in New York. You had better bring a piece of India rubber cloth to lay on, as it will keep the damp out, and you will find buckskin drawers preferable to anything else to ride in. Do not try to conceal your arms while passing through town or country: on the contrary, be careful [to] expose them. Your passport expresses and secures you the right to carry them, and the size of them alone, in the hands of five or more Americans, will keep the *ladrones* or robbers at a respectable distance. These ladrones take care to examine you and your arms as you pass through the town: if you are not well armed they [may] attack you— if you are, they will not. No party of Californians, as far as I can learn, has been attacked. Still it is well to keep your arms always ready to use. A double barreled shotgun is preferable to a rifle, not only for killing game, but also for the purpose of defense, for from the nature of the ground and case, the attack must be a close one, and two barrels loaded with buck shot will do good service.

Treat the Mexicans kindly and you can pass through without difficulty. Persons whom I cannot name, but belonging to crowds which I could mention, have, more than once, after drawing water for themselves and animals, thrown the bucket to the bottom of the well and taken the rope along [with them]. Act like gentlemen, if not for your own sakes, at least for the sake of the country to which you belong. Let not the good name of America or the fair name of its citizens receive injury at your hands.

Powder, shot, tea, coffee, tobacco, etc., which you may want on the journey, are exempt from duty. Tools for working in California, will be charged for. Do not stop in the towns, but if you require a day's rest go to a rancho or hacienda where your mule can have rest and grass; and where you will not have a chance to spend your money in liquor and cigars, or lose at the gaming tables as some have done; and then be obliged to go the land route all through [Sonora, New Mexico, and Arizona]. Although a wagon is a great convenience on the way, especially if you are sick, still I would not advise you to bring one, as you will have to sell it at a considerable loss. If your mule's mouth continues to bleed after you are a few days out, open it and take out the leeches.— Drink a little water or strong drink, eat substantial food, and that sparingly, bathe frequently, and if you are in health, you will likely remain so.

The route I came is, New York to Brazos, Santiago Texas [a small port which was located in latitude N 26-00-24, longitude W 97-09-52, about 3 miles north of the mouth of the Rio Grande and no longer appears on large area maps]; thence by Point Isabelle[157] over the fields of Palo Alto[157] and Resaca de la Palma[157] to Fort Crown [now Brownsville][157] on the Rio Grande, opposite Matamoros[157]; thence through China to Monterey[157], Saltillo[157], across the field of Buena Vista[157] to Parras; thence through Alamo to Queen Camay and Durango, to Mazatlán . If you go to Camargo, you pass Mier to Monterey, thence to Mazatlán , the route is the same. Most of these observations, however, will, I presume, apply with equal course to the Vera Cruz route.

There are ten vessels in port [at Mazatlán], two of them up to sail for California, passage $50 and find [feed] yourself or $70 and found. Persons get shipping as fast as they arrive. None of the mail steamers has a turn here, the two that have gone up are laid up for want of hands.

The engineer of the *California* deserted, but he has been caught and now is in irons on board the United States ship *Ohio*. Gold gets plentier, or is found in great plenty every day.

We met on the road, five days from here, seven Americans returning, who said they could not get shipping here and were going to Durango, to start the land route. We suspected the story, and now find that they had been at the mines from last September to March, and were returning with six hundred thousand dollars in drafts and specie, so at least one of them told in secret a commander of a California party with whom we were acquainted. There are 250 Americans here now, but all of them who can raise the means to pack their passage will leave tomorrow or next day. Some are very hard up here; many are obliged to sell everything they can for whatever it will bring. All our party—that is all of the New Yorkers who left in the schooner *John Castner*, came through in good health [excepting those mentioned earlier who died or turned back], and all of them have, by some means or other, managed to get booked for a passage up [to San Francisco]. I have some notes which I will write out on the passage and send to you.

James McClatchy

---

157. Site of a battle in U. S.— Mexican war of 1846-1848.

James Horace Culver's Grave

It is surmounted by an obelisk and is located in the old Masonic section of the Sacramento City Cemetery. He wrote the first book printed in Sacramento, the 1851 Sacramento City Directory, reproduced in this book.